HEAL
POLICY
ANALYSIS
An Interdisciplinary Approach

CURTIS P. MCLAUGHLIN, DBA
Professor Emeritus
Kenan-Flagler Business School and School of Public Health
University of North Carolina at Chapel Hill
Chapel Hill, NC

CRAIG D. MCLAUGHLIN, MJ
Executive Director
Washington State Board of Health
Olympia, WA

JONES AND BARTLETT PUBLISHERS
Sudbury, Massachusetts
BOSTON   TORONTO   LONDON   SINGAPORE

World Headquarters

Jones and Bartlett Publishers
40 Tall Pine Drive
Sudbury, MA 01776
978-443-5000
info@jbpub.com
www.jbpub.com

Jones and Bartlett Publishers
Canada
6339 Ormindale Way
Mississauga, ON L5V 1J2
CANADA

Jones and Bartlett Publishers
International
Barb House, Barb Mews
London W6 7PA
UK

Jones and Bartlett's books and products are available through most bookstores and online book-sellers. To contact Jones and Bartlett Publishers directly, call 800-832-0034, fax 978-443-8000, or visit our website www.jbpub.com.

Substantial discounts on bulk quantities of Jones and Bartlett's publications are available to corporations, professional associations, and other qualified organizations. For details and specific discount information, contact the special sales department at Jones and Bartlett via the above contact information or send an email to specialsales@jbpub.com.

Production Credits

Publisher: Michael Brown
Production Director: Amy Rose
Associate Editor: Katey Birtcher
Production Editor: Daniel Stone
Marketing Manager: Sophie Fleck
Manufacturing Buyer: Therese Connell

Composition: Jason Miranda,
  Spoke & Wheel
Cover Design: Kristin E. Ohlin
Cover Image: ©bluestocking/ShutterStock, Inc.
Printing and Binding: Malloy, Inc.
Cover Printing: Malloy, Inc.

Library of Congress Cataloging-in-Publication Data
McLaughlin, Curtis P.
  Health Policy Analysis: An Interdisciplinary Approach / Curtis P. McLaughlin,
Craig D. McLaughlin.
       p. ; cm.
  Includes bibliographical references and index.
  ISBN-13: 978-0-7637-4442-7 (alk. paper)
  ISBN-10: 0-7637-4442-5 (alk. paper)
  1. Medical policy--United States. 2. Health planning--United States. I.
McLaughlin, Craig. II. Title.
  [DNLM: 1. Health Policy--United States. 2. Health Planning--United
States. WA 540 AA1 M3783h 2008]
  RA395.A3H4397 2007
  362.10973--dc22

                                              2007008221

6048

Printed in the United States of America
11 10 09 08 07   10 9 8 7 6 5 4 3 2 1

To our talented wives, Barbara Nettles-Carlson and Karen Janowitz, and to the three generations of health professionals in our extended family who patiently share so much with us.

Contents

Part II — The Policy Analysis Process

Preface

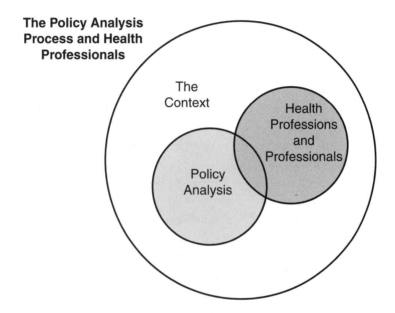

The Policy Analysis Process and Health Professionals

The Context

Health Professions and Professionals

Policy Analysis

This book is about the process of developing health policy relevant to the United States of America. We have included the perspectives of a number of disciplines and professions. Since our country has a lot of actors but no coherent health policy at the federal level, we have drawn heavily on our personal experiences and backgrounds, which include economics, political science, management, communications, and public health. We have also drawn on the experiences of other countries. We have recognized that the states, and even smaller jurisdictions, may end up taking on the bulk of the health planning role. Values, economics, and health risks may vary sufficiently between them to call for independence in planning and execution. Canada's experience with a broad policy and specific health systems for each province has seemed to work as well, or better than, a centralized bureaucracy might have. Even the health services of a number of European countries have tended toward more decentralization as time has gone on.

The book is organized into three sections: Context, Policy Analysis Process, and Professional Response. We have anticipated that this book will be used to review health system issues and policy planning for health in a variety of graduate professional programs of universities. We have not assumed zero knowledge of the health system, but we have not anticipated that the users would have a great deal of background about how and why the U.S. health system developed as it did, nor about the efforts that took place in the past to reform it. Therefore, the Context section explores the current issues with the system (Chapters 1 and 2) and the history of how that system has evolved (Chapter 3). Chapter 4 challenges the readers to ask about where we want to be, while Chapters 5 and 6 review the alternatives that seem to have strong support for getting from where we are to where we might want to be. These chapters do not purport to be "value free," but this book is different from most books on health policy because it does not attempt to push a single solution set. Studying the present is important for research and understanding, but the educational purpose of this book, and presumably of your course, is to prepare you to meet whatever new, and perhaps unforeseen, challenges develop in the future.

The second section, The Policy Analysis Process, develops a set of tools for use in the future. Chapter 7 deals with identification and definition of the issues to be studied. Chapter 8 introduces some of the concepts of technology assessment applicable to health care. Chapter 9 reviews the political processes that influence the planning process in various settings, especially the public sector health arena. Chapter 10 presents the accepted methods of economic and financial analysis that determine the economic viability of health care plans. Chapter 11 addresses the ethical and other value considerations that must enter into the health policy process. In our deeply divided country, value issues are important. They crop up in just about every context and influence outcome of most analyses. We have put this chapter after the other three process chapters to try to offset the tendency of many less sophisticated students to start with the qualitative and never get to the rewarding, but demanding, work of including the quantitative. This section ends with Chapter 12 on implementation. Policies and plans must take into account the capacities of organizations and societies to implement them. At the same time, how the policy making process proceeds becomes a part of the context within which the implementation will take place. Yes, there is a problem of circularity there, but that is real life.

Part III deals with the roles, skills, and leadership that health professionals can bring to the policy making process in their local and national communities. It also acknowledges that one has to act out of a personal set of values and point-of-view, while at the same time preserving one's flexibility to make incremental progress if that is all that can be achieved. Chapter 13 reviews the overall planning processes in our society and suggests some things that professionals might strive for in the short and long run. The emphasis in that chapter is on what is likely to work, rather than the ideal. Chapter 14 suggests that there are important roles for healthcare professionals in the change process. It also discusses the skills that health professionals need to acquire if they are going to be accepted into the process and work effectively on its tasks, either from the inside or the outside. Chapter 15 provides summary and concluding material for the text. It also offers some of our personal suggestions and observations from the point-of-view of the two generations of one family represented by the authors.

About the Authors

Curtis P. McLaughlin, DBA is professor emeritus and adjunct professor at the Kenan-Flagler Business School of the University of North Carolina at Chapel Hill. At the time of his retirement he was also Professor of Health Policy and Administration in the School of Public Health and Senior Research Fellow of the Cecil B. Sheps Center for Health Services Research. Prior to coming to North Carolina he was Assistant Professor at the Harvard Business School and also taught in the Harvard School of Public Health. He is the author or coauthor of some 275 publications including *Continuous Quality Improvement in Health Care* with A.D. Kaluzny, now in its third edition with Jones and Bartlett. He received his BA in chemistry from Wesleyan University and his MBA and his DBA from Harvard Business School. While there, he studied in the initial Harvard interdisciplinary program in health care economics and management and then taught in it.

Craig D. McLaughlin, MJ joined the Washington State Board of Health as senior health policy manager in 2001. He began serving as executive director in 2004. Immediately prior, he served as director of college relations and adjunct faculty for The Evergreen State College. As a newspaper editor and freelance journalist for more than a decade, Mr. McLaughlin wrote and edited articles on a broad range of health issues. He has served as a communications consultant to foundations and as a management consultant to media organizations. Mr. McLaughlin earned his Bachelor of Arts in biology from Wesleyan University and his Masters in Journalism from the University of California at Berkeley. He also completed all coursework toward a Masters in Public Administration with a concentration in health administration at the University of New Mexico.

Acknowledgments

For their assistance with the case studies, the authors would like to thank Beth Melcher and Christina Rausch, formerly of the NC P2P project, for their contribution, as well as Lori Nichols of HInet, LLC and Dr. Michael E. Westley of Virginia Mason Medical Center for reviewing materials related to their respective organizations.

Craig McLaughlin would like to extend his appreciation to the members and staff of the Washington State Board of Health, past and present, as well as the many other talented leaders in state and local public health in Washington State, for their tutelage. In particular, he would like to recognize his present and former supervisors for their patient mentoring—chairs Linda Lake, Dr. Thomas Locke, Dr. Kim Marie Thorburn, and Treuman Katz, and former executive director Don Sloma. Mr. Sloma has the dubious distinction of having recruited Craig into the field of health policy despite a promise to himself that he would never follow in his father's footsteps. Nothing in this book, however, reflects the official views of the Washington State Board of Health or any other Washington State agency.

Curtis McLaughlin would like to recognize a number of individuals who helped steer him in the direction of health policy and administration and supported him to continue in it for over forty years. They include Roy Penchansky and the late John Dunlop while at Harvard; Sagar Jain, Arnold Kaluzny, and the late Maurice Lee at UNC-Chapel Hill; and Bill Judge and Michael Stahl at UT-Knoxville.

CHAPTER 1

Introduction

If everyone is in charge, then no one is in charge. Health policy is a problematic issue throughout the world, but it is particularly challenging in the United States, where there is no consensus about which government agency or social institution, if any, has the legitimate role of developing or implementing national health policy. The U.S. Constitution is silent on the subject of health and health care. Although its preamble promises "to promote the general Welfare," the Tenth Amendment states, "The powers not delegated to the United States by the Constitution, nor prohibited by it to the States, are reserved to the States respectively, or to the people." Neither education nor health care powers are specifically allotted to the federal government in the Constitution. The omission of health, however, cannot be attributed solely to the framers' intent. They lived in a world in which one talked of "evil humours" and visited "barbers and churgeons." Summertime yellow fever epidemics frequently disrupted the government in the capitol, Philadelphia. Relatively little was known about medicine when the Constitution was drafted in 1787. Jenner's discovery of inoculation with cowpox to avoid smallpox did not come until 1796, and Pasteur's germ theory and Roentgen's X-rays came almost a lifetime later.

THE MANY ACTORS

Health care policy making in the United States is also very pluralistic. Any discussion of health policy must account for the fact that policy decisions are made at multiple levels of society:

- National government
- State and local governments
- Health care institutions
- Provider professionals
- Payer organizations (employers and insurers)
- Individuals (consumers).

The boxed tables randomly distributed throughout this chapter (**Tables 1-2** through **1-7**) provide samples of major health policy questions faced at each of these levels. Like most lists in this book, they are meant to be illustrative, not exhaustive.

In such a decentralized environment, the government may take a hands-on approach, treating health care as a public good, or a hands-off approach, favoring market-driven outcomes. The government's stance and specific policies can also swing dramatically as political power shifts. For example, it may or may not encourage the entry of new institutions into the health sector to generate competition among providers as it did by supporting the introduction of family medicine departments and residency programs in medical schools. Any of these shifts can profoundly affect the professional's work life.

This introductory chapter describes what health care policy is, how the policy analysis process works, and the different roles health professionals can play in setting and implementing health policy over time. The role of a policy analyst is described quite completely in the excerpt from the U.S. Office of Personnel Management Operating Manual displayed in **Table 1-1**. As you proceed through the book, you will likely note many parallels between that role description and the organization of this book, even though this book is meant to outline health policy analysis for health care professionals rather than cover the full training needs for a career in policy analysis.

We then provide an overview of some of the major policy issues facing health care in this country. Then we address how certain potentially confusing terms are employed throughout this book and suggest ways to integrate the material that you will be learning with your knowledge from other disciplines.

TABLE 1-1   Excerpts from OPM Operation Manual Qualification
Standard for Policy Analysis Positions

The principal requirements for performing policy analysis functions are listed below, as appropriate to the position to be filled:

- Knowledge of a pertinent professional subject-matter field(s)....
- Knowledge of economic theories including micro-economics and the effect of proposed policies on production costs and prices, wages, resource allocation, or consumer behavior, and/or macro-economics and the effect of proposed policies on income and employment, investment, interest rates, and price level.
- Knowledge of public policy issues related to a subject-matter field.
- Knowledge of the executive/legislative decision making process.
- Knowledge of pertinent research and analytical methodology and ability to apply such techniques to policy issues, such as:
  - Qualitative techniques, such as performing extensive inquiry into a wide variety of significant issues, problems, or proposals; determining data sources and relevance of findings and synthesizing information; evaluating tentative study findings and drawing logical conclusions; and identifying omissions, questionable assumptions, or inadequate data in the work of others.
  - Quantitative methods, such as cost benefit analysis, design of computer simulation models and statistical analysis including survey methods and regression analysis.
- Knowledge of the programs or organizations and activities to assess the political and institutional environment in which decision are made and implemented.
- Skill in dealing with decision makers and their immediate staffs. Skill in interacting with other specialists and experts in the same or related fields.
- Ability to exercise judgment in all phases of analysis, ranging from sorting out the most important problems when dealing with voluminous amounts of information to ensure that the many facets of a policy issue are explored, to sifting evidence and developing feasible options or alternative proposals and anticipating policy consequences.
- Skill in effectively communicating highly complex technical material or highly complex issues that may have controversial findings, or both, using language appropriate to specialists and/or nonspecialists, facilitating the formulation of a decision.
- Skill in written communication to organize ideas and present findings in a logical manner with supporting, as well as adverse, criteria for specific issues, and to prepare material complicated by short deadlines and limited information.
- Skills in effective oral communication techniques to explain, justify, or discuss a variety of public issues requiring a logical presentation of appropriate facts and information or analysis.
- Ability to work effectively under pressure of tight time frames and rigid deadlines.

Source: http://www.opm.gov/qualifications/SEC-IV/A/GS-POLCY.HTM accessed 10/13/06. For more detail see Section IV-A (pp33-34) of the *Operational Manual for Qualification Standards for General Schedule Positions.*

TABLE 1-2 Illustrative Health Policy Issues at the U.S. Federal Level

- What population groups should receive subsidized coverage from tax revenues?
- How should the federal government participate in supporting health care for all when the Constitution does not include health care as a federal responsibility?
- How should the federal government support quality improvement efforts if state professional licensing and disciplinary boards are not addressing medical error rates effectively?
- The cost of malpractice insurance in some states threatens the supply of providers in some specialties and appears to raise the cost of care. What is the role of the federal government in avoiding the negative effects of these suits and awards?
- Progress in information technology implementation in health care has lagged behind most other information-intensive service sectors. Is this good or bad and what should the federal government do about it?
- What services should be covered under Medicare? Medicaid?
- How many health professionals in a subspecialty are sufficient? Who determines that and how do we respond to such findings?

THE SYSTEM IN THE UNITED STATES IS UNIQUE, BUT NOT UNPARALLELED

Many developed countries struggle with the burden of their social programs, including health care. Even in countries with a national health service, there have been recent efforts to decentralize them to make them more responsive to local needs and to tap into tax revenues available at the regional and local levels. Sometimes this transfer of decision-making power carries with it a privatization component. Medical care in the United Kingdom and Scandinavia provides examples of this, as does mental health care in a number of U.S. states. None of the other developed countries, however, spend as much per capita or as a percentage of the national income (gross domestic product) as the United States, and many of them have better health outcomes across the population. The overall results achieved in the United States seemingly should be better, given our relatively high expenditures.

Although this book does not emphasize comparative international health policy, it is important to understand that high-sounding goals such as the World Health Organization's "Health For All by the Year 2000," although promising much on paper, are still far from being achieved. Both developed and less-developed countries have taken rather different routes to more- or less-successful health care systems, leading in turn to different levels of costs and outcomes. These results have been achieved over decades of adaptation to the cultures and institutions of those countries and may or may not be models for the United States. The case study that follows Chapter 3 compares the health care systems in five industrialized nations.

All countries are aiming at targets that shift as basic science knowledge expands exponentially, new technologies become available, and new diseases and environmental threats emerge. Some countries are experimenting with one or more aspects of a market system for health care delivery, while still maintaining that health care is a basic human right. Although health care is not officially a right in the United States, all levels of government and the body politic are concerned about the increasing proportion of the population that lacks health insurance and is forced either to forgo care or to seek some form of public assistance. Even relatively conservative commentators argue for universal participation in national or state-level health insurance schemes, partly to disengage health care financing from employment relationships and partly to avoid adverse selection by employees and underwriting discrimination by insurers.

HEALTH CARE: WHAT IS IT?

The terms, *health* and *health care,* are used somewhat loosely in U.S. policy debates. Often, what people mean by health is absence of notable ailments. The World Health Organization, however, defines health as "a state of complete physical, mental and social well-being and not merely the absence of disease or infirmity."

Similarly, when people utter the phrase the *health care system,* they often are talking about the system for financing and delivering personal medical services—what some refer to as illness care. The entire system that promotes health and wellness is actually much more complex. Other health systems, in addition to the system that delivers medical care, include public health, mental health, and oral health. Moreover, much of our health is the result of *social determinants*—such as housing, education, social capital, our natural environment and the way we construct the *built environment* around us—that are shaped by policy decisions made completely outside the health care system.

Most health care policy debates revolve around issues of medical care access, cost, and quality; however, there are organizational and individual proponents (such as The Blue Sky Initiative) of an approach to health policy where the goal is optimal health status. They would like to see a "move from a health care system to a *health system* that provides vertical, horizontal and longitudinal integration" (Peterson, 2006).

Thinking about health in terms of population outcomes can dramatically shift the way problems are defined and addressed. One example is identifying the leading causes of death. Using a disease model, the leading killers are ailments such as heart disease, cancer, stroke, injury, and lung disease, but McGinnis and Foege (1993), using a population-based, prevention-oriented perspective, identified the "real causes of death" as behaviors such as tobacco use, improper diet, a lack of physical activity, and alcohol misuse. They argued that some 88% of what we spend on health nationally pays for access to medical care, but in terms of influence on health status, it accounts for a mere 10%. This alternative view attributes 50% of our health status to our behaviors, 20% to genetics, and 20% to environmental factors. Yet only 4% of health spending goes to promoting healthy behaviors and 8% to all other nonmedical health-related activities (Robert Wood Johnson Foundation, 2000). Since the mid 1960s, public health spending as a percentage of overall spending on health care has fluctuated between 1% and 1.5% (Frist, 2002), and yet 25 years of the 30-year increase in life expectancy between 1900 and 1995 can be attributed to public health interventions.

Some examples used to illustrate points throughout this book draw on material from outside the realm of medical care finance and delivery. The case at the end of Chapter 10 discusses folic acid fortification of foods, an example of a population-based public health intervention, and the case in Chapter 12 looks at evidence-based, community-centered mental health interventions. This book, however, focuses mostly on access, cost, and quality issues related to personal medical services. That is due largely to the fact that the primary intended audience is health care professionals (people who operate primarily from inside the medical care system) and also to the simple fact that the United State is currently facing many salient and immediate issues related to health care access cost and quality. Readers are urged, however, to keep that intentional bias in mind and to think about how a big-picture view of health might change the way problems and solutions get identified. For instance, one of the health care finance reform proposals currently in vogue, and one discussed in several places in this book, is pay for performance, also know as pay for quality. Pay-for-performance programs provide financial incentives for providers to meet certain process and outcome measures. Kindig (2006, p. 2611) has proposed a "pay-for-population health performance system" that "would go beyond medical care to include financial incentives for the equally essential nonmedical care determinants of population health."

HEALTH POLICY: WHAT IS IT?

Beyond the scope issues just described, most of us are clear on what health policy is about. Simply stated, health policy addresses questions such as:

- Where are we with our health care?
- How did we get here?
- Where do we want to be?
- What other alternatives are available here and throughout the world?
- What is likely to work in the future given our political processes?
- What roles should health professionals and ordinary citizens play in this process?
- How can we become better prepared for such roles?

Can we expect any given set of participants to agree on the answers to those questions? Of course not. Their perspectives vary. Their interests are often in conflict. A goal of this book is to encourage development of an objective, managerial approach to decision making—one that uses precise definitions of terms and relationships and carefully considers the key issues and actors on both sides before reaching individual conclusions. Because of this book's management education approach, you should come away with a set of varied tools for interpreting and analyzing events, situations, and alternatives—tools that you can add to the skills that you have already developed through professional training and experience. You will not be asked to abandon what has worked, but you can probably do a better job with a systematic approach that allows you to use a broader array of methods that fit a greater variety of situations.

THE POLICY ANALYSIS PROCESS

Much of this text is organized around the stages of the policy analysis process, which are as follows:

- Problem identification: Why do we think we need to evaluate and possibly change the way we do things? What kind of actions are

---

TABLE 1-3 Illustrative Health Policy Issues at State and Local Levels

- What services should be provided and to whom under Medicaid options and waivers?
- How should the professional licensure be conducted so as to encourage quality of care, adequate access and appropriate competition?
- How should the public university system decide how many professionals to train to assure adequate access to all sections of the state? To all target groups?
- What should be the balance between local governance and state standards and mandates in the provision of public health department functions?
- What should be the state's role in subsidizing care for the uninsured?
- What should be the roles of the state insurance regulations and oversight boards in assuring access to care for the general public and for special populations?
- How separate should the health care system and the mental health system continue to be? What about insurance parity?
- How do we undertake health care emergency planning: responses to floods, earthquakes, pandemics, or terrorism? What is the relationship between the state systems (public health and military) and local first-responders?

---

people asking for? What are the drivers that require that we commit limited resources to this policy area? What is the intended output? What is the expected result?

- Process definition: What is the current situation, and what is being done about it? What are people citing as the causes of concern? How valid are they? Who are the current actors and what are their roles? Why are the current results unsatisfactory to some? Are people framing the issue effectively? What are reasonable expectations for results over a relevant time horizon?
- Process analysis: What is actually happening in practice? How are outputs and outcomes measured and why? What are the resource inputs? Are they appropriate? Are the outputs distributed fairly? Where, how, and when might new technologies change this process within the relevant time horizon? What are the resource requirements of the really promising alternatives, and what will they cost? What are the impacts of these processes, such as persons served, lives saved, and hospital days avoided?
- Qualitative analysis: Identify and assess the nonquantitative issues related to valuation of benefits, and impacts on quality, equity, and distribution of outcomes.

- Evaluation: Weigh the evidence, quantitative and qualitative, and analyze for the following:
  - Technical feasibility
  - Political feasibility
  - Economic and financial viability
- Recommendation
  - Choice: Consider the value and ethical concerns that must carry weight in your decision and then choose a preferred policy to be recommended.
  - Communication: Prepare to report your findings and conclusions convincingly.

SUPPORTING IMPLEMENTATION

During the design of a health policy study, throughout its conduct, and in its conclusion and reporting stage, the policy process must support its implementation. The objective of policy analysis is not a report but informed choices that lead to an improved health care system. That requires attention to the following:

- Implementation strategy: How do we manage the policy process to gain public, professional, and consumer support for change and backing of the most appropriate alternative(s)? How do we assure that key implementers and consumers buy into the process early enough? How do we mediate conflicting interests?
- Implementation planning: What steps do we need to take to assure successful implementation of the alternative chosen? How will we know that the chosen alternative was an improvement?
- Feedback to our policy processes: Have we been making the right choices? If not, why not? What new understandings should we take away that will lead to better and more efficient policy choices in the future?

HEALTH PROFESSIONALS AND THE POLICY PROCESS

One unusual aspect of health care in the United States is the low level of influence that health professionals generally have on policy formulation. Too often health professionals focus on what policy makers are doing to them, not on what they can contribute to the policy processes. Professionally prepared

---

TABLE 1-4   Illustrative Health Policy Issues for Health
Care Institutions

- How much charitable (uncompensated) care should we provide beyond that which is mandated?
- Should we try to encourage local organizations to participate in a National Health Information Network? Why?
- What efforts should we undertake to encourage local emergency planning?
- How should we go about increasing the proportion of the local population who volunteer as local organ donors?
- How can we rationalize the services provided by local providers, reducing duplication and waste, and still avoid charges of anticompetitive practices?

---

leadership is extremely important if policies are to be accepted and implemented effectively; therefore, we need to consider how and where professionals can exert leadership in enhancing the delivery of the services that are their work and their calling.

One reason for limited involvement of health care professionals in the United States has been the high opportunity cost of any time they spend on policy matters. In most countries of the world, a ministry of health oversees the national health system. Because government salaries for health professionals are relatively low, there is competition for higher administrative posts that offer better pay and better locations. Health professionals hold most key positions below the political level in the ministry, and physicians are the directors of most divisions, departments, and institutions. At one time, U.S. health department directors, as well as many hospital administrators, were expected to be medical doctors. During and after World War II, when physicians were in short supply, those institutions called on other administrators. The nation's schools of public health trained new cadres of administrators. Rapidly rising physician income, especially after the introduction of Medicare and Medicaid in 1965, increased the demand for but not the supply of physician services. That meant that directly providing care paid so much better than administration that fewer health professionals sought health administration training. Educational institutions and health agencies responded by training health administrators without clinical credentials. As managed care has begun to constrain provider income and consolidation into larger organizations has expanded management incomes, professionals have taken a stronger interest in managerial roles. This interest has been reinforced by provider dissatisfaction with changes in professional autonomy, incomes, and working conditions that emerged under managed care. Health professionals are waking up to the need to participate in policy making, but their effective participation has been constrained by their lack of skills and confidence and by the other demands on their time.

BIG ISSUES TO KEEP OUR EYES ON

The United States has experienced rapid inflation in health care costs without attendant relative improvements in key health indicators such as infant mortality and life expectancy. One response has been to note that the United States and South Africa were the only two major countries without a national health service. This response, however, does not account for the fact that many highly developed countries with government health services are now struggling with similar and interrelated issues:

- Relationships between health care financing and employment
- Employment status, compensation, and autonomy of health professionals
- Equity in dealing with underserved populations

TABLE 1-5   Illustrative Health Policy Issues for Provider
                 Professionals

- What services should be provided in addition to those normally provided by one's specialty?
- What managed care organizations should I sign contracts with? Avoid?
- What should I do about the state of local emergency preparedness?
- What positions should I encourage my local, state, and national professional organizations to take on current health policy issues?
- Should I volunteer to serve on local or state committees assessing and advocating on health policy issues? Should I seek or accept a leadership role? How do I prepare for that possibility?
- Should I try to make my practice a leader in the adoption of health information technology? A late adopter?
- Should I go into (or stay in) a private practice or should I join a large group that is tied to a dominant delivery network (hospital, HMO, pharmacy chain, etc.)?

- Adequate supplies of trained health personnel
- Democratic political processes for reaching difficult health policy decisions
- Technology development and dissemination
- Impacts of social meta-issues, such as aging and terrorism, on health policy decisions.

Relationship Between Health Care Financing and Employment

Increasing international competition for jobs has highlighted the high costs of U.S. health care and the impact of concentrating those costs onto large employers who pay for health care for employees and retirees. These costs have been one factor leading international auto manufacturers to select sites in Canada over otherwise lower-cost locations in the southern United States. The proportion of workers covered at their place of employment has been falling in recent years, and this trend is likely to continue. Employers had sought to control costs through the use of managed-care organizations. As this effort seems to have reaped the bulk of its potential savings, more and more the burden is shifting to workers through having high individual premiums, having reduced subsidies for dependents' coverage, moving jobs to independent contractor status, or dropping the benefit altogether under the rubric of consumer-centered health care.

One area where insurance coverage is opposed by many employers is the area of mental health. Many states have passed or tried to pass laws requiring *parity* of coverages for mental illness with coverages for physical illness. Washington State only did so in 2005. There is plenty of evidence that the cost of adding such services would not be all that expensive, but small business organizations have opposed *parity* legislation as costly to them. The existence of publicly funded community mental health centers has complicated the issue. Advocates for the mentally ill have pushed for parity legislation, not only to increase coverage, but also to reinforce the concept that mental illness is a brain disorder that should not be stigmatized and should be handled like any other illness.

Employment Status, Compensation, and Autonomy of Health Professionals

For many years, physicians and pharmacists were almost entirely independent business people. Hospitals employed some specialists (radiologists, pathologists, anesthesiologists), often under profit-sharing agreements, but medical practice acts in many states prohibited the use of employed physicians. With the movement toward managed care and the consolidation and industrialization taking place within the health care industry, more and more organizations began to buy practices and to serve customers that had previously turned to private practices and independent pharmacies. The ability of large organizations to buy and sell goods and services at deep discounts has forced more and more small operations to sell out. Increasingly, health care professionals are employed by large organizations and are experiencing conflicts involving their professional independence and autonomy. This has led to patient concerns about providers' disinterestedness, a concern that has tended to weaken the status of the health professions.

Equity

Healthy People 2010, the federal strategic plan for improving health status, lists two overarching goals. The first is to increase both the quality and the number of years of life. The second is to reduce health disparities. The term *health disparities* refers to a disproportionate burden of disease, disability, and death among a population or group. Disparities can result from genetics, cultural factors, behaviors, social determinants (such as low socioeconomic status), lack of access to care, not seeking or being provided with care when it is accessible and available, and not receiving quality or culturally and linguistically appropriate care when it is accessed. Although the problem of health disparities is not unique to the United States—the term for this policy issue in much of the rest of the world is *health equity*—there is a growing recognition that health disparities are a serious national problem. The *National Healthcare Disparities Report,* released by the Agency for Healthcare Research and Quality in December 2003, identified disparities in health care for "priority populations"—women, children, older people, people of minority races, low-income groups, and people with special health care needs.

A report by the Washington State Board of Health cited examples of health disparities among minorities in that state, including the following (Finkbonner et al., 2001):

- The infant mortality rate for American Indians and African-Americans is more than double the rate for whites.
- African-Americans are more than three times as likely as whites to die from HIV/AIDS, whereas Hispanics are more than 1.5 times more likely to die from the virus.

- The rate of tuberculosis for Asian/Pacific Islanders is more than 15 times greater than it is for whites
- African-Americans are more than three times as likely to die from diabetes as whites; the death rate for American Indians/Alaskan Natives is 2.5 times higher, and for Hispanics, it is 1.5 times higher.

Throughout the world, providers tend to congregate where income and educational opportunities are best for them and their families; therefore, medical care has been plentiful in the major cities, especially those with medical education centers, and scarce in rural areas. The United States is no exception. Providers may also choose to direct their efforts toward consumers who have the greatest ability to pay. They gravitate toward more profitable specialties and may emphasize services that are most likely to generate income. All of these factors can contribute to disparities in care.

There have been many governmental and private programs to bring service to special populations, such as underserved rural areas, the posthospitalized mentally ill, American Indian and Alaskan Native villages, and people with AIDS. In these cases, the nation's focus on a market system has been modified to overcome market failures in health care. Phelps (1997) pointed out that government involvement is one of the four features of the economics of health care delivery that differs from the delivery of most professional services. Three other economic differences that Phelps noted are uncertainty, information asymmetry, and externalities. All of these are explored further.

Adequate Supplies of Trained Health Personnel

Much of the cost of educating and training health professionals is borne by the public sector—public colleges and universities and hospitals are all involved in training health professionals. Because professionals tend to be compensated well above the national average and work for private as well as public companies and institutions, the level of government educational support is frequently called into question. Are we training the right number of the right people with the right degree of specialization for the right jobs? This is an issue in just about every other country because of disconnects between the educational system and the health care system. Because the federal government does not operate either system in the United States, we continue to live with the question of who is in charge of determining how many of what type need to be trained.

TABLE 1-6   Illustrative Health Policy Issues for Payer Organizations
(Employers and Insurers)

- What options should I offer as health benefits? Given that employees need choices, should I offer medical savings accounts?
- How much money and effort should we be allocating to prevention? What about the argument that people change plans so often that our investment in prevention won't pay off?
- We have a lot of data on health care utilization? Should we mine that data and suggest choices of procedures? Providers? Lifestyle changes?

Democratic Political Processes for Reaching Difficult Health Policy Decisions

Time and time again, attempts to rationalize the health care system have been stymied by those who prefer the *status quo ante.* Opposition may be due to self-interest in some cases, but it can also be due to fundamental disagreements about how and where decisions are best made. The debate over the role of central government versus local units split the Founding Fathers and still is ongoing and so is the debate over whether the health care system needs considerable oversight or whether a suitable case can be made instead for relying on market approaches. In thinking about where the nexus for decision making about health care should lie in today's United States, several complex economic, ideological, and managerial issues must be considered:

- Centralization versus decentralization: This is both a strategic and a tactical issue. Often it is considered in an ideological context with one side arguing that management is more responsive when it is closer to the people. The opposing side is likely to argue that local management is much more likely to be captured by local interest groups and is inefficient because of its small scale of operation.
- Unequal power in the markets: There are circumstances in health care that may limit the usual free market conditions of commerce. These include the following:
  - Monopoly power: The ability of the seller to control a market. This is of concern where there are only one or two providers of a specific service in a community. Under federal and most states'

laws, obtaining a true monopoly position is illegal. In rural and other underserved areas, however, a lack of provider interest may allow a monopoly to exist.

- Monopsony power: A counterpart of monopoly in which the buyer rather than the seller has control of the market. Although this is not illegal, it is a market failure. The most common illustration in the United States has been the market power of the federal government. As a purchaser through Medicare, Medicaid, veterans' health care programs such as CHAMPUS/TRICARE, and federal employee health insurance, it has been able to insist on maximum price discounts. In some locales, major managed-care organizations, such as the former Blue Cross and Blue Shield organizations, may also hold such pricing power.

- Collusion: Tacit or explicit agreement by a group (usually of sellers) to follow a common strategy. While joint price fixing is a crime, there are many other legal practices that may limit the supply of services. For example, one hospital in a two-hospital city may decide to stop offering obstetrical services after receiving assurances that the other hospital will in turn stop offering level I trauma care, allowing both to increase occupancy in their respective units and to keep the physicians in the community with those specialties from playing off one hospital against the other.

- Professionalism and information asymmetry: Information asymmetry occurs when one party to a transaction has more or better information about markets and values than the other. One of the underpinnings of professional status is the reality that the professional has information that is not possessed or understood by the client, thereby assuring information asymmetry. The client must then defer in decision making and the delivery of service to the professional.

- Public good vs. competitive market: The conditions of a competitive market require many buyers and many sellers, complete information for both buyers and sellers, and the capacity to make rational decisions on both sides. It can be argued that because of information asymmetry, the provider has a distinct advantage in the health care market, leading to market failure. Because the market is not functioning effectively and health care is a necessity for many, some argue that health care should be considered a public good to be regulated and perhaps provided by the government. If one assumes that health care is a public good and the market is failing, where and how should the government flex its economic and regulatory muscle? There are those who think that the market or consumer approach is the way to solve our health care national problems. Others argue that health care is not very adaptable to an unmanaged marketplace. That will be an important theme throughout any discussion of health policy analysis. Reagan (1999) referred to this as an aspect of the basic dilemma of health policy.

We in the United States want health care for everyone, and yet we prefer that it delivered through a virtually unregulated marketplace with lots of consumer choice. The unregulated marketplace proves to be a double-edged sword. Those who want to support consumer responsibility and choice believe that careful shopping behavior will reduce costs. Current experience with medical tourism bears that out. On the other hand, the difficulties of those who do shop in gaining access to price and quality information suggest how far we are from suitable market conditions. Although one hears from strong advocates on one side about the need for universal coverage and on the other about consumer-driven markets, the vast bulk of this industry gradually industrializes and continues silently with its current course of growth with disconnectedness, high cost, withheld price and quality information, and dominance of local markets by powerful local actors.

Technology Development and Dissemination

A key issue in health policy is how to evaluate and rationally adopt new health care technologies. In manufacturing terms, how and when do we deploy the products of our research and development? Much of the recent

TABLE 1-7   Illustrative Health Policy Issues for Individuals

- Should I participate in my employer's health benefit plan and, if so, which option?
- How much should I plan to rely on Medicare when I retire in 2030? What alternative strategies should I be considering?
- Certain medical specialties are not available in my area. My county government wants to issue tax-exempt bonds to finance a new doctors' office wing on the county hospital site. Should I support the referendum on the bonds?

increase in health care costs has been attributed to the introduction of health care technology, much of which leads to positive improvements in our ability to deal with disease but also costs more to provide.

Because the health care marketplace is highly fragmented with mostly local providers, individual providers cannot undertake research and development unless the development can be patented, as is the case with new drugs. Individual providers can only amortize the costs of such development over their own client base, and thus the cost would take too long to recoup. Alternatives are to turn to the federal government or to vendors who have access to multiple providers. Areas of research and development where government already plays some role in the United States include the following:

- Basic science: Our society has decided to fund basic research in health care through the National Institutes of Health and other government agencies. Much of this takes place in universities that receive grants to conduct proposed research efforts.

- Clinical applications: Some federal funding is available for clinical research, but much of it takes place with the support of vendors or individual or institutional providers. In areas, such as surgery, which often is not subject to Food and Drug Administration approval, a great deal of individual experimentation goes on and innovation spreads rapidly. In the new drug field, the Food and Drug Administration tightly controls experimentation. This helps assure consumer safety but slows the pace of innovation considerably.

- Testing for efficacy and safety: Here there is joint responsibility of the vendor, the provider, and government regulators, depending on the nature of the innovation. If the technology does not offer a "blockbuster" or high-volume good or service, there is limited support for this type of research. The Agency for Healthcare Research and Quality has the function of studying "evidence-based medicine" applied to existing treatments and practices, but its funding is not sufficient to do many needed studies.

Impact of Meta-Issues on the Health Policy Decisions

Health care policy making does not occur in a vacuum. It takes place in the context of society at large, and its debates reflect issues in the larger society. Health policy is profoundly influenced by value-driven issues that cut across the entire U.S. policy landscape. These include, especially, debates over the role of free versus managed market mechanisms and pro-life and right-to-die ideologies. The battle over embryonic stem cell research is a case in point. The idea of using cells from fertilized eggs that were going to be thrown out anyway might not have attracted attention if it were not for the continuing debate about abortion, much of which turns on the definition of when life begins. If "life" begins at birth, then the opposition to early abortion—and the objection to using embryonic stem cells—is greatly weakened. If "life" begins with the union of the egg and sperm, then embryos are to be protected. Similarly, strong clashes among value frameworks affect other health care issues such as physician-assisted suicide or executions, contraception for minors, morning-after pills, concerns of institutional review boards, and direct-to-consumer pharmaceutical marketing.

THE ROAD AHEAD

Virtually all of these issues are revisited in the process chapters of this book. As central themes, we have developed brief cases offering 10 health policy examples that accompany their relevant chapters:

- International comparisons of health care systems
- A standard for culturally and linguistically appropriate care
- Subspecialty versus community hospitals
- Global medical coverage
- Marked small area variations in treatments
- The development of the National Health Information Network and regional health information organizations
- The Clinton health plan experience
- Folic acid fortification
- Voluntary versus governmental standards
- Evidence-based medicine and mental health.

These illustrate the types of issues and activities that cluster around health care policy debates and decisions and serve as examples for classroom discussion as we follow the stages of the policy analysis process.

The next five chapters (Part I) review the context in which American policy analysis is likely to take place, the status of our health system, and its apparent performance in recent years. Chapter 2 reviews where we are. Chapter 3 recounts how we in the United States got there, whereas

Chapter 4 discusses what various actors would like to see occur. Chapter 5 outlines some of the government options that are under consideration for the country's future course. Chapter 6 presents some alternative responses and initiatives open to institutions and professions. Discussion case studies are attached to Chapters 3 through 6. Part II presents specific aspects of the policy analysis process. Chapter 7 begins the presentation of this process with issues of process identification and definition. Chapters 8, 9, and 10 deal, respectively, with the three major areas of evaluation in the analysis process: (1) technological, (2) political, and (3) economic. Chapter 11 returns us to the additional value issues that dominate today's headlines, whereas Chapter 12 points out how the policy analysis process must support the implementation of the policy after it is accepted. Discussion cases are attached to each of the six chapters in this part. Part III moves us to a focus on the roles of professions and professionals in the world of health policy. Chapter 13 reviews what is likely to work, given our political processes, and Chapter 14 outlines the ways that professionals can become further involved in the policy process. Chapter 15 wraps things up and suggests some strategies for staying involved with policy issues beyond the completion of this course of study.

PART I

The Context

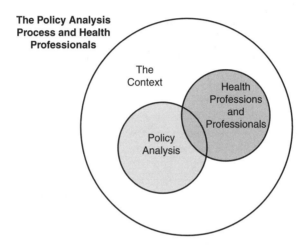

The Policy Analysis Process and Health Professionals

The Context

Policy Analysis

Health Professions and Professionals

Although this book is designed to be valuable to anyone engaged in health policy development, its primary purpose is to enable current and future health professionals to understand and then participate in the health policy process. The diagram above shows policy analysis and the work of the health professions taking place within the context of the health care system. The first section of this book develops that context through a discussion of the current status of the U.S. health care system (Chapter 2) and a review of factors that influenced its development as the decentralized system we have today (Chapter 3). The case accompanying Chapter 3 provides a chance to look at the experiences of other countries and develop some hypotheses about how these countries achieved their current status. Chapter 4 reviews the many and varied objectives for the U.S. health care system being expressed by various policy participants. Chapter 5 presents some of the recommendations for government action being suggested. One educational outcome you should try to achieve is to understand these positions, their underlying assumptions, and their strengths and weaknesses. This is followed in Chapter 6 by a discussion of the responses that service delivery organizations, providers, payers and employers, and patients have undertaken.

These chapters provide both the context and vocabulary for moving on to the second part of this book, which outlines available tools for rational policy analysis—one of the circles within a circle in the diagram. The third part of this book looks at the role of the health professions and professionals, and in particular, how they can and should participate in policy analysis.

Where Are We?

As more of us are being told we are sick, fewer of us are being told we are well. People need to think about the benefits and risks of increased diagnosis: the fundamental question they face is whether or not to become a patient (Welch et al., 2007, p. 2).

American health care is always in a state of flux as new scientific knowledge and clinical experience change our prescriptions for illness and wellness. As a society, we respond by changing the ways health care is delivered. The way we choose to provide those services increasingly impacts many aspects of our society, from health status to employment to economics to recreation to professional concerns to our perceptions of our own well-being. This chapter reviews the current status of the U.S. health care system from three points of view:

- Current outcomes and costs
- Industrializing structures for delivery
- Medicalization of our society.

CURRENT OUTCOMES AND COSTS

There is a growing consensus that not all is well with U.S. health care. Medicare trust funds are forecast to disappear over the next decade. Health care expenditures are projected to rise to around 20% of the gross domestic product (GDP) by 2015 (Borger et al., 2006). More and more small companies do not provide health benefits, whereas larger companies are shifting significant portions of health insurance costs onto employees and retirees. Politicians on both sides of the aisle are calling for change (Clinton,

2004; Gingrich, 2003; Gingrich & Kennedy, 2004). At the same time, health professionals' control over health care is being threatened by outsiders calling for more reliance on government programs, more consumer-centered care, or both. Each recommendation has the potential to change markedly the roles and status of health care professionals.

High Comparative Costs and Low Comparative Outcomes

The United States spends far more on health care per capita and as a percentage of GDP than other developed countries, but does not seem to be much better off for it. **Table 2-1** illustrates this by comparing a dozen countries on these two resource input dimensions and on two outcome dimensions, male life expectancy at birth and infant mortality rates. Similar rankings result when looking at a number of other outcome variables. The health care systems of these other countries offer virtually universal coverage but range from mostly private insurance to a national health service. The high U.S. costs and low U.S. outcomes do not seem to be associated with any one specific organizational or financing approach. Yet that is about all that experts seem to agree on.

Consumers in six countries (Australia, Canada, Germany, New Zealand, the United Kingdom, and the United States), especially those experiencing illness, were asked to rate their experience in terms of several factors (Davis et al., 2006; Frogner & Anderson, 2006):

- Patient safety: Perceived error rates were highest in the United States; laboratory errors highest in Canada.
- Effectiveness: The United States ranked best overall and best on preventive care and care for the chronically ill.
- Patient-centeredness: The United States ranked last in almost all respects.
- Timeliness of care: The United States and Germany were quick to receive specialist and elective surgical care, but the United States and Canada had the longest waits for primary care visits.
- Efficiency: U.S. patients reported use of emergency departments because a primary care provider was not available and also reported unavailability of medical records and test results and duplication of tests.
- Equity: The United States lagged in terms of perceived inequities for both poor and average income respondents.

TABLE 2-1 Selected International Comparisons of Health Inputs and Outcomes

	Health Expenditures as % of Gross Domestic Product 2004	Health Expenditures in US Dollars per Capita 2004	Practicing MDs per 1,000 2004	Inpatient and Acute Care Beds per 1,000 2004	Population Life Expectancy at Birth 2003	Infant Deaths Per 1,000 2004
United States	15.3	$6,120	2.4	2.8	77.5	6.9*
Switzerland	11.6	4,077	3	3.8	80.6	4.2
Canada	9.9	3,165	2.1	3*	79.9	5.3*
France	10.5	3,159	3.4	3.8	79.4	3.9
Australia	9.6	3,120	2.6*	3.8	80.3	4.7
Belgium	10.1*	3,044*	4	4.8	78.8	4.3
Germany	10.6	3,043	3.4	6.4	78.6	4.1
The Netherlands	7.7	3,041	3.6	3.3	78.6	4.1
Sweden	9.1	2,825	2.9*	2.2	80.2	3.1
United Kingdom	8.1*	2,508	2.3	3.6	78.5	5.3
Japan	8.0	2,249	2	8.4	81.8	2.8

* 2003 data
UK expenditure data is for the United Kingdom, but life expectancy and infant mortality is for England and Wales.
Source: OECD Health Data 2006. Copyright OECD 2006.

The number of physician visits and hospital days per capita was lower in the United States than the Organisation for Economic Co-operation and Development median, and input prices for health care worker wages, hospital supplies, and drugs were much higher in the United States. Anderson et al. (2003) noted, "U.S. policy makers need to reflect on what Americans are getting for their greater health care spending." They conclude, "It's the prices, stupid." Administrative costs for our system, estimated as high as 30% of overall health care costs, are also high when compared with the rest of the world (Woolhandler et al., 2003).

Overinsurance and Overutilization Arguments

Cannon and Tanner (2005) argued that the basic American problem is overutilization and would explain away comparative international differences because:

- Data definitions and collection methods are not comparable
- Health care is partly a consumption good that normally rises with income
- The U.S. infant mortality is increased by our efforts to save low-birthweight infants that would be stillborn elsewhere
- There is little proven relationship between longevity and health care expenditures
- Our cost figures include the costs of medical research and innovation that are not incurred elsewhere.

They argue that disease-specific data are a better measure. On the mortality-to-incidence ratios for AIDS, breast cancer, colon cancer, and breast cancer, for example, the U.S. system looks very good.

Alan R. Hubbard (2006), assistant to the president for economic policy and director of the National Economic Council in the George W. Bush Administration, opened an April 3 *New York Times* Op-Ed column entitled "The Health of a Nation" by noting that private health care premiums had risen 73% in the most recent 5 years. He observed the following:

> *Health care is expensive because the vast majority of American consumers use it as if it were free. Health insurance policies with low deductibles insulate people from the cost of the medical care they use—so much so that they often do not even ask for prices* (p. A17).

Ironically, relevant prices for major interventions are not usually available to consumers, even when they do ask for them.

A similar point of view has been expressed by R. Glenn Hubbard (2006), former chair of the Council of Economic Advisers, who saw rising health care costs as one of the biggest threats to the nation's future prosperity. "Despite our national investment of $1.9 trillion, we get highly inefficient care—spectacular in certain respects, but rife with error, disorganized, and unaffordable or inaccessible to many." He proposed that all health care costs be individual (rather than corporate) tax deductions. He believed this would accelerate the use of health savings accounts (HSAs). To support this, he argued for uniform national health insurance standards and open national health insurance markets. He used the banking reforms that allowed multistate banking as a positive parallel example and disagreed with the President's Advisory Panel on Tax Reform, which had recommended a cap on the tax deductibility of employer purchases of health insurance. That recommendation was aimed at motivating employers to offer only basic, more affordable plans. He recommended giving consumers more choices of providers, greater use of health information technology, and medical liability law reforms (Cogan et al., 2005).

If the United States spends more on health care than any other nation without topnotch results, does that mean we are spending too much? The overspending can be in price or the quantity of services provided, probably some of both. U.S. health care wages are the highest in the world. Research also shows that an increased supply of health professionals leads to more utilization, some of which may be unwarranted, yet attempts to restrict the supply of specialists using licensing systems have led to charges of illegal restraint of trade. Like health care, professional education is a confusing mixture of a public good and a matter of personal consumption. There are many alternative ways—certificate of need regulations, for example—to try to control overuse or underuse by trying to influence the supply or demand for heath care services.

Cutler et al. (2006) concluded that if 50% of the increase in longevity between 1960 and 2000 is attributable to our increased medical care expenditures, we have gotten an acceptable return on our money. They suggest that the cost of a life year gained was reasonable, especially for those less than 65 years old. They caution, however, that the returns from added expenditures, especially for older people, have diminished over time.

Continued High Cost Inflation Rates

The Office of the Actuary, Centers for Medicare and Medicaid Services, and the Department of Health and Human Services are responsible for providing estimates used to assess the financial viability of those two huge government programs. Its report, *National Health Care Expenditures Projections: 2005–2015,* concludes that health care spending is likely to outstrip economic growth (GDP growth) throughout the next decade. Although there will be ups and down because of specific interventions such as Medicare Part D drug coverage, there will be little affect on aggregate health care spending, which will grow at a rate 2% higher than the overall economy. By 2015, it forecasts, national expenditures on health care will reach 20% of the GDP. The government share will gradually increase, leaving health expenditures financed about equally between government and private sources (Borger et al., 2006). **Table 2-2** summarizes historical and forecast data on health expenditures in terms of dollars, dollars per capita, percentage of GDP, and price deflators for both health expenditures and GDP.

Except for the period from 1995 to 1998, the inflation rate for health care costs and health insurance premiums has been well above the inflation rate of the consumer price index and of workers' earnings for at least the last 18 years, as **Figure 2-1** illustrates. No wonder workers and employers feel squeezed by the rising costs of health care.

Disappearing Health Benefits

Employee health benefits (75% paid by employers, including government employers, in 2003) are disappearing at an increasing rate. Between 2000 and 2004, the percentage of insured nonolder people (0 to 64 years old) in employment-based health programs dropped 5% to 61%. In Indiana, Missouri, South Carolina, and Wisconsin during that period, the percentage dropped 9% to 10% (State Health Facts, 2005).

Official federal policy has been to encourage employees to participate in HSAs. The theory is that workers will choose health insurance coverage with high deductibles and coinsurance and will put the premium money saved into tax-exempt (income and interest) savings accounts that could be used in case of heavy expenses, for retirement income, or for other uses. These plans have gotten off the ground slowly because employers have been concerned about the problem of *adverse selection,* namely that younger, healthier employees would choose the HSA option, leaving employees who are at

TABLE 2-2   U.S. National Health Expenditures (NHE), Share of GDP and Price Deflators, Selected Calendar Years 2000–2015

NHE Spending Category ($ billion)	2000	2005*	2007*	2010*	2015*
Total	1358.5	2016.0	2325.7	2887.3	4043.6
Physician and Clinical Services	288.6	429.9	496.5	610.7	849.8
Other Personal Health Care	37.1	58.1	67.8	89.2	134.8
Dental Services	62.0	87.4	101.3	124.9	167.3
Other Professional Services	39.1	55.8	64.0	78.5	109.4
Hospital Care	417.0	616.1	709.1	882.4	1230.9
Nursing Homes, Home Health Care	125.8	170.6	192.2	232.8	320.5
NHE Per Capita ($)	$4,729	$6,683	$7,376	$9,173	$12,357
NHE as % of GDP	13.8%	16.2%	16.8%	18.0%	20.0%
HCFA Implicit Medical Price Deflator (2000 base)	1.000	1.205	1.248	1.453	1.752
GDP Implicit Price Deflator (2000 base)	1.000	1.119	1.171	1.260	1.298

*Projected

Source: Author created. Data from CMS accessed 02/05/06 at http://www.cms.hhs.gov/NationalHealthExpendData/downloads/proj.2005.pdf

higher risk drawing from a different and smaller risk pool. Early returns from postal employees showed that the employees signing up for HSAs were much younger than those who chose or kept traditional coverage.

Some employers are also concerned about the "portability" feature of HSAs. If the worker leaves, the premium dollar saved goes with the worker rather than staying to help cover the remaining employees' health insurance claims. Many employers see health benefits as a cost necessary to attract good employees and reduce employee turnover. Portability can run counter to that objective (Freudenheim, 2006a).

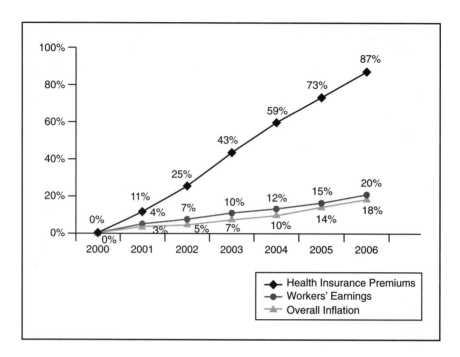

FIGURE 2-1   Cumulative Changes in Health Insurance Premiums, Overall Inflation, and Workers' Earnings, 2000–2006

Source: "Employer Health Benefits 2006 Annual Survey—Chartpack," (7451), The Henry J. Kaiser Family Foundation and Health Research & Educational Trust, September 2006.

A MORE SYSTEMATIC EVALUATION

Taking stock of where we are means that we must evaluate our health care system systematically according to a number of criteria—cost, quality, outcomes, and equity. In 1980, Donabedian suggested the following classification when evaluating quality of care:

- Access
- Technical management
- Management of interpersonal relationships
- Continuity of care.

One could easily amplify these categories, but they are a useful starting point (McLaughlin, 1998). All of these factors involve tradeoffs with the cost of care and with one another.

Access and Availability

If you were in a serious auto accident, you would want the ambulance there fast to stabilize you and transport you to a trauma center. You would want that ambulance *available*. If we are in danger, we supposedly are guaranteed *access*. If the situation is life threatening and the hospital participates in Medicare or Medicaid, it must take us regardless of ability to pay. For less serious situations, for emergent medical conditions, and for prevention, there are no such guarantees. The local capacity to care for us and the ability to ensure that payment will be made (either through insurance coverage or out of pocket) are both necessary conditions of obtaining care. Unfortunately, a significant proportion of our population lacks access, availability, or both. **Figure 2-2** shows the number of nonolder U.S. residents lacking health insurance coverage from 2000 through 2004. That number has risen from more then 39 million to more than 46 million. Although federal safety net spending, including Medicare, has increased 15% over the same period, spending in real dollar terms has expanded only slightly because of a 14% inflation in health care costs. Spending has failed to adjust for the additional uninsured, most of whom are young and poor (Holahan & Cook, 2005; Kaiser Commission on Medicaid, 2005). As employers shift more and more of the costs of health care to their employees or to public sector programs and as Congress and the Administration try to reduce budget deficits by cutting "entitlement programs," access problems mount.

There are numerous other perceived access problems. Although coverage for children has improved and the older population receives considerable benefits from Medicare and Medicaid, the working population has become worse off. Even before employer coverage decreased, the biggest access problem was with the *working poor*—those who earn too much to qualify for Medicaid but have little or no access to employer-subsidized health insurance and are unable to pay their share of the costs, even when employment-based insurance is available. Even under subsidized programs such as the Maine and Massachusetts programs, there has been slow enrollment by the working poor (Belluck, 2007).

Many improvements in coverage for children came with the State Children's Health Insurance Program in 1997 and have occurred despite reduced private insurance coverage for children. Racial disparities in insurance coverage remain, with the highest rate of uninsurance occurring among Hispanic children (21% in 2004) and African American children (13.4% in 2004). Overall, 11.3% of U.S. children remained uninsured

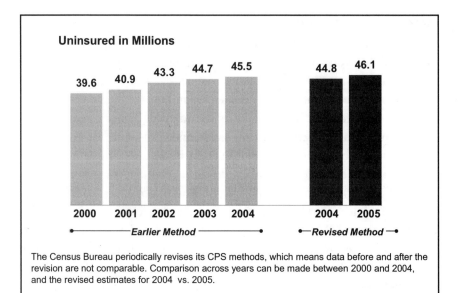

Uninsured in Millions

39.6	40.9	43.3	44.7	45.5		44.8	46.1
2000	2001	2002	2003	2004		2004	2005

●————————*Earlier Method*————————● ●——*Revised Method*——●

The Census Bureau periodically revises its CPS methods, which means data before and after the revision are not comparable. Comparison across years can be made between 2000 and 2004, and the revised estimates for 2004 vs. 2005.

FIGURE 2-2 Number of Non-Elderly Americans Uninsured 2000–2005

Source: "Covering the Uninsured: Growing Need, Strained Resources" (#7429-02), The Henry J. Kaiser Family Foundation, January 2007.

throughout 2004, but 25.6% were uninsured at least part of the year. Children uninsured for all or part of the year were more than twice as likely to receive no medical care that year (SHADAC, 2006).

Meanwhile, racial discrepancies still abound. Why are black infants as much as three times as likely to die as white infants in many states? Why was a child between 1 and 14 years old about three times as likely to die in 2003 in Alaska, Wyoming, and South Dakota as a child in New Hampshire, Massachusetts, or Rhode Island and more than twice as likely to die in Arkansas, Alabama, Oklahoma, New Mexico, and Mississippi? Why in the same year was the heart disease age-adjusted death rate in Mississippi and Oklahoma virtually twice what it was in Minnesota and some 30% above the national average (State Health Facts, 2006, 2007)?

One hopeful sign is the report from Centers for Disease Control and Prevention that there was no statistically significant difference in the vaccination rate of children 19 to 35 months in 2005, whether black, white, Hispanic, or Asian/Pacific Islander (Centers for Disease Control and Prevention, 2006).

Access—Structure

The United States stacks up pretty well in the developed world in terms of the total supply of services available, but services are distributed very unevenly. This is, however, a problem almost everywhere in the world. Urban centers attract trained personnel with job opportunities and educational and cultural opportunities for their families. Rural areas everywhere tend to lack personnel and facilities. That is why in 2004 a third of U.S. patients could see a primary care physician the same day; however, a sixth had to wait 6 or more days, and 16% reported going to the emergency room for a condition that could have been treated elsewhere if a regular doctor or source of care was available (Schoen et al., 2004). Over time, this rural problem has lessened as the supply has increased and primary care physicians and even some specialists have moved to smaller communities in response to market forces (Rosenthal et al., 2005).

Access—Process

For U.S. respondents, the limitations on access were perceived primarily as financial. When asked in 2001 about prescriptions not filled, doctor visits needed but not made, and treatments, tests, or follow-ups missed, all because of costs and problems paying medical bills, 35% to 40% of U.S. respondents with incomes below average reported experiencing such problems, almost double the rates in Australia, Canada, and New Zealand and six to nine times as large a proportion as in the United Kingdom. For the U.S. uninsured, the rate exceeded 50%. More than half of below-average income U.S. respondents and a quarter of those with above-average income were delaying dental work because of the cost; however, these rates were also high in all of the five countries except the United Kingdom (Blendon et al., 2002). People everywhere seem to use every reason possible to avoid going to dentist.

Access—Outcomes

Americans report that the barriers to health care access are predominantly economic. Morbidity in the nonolder population is concentrated in the lower socioeconomic strata. Certainly, high morbidity contributes to loss of income, but that effect is small compared with the effects of social status on access to care. A study of white, middle-class males in the United States and the United Kingdom showed that the Americans considered themselves less healthy, and thus, the problems apparently are not confined to one socioeconomic class (Banks et al., 2006).

Technical Management

The heaviest efforts to improve U.S. care have focused on the processes of care delivery. The 100K Lives campaign (see **Case 11-1**) was aimed at implementing effective measures that improve patient survival and quality of life. Still, our care system is wasteful in many ways, inconsistent in treatment and outcomes, and focused on revenue maximization rather than delivering maximum quality at a reasonable cost.

Technical Management—Structure

In the United States, most health professionals are well trained. Their credentials are carefully checked by the institutions where they work, and their licensing boards and certifying bodies require some continuing professional education. Entry by foreign physicians is relatively tightly controlled, with requirements for additional postgraduate training and testing before practicing; however, the results of this process still show providers and institutions to be poorly distributed. Poor states, rural areas, inner cities, and areas with high minority concentrations and low incomes have very different health care utilization rates from the more privileged areas of the country.

Technical Management—Process

Most systems to assure quality of care focus on the process of care delivery. They concentrate on the variability in treatment approaches among practices, among various areas of the country, and on failure to implement evidence-based practices. This focus on specific care processes, supported by measurement and reporting systems such as National Committee for Quality Assurance's Health Plan Employer Data and Information Set system, has improved the rate of conformance in the areas measured, but there is still a long way to go.

One indicator of poor resource allocation and questionable quality is variability in medical care delivery from one area to another. Wennberg et al. (2002) showed, for example, that Medicare spent twice as much per enrollee in Miami than in Minneapolis without any apparent improvement in results. Miami patients might be sicker to start with, but case mix differences are unlikely to justify a doubling of average costs in a fee-for-service program. They suggest that there is relatively little variability where the medical evidence is strong and much more where the evidence is less so, such as with hospital-based care during the last 6 months of life.

Estimates of waste in the U.S. health care system run to 30% to 40% (Milstein, 2006). Not only are tests duplicated and medical records unavailable, but there is little attempt to optimize processes and coordinate activities to maximize the use of personnel. Each specialty and department tends to operate to meet its own preferences and maximize revenue, rather than to improve system efficiency. Staff departments assigned to improve processes have fallen by the wayside during cost-cutting drives (Sahney, 1993).

Technical Management—Outcomes

Much attention has been paid to medical error rates in recent years. The 2000 Institute of Medicine report *To Err Is Human* and the follow-up report *Crossing the Quality Chasm* focused the attention of the government and a reluctant medical profession on this problem (IOM, 2000, 2001). The Leapfrog Group, an employer-oriented organization, has suggested several measures that are in the process of being implemented, including computerized physician order entry and widespread use of intensive-care hospitalists. The experience with the 100K Lives program illustrates the magnitude of the improvements that can be achieved.

Management of Interpersonal Relationships

One area the American public has emphasized has been the importance of a relationship with a personal physician. Members of the public do not want to be told whom they may or may not see. They will even pay extra to have the relationships that they think suits their needs.

Management of Interpersonal Relationships—Structure

Americans rebelled at the idea that their health maintenance organizations (HMOs) could interfere with their existing relationships with their personal physicians. They clearly value that relationship where it exists; however, a substantial number of Americans report financial and spatial access problems and use less personal services such as emergency rooms or urgent care centers. Even those with relatively poor access to care triage their own care considerably, driving greater distances for more sophisticated care, if they believe a problem may be serious.

Management of Interpersonal Relationships—Process

Much of the expressed dissatisfaction with interpersonal relationships in U.S. health care has to do with the brevity of encounters. Patients feel rushed by their primary care providers, who are under pressure to see more patients as preferred provider contracts and government discount pricing have eroded income per visit. This weakens patients' confidence that their providers have their welfare at heart. Clinically, it means many emotionally fraught issues— issues that used to be addressed when the provider listened carefully for the "by the way" comment toward the apparent end of the visit or at what some counselors call the "doorknob moment"—are no longer addressed.

Management of Interpersonal Relationships—Outcome

Increasingly, payers evaluate providers on the basis of questionnaires that measure consumers' satisfaction with the interpersonal aspects of their encounters. For example, the Hospital CAPS 27-Item Survey Instrument asks questions such as these:

- During this hospital stay, how often did nurses and doctors treat you with courtesy and respect?
- During this hospital stay, how often did doctors and nurses listen carefully to you?
- During this hospital stay, did doctors, nurses, or other hospital staff talk to you about whether you would have the help you needed when you left the hospital?

Other Factors to Consider

Donabedian's structure was developed ahead of most of our concerns about costs and at a time when the health community shared a more homogeneous value system; therefore, we must consider the additional factors relating to costs and values, especially notions of equity in health care delivery. The values issues will be addressed in subsequent chapters.

Costs—Structure

The unit costs of health care inputs are high in the United States, especially professional salaries, drugs prices, and the costs other medical supplies and devices. This is leading to a burgeoning international trade in health care. Costs would go even higher if unmet needs were addressed. There is a shortage almost everywhere of registered nurses, which may be constraining some hospital use. There are huge untapped needs in the field of child psychiatry and community psychiatry. People report being constrained on their consumption of psychotherapy because of the limitations on insurance reimbursement. We also know the poor do not see physicians and other providers as much as those with adequate insurance, although that can beg the question of whether the problem is overutilization by those with health insurance or underutilization by the poor or both. Given that a significant proportion of the poor are poor because of their health status, one would expect higher utilization on their part if they had sufficient insurance.

Costs—Process

Variability in processes is evident through differences in costs across areas and institutions. A substantial amount of gaming goes on between providers and the payment system. Where the system will not pay for a diagnosis and an office procedure on the same visit, a dermatologist may schedule two visits. If the patient needs multiple minor procedures but the payer will not pay for each one separately, there again may be as many visits as procedures, wasting patient time and payer money. Kleinke (2005) reported that the three large independent clinical laboratory firms have failed to adopt a common reporting system that is available to them because they do not want to support electronic data interchange that might avoid tens of billions of dollars in duplicate laboratory tests.

> *In an industry rife with dirty little secrets, this is health care's dirtiest: Bad quality is good for business and the surest road to bad quality is bad information or no information. The various IT systems out there are expensive to buy, implement, and train staff to use, but this expense pales in comparison to all of the pricey and billable complications those systems would prevent.... As Walker et al. pointed out with this agonizing understatement, "Those who depend in subtle ways on redundancy could find such change costly." This is health care's second-dirtiest little secret: One organization's unnecessary medical product or service is another's revenue source* (Kleinke, 2005, pp. 1250–1252).

Costs—Outcome

Earlier sections of this chapter provided information on health costs and outcomes for the United States compared with other developed nations. They also noted that perceived cost and inability to pay were major impediments to obtaining needed health care. The magnitude of those costs is also motivating major corporations to dismantle their employment-based insurance plans for employees, families, and retirees and keeping many smaller employers from offering health care plans to their staff.

COMPLEXITY

One barrier to access may be the complexity of publicly financed programs. Some programs are available only to those who at are below the federal poverty level (FPL), whereas other specific state programs can enroll families up to 300% of FPL. Programs also have requirements for cost-sharing with premiums, co-payments, and deductibles. For example, the Medicaid working group of the National Governors' Association has suggested that the states be allowed to impose and enforce cost sharing provisions up to 5% of family income for those below 150% of FPL and 7.5% for those above 150% of FPL. Take a look at the implications of this as outlined in **Table 2-3** for a minimum wage worker. First, note how complex it all is. Assume that a worker at a minimum wage job has the alternative of either accepting the typical employer plan with payroll deductible annual premium of $610 for personal coverage only and $2,713 for family coverage (approximately the national average). The latter is over 25% of one worker's annual wages for the family. Even with two minimum wage workers in the family, the premium percentage is still large. The worker is likely to go without family coverage in just about every conceivable scenario unless there is high-cost chronic illness in the family. The individual worker is not likely to pay the $610 premium either, as the $536 cost share is less than the premium. Table 2-3 oversimplifies things considerably. A person changing employers may experience gaps in coverage or may lose benefits if he or she works less than full time. There are waiting periods for new employees to become eligible, and complex descriptions of coverage that can be off-putting to many employees. Usually the company human resources department tries to help out with the enrollment process, but the economics of the process can only be understood in retrospect by most individuals. After all, very few of us plan to get sick.

The result is the following snapshot of insurance coverage as of 2004: employment-based insurance coverage, 174 million; individually purchased coverage, 27 million; Medicare coverage, 40 million; Medicaid coverage, 38 million; and uninsured, 46 million.

TABLE 2-3 Example Based on the 2005 National Governors
Association Working Group Proposal

Worker's Income	One Earner	Two Earners
Single Worker Income 100% of Poverty Level	$ 9,570	
Minimum Wage One Full-time Worker ($5.15/hr.)	10,712	
Family of Four Income 100% of Poverty Level	19,350	
Two Minimum Wage Workers		$21,424
Premium in Employment-Based Programs		
Total Annual Premium Single Worker	$4,024	8,024
Total Annual Premium Family Coverage	10,880	10,880
Employee Annual Premium Single Worker	610	
Employee Annual Premium Family Coverage	2,713	2,713
Cost of Care—Medical Loss Ratio of 85%		
Single Worker Premium	$3,420	
Family Coverage	9,248	9,248
Cap on Cost Sharing Requirement 5% of Income	536	
Cap on Cost Sharing Requirement 7.5% of Income		1,607

Compromise and Complexity

The political give and take that has marked the development of health care policy in the United States has left us with incredible financial complexity in our health system. **Table 2-4** shows the primary federally financed programs, each of which has its own often-changing sets of regulations.

In the Medicaid program, we have at least 52 distinct governmental health care systems, one for each state, Puerto Rico, and the Virgin Islands.

There are more than 1,100 current waivers of the rules granted to indi-vidual state programs to allow expanded coverage and use of managed care approaches. Each state system has it own reimbursement rate, the Federal Medicaid Assistance Percentage, which is based on a complex formula involving income levels in the state. For 2006, this ranged from 50% federal payment in a number of wealthier states to 76% in Mississippi and 73.77% in Arkansas (**Table 2-5**).

Whether a person is eligible for Medicaid depends on the state that he or she lives in, as income eligibility and some coverages vary by state. For exam-ple, a pregnant woman may be covered in one state if her family income is at or below 133% of the FPL or 150% in some others, or 166% or 185% or 200% or 250% or 275%, depending on where she is enrolled (State Health Facts, 2007). Those covered by Medicaid may include the following:

- Categorically needy
  - Families receiving Aid to Families with Dependent Children
  - Pregnant women and children under 6 years old with family income up to 133% of the FPL
  - Children ages 6 to 19 with family or caretaker incomes up to 100% of the FPL
  - Supplemental Security Income (SSI) recipients or aged, blind, and disabled persons whose requirements are more restrictive than SSI
  - Individuals and couples living in medical institutions who have monthly income up to 300% of the SSI income standard
- Medically needy individuals whose income or assets exceed those of the categorically needy
  - If a program exists, it must cover pregnant women through 60-day postpartum period, children under 18, certain newborns for first year, and certain protected blind persons.
  - The program has the option of covering:
    - Selected groups of full-time students between 18 and 21 years old
    - Caretakers (relatives and legal guardians) living with children
    - Aged persons over 65 years old
    - Blind persons
    - Disabled persons meeting state or SSI standards
    - Persons who would be eligible if they were not enrolled in an HMO

TABLE 2-4 Major Federal Programs

Medicaid is health insurance for the poor and disabled. It can cover pretty much all their medical bills, including nursing home care and drugs. Eligibility levels and services vary by state.

Medicare is health insurance for those over 65, some disabled younger than 65, and individuals with end–stage renal failure. It consists of three programs:

- **Part A** is hospital insurance and is covered by payroll taxes. In addition, it may cover hospice care, some home health care, and brief post-hospitalization nursing home care.
- **Part B** is medical insurance for which the premium due is deducted from one's Social Security check. It pays parts of the physician's and other providers' fees, home health care, outpatient services, medically necessary physical and occupational therapy, and some home health services.
- **Part D** is insurance for prescription drugs coverage. Most participants pay a monthly premium to a private insurer for coverage under a plan-specific formulary.

Dual eligibles are poor disabled or elderly persons eligible for both Medicare and Medicaid. This population accounts for 18% and 16% of the respective beneficiaries of these two programs. Medicare pays for physician, prescription drug, and hospital care, while Medicaid pays the Medicare premiums and cost sharing and covers other health needs such as long-term care. Dual eligibles accounted for 42% of Medicaid costs in 2000.

- Special groups
  - Medicare premiums, coinsurance, and deductibles may be covered for Medicare beneficiaries with incomes below 100% of FPL and resources below 200% of the SSI allowable. States can also cover groups up to 135% of that level.
  - States may provide extended Medicaid eligibility while disabled persons learn to work and seek employment and as their conditions improve.
  - Individuals with tuberculosis may be covered for tuberculosis-related treatments costs.
  - Women with cervical or breast cancer may receive time-limited full coverage for cancer-related care.
  - Long-term care (institutional and home health) is covered in all states, but eligibility requirements varying by state.

Until very recently, Medicaid covered prescription drugs, but Medicare did not. Medicare still does not cover long-term care.

TABLE 2-5   FY 2007 Federal Medicaid Assistance Percentage
(FMAP) By State and Territory

Percentage Grouping	States and Territories in Category
50.0	California, Colorado, Connecticut, Delaware, Guam, Illinois, Maryland, Massachusetts, Minnesota, New Hampshire, New Jersey, New York, Virginia, Puerto Rico, Virgin Islands
50.01–50.99	Alaska, Nevada, Rhode Island, Washington, Wyoming
54.00–57.99	Hawaii, Michigan, Nebraska, Pennsylvania, Wisconsin,
58.00–60.99	Florida, Kansas, Ohio, Texas, Vermont
61.00–64.99	Georgia, Indiana, Iowa, Maine, Missouri, North Carolina, North Dakota, Oregon, South Dakota, Tennessee
65.00–67.99	Arizona
68.00–69.99	Alabama, Kentucky, Louisiana, Montana, Oklahoma, South Carolina
70.00–73.99	Arkansas, District of Columbia, Idaho, New Mexico, Utah, West Virginia
76.0	Mississippi

Data Source: Federal Register 2005 Vol. 70, No. 229, p. 71857.

LEADERSHIP AT THE STATE AND LOCAL LEVEL

A state is responsible for health insurance regulation as well as paying up to half the costs of Medicaid. Complexity is increased by the fact that each state has its own system of insurance regulation. Yet this has enabled a wide variety of innovative responses to access and cost issues at the state and local levels. Medicare is often the largest expenditure category in their budgets and is an open-ended commitment. Jurisdictions that rely heavily on property taxes have major problems dealing with such unpredictable expenditures. State and local governments also end up covering most of the acute care costs of the uninsured. The many approaches that they are using are discussed in Chapter 5.

The ERISA Barrier

Insurance regulation is a strong lever for mandating coverage and access and for taxing premiums to cover uncompensated care and fund high-risk pools; The Employee Retirement Income Security Act (ERISA) of 1974, however, exempted self-insured plans from much of state insurance law because self-funded insurers would not have insurance as a primary line of business. Generally, the courts have upheld this law. One exception is a 1995 Supreme Court decision allowing New York State to place a surcharge tax on health premiums, including self-insured plans, to cover uncompensated hospital care.

Park (2000) reported that in 1993 about half the nation's insured workers were in self-insured plans (also called Section 125 plans), mostly in large companies. The exemption allows companies to offer a consistent benefit package to all of their employees in various states and to avoid state taxation of premiums and incurring the costs of regulation, as well as keeping any returns on their capital reserves. A self-funded company takes the underwriting risk for its own pool of generally healthy employees. These plans were most popular in the 1980s and early 1990s, but then lost market share as companies turned to managed care organizations to reduce costs. They are further losing share as companies cut back their plans and offer defined contribution plans, if anything at all.

ERISA constitutes a barrier to states attempting to achieve universal coverage. It leaves each state with two health care insurance systems, one regulated and one not. Other arguments against the ERISA exemption point to the possibility that unregulated plans might fail because of mismanagement, might abuse sick employees, and would put employees at a disadvantage whenever employers discontinue their self-funded plans.

INDUSTRIALIZING STRUCTURES FOR DELIVERY

The terms *industrialization* and occasionally *commoditization* keep coming up in current discussions of how to fix health care (Holstein, 2006). When applied to manufacturing early in the 20th Century, industrialization meant (1) breaking complex tasks performed by individuals down into simple tasks assigned to different members of a team and (2) studying, analyzing, and specifying the best way to do each of those tasks. The result was that work moved from the control and *artistry of the craft person* to a systematic process that was perhaps more efficient and less personal. Specialization in the industrialized system can imply *deskilling* for some and much higher, but narrower, skill levels for others. Managerial control of the system involves both allocating duties and specifying the right way to do them. Usually management includes two groups: (1) line managers who allocate the work and (2) staff specialists whose job is to specify and improve processes. Where the process is well defined and skill requirements can be reduced, *labor substitution* takes place—routine work is done by less expensive personnel with more limited training and less autonomy. Primary care physicians particularly report the frustration with their loss of autonomy and with the pressures for efficiency expressed as a measure of the number of patients seen (Rastegar, 2004).

Clayton Christensen has expressed the industrializing view most strongly.

> *In health care, rather than replicating the expensive expertise of Mount Sinai Medical Center or Mass General Hospital, or replicating the expensive expertise of doctors, we have to commoditize their expertise. That comes through the precise ability to diagnose the diseases that people have. Our ability to diagnose diseases is moving ahead at a breathtaking pace, but regulation and reimbursement are trapping the delivery of rules-based medicine in high-cost models.*

Referring to the mastery of consumption he argued,

> *You had tuberculosis there, at least three types, and you had pneumonia. We thought it was all one disease. So the care had to be left with doctors because they were the ones with the training and judgment, but once you could precisely diagnose the cause of the disease, you could then develop a cure. It was so rules-based that you didn't need a doctor any longer. Today a technician can diagnose those diseases and a nurse can treat them* (Holstein, 2006).

Other symptoms of industrialization in health care include the following:
- More physicians employed (under management) rather than partners in practices
- Institutional emphasis on process development, including evidence-based medicine and continuous quality improvement
- External exchange of information on relative experience, outcome quality, and prices and costs
- Emphasis on process conformance and transparency, including preauthorizations, carve outs, utilization review, and clinical pathways.
- Increasing labor substitution

- Development of focused factories that specialize in a limited range of procedures, such as specialty hospitals and ambulatory surgery centers
- Increasing fragmentation of patient care with offsetting efforts aimed at coordination and teamwork
- Increasing substitution of capital for labor
- Less of a personal relationship between the server and the served.

Managed care has become a major form of organization for care delivery. Practices and institutions have merged or sold out to a wide array of health care organizations. Physician incomes, especially those of specialists, have dropped rapidly. These are all symptoms of the industrialization of what had been a cottage industry organized along craft lines despite being 14% to 15% of our country's economic activity.

Figure 2-3 suggests one way of thinking about industrialization and the various process requirements that analogy suggests. Two dimensions are identified: Type of Case: Simple to Complex and Knowledge Base: Science-based (Codified) to Art (Tacit). The drivers of industrialization in health care have been the expansion of the science base of medicine and the codification of

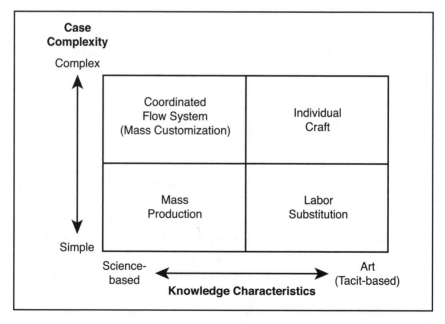

FIGURE 2-3   Suggested Impact of Case Complexity and Knowledge Characteristics on Process Choices in Health Care

product definitions and process specifications. For more about art (tacit knowledge) versus science and product and process improvement trajectories in general, see Victor and Boynton (1998). Their applicability to health care is discussed in greater detail in McLaughlin and Kaluzny (2006).

The craft/guild system attributed to medicine before World War II implied that medicine was primarily an art lacking decisions rules that could be communicated effectively (tacit knowledge) (Ferdows, 2006). With more and more scientific and/or codified knowledge, it was possible to differentiate between simple and complex cases. Where activities were simple, they could be turned into mass production systems that repeated the same process over and over. If the knowledge was still pretty much an art but the case simple, the work could be delegated to less experienced or less trained personnel (like in the old *apprentice* system in which much of the simpler work was delegated to others, but the master craftsman maintained control and handled the trickiest parts). Part of the training process was learning what not to treat and what to hand off to appropriate experts. Where processes are codified but the cases are complex, and hence varied, they need to be processed in a coordinated flow between provider subsystems, a process referred to today as *mass customization.* The modern hospital can be visualized as such a process, with patients (all or in part) moving from the bed tower to the X-ray department to the blood laboratory to surgery to the intensive care unit to the step-down unit and back to the bed tower. However, we all witness the consequences of matches and mismatches between situations high in art that fit with craft (apprenticeship and job costing or fee-for-service) and those high in science that fit with industrialization (bundled payments, use of clinical pathways, length-of-stay controls).

Mass production does exist in areas such as cataract surgery and other "centers of excellence," but there is a widespread desire to avoid mass production of medical services. That desire is legitimate given the high inherent variability in patient anatomy, physiology, and psychological needs and preferences. Mass customization is the logical end point for this process. Health care is a mixture of art and science; however, health care differs from classic mass production in the sense that patients present themselves with both simple and complex problems (multisystem problems or comorbidities). Problems that have a clearly optimal treatment regimen and those for which medical knowledge is limited can appear simultaneously in the same individual.

What has kept this from being a well-coordinated process has been the absence of development of process codification and inadequate investment in information technology, as well as a lack of provider commitments to share knowledge and to abide by specified process parameters. This is often attributed to lack of sufficiently aligned professional and institutional incentives.

Ownership of Intellectual Capital

As work is industrialized, work methods are specified by the organization rather than the individual artisan. In health care, we have historically assumed that intellectual capital resides with the professional. This stems from an assumed inability of the public (including lay administrators) to understand the technical processes of health care. This notion is the underlying foundation of medicine's claims of professional autonomy, but that autonomy is threatened by recommendations such as those of Einthoven and Tollen (2005), who argue for reliance on integrated delivery systems for cost control. They argue against provider-level competition and for system-level competition because integrated delivery systems:

- Can better motivate and hold accountable clinicians to use best practices
- Do a better job of achieving coordination and continuity of care, especially for the chronically ill
- Are more likely to invest in and implement interoperable information technology
- Are more likely to adopt and successfully implement "large scale efficiency measures"
- Are more likely to compete directly with each other on quality and price
- Are more likely to be selective among providers than loose and inclusive provider networks serving most insurers in a community.

These authors want employers to offer employees a choice of carriers to motivate insurers to avoid providers of low quality and high costs. Haislmaier (2006) argued that a key innovation of the Massachusetts reforms was the "Connector" exchange system, which allows individuals insurance portability and enables them to change carriers without reunderwriting.

As competition increasingly depends on the implementation of evidence-based practices by an institution and rapid dissemination and adoption by practitioners, organizational rather than professional learning becomes the focus. That raises new questions about the provider–management conflicts (often called *suits versus coats*), the role of continuing graduate medical education, and access to clinical records and research outputs. Professionals must be prepared to take leadership in issues around developing, disseminating, and compensating for intellectual capital or lose even more autonomy.

The Professions

One interesting aspect of the U.S. medical system is that it did not industrialize under either corporate or government control. Many U.S. services industry sectors have concentrated into large corporations emulating the oligopolistic model of dominant multinational firms. Starr (1982) discussed how the medical profession gained control of health care and maintained it in the presence of pressures to consolidate into corporate forms of organization. The cover of his book, *The Social Transformation of American Medicine,* states that it is about "the rise of a sovereign profession and the making of a vast industry." Writing in the early 1980s at the height of the interest in HMOs, he foresaw rapid growth in the corporate form of care delivery.

Much of the ebb and flow of employer, insurer, and government attempts to solve health care system issues flows around issues of industrialization and corporate delivery of medical care. Starr (1982, pp. 229–231) cited five structural changes in American medicine before World War II that strengthened the sovereign position of physicians in health care and enabled them to avoid working in a corporate structure. They were as follows:

1. An informal control system based on dependence on colleagues for referrals and hospital privileges
2. Formal control of labor markets through the licensing process
3. Transfer of many of the overheads and investments that a typical private corporation would make should it provide medical services to societal organizations such as hospitals, public health departments, and educational institutions
4. A lack of countervailing organizations that could choose to challenge the political and economic influences of the medical profession
5. Few attempts to develop integrated care organizations that would attempt to rationalize the highly fragmented, but insulated delivery system.

In 1934 the American Medical Society claimed that "all features of medical service in any method of medical practice should be under the control of the medical profession." Elsewhere in the world the response to that assertion is that control should rest with the government. In the United States, we increasingly hear that it should rest on "consumer sovereignty."

Is there something inherently different about health care? Nobel economics laureate Kenneth Arrow addressed this question in his influential 1963 article entitled "Uncertainty and the Welfare Economics of Medical Care." He argued that some functions, such as insurance, exhibit typical market behavior, but he also observed that the buyer is not a rational optimizer in a perfect market, but is a vulnerable, trusting patient who seeks information in an uncertain world from a physician who is also dealing with many uncertainties. He emphasized elements of uncertainty and market failure such as the following:

- Inequality of information (today called *information asymmetry*)
- Inequality of resources, especially income
- Professional ethic demanding that treatment be independent of ability to pay
- Importance of trust to the effectiveness of the care
- Vulnerability and psychological state of patients
- Longer term implications of the ongoing physician–patient relationship.

Arrow pointed to a number of the unique structural elements of the health care marketplace such as professional licensure, nonprofit institutions, sliding fee scales, and government intervention as responses to these elements. He argued that much of the uncertainty could be handled through insurance and government intervention. His postscript concluded,

> *The failure of the market to ensure against uncertainty has oriented many social institutions in which the usual assumptions of the market are contradicted. The medical profession is only one example, though in many respects an extreme one.... The economic importance of personal and especially family relationships ... is based on non-market relations that create guarantees of behavior which would otherwise be afflicted with excess uncertainty.... The logic and limitations of ideal competitive behavior under uncertainty force us to recognize the incomplete description of reality supplied by the impersonal price system.* (Arrow, 1963, p. 967)

Criticisms of Arrow and of how that article is interpreted are many, but it remains very relevant and very influential. Sloan (2003, p. 58) argued that the article is used by those who oppose markets and argued that "an alternative approach—in my view, a much more fruitful one is to recognize the market imperfections and devise various interventions to empower consumers. . . . Consumer ignorance should not be taken as a given." Rice (1998) raised 15 questions about the assumptions of the competitive market model applied to health care, such as lack of externalities, fixed preferences, absence of monopoly, complete and accurate information availability, and rational decision making. Henderson (2002, pp. 109, 111) accepted the market failure examples but counters normatively,

> *On the other hand, no credible evidence supports government reme-dies as the answer to the perceived inequities either. Markets may fail, but governments may be just as prone to failure. And correct-ing government failure is inherently more difficult than correcting market failure. . . . Criticism directed at market failure without at least admitting the possibility of government failure is dishonest, or at minimum naïve.*

Starr interpreted many of the social institutions that Arrow cited not as social responses to uncertainty but as steps that organized medicine used to establish its monopoly control over health care and stave off industrial-ization and cites examples of them increasing uncertainty.

Why has it remained a cottage industry? The medical profession has been very protective of its control over health care. Yet there have been a number of moves in the direction of consolidation and corporate struc-tures. Starr (1982, p. 420) suggested five dimensions likely to change should the practice of medicine move toward a more typical American corporate structure. They are:

1. Change in ownership and control
2. Horizontal integration into multi-site organizations
3. Diversification and public restructuring with holding companies and subsidiaries with differing product lines
4. Vertical integration involving multiple stages and levels of care
5. Industry concentration of ownership and control of services.

Interestingly, all of these have been taking place, albeit slowly and selectively. In fact, many of the implemented proposals and experiments have accomplished aspects of each of these and created efficiency, effectiveness, and wealth. They have each had their day, yet they have not stemmed the inflationary trends nor overwhelmed the smaller operators. Hospitals and corporations that bought up physician practices in the 1990s experienced problems in recouping their investments. For-profit hospital chains have had their ups and downs. Integrated health systems do dominate in many specific areas, but have not been terribly successful in replicating their approach elsewhere.

Status of Professions and Professionals

It may seem odd to think of professional status as a variable to manipulate in establishing health policy; however, professional roles are not immutable. New professions emerge as technology changes and others lose ground. Professions are a combination of knowledge, political power, and custom. It is the public that either accepts or denies one group's dominance over a knowledge domain and the delivery of services.

Health workers existed long before the modern medicine era. Most societies have had shamans, birth attendants, and indigenous healers. Before 1850, physicians did not seem to enjoy any consistent status in the United States. With the advent of modern science and modern medicine, governments became alarmed at the amount of quackery going on. They cooperated with the medical profession and conferred on the profession a near monopoly, which has been buttressed by our system of licensing and credentialing.

Starr (1982) traced in detail the parallel political and social development of monopoly power by American physicians. Freidson (2001) saw the professional model as a third alternative to the hierarchical (corporate) model and to "free market autonomy." In the professional model the professionals maintain considerable control over (1) the information and (2) the means of delivery in their domain; however, as we see in Chapter 5, many proposed and implemented alternatives have the effect of weakening the existing status of health professionals. This is a natural result of the emphasis on market mechanisms and an informed consumer, as well as the vastly increased access to information that the public now has, especially through the Internet.

Given that professional status and credentials offer privileges with economic value, health policy analysts must consider how that value and power might be allocated to serve the public interest. The literature suggests a number of issues of interest related to professional status decisions:

- Labor substitution
- Outsourcing
- Rising educational barriers
- Disintermediation
- Consumer-centered care based on quality report cards, etc.
- Incentive systems for quality, cost, and access.

As potential policy alternatives, all of these warrant further consideration.

Labor Substitution

Despite the monopolies offered by licensure and credentialing, many health care tasks can be done by more than one level of health care worker. For example, there were midwives before there were obstetricians. That function nearly disappeared in the United States but is undergoing a resurgence. Nurse practitioners and physician assistants now are the first level of care for many patient encounters. In many psychiatric practices, the psychiatrist handles the patient's medications but delegates most other care activities to psychologists, social workers, and other counselors. Pharmacies now use pharmacy technicians as well as pharmacists. Dental practices have their own dental hygienists and technicians working in parallel with the dentists. Primary care physicians perform procedures once limited to specialists. The key to further substitution is whether the alternative type of worker is qualified for the problem at hand and whether their unit cost is less. The main drivers for labor substitution are availability and cost. Most substitutions were initially proposed to overcome a shortage of personnel in one area, but after the experiment has worked, more and more organizations adopt it to increase access and reduce cost.

Outsourcing

This is a relatively new phenomenon in health care, but is driven by the same factors as labor substitution. A shortage of radiologists in rural areas has led to networking arrangements in which radiologists in urban areas read the images from rural hospitals in their offices or homes without going to the patient. Technicians produce the images and radiologists read them off site. After the information is digitized, it can be read anywhere in the world and it is not unusual to find that U.S. imaging and electrocardio-grams are farmed out to Asian locations where salaries are much lower. More and more patients who lack adequate insurance coverage but have reason-able incomes are choosing to have elective surgery done in reputable over-seas hospitals where the cost is much lower. Pharmaceutical companies are also moving medical research and clinical trails offshore to reduce costs.

Rising Educational Barriers

The force that runs counter to labor substitution is the pressure within each profession to raise the bar that one must clear in order to achieve profes-sional status. The biggest suppliers of nursing labor in the United States are the community colleges, which have programs that do not always end up with a baccalaureate degree; however, nursing leadership has argued for the need to have more, if not all, nurses with 4-year degrees. At the same time, nursing subspecialists proliferate, requiring master's level degrees. The phar-macy schools that once offered pharmacy bachelor degrees now produce Pharm. D. recipients. All of these moves require more training and in turn constrain the supply of personnel in a field and seemingly justify higher wages and greater professional status. One casualty of this trend in the university is the use of cross-disciplinary faculty to teach in the health profes-sions. Rather than training in common or using common faculty from other departments to teach their anatomy, pharmacology, and behavioral science, for example, they increasingly insist on having it done by individuals with doctorates in their own field. In-sourcing all of the teaching increases the demand for their own doctoral-level graduates.

Disintermediation

The term *disintermediation* means removing the person in the middle, the intermediary. One prime example is the recent emphasis on direct-to-consumer pharmaceutical advertising. Ten years ago, companies selling efforts focused entirely on the prescribing physician. That has changed markedly. Ad after ad suggests a treatment, syndrome, disease, or risk factor that the patients might not even be aware of (i.e., hypercholesterolemia, acid reflux disease, toenail fungus) and urges them to ask their physician about the branded treatment. This advertising bypasses the physician initially and, given the availability of imported drugs, may bypass the physi-cian entirely. **Table 2-6** shows situations in which primary care physician control of medical information and/or of the means of delivery of care are being bypassed today.

TABLE 2-6   Disintermediation Activities Affecting the Primary
Care Physician

Actor	Activities Affecting Information Control	Activities Affecting Transaction Control
Pharmaceutical Companies	Direct-to-Consumer advertising (DTCA) Web sites	Moving patent-expired drugs over the counter (OTC)
Screening Centers	DTCA Direct patient reporting	No referral required Direct patient pay
Nurse Practitioners Physician Assistants	Independent practice	Independent practice
Psychologists	Independent practice	Gaining prescribing authority
Insurers	Deep portals for enrollees Case management	Forcing drugs OTC Case management
Case Management Firms	Taking over patient management Self-care advice	Patient advocacy in community
Pharmacy Benefits Management Firms	Formulary feedback to patients	Multi-tiered copays
Employers	Educational programs and web portals	Screening programs
Academic Medical Centers	Newsletters/Web sites Telemedicine programs	Telemedicine programs
Government Agencies	Web sites/Advertising Screening recommendations Case management	Preferred drug lists Screening programs
Patient/disease Advocacy Groups	Web sites/Advertising Screening recommendations	Screening programs
Pharmacists	Counseling centers	Screening programs
Hospitals	Protocols share with patients and their families Formularies	Formularies Screening programs

Source: Table 1, p. 72 from C.P. McLaughlin et al., Changing Roles for Primary-Care Physicians: Addressing Challenges and Opportunities." *Healthcare Quarterly*, Vol. 8, No. 2, 2005 Copyright Longwoods Publishing Corp.

The primary care provider is not the only intermediary that can be targeted. The decentralized and disjointed nature of the health care industry has allowed the rise of an array of middlemen who have profited greatly by aggregating the demand of small actors and obtaining discounts or who have achieved at least a temporary knowledge advantage that has enabled them take advantage of the market (sometimes called *arbitraging*). The *Wall Street Journal* ran a series of articles on these highly profitable intermediaries in 2006, focusing on pharmacy benefits managers, billing consultants, catastrophic case care managers, Medicaid HMOs, nursing home pharmacy firms, and insurers (Wessel et al., 2006). Large self-insured employers have been attempting to get them to make their operations more transparent or eliminate them entirely.

Consumer-Centered Care Based on Quality Report Cards, Etc.

Quality reporting is relatively new in health care. Diagnosis-related groups, introduced in the 1980s, classified hospital services in 467 bundles of care. A parallel relative value scale system was also developed to evaluate professional fees. It had not been possible to adjust cost data for severity and patient characteristics nor to maintain quality control records until those product definitions were established and widely adopted. After data on costs could be associated with specific diagnoses and compared across cases, providers, regions, and institutions, the tools began to fall in place for a corporate-level analysis, allowing a more industrial approach to health care management.

Incentive Systems for Quality, Cost, and Access

Once cases could be assessed for process quality, outcomes, and costs, payment could be based on overall experience rather than on the inputs utilized in the specific case (fee for service). We discuss pay for performance more extensively in Chapter 3.

MEDICALIZATION OF SOCIETY

A 2006 study showed that white, middle-aged British patients reported better health status than Americans, despite spending much less per capita on health care. Some attribute the differences to high U.S. stress levels; however, an alternative point of view is that the high rate of expenditure on medical care, especially the amount of screening taking place and the constant barrage of health-care-related advertising, has resulted in a reduced perception of wellness. In essence, the greater the proportion of our economy that goes into health care–related activities, the more "sickness" we experience (Welch et al., 2007). This goes back to the definition that we have heard attributed to any number of sources—that a healthy person is one who has not been sufficiently examined by a physician. Consider, for example, comparisons of high blood pressure and high cholesterol levels in U.S. and British 40 to 70 year olds. Americans self-reported more of these problems; however, measured blood pressures were the same, and Americans had lower cholesterol levels. Some attribute lower levels of reported illness among Britons to the fact that British primary care physicians do much less routine screening (Hadler, 2004; Kolata, 2006a). Some see the U.S. screening penchant as a transfer of scarce medical resources from the sick poor to the worried, insured well and as a logical outcome of the medicalization of life together with the industrialization of medicine (Heath, 2005).

Other issues related to the medicalization of U.S. society include the dependence of the economy on the growth of this sector. A 2006 cover story in *Business Week* asserted that two sectors, construction and health care, accounted for all the growth in private sector employment over the preceding five years and that growth in health care employment was the greater of the two. "Since 2001, the health care industry has added 1.7 million jobs. The rest of the private sector? None." (Mandel, 2006, p. 55). Career choices and educational offerings have changed in response to the perceived demand.

Health issues have received increased emphasis in news reporting, television programming, television advertising, and recreation facilities. We have had visitors from other countries ask, unprompted, why we have so much medical and pharmaceutical advertising. There are pluses and minuses to this increasing presence of health care issues throughout our society. We are not arguing that it is good or bad; however, the analyst must take this trend into account when making recommendations. Overall, medicalization tends to increase both the political and economic risks of rapid or radical change to our health care system.

CONCLUSION

This chapter examines the status of the American health care system in terms of access, technical management, management of interpersonal relationships, and costs. It offers comparisons of per capita expenditures, GDP, life expectancy, perinatal mortality in many countries. It also outlines the linkages between these variables or lack thereof. With such data available, the educated citizen can join the debate about where the United States wants to go.

Other concerns in such a debate could include the impacts of changes and trends in the professional environments of health care. Two related constructs discussed in this chapter are the industrialization of health care and the medicalization of American society.

How Did We Get Here?

A history of health care financing and policy making in the United States could well start in 1791 with passage of the Bill of Rights. The Tenth Amendment to the U.S. Constitution declares that those powers not expressly given to the federal government belong to state and local governments. Health and education were not expressly given to the federal government; however, some federal involvement has been justified under the welfare clause of the Constitution and also through Jefferson's argument of implied powers.

With minor exceptions, the federal government has limited itself to financing national programs of health and education, rather than delivering services directly. Yet the federal financial share is fast approaching half the direct cost of health care, even without counting the tax deductions allowed to individuals for health care spending and to corporations for employee health insurance premiums. If you count tax subsidies, health insurance provided to government employees and public dollars spent at all levels of government, government funds account for close to 60% of all health spending.

This chapter looks at the co-evolution of two inextricably linked U.S. systems—one for delivering medical care and one for financing it. The primary focus is on medical care financing, namely the health insurance system, and ways it has impacted delivery systems, for instance, by creating incentives for overutilization or underutilization. Other insurance systems exist to cover expenses for particular types of health care, specifically dental, vision, and long-term care. Public health is financed primarily through state, local, and federal tax dollars (taxes and fees), although the mix has varied greatly. In 1968, roughly half the spending came from the federal government. Today, even after increased federal investment in public health emergency preparedness after 9/11, state and local governments pick up much of the governmental costs (Frist, 2002). The evolution of our system for financing mental health services is discussed in several later sections of this book, including the case at the end of Chapter 12. The case study that follows this chapter looks at where else we might have gone by describing the financing and delivery of health care in five other industrialized countries.

CONTENDING VISIONS OF A SYSTEM FOR DELIVERING HEALTH CARE

Contending visions of how the health system should operate have dominated U.S. health care policy making at different times. Yet there has not been a dominant viewpoint since the 1960s, and all of the contending approaches remain on the table. We focus on three characterizations that contrast the contending points of view while recognizing what we are really talking about is a continuum of alternatives as represented in **Figure 3-1**. There are five potential characterizations of the health care market in Figure 3-1, but one, a provider monopoly, has been ruled out by our legal system, although it said to have characterized the U.S. health system between World Wars I and II (Starr, 1982). A monopoly is control by a single provider and is usually illegal, whereas a monopsony is control by a single buyer. In Figure 3-1, the extreme monopsony position is represented by the U.K.'s original National Health Service. It is not currently a realistic contender for adoption in the United States.

Administered competition means that there are multiple suppliers, but the market is controlled by a primary buyer, usually a government creation. It could involve universal coverage, a single payer, and/or a single underwriter.

Oligopolistic competition involves a relatively open market dominated by a few large sellers and is characteristic of many U.S. industrial sectors. Usually there are three or four sources of goods or services that control at least 40% of the market. In health care, which appears to be so decentralized, these three or four vendors may control state or local markets rather than the national market, although national oligopolies exist in many areas

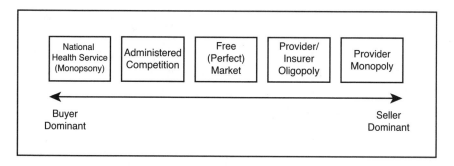

FIGURE 3-1   Stages of Health Care Market Power

such as pharmacy benefits management, Medicare-managed care, replacement joints, imaging equipment, and pharmaceuticals distribution. In California, three insurers control 62% of the commercial market for enrollees under age 65 years, and four control 74% (Fuhrmans, 2007a). Two or three hospital groups often control most of the relevant local market. Concentration in hospital markets has been increasing sharply enough to become a concern of the Federal Trade Commission, although available studies of hospital concentration yield ambiguous findings (Gaynor, 2006). In many state markets, the same is true of health insurance providers.

Perfect (free market) competition assumes the following conditions:

- There are large numbers of buyers and sellers so that no one controls prices
- All buyers and sellers have complete and accurate information about the quality, availability, and prices of goods
- All products have available perfect substitutes
- All buyers and sellers are free to enter or leave the market at will.

A CHRONOLOGY

Centuries ago, medical care was a religious calling, not a scientific field. The term *hospice* was much more representative of the process in health care institutions than *hospital*. Gradually, health care has become a calling *and* an industry. Well into the 20th century, U.S. physicians took whatever people could pay. Teaching institutions provided free care in return for allowing learners to work on those who could not pay. This system of combined fee-for-service and charity care existed before the Great Depression and World War II. From there, one can trace the development and gradual introduction of employment-based health insurance and prepaid group practices leading then to health maintenance organizations (HMOs) and industrialization of parts of the delivery system with pharmaceutical giants, hospital chains, pharmacy chains, and large integrated health care systems.

The Health "Insurance" Approach: Moving From Provider Monopoly Toward Provider/Insurer Oligopoly

Health care insurance systems in the United States were started in the Great Depression to stabilize the cash flows of providers. The concept existed in Europe much earlier. For a discussion of the origin of health insurance there, see Starr (1982). These early efforts ultimately became the not-for-profit Blue Cross/Blue Shield organizations.

Some people credit Dr. Justin Ford Kimball, the administrator of Baylor Hospital in Dallas, with starting the U.S. medical insurance movement in 1929. He conceived of the idea of collecting "insurance premiums" in advance and guaranteeing the hospital's service to members of groups subscribing to this arrangement. Furthermore, he found a way to involve employers in the administration of the plan, thus reducing expenses associated with marketing and enrollment. The first such employer was the Dallas school district, which enrolled schoolteachers and collected the biweekly premium of 50 cents (Richmond & Fein, 2005, p. 31).

About the same time, prepaid group practices began in Oklahoma, but they were bitterly opposed by local medical societies. Prepaid group practices, forerunners of today's HMOs, were also started to provide stable cash flows, but remained a relatively minor factor for a number of decades because of medical society opposition.

State hospital associations controlled the Blue Cross organizations, and medical societies controlled the Blue Shield organizations. Well into the 1940s, state laws in 26 states said that only medical societies could offer prepayment plans for physician services. In 1934, the American Medical Association (AMA) set forth conditions that it argued should govern private insurance for physician services (Starr, 1982, pp. 299–300):

- "All features of medical service in any method of medical practice should be under the control of the medical profession."

- This included all medical care institutions, and thus, only the medical profession could determine their "adequacy and character."
- Patients were to have absolute freedom of choice of physician.
- "A permanent, confidential relation between the patient and a 'family physician' must be the fundamental, dominating feature of any system."
- No form of insurance was acceptable that did not have the patient paying the physician and the patient being the one reimbursed.
- Any plan in a locality must be open to all providers in a community.
- Medical assistance aspects of a plan must be limited to those below the "comfort level" of income.

Group Health Association of Washington DC, a prepaid group practice, began in 1937, but faced strong opposition. In 1943, the Supreme Court (AMA v. U.S., 1943) upheld a lower court in a case brought by the Federal Trade Commission, finding that the AMA and the DC Medical Society were guilty of "a conspiracy in restraint of trade under the Sherman Anti-Trust Act" and had hindered and obstructed Group Health "in procuring and retaining on its staff qualified doctors" and "from privilege of consulting with others and using the facilities of hospitals" (Richmond & Fein, 2005, p. 34).

Expanding Participation

World War II saw industrialization of all available hands, breaking the Great Depression, inducing migration from rural areas to industrial cities, increasing the power of industrial unions, and inaugurating the era of big science. It also led to an era of optimism that together Americans could accomplish collectively anything that they wanted (Strauss & Howe, 1991).

Many employers had established their own industrial health services to support their employees and the war effort. Some of these services, such as Kaiser Industries' medical department, evolved into prepaid group practices. The Kaiser Permanente Group opened up to outside enrollees at the end of the war. Others, like the Health Insurance Plan in New York, which started in 1947, sprang up independently.

The government imposed wage and price controls during World War II. As labor became scarce and the war turned in the Allies' favor, workers pressed for better compensation. The Office of Price Administration held the line on wage increases, but allowed improved benefits through collective bargaining. This led to the rapid expansion of health insurance among unionized industrial and government workers. This was also consistent with the provision of medical benefits to the vast military establishment. Unemployment fell from 17.2% in 1939 to 1.3% in 1944, and the real gross national product grew by 75% (Richmond & Fein, 2005). Health insurance costs were not yet a serious concern of corporate managers nor of government. In 1948, the National Labor Relations Board ruled that refusal to bargain over health care benefits was an unfair labor practice.

Collective bargaining was the basic vehicle for determining health benefits. Because union officers were elected by their membership, union leaders did not choose catastrophic coverage but sought to maximize the visibility of benefits to their rank-and-file (voting) members. This led them to bargain for first-dollar, fee-for-service coverage for everyone and to put limitations on lifetime benefits for those who were born with or developed catastrophic or high-cost chronic conditions. It also led them to emphasize employment-related coverage for dependents. They wanted most union members to experience regular payouts from that benefit. If their workers were young and healthy, they would still see payment for services such as obstetrical and pediatric care that their families consumed. Employers did not much care how their workers divided the contract settlements between wages, health benefits, and other fringes. If workers and their families already had individual health coverage, they still gained a tax advantage after the employer paid the premium directly. Blue Cross enrollments tripled between 1942 and 1946, while enrollment in commercial health insurance plans more than doubled (Becker, 1955).

Postwar Responses: Adding Administered Competition

Following the major expansion of health insurance during World War II, most U.S. presidents suggested health care reforms of some sort. The Hill-Burton Act of 1946 expanded hospital facilities. President Truman recommended developing a system of universal health insurance based on the report of the President's Commission on Health Needs of the Nation; however, it was opposed by entrenched interests and lapsed when President Eisenhower was elected. In 1950, Congress approved a grant program to the states to pay providers for medical care for those receiving public assistance. Proposals for a Medicare-type system under Social Security appeared in Congress as early as 1957, but it took 8 years of debate for Congress and the White House to reach a consensus.

In 1960, the Kerr-Mills Act created a program administered by the Welfare Administration and the states for "Medical Assistance to the Aged," which also covered the "medically needy" older population who did not necessarily qualify for public assistance. Richmond and Fein (2005) described Kerr-Mills as an attempt to stave off Medicare-type programs.

The Joint Commission on Mental Illness and Health, formed under Eisenhower, did not issue its final report until 1961, under the Kennedy administration, which oversaw the passage of the Mental Retardation Facilities Construction Act of 1963 and the Community Mental Health Centers Act of 1963.

Early in his term, President Johnson announced formation of a Commission on Heart Disease, Cancer, and Stroke. Its recommendations led to the Regional Medical Programs legislation to advance training and research. Congress, however, added a provision that this work was not to interfere in any way with "patterns and methods of financing medical care, professional practice, or the administration of any existing institutions" (Richmond & Fein, 2005, p. 44).

While the Medicare debate continued, Congress passed many health measures as part of Johnson's War on Poverty. Given the highly visible opposition of organized medicine, however, health components of these new programs were not housed in the U.S. Public Health Service. For example, the Office of Economic Opportunity started neighborhood health centers, and its Head Start program included health assessment and health care components for children.

When the Johnson administration finally secured passage of the Social Security Amendments of 1965, it accommodated AMA concerns by offering three separate programs: (1) Medicare Part A, providing hospital coverage for most of the older persons; (2) Medicare Part B, a voluntary supplementary medical insurance program; and (3) Medicaid, which expanded the Kerr-Mills program to help with out-of-pocket expenses such as nursing home care and drugs and extended potential eligibility to families with children, the blind, and the disabled under the Welfare Administration.

There were other compromises in the legislation. For example, at the time, hospital-based physicians were being placed on salary so that hospitals could use some of their medical fee revenue to cover the capital costs of their practices. The Medicare bill specifically required that anesthesiologists, radiologists, and pathologists be paid directly, not through a hospital. That law also stated, "Nothing in this title shall be construed to authorize any federal officer or employee to exercise any supervision or control over the practice of medicine." Some have questioned whether the government's 1.5% pay-for-performance bonus program violates this provision (Pear, 2006b).

Bodenheimer and Grumbach (2005) labeled the years from 1945 to 1970 as those of the "provider-insurer pact" (p. 167). Starr (1982) referred to the period before 1970 as one of accommodation between the insurance industry and the medical profession. He noted that it was a period in which most employed Americans were covered because union shops were dominant. "The government supported this private tax system by making employers' contributions into it tax exempt from the government's own taxes. Private voluntary insurance was neither strictly voluntary, nor strictly private, but its compulsory and public features were hardly noticeable" (p. 334). That system, however, left out the poor, the unemployed, agricultural and domestic workers, most farmers, the disabled, and older persons. It was the needs of some of these uninsured populations that the 1965 Great Society legislation addressed.

The Great Society

When implemented in 1965, Medicare mirrored the structure of health insurance in the industrial sector, but without lifetime limitations. It did not provide adequate coverage for drugs or for long-term care (nursing homes, hospice care, home health) or much for prevention. Many employment-based health plans paid for prescription drugs, but not for long-term care. Medicare did not cover prescription drugs until 2006.

It may be hard to believe today, but before 1965, academic medical centers delivered a large amount of the urban charity care. Local volunteer physicians supervised the clinics, and patients received care at no charge or at nominal fees in return for letting learners practice on them. Because many people covered by Medicare and Medicaid had been receiving charity care, the net effect of Medicaid and Medicare was to pay in full for services once provided free or with income-based discounts. It also gave the urban poor a choice of institutions, a choice they quickly exercised.

Rapid Expansion of Capacity

The full fee-for-service payments for visits previously provided free, or nearly so, increased physicians' incomes without increasing supply. At the same time, availability of insurance to underserved populations increased the demand for services. Academic medical centers added new full-time salaried medical staff that billed for their services to all insurers and cross-subsidized education and research. Heavy investments in medical research increased the variety, cost, and effectiveness of what providers could offer. Hospitals also had to cover the capital and support costs of hospital-based physicians now that they could not bill for them directly. A limited supply of resources, new demand, and rapid increases in volume because of technological advances led to rapid price inflation.

The primary policy response to this increase in demand for health services in the 1970s and 1980s was to increase the supply of resources. As personnel shortages appeared, governments increased the supply of providers and facilities. For example, it launched the Community Health Center and Migrant Health Center programs. Then, in 1970, it established the National Health Service Corps to increase provider supply in underserved areas via scholarships and loan forgiveness. Many new programs were established to train health professionals, and existing ones expanded with financial assistance from state and federal governments

The Private Sector Responds

At the end of World War II, the health care sector accounted for 4.5% of the gross domestic product (GDP). By the mid 1980s, it was up to 11%. With the cash flows from private insurance and Medicare and Medicaid, community hospitals expanded rapidly but no longer relied on philanthropy for capital. Wall Street was happy to finance their expansion by selling bonds. Interest was considered a reimbursable cost by rate setters. Health care attracted entrepreneurs and for-profit hospital chains grew rapidly. Similarly, the nursing home industry and kidney dialysis centers attracted new capital. The medical establishment, which had fought against corporate control of hospitals and other institutions, was relatively helpless. The AMA's stance on Medicare and Medicaid had cost it credibility, and its constituency was now spread out between the AMA, specialty and subspecialty societies, and the academic medical centers, each of which had their own interests.

Costs and Concerns Mount

As health care costs mounted and became a much more significant share of the economy, more and more observers expressed concern about the lack of competition in portions of the industry and began suggesting ways to control costs. One suggestion was the prepaid group practice or HMO, which shared some of the cost risk with the employer, thereby inducing reduced costs. The success of Kaiser Permanente and others in delivering care at a lower premium cost without evident diminution of quality drew much attention. This led the Nixon administration to support the Health Maintenance Organization and Resources Development Act of 1973. Although that legislation had little immediate impact, later amendments opened the way for the explosion of HMOs and other vertically integrated health care systems in the 1980s. In 1974, the administration also proposed the Comprehensive Health Insurance Program, which sought to provide health insurance to all employees. Congress debated this and a similar measure, the Kennedy-Mills bill, but did not enact either. Richmond and Fein (2003) argued that 1974 was the closest the nation ever came to universal health insurance and that those proposals, although eclipsed by the Watergate coverup and Nixon's resignation, were the basis for successive calls for congressional action by Presidents Ford, Carter, and Clinton.

Charges and Cost Shifting

Originally, Blue Cross organizations, owned by state hospital associations, were interested in a management cost-finding system that fairly allocated the full costs of services among the users of those services. Because they understood that most costs in a hospital system are (1) fixed and (2) joint,[1] they did not attempt to find out the marginal cost of a service (*marginal cost* is the additional cost of producing one additional unit of a product). They established an estimated average direct cost for each unit of service (bed day, laboratory test, operating room hour, X-ray) and then allocated the overhead costs on the basis of the number of units consumed by the payer's enrollees. The largest expense in the institution, nursing time, was treated as an overhead and not allocated to the individual patient. The resulting charges included all the overhead costs, allowing each institution to break even on its Blue Cross patients. If the patients in your health plan used a quarter of the X-rays produced by the radiology department, the plan paid a quarter of the full costs of that department (including allocated overheads). If institutions offered discounts, they tended to favor the Blues, not the other insurers, and certainly not the directly paying patients. This resulted in what is called *cost shifting*.

---

[1] The cost of a nurse's time is incurred when she or he reports to work, and thus, it is *fixed* regardless of whether there are six patients rounded or three or whether a team approach is used. That time is also jointly shared among all the patients the nurse serves. Few systems recorded nursing time by specific tasks.

More patient care costs were not covered by insurance contracts, and thus, hospitals added the cost of this uncompensated care to the overhead rate and increased charges accordingly. It was easy to manipulate charges to mark up costs and either make a profit or provide deeper discounts to preferred customers. First the Blues and then the federal government exerted pressures on their providers, obtaining substantial discounts in return for their business. This shifted the costs of uncompensated care to private insurers and the uninsured. Reinhardt (2006, p. 64) observed, "What prevailing distributive ethic in U.S. society, for example, would dictate that uninsured patients be billed the highest prices for hospital care and then be hounded, often mercilessly, by bill collectors?"

THE CURRENT "ERA" EMERGES

Fox (2001) described three eras of managed care:

- Pre-1970, early years
- 1970 to 1985, the adolescent years
- 1985 to the present, managed care comes of age.

Richmond and Fein (2003) described the period 1965 to 1985 as a time of emerging tensions between regulation and market forces and the period after 1985 as the "Entrepreneurial Revolution." Bodenheimer and Grumbach described the 1970s as a period of developing tension, the 1980s as the "Revolt of the Purchasers," and the 1990s as the breakup of the provider–insurer pact. The changeover to managed care slowed the growth of premiums from the mid 1990s into the first 2 years of the new century, but then they took off again. In the meantime, both providers and patients expressed displeasure with HMO constraints on treatment choice and provider choice. New state laws sprang up limiting control of professionals and patients by insurers and HMOs. Some thought managed-care control mechanisms had already picked the low hanging fruit, stopping the most egregious cases of inappropriate utilization. One of these mechanisms, capitation (a fixed payment per enrollee per time period), although widely promoted because it shifted the cost risk to providers, became less fashionable as providers were unable to manage it or lacked sufficiently large risk pools and capital reserves to handle it. Insurers moved toward preferred provider plans where patients and providers had more freedom of choice; however, providers gave deeper discounts, and enrollees were subject to higher premiums and greater deductibles and co-payments (HDHP/SO). **Figure 3-2** illustrates the magnitude of these shifts in the insurance contracts in force.

Breaking the Old Social Contract

Employers fought back as their premiums jumped at rates well above the overall inflation rate and as competition from foreign firms that did not provide such benefits ate into their markets. They demanded that insurance companies begin to control premiums (Starr, 1982; Mayer & Mayer, 1985). Bills based on the published price lists of doctors and hospitals typically appeared on the accounts sent to patients and others. People with no insurance were asked to pay full charges. Commercial insurance companies had

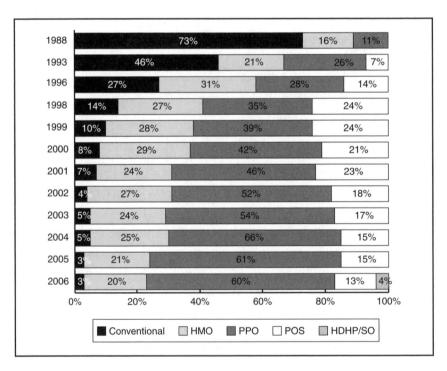

FIGURE 3-2   Health Plan Enrollment for Covered Workers by Plan Type, 1988–2006

Source: "Employer Health Benefits 2006 Annual Survey—Chartpack," (7451), The Henry J. Kaiser Family Foundation and Health Research & Educational Trust, September 2006

contracts that discounted the charges. The Blues and large HMOs enjoyed even bigger discounts, and the federal government got the biggest discount because it demanded the lowest rate allowed to any customer. Because of the inflated charge figures posted to most bills, the public thought their unit care costs were a great deal higher than they really were and that their insurers were picking up a higher proportion of their costs. Real transfer prices for medical services were kept under wraps. This also had the effect of making deductibles and co-payments appear to be a much smaller proportion of actual costs than they really were. Under pressure from the public for greater transparency, that has gradually changed. The public now sees more of what is actually paid and by whom, but real transparency is still lacking. **Table 3-1** shows recently released information on Medicare charges billed by hospitals and payments made by Medicare and the patients by procedure type. This is part of the federal government's efforts at price transparency.

When you read the financial reports of health care institutions, you get a picture of the size of these discounts and the amount of charity care. Many institutions book their full charges as revenue and then deduct for trade discounts under discounts and "allowances" and for charity care under bad debt written off and under "uncompensated care." Tomkins et al. (2006) reported that the ratio of gross revenue (charges) to net revenue (payments received) has grown from 1.1 to 2.6 over a 25-year period. They report that cross-subsidization of services and differential pricing might be difficult to change in the current marketplace.

Currently, every hospital has a price list called a *chargemaster* that may have as many as 20,000 items. These are the charges that the patient usually sees. Terms are not standardized, and some items are really bundles of services so that patients still have trouble comparing prices between institutions. In California hospitals, reported charges for the same procedure at one hospital might be four times that of another, but on average, hospitals received reimbursements for only about 38% of charges from patients and insurers in 2004. Reinhardt (2006) argued that pricing practices would have to change radically if patients were to make rational buying decisions, and he seemed to support the recommendation of Porter and Teisberg (2006) that hospitals post one set of bundled prices per disease entity and charge the same to everyone. However, Altman et al. (2006) wondered whether transparent pricing and customer sensitivity to pricing might send hospitals down the same path as the unstable airline industry.

TABLE 3-1   2005 Medicare Charges and Full-Load Payments for
High Volume Inpatient Admissions

DRG No.	DRG Label	Cases On File	National Average Charges	National Average Payments
088	Chronic Lung Disease	422,677	$16,360	$5,176
105	Heart Valve Operations	32,433	115,221	38,528
109	Heart Bypass Surgery	47,445	75,536	24,506
127	Heart Failure	661,056	19,321	5,999
143	Chest Pain	234,338	10,965	3,405
160	Hernia Operation in Adults	11,867	16,310	4,991
209	Replacement of Hip or Knee	487,232	36,644	11, 761
233	Major Arm and Shoulder Operations With Complications or Preexisting Conditions	12,579	21,942	6,518
294	Diabetes in Adults	36,334	14,876	4,749
337	Removal of Prostate via Urethra	21,334	10,993	3,446
359	Uterus and Ovary Operations	28,530	15,084	4,855
494	Gall Bladder Removal by Laparoscope	24,308	19,314	5,971
515	Insertion of Heart Defibrillator	43,880	97,306	35,116
527	Angioplasty Procedures & Insertion of Drug Coated Stent into Heart Artery	238,967	43,096	14,047

Payment includes Medicare Teaching, Disproportionate Share, Capital and Outlier payments plus
co-payments and deductibles paid by patients.

Source: December 2005 update of Fiscal Year 2005 Medicare Provider Analysis and Review File (MedPAR 2005).

Responding to Cost Shifting

Employers and private insurers became increasingly aware of the effects of cost shifting and adopted a number of measures to counter it and combat the overall inflation in the costs of care under the general heading of *managed care.* Most of these measures already existed in one form or another somewhere in the country, but they had been spreading slowly until the 1980s. Employers moved away from contracts that accepted provider-established fees from any provider and instead signed up with health maintenance organizations. Figure 3-2 illustrates the roughly 60% decline in market share for traditional indemnity plans from 1988 to 1998. The HMO/POS (HMO plus point-of-service) and PPO (preferred provider organization) plans appeared much better able to control health care costs by exacting their own discounts and by constraining what patients and providers would be able to do.

The Blues began to lose their not-for-profit identity and their focus as community-based cooperative organizations as they competed with the newer for-profit insurers. They often developed their own HMO organizations. By now, the concept of the HMO was no longer a prepaid group practice. It had become an organization that managed the insurance risk and the delivery of care either directly or through a designated provider network. HMOs (for–profit and not–for–profit) continued to negotiate with individual providers, group practices, hospitals, pharmaceutical companies, and all other types of providers for deeper and deeper discounts.

1985 (Not 1984): The Big Step Toward Industrialization

George Orwell warned about Big Brother watching us in his novel *1984.* For health care, he was a little early, but not much. While HMOs existed, they really lacked an effective classification system to make comparisons on a scale suitable for managing care. The introduction of diagnostic-related groups led to *prospective payment* (payment per admission by diagnosis) systems that eliminated some cost *outliers* first for Medicaid and Medicare and then for the HMOs. Having a uniformly defined cluster of cases to follow allowed for the development of classification and information systems and for internal and external oversight of care. Utilization review became a major activity of insurers, and decisions about whom to retain in the service network could be based on profiles of the cases treated by providers and institutions.

EMPLOYERS WANT OUT: BACKING FOR CONSUMER–DRIVEN HEALTH CARE

Throughout the 1990s, observers argued that the United States should move rapidly in the direction of a less regulated national market in health care, as the Reagan Revolution and success in the Cold War led economists and politicians to seek deregulation and consumer sovereignty in all areas. Commentators, such as Herzlinger (1997), pointed to the disappointing results coming out of managed-care contracts and argued that the only way to control health care costs would be to motivate consumers to take more responsibility for their own buying decisions. They noted that neither patients nor providers were fully aware of what things cost, and patient pocketbooks were not affected significantly by the choices made. Providers were likely to benefit from waste and overutilization that were not of concern to consumers who were not payers. The only way to get costs under control, they argued, was to create as much of a market system in health care as the nation had begun to make in other professional services areas. At the same time, the Internet was opening up relatively painless access to medical information for consumers. Payers and insurers established standard sets of provider report cards that purported to rank local providers in terms of their quality of care and costs. They increased deductibles and co-payments and launched experiments to test various pay-for-performance schemes that rewarded desired quality and cost-related behaviors.

Corporations began to assess the impact high employee and retiree health care costs had on their ability to price goods competitively. Increasingly, their competition came from countries where the overall tax system supported much of the costs of health care. They began to support strongly the notion of a defined benefit package (a set dollar amount) and move toward a health care market in which employees would take more responsibility for expenditures and for selecting effective care.

Consumer-driven health care insurance contracts fall into two groups: tiered programs and *reimbursement accounts.* Tiered programs are of two types: (1) tiered premiums and (2) tiered point-of-care cost sharing. The first type gives employees premium benefits in return for accepting higher co-payments and deductibles, a more-restrictive network, or less freedom from utilization review. The second type allows cost sharing for those who choose providers deemed to be preferred providers based on cost and/or quality measures. The publicity, of course, has been attached to the health reimbursement account arrangements, especially tax-sheltered health savings accounts. Typically, the employer establishes an account for the employee to spend on health care. Then a large deductible comes into play and insurance kicks in when the total of these two is exceeded. Unexpended money in the initial account often can roll over from year to year. So far, employer payments under these programs seem to be considerably less than under traditional health insurance. It is unclear how much of the difference comes from reduced utilization, from higher out-of-pocket payments, or from more knowledgeable purchasing decisions (Rosenthal & Milstein, 2004). Davis (2004) suggested that the success of these innovations will ultimately hinge on whether the public sees it as measure to shift costs from employers to employees or whether it motivates provider institutions to "identify, demand and reward high performance, with positive incentives for consumers in a complementary role" (p. 1230).

The Resulting Picture

Currently, the U.S. government and private sector are operating with a hodgepodge of approaches. Medicare and Medicaid are monopsonistic, administered systems. The George W. Bush administration has emphasized consumer-driven health care, a free-market concept focused on health savings accounts. Federal health care policy since the Nixon administration has also tended to support development of large HMOs, examples of oligopolistic competition. Consolidation into larger multisite firms continues to take place both locally in hospital markets and nationally in subsectors such as kidney dialysis centers, nursing home chains, pharmaceutical distribution, medical oxygen distribution, and rehabilitation centers. Three firms of some 80 dominated enrollment for Medicare Part D in 2006. At the same time, successive congressional budgets have reduced funding for Medicare and Medicaid, creating new concerns about cost shifting to insurance programs already burdened with the costs of the uninsured and underinsured.

Each of these contending metaphors and philosophies—administered competition, oligopolistic competition, and free-market (consumer-directed) health care—is rooted in our health care system's past and present. It is not clear what role they will play in that system's future.

CONCLUSION

Like any other democracy, the United States has a system of health care that evolved through a political process influenced by trends in culture, technology, demographics, political ideology, and economic development and through experimentation. When something did not work or stopped working, other things were tried. Those countries coming out of a socialist background have been moving toward decentralization and allowing more of a private sector. Those who started out with a private insurance system have had to add more and more government funding to deal with aging populations and burgeoning technology. There is little reason to believe that what has worked in one time and place will necessarily work in another, nor that what has not worked in one time and place could not be made to work in another. A review of the efforts in many countries shows that there is no magic bullet, that the health care system is the product of a social context, and that many measures and many accommodations are needed to achieve good care at reasonable cost. Where the United States has paid a high price is in its lack of ongoing health policy development with adequate testing of potential interventions and adequate study of new alternatives before the political system becomes disappointed and acts again, often without sound, disinterested policy advice.

Case 3-1

INTERNATIONAL COMPARISONS: WHERE ELSE MIGHT WE HAVE GONE?

It can be useful to consider the roads not taken—the different systems that have evolved in the other developed countries. This case study briefly reviews the health systems of five developed countries for which data are readily available: Canada, the United Kingdom, Australia, Germany, and Japan. The discussion questions at the end ask you to contrast and compare these systems with the U.S. system and among themselves. The variety of approaches taken is amazing, yet all seem to be producing similar results (except costs). Satisfaction surveys for the four English-speaking countries show similar ratings of consumer satisfaction and quality of medical and hospital care; however, self-reported access and expenditures differ widely.

DIFFERENT CULTURES, DIFFERENT SYSTEMS

Canada

Canada started out with a health system very similar to the United States but consciously switched to a very different system in 1971. The key differing aspects of the Canadian system are as follows:

- Universal coverage under provincial health plans financed through value-added and income taxes. Many Canadians have private insurance to cover costs the government does not pay for and to provide more rapid access to scarce services.

- Private medical practices and regional hospitals. Hospital authorities have a fixed budget. Physicians are paid according to a government-established fee schedule. Prices of prescription drugs are also affected by government regulation.

- Hospital financing of new technology or facilities through the provincial budgeting system, not capital markets. Adoption of new technology such as imaging equipment and surgical capacity is slower than in the United States.

- Rationing through delays in elective services, not through ability to pay. Lengths of hospital stays have not gone down as rapidly as in U.S. hospitals. Physician visits per person are similar in both countries, but the percentage of GDP devoted to health care has grown much more slowly than in the United States. Canada has fewer physicians per 1,000 population (2.1 vs. 2.4) but more nurses (9.9 vs. 7.8).

- Concerns about access to specialists and primary care after hours. Canadians express about the same level of satisfaction with their health care as U.S. respondents, but complain a little more about the shortness of physician visits.

- Accelerating growth in per capita spending on health care. Although it slowed sharply after 1971, it has picked up since, despite long waits for scanning procedures and "elective" surgery such as hip replacements, cataract removal, and cardiovascular surgery.

- Per capita health care spending is somewhat lower than in the United States and health outcomes slightly better (Table 2-1). No one is sure how much leakage of services and expenditures takes place across the border between the two countries, with U.S. citizens purchasing pharmaceuticals in Canada and Canadians purchasing scarce physician and hospital services in the United States.

United Kingdom

The British National Health Service (NHS) became a socialized system in 1948 after a gradual movement through voluntary and then mandatory health insurance. The government then owned the hospitals and employed physicians and other provider staff. A very small private insurance market was allowed. It has grown in recent years, and a number of physicians practice outside of the NHS. In London, they are referred to as the "Harley Street" physicians catering to the wealthy.

- In 1995 (under Margaret Thatcher), administration of the system shifted to local authorities that administer the tax revenues allocated to health in areas that cover about a half-million people each.
- Partly because of outmigration, the number of physicians per thousand patients is slightly lower than in the United States; however, British nurses do many things physicians would handle in the United States, including delivering babies, and more are available (9.1 per 1,000 in the United Kingdom vs. 7.9 in the United States).
- Rationing has been based on waiting times for treatments for nonacute conditions. These have included cataract removal, hip replacement, and coronary artery bypass surgery, for which patients may wait as much as a year.
- Primary physicians—general practitioners—are the entrepreneurs of health care. They are grouped together into primary care fund-holder trusts that cover about 100,000 individuals. The trusts accept capitation, incentives, and allowances, and then negotiate contracts with specialist physicians and local hospitals. These primary care fund–

holders are similar to U.S. independent practice associations, except that they are geographically focused, they are responsible for community health and quality improvement activities as well as acute primary care, and primary care physicians can belong to only one trust and each enrollee has a designated primary care provider.

- In 2004, the NHS adopted a pay-for-performance system for family physicians that involved 146 quality performance measures. According to Doran et al. (2006), primary care practices met targets for 83% of patients and achieved 97% of the possible points, much more than the 75% anticipated in the budget, resulting in an average of more than $40,000 in additional payments per physician. The result was a substantial budget overrun. One question still open, because a major baseline study was not performed, is how much of the improvement was due to changed medical care and how much was due to improved documentation.

- Consultants (specialists) are usually salaried by the NHS and have their offices at hospitals. General practitioners do not follow patients into the hospital. Specialists may also be allowed to take some private-pay patients.

- Long queues were a major political issue in the 1997 elections that brought back the Labour government. That government increased NHS funding, and waiting times dropped. Some management decision making was also decentralized from the regional health authority to the local hospitals, whose accountability for quality and cost was increased. At the same time, the government established the National Center for Clinical Excellence to evaluate procedures, treatments, and technologies and to speed their adoption if the evidence is adequate and favorable. This was in response to reliable evidence of differences in treatments and outcome differences among various geographic areas, regional health authorities, and fund-holder groups.

- The primary care trusts have been successful and survived economically.

Australia

Australia has a hybrid public–private health care system. A national health care system called "Medicare" is financed out of taxation, including a Medicare levy based on taxable income. When established in 1984, the Medicare fund supported government hospitals and medical care and prescription drugs for the indigent, and it provided grants to state and territorial governments to operate hospitals. The addition of 1.5% to 2.5% to the levy in 1999 extended the same benefits to the general population. Private insurance is used to pay "cost sharing" fees and provide access to private hospitals, specialists, and physicians. About 40% of Australians have private insurance, which the government says pays 11% of health care costs.

- Australians seem to have less access problems overall than Canadian and U.S. patients, but they report problems accessing care on nights and weekends and paying for prescription drugs.

- An Australian entering the local public hospital can decide whether to do so as a public or a private patient. A public patient receives free hospital and physician care. A private patient receives a choice of doctor and must pay some minor charges, but most charges are covered by a combination of Medicare and private insurance.

- Under a program called Lifetime Health Cover, those who join a private health plan before the age of 31 pay a lower premium over their whole lifetime. Two percent is added to the premium for each year of delay. This is to prevent "hit-and-run" enrollment when major expenses are forecast and maintain a larger, healthier overall risk pool.

- Community rating is required for private health insurance funds. A system of "reinsurance" redistributes the costs of claims among insurers to avoid winners and losers among funds.

- To reduce reliance on the public funding, a 30% government rebate on private health insurance was introduced in 1999.

- There is also a government subsidy for long-term care of older persons, which includes institutional, community-based, and in-home support. In return, the government controls the supply of long-term beds.
- In 2003, Australia had 2.6 physicians and 10.2 nurses per 1,000 population compared with 2.4 and 7.9, respectively, in the United States.

Germany

Chancellor Otto von Bismarck is credited with starting the first national health insurance program in the 1880s. It is centered in 252 not-for-profit sickness funds that negotiate with labor unions, employers, and providers. Employer associations, labor unions, and provider associations interact quite formally. Some physicians are partners, and some are employed. All individuals must have some form of health insurance.

- The premiums of the unemployed (currently a high percentage in Germany) are paid by the federal unemployment insurance fund. For retired workers, premiums are paid by the worker's pension fund. Coverage is universal one way or another. Workers have choices among funds, but they tend to be linked to an industry or a locale. Premiums are assessed on a graduated scale based on income. Co-payments have increased in recent years to cover revenue shortfalls.
- Physician associations receive a fixed amount per person per year, as do hospitals. Hospitals pay hospital-based physicians' salaries from their capitation income. Ambulatory-care physicians are paid either a fee for service or the physician associations pay them a salary from capitated revenues. They generally cannot follow patients into the hospital.
- Doctor visits are shorter and more frequent than in the United States, and hospital stays are longer; however, the hospital staffing ratios are much, much lower.
- Germany had 3.4 physicians and 9.7 nurses per 1,000 population in 2004 compared with 2.4 and 7.9, respectively, in the United States.

- Germany has the third highest percentage of GDP devoted to health care after the United States and Switzerland. Because of cost increases, high unemployment, and an aging population, a 2006 political compromise increased premiums to an average of 14.7% of salaries in 2007. Premiums are pooled, and each insurer receives the same premium per enrollee in an attempt to force some efficiency improvements.

Japan

Employment-based health insurance is at the core of Japan's health system, and it continues to produce the best health outcomes of any of the systems mentioned here; however, some ascribe much of the differential outcomes to demographic and lifestyle issues, especially diet.[2] There is also a national health insurance program financed with national and local taxes. Premiums are scaled to family income. Households not covered by employment-based insurance must belong to community insurance programs under the national plan. Retirees are covered by their employers or their community plans.

- The government sets fee schedules for physicians at a level much below U.S. rates. Fees are identical for all plans; however, patients often add 3% or 4% "gifts" to their payments.
- Hospitals are both nonprofit and for–profit and may be owned by doctors.
- Most physicians work out of large clinics, some associated with hospitals, and are reluctant to send patients into the hospital, as they cannot follow them inside.
- Specialists are hospital employees and earn less than primary care physicians.
- Clinics usually dispense their own drugs.

---

[2] Henderson (2002), while agreeing with this, also cited cultural aversion to invasive procedures and underreporting by at least 1.5% of GDP, by excluding medical care preventive services, under-the-table payments for access, maternity care, and private room charges.

- Japanese patients have many more, briefer visits and many more prescriptions than their U.S. counterparts. They also have many fewer admissions, although lengths of stay tend to be much longer.
- There are much fewer doctors per capita in Japan than in the United States, and waiting lines tend to be managed on a first-come, first-served basis.
- Japanese hospitals are considered by many to have somewhat outdated equipment and shabby facilities. Physicians do not seem to be customer oriented or highly motivated to meet patients' affective needs.

Other OECD Countries

Most other Organization for Economic Cooperation and Development (OECD) countries have more physicians and nurses per thousand population than the United States. The Netherlands has one of the highest ratios of nurses (13.6 per 1,000) and recently increased the roles of nurses in primary care. France, Sweden, and Spain had high ratios of physicians per 1,000 population (3.4, 3.3, and 3.2, respectively) (Grol, 2006).

SOME REPEATING THEMES

A number of themes seem to recur in the systems of these various countries. Some represent ideas tried already in the United States, but all might be considered as possibilities as the U.S. system changes over the next 10 to 20 years.

Universal Coverage

Health care is provided to all. Often it is through a patchwork of public and private funds, but every effort is made to have everyone in the system. General tax revenues (income and value added taxes) are used extensively to fund health care, but in most cases, there is a mixture of additional revenue sources, including patient co-payment, employment-based insurance, retirement funds, local government revenues, and private insurers. This patchwork of payment mechanisms does not leave large gaps of uninsured or underinsured citizens. Private insurance and private care are available to those who choose to pay more. Where co-payments are required, a careful effort is made to make sure that ability to pay does not control access to basic care.

Hospitals Are Budget Constrained

Since the introduction of prospective payment based on diagnostic-related group classifications, hospitals in the United States have operated more as cost centers than revenue centers. A number of countries have established global hospital budgets or capitation budgets for hospitals, often administered through local authorities or trusts. Capital investment is constrained to avoid a hospital arms race.

Specialists Are Salaried and PCPs Are Incentivized

Income of the universal coverage system is used to pay the salaries of specialists, whereas fee-for-service payments reimburse the primary care providers. They serve as gatekeepers for referrals to specialists and hospitals and do not follow patients into the hospital. They are motivated, therefore, to avoid unnecessary hospitalizations. The British experiment with pay-for-performance was sufficiently successful that Epstein (2006) argued that its time has come for the United States. One might also see it as a way to boost the incomes of primary care physicians in the United States sufficiently to attract new practitioners to bolster the currently dwindling supply (Basch, 2006).

Large Premium and Risk Pools Are Maintained

Individuals are compelled to belong to one health plan or another. Young and healthy individuals cannot opt out, or where they can, incentives are provided to try to keep them in. Trusts serve very large employers, but the needs of small businesses and individuals are met through required community rating, local community health plans, and tax subsidies. Large premium and risk pools are built in to level the playing field and hold down administrative and marketing costs.

Systems Integration

The integration of the system is provided at the governmental rather than the institutional level. Circuit breakers in the system, especially between hospitals, specialists, and primary care practices, keep individuals and institutions from maximizing utilization. Incentives focus on motivating primary care physicians to control costs and improve quality.

Rationalization and Standardization

A trend toward decentralization of health care services is offset in part by setting up staff units that analyze and report on current medical technology, evidence about best practices, and evaluation of the cost-effectiveness of common interventions. These recommendations will probably be worked increasingly into pay-for-performance systems.

Labor Substitution

Many countries with lower costs seem to have not only lower professional incomes, but also substitute nurses and pharmacists for physicians, and physician generalists for specialists in their delivery systems.

Pharmaceutical Costs

Some countries constrain or ban direct-to-consumer advertising for prescription drugs, a cost that has grown to $4.8 billion annually in the United States, and rely on recommendations to physicians for decision making. The profit margins of pharmaceutical companies are constrained through a number of mechanisms, depending on what alternatives exist for payment in the national system. In a few cases, physicians are allowed to supplement their revenue by dispensing in their practices.

DISCUSSION QUESTIONS

We have intentionally omitted some recurring themes from our discussion. We invite you to discuss recurring themes that relate to the following questions:

1. In most of these countries, does universal coverage provide the gold standard of care?

2. Does rationing occur in these countries and how is that different from rationing in the United States?

3. Do revenues used to pay for health care tend to come from a single source or many?

4. What steps do these countries take to assure that payments required of individuals do not become a barrier to access?

5. What other patterns of similarities and differences do you notice?

CHAPTER 4

Where Do We Want to Be?

Even in a country that lacks an overall health policy, this is a useful question: How unhappy are we with our health care and what do we want to change? Do not expect the American public to respond consistently. When the Clinton health plan was being debated, a number of organizations surveyed the public. The public reported that they believed that the health care system was in trouble. At the same time, they expressed satisfaction with their own largely employer-financed health care programs. Public support for universal coverage was strong, but individuals did not want to pay higher taxes to support it (Peterson, 1995). An *ABC New/Washington Post* poll in October 1993, showed the following (Schick, 1995):

- 51% of the public favored the Clinton health plan
- 59% thought that it was better than the existing system
- Only 19% thought that their care would get better under it, and 34% thought worse care would result
- However, 57% were against tax increases to pay for it, whereas 40% would be willing to pay.

This parallels the common situation where voters report that they want to throw out the rascals in the capitol, but their own incumbent, whom they know, is all right.

ALIGNMENT WITH THE REST OF SOCIETY

The democratic process is likely to generate many policy experiments as we cope with changing technology, changing demographics, political pressures, and economic fluctuations. These experiments will continue to stir debate about the merits of the many delivery and payment alternatives available today in the United States and elsewhere.

For professionals in leadership positions, this is probably an unpleasant reality because it makes it much harder to plan and implement any institutional strategy. Even the most prestigious institutions are affected by these external drivers. For example, the Finnish national orthopedic hospital, the Orton Hospital in Helsinki, had to downsize and reach out to private pay individuals when the Finnish federal government chose to decentralize its jointly financed government health care program and pass administration on to local governments (Masalin, 1994). These local governments then attempted to control the rising cost of health care by reducing referrals to central specialized hospitals. Orton Hospital was a national resource of high quality, but as the referral patterns of the country changed, it too had to change the way it functioned in order to survive.

WHO IS THE "WE" IN "WHERE DO WE WANT TO BE"?

There is no universal "we" in health policy. There are interest groups, each of which has a central point of view. Within each group are many individuals with some diversity of views. They may be willing to compromise on some issues but not on others.

What Do Providers Want?

Providers are aware of their responsibility to act in the best interests of their patients. They are also inculcated with the "first do no harm" dictum. Even among the "disinterested" parties, some care most about individuals, whereas others focus on populations. This is often a vexing problem for those clinicians who, although committed to the needs of individual patients, are also trained in statistical thinking and population-based approaches.

Provider professionals want professional autonomy, income stability, and growth comparable with their peers, successful outcomes for their patients, a sense of mastery of their field, and the respect of the public. They know that they will make some mistakes but will work very hard to avoid them. They do not want to put their careers on the line with every decision. They do not want to waste energy in silly bureaucratic exercises that consume resources and distract them from effective care. They also would like to see provisions to pay for care for the uninsured. They are aware that these individuals often forgo normal care and may end up later with more serious and costly problems. That is why some hospitals and health maintenance organizations (HMOs) have strongly endorsed state plans to cover the uninsured, even when they involve adding a tax on their bills to paying patients. **Table 4-1** illustrates some of these desires as expressed in the American Nurses Association's *Bill of Rights for Registered Nurses*.

Professional Autonomy

The professional mystique of physicians in the past rested on their control of information. Those who favor a consumer-centric, free-market approach to health care decision making want to maximize the amount of information

---

TABLE 4-1 American Nurses Association's Bill of Rights for Registered Nurses

---

1. Nurses have the right to practice in a manner that fulfills their obligations to society and to those who receive nursing care.
2. Nurses have the right to practice in environments that allow them to act in accordance with professional standards and legally authorized scopes of practice.
3. Nurses have the right to a work environment that supports and facilitates ethical practice, in accordance with *Code of Ethics for Nurses with Interpretive Statements*.
4. Nurses have the right to freely and openly advocate for themselves and their patients without fear of retribution.
5. Nurses have the right to fair compensation for their work, consistent with their educational preparation, knowledge, experience, and professional responsibilities.
6. Nurses have the right to a work environment that is safe for themselves and their patients.
7. Nurses in all practice settings have the right to negotiate, either as individuals or collectively, the conditions of their employment.

Source: Reprinted with permission from American Nurses Association, *ANA Bill of Rights for Registered Nurses*, © 2001 Nursesbooks.org, Silver Spring, MD.

available to consumers. This has led many physicians to argue for privacy in the conduct of their practices, often in the name of protection of business secrets and personal privacy. Many physicians object, for example, to the fact that a drug company's local sales representative has data on their prescribing behaviors (Saul, 2006). Insurers certainly profile physicians and institutions for costs and outcomes regularly, and they make aggregated data available to employers and the National Committee for Quality Assurance (NCQA).

Employer representatives want more information to be available to consumers. One thorny issue is information on individual physicians. President George W. Bush has called for "transparency in the marketplace" and urged private insurers to disclose data on physician costs and outcomes; however, when the Business Roundtable called on the federal government to make its Medicare databases available, the administration cited a 1979 court ruling protecting the privacy of physicians and prohibiting disclosure of Medicare payments to individual physicians (Pear, 2006). NCQA has offered the following conclusions and policy recommendations:

1. Conclusion: Measurement and public reporting reduce variation and improve quality, but the effects have been limited because the practice is not widespread. The shift of consumers into health plan models that are less accountable than HMOs threatens continued improvements. Recommendation: Encourage and reward public accountability from *all* sectors of the health care system.

2. Conclusion: The U.S. health care system is still saddled with anachronistic payment systems that reward quantity, not quality, of care. This contributes to widespread variations in the way health care is delivered—from failure to deliver needed care to huge numbers of unnecessary procedures that drive up costs and endanger patients. Recommendation: Support pay-for-performance strategies that reward physicians, hospitals, and health plans for improving quality.

3. Conclusion: Because measurement and public reporting are not yet commonplace except among HMOs, consumers lack information with which to make informed and fiscally sound decisions on their own. Recommendation: Encourage and offer incentives to doctors, hospitals, and health plans to take part in public accountability efforts and steer consumers to only those plans and providers that participate (NCQA, 2006).

This is a difficult area. Professionals, like other business people, have some rights to privacy and to the prying eyes of competitors, but some observers see the current tensions as the last gasp of a professional monopoly and an attempt to withhold information that bolsters purchaser sovereignty at all levels. Yet the public lacks sufficient knowledge to interpret much of this information effectively. Current techniques for evaluating case mix and adjusting for risk are crude at best. Measuring the outputs of medical interventions is difficult unless one knows that the inputs are comparable or unless there is a way to adjust the data to reflect those differences in inputs, especially the condition of the patient going in.

Other professions fight hard to overcome the dominance of physicians. In many countries, pharmacists are much freer to dispense independently. Nurse practitioners and midwives have fought state by state for the right to practice independently. Psychologists have been fighting some of the same battles with respect to prescribing for the mentally ill, whereas more and more types of counselors want to be able to bill Medicare, Medicaid, and private insurance.

What Do Patients and Their Families Want?

Patients want to beat the odds. They and their families want the best possible outcome, and they want to know that everything that was possible was done to assure recovery or a comfortable death for their loved ones. Some want miracles. All want respect and caring. Most know that they need experts to look after their interests, but still want to be kept informed of what is going on so that they can make sense of what is happening and avoid serious medical errors. Again, the issues are complex. Patients and families want to have access to quality information if they have the time and energy to make their own decisions. At the same time, they employ the provider as their agent, and the sicker they are, the more they tend rely on the clinician's judgment.

When they are not terribly sick, they also worry about the cost of their care. They do not want to spend a lot of time in the waiting room or figuring out how to fill out paperwork. That is a nonmonetary cost, but a cost to them, nevertheless. It can also be a monetary cost if they lose work hours or reimbursement opportunities because of it.

They want to know that they were not treated unfairly by any part of the health care system and that their treatment was not affected by their gender, their ethnicity, or the color of their skin. They would like to think that it was not affected by their pocketbooks, but probably believe that to be a bit unrealistic.

They also become concerned when they believe that profitability concerns or payment mechanisms are biasing the selection of treatments they receive. An example has been the debate over whether the drugs chosen by oncologists for outpatient treatment have been chosen for their effectiveness or their profitability (Abelson, 2006a). Increasingly patients are aware of the financial incentives affecting providers that in the long run can undermine provider legitimacy (Schlesinger, 2002).

Individuals do not want to be denied insurance on the basis of prior medical conditions over which they have little or no control. Yes, some, particularly those sometimes referred to as the "young immortals," are willing to gamble and "go bare" (not carry insurance) if they perceive a relatively low probability of a catastrophic event. This raises the issue of *free riders* getting emergency care even though they are not making provision for paying for it ahead of time. An even thornier problem is the *moral hazard* of those who knowingly indulge in high-risk behaviors for which the general public will have to pick up a share of the costs.

What Do Insurers Want?

They want to be free to play the odds. They want to be able to make an acceptable level of profit whether they are a for-profit or a not-for-profit organization. They want to be able to compete in the marketplace on a "level playing field." Their customers are the payers—the employers and the group and individual enrollees—and they want to maintain a good reputation with them. In the HMO and preferred provider organization (PPO) world, payers want the biggest possible discounts from providers to keep their medical loss ratios competitive.

Insurers also want to avoid adverse selection. They want protection against having those who know they have a higher than average probability of a claim joining their system, whereas those with a below-average probability of a claim do not. They do not want to be in a situation in which they are disadvantaged vis-à-vis other insurers. They would like to continue to compete on marketing skills, on underwriting ability, on investment returns on their reserves, and on their operating efficiencies.

Insurers, however, are very sensitive to market shifts. For example, many are currently developing new insurance products for individuals and small groups as the notion of consumer-oriented care increases customer demand for those products (and as employers reduce their contributions and coverage). They suddenly seem interested in the individual subscribers that they ignored a few years ago.

What Do Employers Want?

They want competent, productive employees and competitive cost structures. They are not in the health care purchasing business for any other reason. They are generally supportive of consumer-driven health care that allows individual consumers, rather than employers, insurers, or provider organizations to make more decisions than in the past. This effectively shifts more of the costs onto the employees and from the lowest paid employees onto Medicaid.

Large Employers and Unions

In unionized firms, premium payments are set through collective bargaining between the company and the unions. This bargaining can expand or contract the health care benefits, depending on the wants and needs of the employer and key groups within the union. After a period during which many of our bitterest strikes were waged over health benefit issues, both sides are now recognizing that employment-related health care costs can reduce domestic employment by encouraging companies to shift production to other countries. Employers are rapidly limiting their liabilities to specific dollar contributions toward health care for employees and retirees.

Galvin and Delbanco (2006, p. 1549) summed up the desires of large- and mid-sized firms as follows:

- Cost control without jeopardizing their ability to attract and hold good workers
- Immediate improvements without heavy investments
- A more productive workforce through health improvement
- Approaches that "focus on individual responsibility, competition, and market forces"
- Avoiding government mandates or other interventions that "bar customized solutions for their firms."

Small Employers

Because health care insurance risks are reduced by pooling large numbers of beneficiaries and because administrative costs and insurance prices are very sensitive to the number of individuals being covered, small businesses find it hard to provide competitive health benefits to their workers. They need either subsidies or effective ways of pooling their people with others to make a viable enrollee population.

What Do Governments Want?

They want a satisfied public. They want health care expenditures to be predictable and at a level that does not disadvantage economic growth in both domestic and international competition. The system should work within the parameters of accepted cultural norms of equity and fairness so that it does not foment unnecessary voter dissatisfaction. All levels of government want to keep costs down, especially Medicaid costs, so as not to crowd out other programs or increase taxpayer unhappiness. Federal, state, and local governments are also concerned about their longer term liabilities for the viability of Medicare trust funds, Medicaid costs, and their accrued liabilities for government retiree health benefits.

Federal Government

It purchases health care on behalf of special populations: the poor, the older populations, veterans, active duty military, Native American, and so forth. It pays for more than 40% of health care purchases (and covers more than 60% of patients in some markets). Children have actually fared better in federally purchased health care since 2000 because of the 1997 startup of the State Children's Health Insurance Program. Federal programs, which are highly sensitive to political pressures, have tended to rely on their purchasing power to garner deep discounts. (Only recently have governments begun to demand and pay only for the use of best practices.) Because of the low federal reimbursement rates, some providers refuse to participate in federal and state programs, further reducing access and availability.

State and Local Governments

Their interests are much more limited, involving Medicaid and local programs for the uninsured poor. Their revenue streams are limited and inflexible, often being tied to real property taxes that cannot adapt rapidly to changing economic conditions. On the other hand, revenue restraints have encouraged innovation. State and local governments cannot print money to cover deficit spending. Despite all of the rhetoric at the national level, most experiments that have been implemented to control health costs have occurred at the state level. States concerned about access issues are increasingly discouraged about the prospects of a coherent national health policy coming out of Washington DC anytime soon, so states such as Maine, Vermont, and Massachusetts are experimenting with systems to provide universal coverage using a variety of funding sources. The governors of more than half the states have proposed measures that include one or more of the following approaches:

- Mandated insurance coverage for all citizens
- Mandated employer coverage or payments into insurance pools in lieu of coverage
- Mandated lower premium individual policies from insurers
- State coverage for all uninsured children
- Tax credits and deductions for individual insurance premiums
- Special discounts for prevention and healthy lifestyles
- Calling for expansion of Medicare to cover the uninsured (Barry & Basher, 2007; Solomon & Wessel 2007).

Governments are also concerned about appropriate access for their constituents. **Case 4-1** provides the example of U.S. Department of Health and Human Services standard for Culturally and Linguistically Appropriate Services (CLAS). Some parts of this standard are mandatory for services paid for with federal government funds, whereas others are guidelines.

What Does the General Public Want?

Members of the general public want to feel that they and their families are safe and that the system will treat them fairly and effectively if and when they need it. That calls for assured access to health care which means assured health insurance coverage. They also do not want to feel guilty about the suffering of their 47 million uninsured fellow citizens. At the same time, they are not enthusiastic about using the tax system to cover the needs of others. They do not want to be treated in a way that marks them as a member of any underclass, but want to be treated as middle class or above.

Americans seem unwilling to pay more than the current proportion of national income (about 16%) for health care, yet the inflation rate in health care continues to exceed the rate of growth in our overall economy (growth in gross domestic product). International economic comparisons have shown a close relationship between national income and per capita health expenditures. Wealthy nations spend more per person. This would seem to indicate that part of the cost of health care is related to need, part is related to availability, and part is related to decisions people make as consumers.

Individual Insurance Purchasers

The problems affecting small business are even worse for the self-employed seeking coverage. Premiums are highest and rejections frequent. Those with preexisting conditions are essentially excluded from the market. Many end up going without coverage. Yet the self-employed often have an advantage over the working poor who are unable to obtain insurance through their employer—either because it is not offered, because they only work part time and are not eligible, or because it is optional and they cannot afford the added expense.

What Do Policy Wonks Want?

They want a system that is efficient, coherent, and rational and that provides effective care to the relevant populace. Health care competes with other services for scarce resources. Money spent on health care cannot be spent on transportation or public amenities; therefore, there must be some calculus for allocating scarce resources to health care and other meritorious causes on a consistent basis. Analysts are sharply divided on many other issues. For example, although many argue for measures to forestall continued growth in health care expenditures, others say, "Don't worry—the U.S. citizenry can afford it and it constitutes economic growth and increasing employment even if it were to approach 25% of our economy." Others say, "Yes, that is growth, but it represents a transfer of assets from the young to the elderly that is not sustainable." Much care is effective and worth doing, but there is agreement that there is considerable waste and inefficiency, even though waste and inefficiency are income-enhancing for someone.

Examples of other areas of concern to policy analysts include the following:

- Free riders—individuals who could otherwise pay but avoid doing so while still relying on the system for help in case of a catastrophic event. Two possible solutions to the free rider problem are (1) universal coverage with a mandated payment and (2) mandated catastrophic insurance, usually with a very high deductible and low premium. Consider for example the contentious issue of motorcycle helmets. Those who do not want to wear them could be required to post a bond to cover their bills and perhaps sign an organ donor agreement to compensate society for the unnecessary risks taken.
- Overserved and underserved areas: Not only are health care resources limited by the willingness and ability of governments, firms, and individuals to pay, but available resources can be poorly distributed, result-

ing in surpluses in some areas and shortages in others. Governments and payers have attempted to regulate the supply of health services as well as the demand. One example of the regulation of supply is *certificate of need* legislation. In an attempt to regulate against an oversupply of health care capital investments, many states have legislation that requires independent review to determine whether additional investments are warranted. If not, the services they provide cannot be compensated for from state and federal funds. Examples of the types of capital investments reviewed include hospital beds, nursing home beds, cardiac catheterization units, and expensive imaging equipment. Legislation has also subsidized the building of hospitals and the posting of health professionals to serve needy populations.

- Withdrawal of services: Demand is constrained when payers restrict what they will pay for and how much they will pay for what is delivered. The absence of sufficient demand or reimbursement for services can lead professionals and provider institutions to withdraw from the market, downsize, or file for bankruptcy. Because of high malpractice insurance costs for obstetrical procedures, for instance, many obstetricians have stopped doing deliveries and only provide gynecologic services. Many hospitals have reduced their psychiatric beds, shifting the burden to the state institutions. Some withdrawals are responses to overcapacity in an area, but some are also the result of decisions that a particular line of services is bound to lose money.

Consensus Does Not Necessarily Lead to Action

By 2007 there seemed to be a consensus that we must do something about our 47 million uninsured. Coalitions, often of strange bedfellows, sprang up everywhere. States were experimenting with universal coverage plans and governors were proposing even more. Many groups urged the federal government to join in the solution. It has done so already by allowing federal monies, including Medicaid funds, to be used more flexibly by the states. There was, however, no consensus as to how universal coverage should be achieved. Some want national health insurance. Others want individuals to buy individual health insurance using vouchers and tax subsidies where necessary. Still others want the states to provide it with employer mandates, special taxes on insurers and providers, and/or subsidies for the poor and near poor (Solomon & Wessel, 2007). These will all likely be debated in the 2008 election.

Proposals to solve the access problem seldom mentioned much about the supply of services available or the impact of a large increase in volume on prices and costs. In the minds of many, universal coverage and costs seem to be separable issues. We learned that that certainly was unlikely to be the case when Medicare and Medicaid were introduced.

CONCLUSION

There are specific things that a majority or a plurality among each set of actors want to see happening in the health care system. For the most part, there are clear majorities on the need for providing insurance for all, controlling the rate of inflation, eliminating waste, improving quality, investing in the most beneficial programs, taking care of children and the older population, and pushing ahead with research to find cures for diseases. Yet there will be a vocal minority on just about every issue, from special interests and from people strongly representing economic and social ideologies. That is why the authors of this book believe in the importance of policy analysis as a way toward maximum possible rationality in decision making, reducing the number of ungrounded assertions and increasing our ability to deal with new evidence and new opportunities.

Case 4-1

NATIONAL STANDARDS ON CULTURALLY AND LINGUISTICALLY APPROPRIATE SERVICES (CLAS)

In 1997, the Office of Minority Health (OMH) in the U.S. Department of Health and Human Services began work on national standards for culturally and linguistically competent health care. The stated goal was to help reduce health disparities. OMH published draft standards in December 1999 and solicited public comment through a variety of channels over a 4-month period. On December 22, 2000, it published the final standards. Although the standards are primarily directed at health care organizations, OMH encourages their use by individual providers as well as by policy makers, accreditation and credentialing agencies, purchasers, patients, advocates, educators, and the health care community in general (OMH, 2001).

CULTURALLY COMPETENT CARE (GUIDE-LINES FOR ACTIVITIES RECOMMENDED BY OFFICE OF MINORITY HEALTH FOR ADOPTION AS MANDATES BY FEDERAL, STATE, AND NATIONAL ACCREDITING AGENCIES)

Standard 1

Health care organizations (HCOs) should ensure that patients/consumers receive effective, understandable, and respectful care from all staff members that is provided in a manner compatible with their cultural health beliefs and practices and preferred language.

Standard 2

HCOs should implement strategies to recruit, retain, and promote at all levels of the organization a diverse staff and leadership that are representative of the demographic characteristics of the service area.

Standard 3

HCOs should ensure that staff members at all levels and across all disciplines receive ongoing education and training in culturally and linguistically appropriate service delivery.

LANGUAGE ACCESS SERVICES (MANDATED REQUIREMENTS FOR ALL RECIPIENTS OF FEDERAL FUNDS)

Standard 4

HCOs must offer and provide language assistance services, including bilingual staff and interpreter services, at no cost to each patient/consumer with limited English proficiency at all points of contact in a timely manner during all hours of operation.

Standard 5

HCOs must provide to patients/consumers in their preferred language both verbal offers and written notices informing them of their right to received language assistance services.

Standard 6

HCOs must assure the competence of language assistance provided to limited English-proficient patients/consumers by interpreters and bilingual staff. Family and friends should not be used to provide interpretation services (except on request by the patient/consumer).

Standard 7

HCOs must make available easily understood patient-related materials and post signage in the languages of the commonly encountered groups and/or groups represented in the service area.

ORGANIZATIONAL SUPPORTS FOR CULTURAL COMPETENCE

Standards 8–13 are guidelines for activities recommended by the Office of Minority Health for adoption as mandated by federal, state, and national accrediting agencies. Standard 14 is suggested for voluntary adoption by HCOs.

Standard 8

HCOs should develop, implement, and promote a written strategic plan that outlines clear goals, policies, operational plans, and management accountability/oversight mechanisms to provide culturally and linguistically appropriate services.

Standard 9

HCOs should conduct initial and ongoing organizational self-assessments of CLAS-related activities and are encouraged to integrate cultural and linguistic competence-related measures into their internal audits, performance improvement programs, patient satisfaction assessments, and outcomes-based evaluations.

Standard 10

HCOs should ensure that data on individual patient's/consumer's race, ethnicity, and spoken and written language are collected in health records, integrated into the organization's management information systems, and periodically updated.

Standard 11

HCOs should maintain a current demographic, cultural, and epidemiological profile of the community as well as a needs assessment to accurately plan for and implement services that respond to the cultural and linguistic characteristics of the service area.

Standard 12

HCOs should develop participatory, collaborative partnerships with communities and use a variety of formal and informal mechanisms to facilitate community and patient/consumer involvement in designing and implementing CLAS-related activities.

Standard 13

HCOs should ensure that conflict and grievance resolution processes are culturally and linguistically sensitive and capable of identifying, preventing, and resolving cross-cultural conflicts or complaints by patients/consumers.

Standard 14

HCOs are encouraged to regularly make available to the public information about their progress and successful innovations in implementing the CLAS standards and to provide public notice in their communities about the availability of this information (OMH, 2001).

DISCUSSION QUESTIONS

1. Some standards are mandatory, and some are not. Try to explain the differences in these requirements.

2. A number of newspaper articles indicate that HCOs are having trouble meeting the letter and the spirit of these requirements, especially in office-based practices where the cost of interpretation may exceed the revenue per visit. What can be done about this?

3. Which are the most important standards as far as you are concerned and why? What are least important and why?

4. What would you change about these regulations if you were in charge at the U.S. Department of Health and Human Services?

CHAPTER 5

What Are the Governmental Alternatives? Many Actors, Many Proposals

The United States has tried an entire alphabet soup of health policy options: HSAs, HMOs, IPAs, PPOs, POS's, IPAs, etc. Some have helped the system, and some have not; however, health care analysts must also look beyond specific organizational and financial alternatives and address issues at a higher level—dealing with the threads of economic and political thought that are behind individual proposals and with the overall criteria of access, cost, and quality of care.

Political and business figures from outside the health care sector currently advocate many alternatives. To offset their tendency to ignore professional issues, we designed Chapters 5 and 6 to include alternatives affecting professional status and roles and institutional responses to them, as well as the usual suspects—alternatives various actors would like impose from the outside. **Table 5-1** presents an array of federal alternatives organized by their primary foci—access, quality, or cost—and then by the economic philosophies behind them. They are not intended to be either mutually exclusive or collectively exhaustive, but to provide a framework for looking at both the broad policy picture and specific health care actions taken at various times and places.

Further into this chapter, a second table summarizes policy alternatives added by state and local governments. Chapter 6 considers other actors, including payers, providers, and consumers. One can think of still others, but these seem sufficient for a review of current policy alternatives.

TABLE 5-1   Illustrative Federal Government Health Policy Options

---

Access to Care
- Administered systems
  - Universal coverage
  - Captive providers
  - Single (or captive) payer system
  - Expanded/reduced eligibility and benefits

- Oligopolistic competition
  - Expand and contract coverages in entitlement and categorical programs
  - Allow states to reallocate federal uncompensated care funds
  - Eliminate ERISA constraints on the states
  - Expand the capacity of the system
  - Fund services for special populations

- Free-market competition
  - Allow states flexibility to reallocate federal funds for vouchers
  - Encourage basic plans with very low premiums for low-income workers and "young invincibles"
  - Encourage portability of health benefits

Quality of Care
- Administered system
  - Mandate participation in quality improvement efforts in federal plans and programs
  - Add more pay-for-performance incentives
  - Select providers and programs on the basis of quality excellence

- Oligopolistic competition
  - Encourage or mandate transparency of quality reporting in federal plans and programs
  - Encourage wider use of health information technology
  - Conduct research on evidence-based practices with high-cost illnesses and procedures and facilitate dissemination and adoption

- Free-market competition
  - Work reporting of quality care and adverse events into purchasing specifications for federal programs
  - Oversee licensure and credentialing of foreign-trained providers

Cost of Care
- Administered system
  - Reduce fees and subsidies
  - Use full bargaining power in negotiation of fees and discounts
  - Limit eligibility and covered services in entitlement and categorical programs

(continues)

- Oligopolistic competition
  - Expand managed care/disease management
  - Bundle payments for services
  - Subsidize capacity reductions
  - Constrain anticompetitive practices
  - Support community-wide development of health information networks
- Free-market competition
  - Change policy on tax deductible status of employer-paid health premiums and individual health expenditures
  - Support individual medical savings accounts
  - Privatize parts of Medicare, Medicaid, and other federal programs
  - Implement information and price transparency in federal programs and promote parallel industrial efforts
  - Support consumer information reporting and database availability
  - Constrain anticompetitive practices

Other Interventions
- Research, development, and deployment
  - Treatment methods (e.g., National Institutes of Health)
  - Delivery system methods (e.g., information technology)
- Provider quality and availability
- Health and safety regulation
- Special situations and opportunities

Governmental alternatives are grouped according to their approaches to the health care marketplace: (1) administered system (monopsonistic), (2) free-market competition (assuming near perfect markets), and (3) oligopolistic competition. Figure 3-2 has already illustrated these market positions, as reflected in the distribution of buyer versus seller market power.

The federal government especially also has a large number of programs that make indirect investments in health care, such as research and development (National Institutes of Health (NIH), Agency for Healthcare Research and Quality (AHRQ), Centers for Disease Control and Prevention (CDC)), educational programs, and health care information technology initiatives. State and federal spending programs also influence the supply and training of health professionals and provide for traditional public health services. These have been put into a fourth section, as they seem to pertain to all alternative economic value systems.

FEDERAL LEVEL ALTERNATIVES

Access to Care—Administered System Alternatives

Under this approach, the government assumes the primary risk. The government certainly may try to influence the behaviors of the other actors, but in the end, it is patient pay, insurance premiums, and tax revenues that cover the costs of the health care system with the risks falling heavily on the tax system. Because a national government tends to respond to political pressures, administered systems tend to focus on access needs and then on costs. These two may take priority over other quality-of-care criteria such as continuity of care (McLaughlin, 1998).

The public sector in United States makes very heavy expenditures in health care, even though the private sector portion is large. In fact, recent World Health Organization data indicate that the United States not only spends more per capita on health care than most other countries, but actually spends more public money per capita than Sweden and the United Kingdom, which ostensibly have public systems (see **Table 5-2**). Similar results were reported by Grol (2006) based on Organization for Economic Cooperation and Development data.

Universal Coverage

Many countries operate with a nationally funded, controlled, and administered health care system. Despite the fact that nearly all countries have a policy on paper that promises universal coverage, only the developed countries have the resources to come close to fulfilling such promises.

Under a single-payer system, coverage is provided almost exclusively through tax revenues, although in practice there is often a parallel private sector based on private insurance or personal payments and a set of private providers. This allows those who can afford it the option of bypassing any supply constraints. In many less wealthy countries, health professionals work for the government part of the day and see private pay patients at other times. This is because government revenue is not sufficient to pay health professionals even a middle-class wage for their government service. Even where this private sector is technically illegal, it is usually tolerated as a reality of life. Where the coverage is universal and the resources are not sufficient, the services are just not delivered and/or a rationing scheme is put in place, especially for procedures that can be postponed.

TABLE 5-2 Comparison of Public and Total Expenditures in Selected Countries, 2003

Country	Health Expenditure as Percentage of GDP	Total Per Capita Heath Care Expenditures*	Total Per Capita Public Health Care Expenditures*	Governmental Percentage of Health Care Expenditures
Australia	9.5	2,874	1,821	67.5
Canada	9.9	2,989	2,098	67.9
France	10.1	2,902	2,214	76.3
Germany	11.1	3,001	2,284	78.3
Sweden	9.4	2,825	2,305	85.2
United Kingdom	8.0	**2,289**	2,047	85.7
United States	15.2	5,711	**2,598**	44.6

* Using adjusted international dollar rate
Source: Author created. Data from *World Health Report 2006* accessed 02/05/07 at http://www.who.int/whr/2006.

Universal coverage is not synonymous with single payer. It can be financed by direct government payment, by mandatory insurance schemes (with mandates placed on employers, consumers, or both) or vouchers allowing subsidized purchase of insurance directly by the consumer, or by a combination of more than one of these. President Clinton's Health Security plan, for instance, was designed to provide universal coverage but preserved the existing system of employer-based coverage. Those favoring consumer-centered care tend to favor vouchers because they believe that vouchers would lessen the tendency of insured patients to ignore costs and allow the recipients a better match between their preferences and the coverage they purchase (Feldstein, 2005).

Captive Providers

Providers can become captives of the governmental system either through employment or government control of the marketplace. Canadian physicians are not employed by the federal or provincial governments, but are unlikely to have much of a domestic practice unless they participate in their province's single-payer system. In the United States, a number of governmental systems employ physicians, including military services, the Department of Veterans Affairs, the U.S. Health Service, and the National Health Service Corps, but altogether, the federal government employs less than 3% of the nation's physicians. The majority of employed U.S. physicians work in the private sector for physician practice management companies (PPMs), health maintenance organizations (HMOs), academic medical centers, and other integrated service organizations.

Single (or Captive) Payer

Common use of "single payer" refers to a unitary health system such as British National Health Service; however, that need not be the case. Medicare is a single government payer for older people and those with disabilities in the United States, but one must meet eligibility criteria and must opt to pay for some specific coverages—for example, physicians and drugs. The government may also set up captive organizations or contractors to administer its programs or handle program disbursements.

Expanded or Reduced Eligibility or Benefits

If coverage is not universal, it may be selective. U.S. government health programs pay directly for more than 40% of health care costs. In recent years, the proportion covered has been slowly increasing as more children are covered each year and the Medicare drug benefit has begun to take effect. Some federal programs are paid from trust funds and some by taxation. A number of optional services can be provided under Medicaid if the states decide to participate. As their budgets dictate, governments may add or subtract from their list of optional services and covered populations. For example, the Trade Act of 2002 created a new category of coverage— displaced workers who became uninsured—in the form of Health Coverage Tax Credits, which paid 65% of the premiums for most COBRA continuation coverage plans of former employers or private health plans arranged by the states. The credits could go directly to the households or be advanced monthly to the insurer. Uptake has been slow, however, because the enrollees facing reduced incomes still have to fund the other 35%.

Access to Care—Oligopolistic Competition Alternatives

Oligopolistic competition is the normal state of affairs in American industry. It is also the case in health care, as many communities have only a couple of hospital groups and a few dominant practices. In the ideological battle between administered systems and consumer-centered care, this fact has gone largely unnoticed.

The federal government's role under oligopolistic competition is limited, but it does have to be concerned about monopolistic practices and enforce the regulations governing commerce overall and health care in particular. It can also provide incentives for specific corporate responses. An example of government encouragement of industry change was the HMO Act of 1973.

Expand and Contract Coverage in Entitlement and Categorical Programs

Most American health care is delivered on a fee-for-service or managed care basis by private providers. The federal government, however, writes or at least approves the regulations that determine eligibility and benefits under programs such as Medicare and Medicaid and the end-stage renal disease (ESRD) program. It can expand or contract the groups to be covered in those programs, directly or by allowing waivers of regulations to the states.

Allow States to Reallocate Federal Uncompensated Care Funds

Many alternatives being worked out by the states involve reallocation of federal monies that have been going to the states to fund uncompensated care. The states may be allowed to reallocate these monies directly to purchase insurance or provide services for the uninsured, or they may pull them back from institutions through special taxes. Federal programs that currently fund uncompensated care, mostly through Medicare and Medicaid, include the following (McClellan, 2005):

- Disproportionate share hospital payments
- Indirect medical education payments
- Bad debt payments
- Section 1115 Medicaid waivers
- Section 1011 of the Medicare Modernization Act for emergency medical treatment

Eliminate ERISA Constraints on the States

Because the Employee Retirement Income Security Act (ERISA) of 1974 sets up two insurance systems, only one of which is under state regulation, a number of promising state and local initiatives have not gotten off the ground. Congress could amend this legislation to remove or weaken this exemption for self-insured employers.

Expand the Capacity of the System

Federal funding can be used to fill in any number of gaps in service programs and facilities. The Hill-Burton program (Hospital Survey and Construction Act of 1946), which funded so many small rural hospitals, is one example. Interestingly, that legislation called for the states to undertake systematic health planning to establish population-based needs for hospital beds and to create a licensing system for hospitals, and then it provided construction assistance to bring shortage areas up to a standard level of services. Many of these new hospitals had fewer than 50 beds and were located in rural areas that had completely lacked hospitals. Between 1946 and 1975, when Hill-Burton funding ended, about a billion dollars of facilities construction was put in place, with about 35% paid for with federal funding, and hospital beds per capita increased about 50%. Hospitals receiving Hill-Burton funding are still mandated to serve the local population with a certain amount of charitable care and care provided on a sliding-fee scale, although government enforcement of that provision has been limited.

Fund Services for Special Populations

The federal government has many categorical programs that support local case finding and service delivery to specific populations and disease groupings, including Native Americans, low-income children, ESRD, and HIV/AIDS. Access could be expanded by adding more such populations or programs.

Access to Care—Free-Market Competition Alternatives

Under this philosophy, the national government's role is to try to mitigate those factors that might make the market imperfect. These include further reduction of regulations that influence the market, making sure that there are adequate numbers of competing providers (the supply side), making sure that buyers and sellers are free to move in and out of the market, and assuring that both buyers and sellers have maximum access to both services and information about price and quality.

Allow States Flexibility to Reallocate Federal Funds for Vouchers

One recommendation from those who would like to see greater consumer choice in programs aimed at improved access would be to give targeted individuals vouchers with which to purchase insurance or services directly. The arguments for this approach parallel those for school vouchers in education.

Encourage Basic Plans With Very Low Premiums for Low-Income Workers and "Young Invincibles"

One of the thornier problems in health policy is the free rider issue. Among the uninsured population are many young, healthy adults who have access to insurance but choose to go without it because their expected health care costs are considerably below the premium levels available. They might be lured back into the insurance market by very low-premium plans that cover only their likely health events, such as trauma and infectious disease. This is, of course, a two-edged sword because such programs might also motivate other healthy workers to leave existing programs, thus exacerbating the adverse selection problem for the remaining enrollees.

Encourage Portability of Health Benefits

A significant number of the uninsured are in and out of the labor force and in and out of employment-based plans. Efforts have already been made to help with interim coverage and portability from one employer to another, but much more could be done.

Quality of Care—Administered Systems

Mandate Participation in Quality-Improvement Efforts in Federal Plans and Programs

Increasingly, the Centers for Medicare and Medicaid Services (CMS) has insisted that institutional providers participate in quality-improvement programs. Often these quality improvement requirements are indirectly enforced through the third-party accreditation procedures of organizations like the Joint Commission on Accreditation of Health Care Organizations (JCAHO).

Add Pay-for-Performance Incentives

The federal government has supported a number of pay-for-performance demonstrations and appears to be committed to national implementation of this approach (Epstein, 2007). Not only can its proponents point to the experience of the United Kingdom with such a plan, but there is increasing evidence from the demonstrations that this may work here. However close this innovation may be to a tipping point, there is still concern that the level of hospital sector improvement may not be sufficient to warrant the investment (Epstein, 2007; Lindenauer et al., 2007).

Select Providers and Programs on the Basis of Quality Excellence

Insurers profile providers on the basis of quality, but the federal government has been reluctant to get involved unless fraud and abuse or specified adverse events are involved; however, the opportunity for greater selectivity is still there.

Quality of Care—Oligopolistic Competition

Encourage or Mandate Transparency of Quality Reporting in Federal Plans and Programs

On August 28, 2006, President Bush issued Executive Order 13410, entitled "Promoting Quality and Efficient Health Care in Federal Government Administered or Sponsored Health Care Programs." U.S. Department of Health and Human Services Secretary Michael Leavitt interpreted the orders as promoting "value-driven health care." In a letter addressed to employer CEOs, Secretary Leavitt (2006a) wrote, "I am writing to invite you to play a leadership role in the movement toward transparency and value-driven health care." He asked for support of the "four cornerstones" of the Executive Order:

- Interoperable health information technology
- Transparency of quality
- Transparency of price
- Incentives for high-value health care.

Encourage Wider Use of Health Information Technology

The same executive order calls for government agencies to require in contracts and agreements that whenever a health care provider, health plan, or health insurance issuer "implements, acquires or upgrades health information technology systems, it shall utilize, where available, health information technology systems and products that meet recognized interoperability standards." Interoperability is a cornerstone of any efforts to collect information on quality of care, costs, and outcomes for reporting to consumers.

Quality of Care—Free-Market Competition

Work Reporting of Quality Care and Adverse Events Into Purchasing Specifications for Federal Programs

Quality reporting for public consumption was also envisioned in Executive Order 13410 and by the "transparency" efforts of the Secretary Leavitt. Reporting of adverse events is required by JCAHO and is also subject to CMS scrutiny.

Oversee Licensure and Credentialing of Foreign-Trained Providers

Foreign medical graduates who are citizens or immigrants must now go through a series of hurdles to achieve licensure in the United States. These evaluation programs will have to continue to balance off the quality aspects of their credentialing process and yet avoid restricting the supply of providers. Given the fact that primary care residencies are not being filled by domestically trained graduates, the country will be relying heavily on outsiders for those services for some time to come.

Cost of Care—Administered System

Use Full Bargaining Power in Negotiation of Fees and Discounts

One bone of contention in the 2006 election was whether the federal government should use its full bargaining power in dealing with the pricing of prescription drugs under federal programs, especially Medicare Part D. Some government programs such as the Veterans Administration Health System bargain for and receive much lower prices than Medicare and Medicaid. Federal government policy about use of its monopsony buying power has been very mixed in terms of how strongly prices for federal programs are negotiated for purchases such as physician services, hospitals, home health, and pharmaceuticals. It would appear that the lobbying and political power of the affected providers have a lot to do with the intensity of bargaining.

Limit Eligibility and Covered Services in Entitlement and Categorical Programs

The federal government in addition to negotiating prices, also established what it will pay for by exercising its legislative and administrative powers. In the budget process, many changes get made in who and what gets covered in what program from year to year. Some of these changes are political, but some can be technologic as well. For example, the ESRD program has added alternatives such as outpatient dialysis centers, home dialysis, and transplantation to its original program of dialysis in hospitals. It has taken steps to encourage less expensive technology, including national support for organ donation and transportation.

Cost of Care—Oligopolistic Competition

Expand Managed-Care/Disease-Management Programs

Although the federal government began with and still maintains a fee-for-service philosophy for Medicare and Medicaid, it has encouraged states efforts to move more and more Medicaid recipients and dual eligibles (for both of the programs, mostly the disabled) into managed-care programs and adopt disease-management programs to control the costs of the 20% of the under 65 population who account for 80% of health care claims from that group. Medicare Part D, the prescription drug benefit, represented a major change for that fee-for-service program in that those who want the benefit must enroll in a Medicare prescription drug plan. Furthermore, many large HMOs are working to recruit Medicare patients by offering to waive the Part D premium, at least temporarily, if older persons also join their Medicare HMO. At the same time, the Medicare program is taxing the states for their share of the drug premiums for some seven million enrollees, most of whom are active patients whose drugs were previously covered by Medicaid. This tax is a called the *clawback*. In essence, the clawback makes the states partially responsible for funding Medicare. Several governors are resisting the clawback provision and court cases are pending. States have also been concerned about the drug benefit attracting more enrollees, sometimes called the *woodwork effect*, and about the potential loss of federal waivers that had allowed some states to receive matching federal funds for their existing pharmacy benefit programs.

Bundle Payments for Services

Porter and Teisberg (2006) have suggested that we need to move to a system in which the full cost of treating a disease entity is made fully transparent by bundling various necessary services into a single price. Although prospective reimbursement systems have accomplished some of this for insurers, including the federal government, they have not translated into transparency for the buying public. It is not clear whether the transparency approach outlined by Secretary Leavitt (2006b) will capture both physician and hospital and other provider costs into a single figure unless the providers are integrated into a single billing institution.

Subsidize Capacity Reductions

There are some areas and some services that are over capacity and therefore likely to have high costs and high prices and deliver unnecessary services. For example, on November 28, 2006, New York State's Commission on Health Care Facilities in the 21st Century recommended closing 7% of the state's hospital beds. This would involve closing nine hospitals and reconfiguring 48. The Commission operated under a law setting up a process similar to the federal government's procedures for closing military bases. Its entire recommendation had the force of law unless the Legislature or the Governor turned down the proposal in its entirety by the end of the year. The state would receive $300 million per year for five years to defray the transition costs from the Federal-State Health Reform Partnership (Cooper & Chan, 2006).

Support Community-Wide Development of Health Information Networks

The National Health Information Network program outlined in **Case 8-1** is an example of this policy approach. That case discusses some pros and cons of the current federal government approach.

Cost of Care—Free-Market Competition

Change Policy on Tax-Deductible Status of Employer-Paid Health Premiums and Individual Health Expenditures

President Bush's 2007 State of the Union message proposed a number of changes in the tax code pertaining to the deductibility of employer-paid and individually paid health care premiums. These proposals would make individual premium payments fully deductible just like employer payments, but put a cap of $7,500 per individual or $15,000 per couple on the overall deductibility of premiums. As of 2006, individual health care premiums were included with other health care costs, which could be deducted only if they exceeded 7.5% of adjusted income. The cap would be new and would be designed to reduce the incentive to purchase policies that are deemed to encourage overutilization.

Support Individual Medical Savings Accounts

Market-oriented strategies for controlling costs have gone through a number of phases. In the 1980s and early 1990s, HMOs were encouraged and were temporarily successful in slowing down the rise in costs; however, as costs rose again, policy makers looked for an alternative approach. In the late 1990s, the concepts of consumer-centered care gained greater acceptance. More and more companies, faced with increased international competition and increasing inflation in their insurance premiums, felt a need to reduce or eliminate health care benefits. At the same time, there was greater acceptance of a philosophy of defined contribution pension plans rather than defined benefit plans. That made it easier to accept the similar transition for health insurance benefits. Because health care benefits are fully funded annually, the underlying drivers were not quite the same, but that paved the way conceptually for employers to pay a fixed amount regardless of the amount of cost inflation in health care.

There are two basic approaches to the limited-benefit approach. The older approach was to fund a basic plan with limited benefits and one or more premium plans with the employee responsible for paying the difference. This usually included the option of enrolling one's family and purchasing additional services such as dental and long-term care insurance. The other approach is characterized by the health savings account, which allows the consumer to assume more of the risks of health care costs, but to keep the winnings if the gamble pays off.

Where the basic plan limits the employee to a preferred-provider panel, one enhanced alternative is a point-of-service plan in which the employee can go to any provider and pay the difference between the negotiated rate and the provider's bill. This has been a popular option because American patients strongly value having the freedom to choose their own providers.

Recent federal legislation supports the second alternative, the consumer-driven health plans approach, which often includes the following elements:

1. The employer pays a fixed amount toward each employee's health benefit.
2. It is paid into the employee's tax-sheltered health account, which he or she controls and uses to pay for care (called a health savings account).
3. The money in that account that is not spent is allowed to accumulate from year to year.

4. The employee is also covered by a high-deductible health insurance policy that protects him or her from the worst effects of a catastrophic health event.
5. The employee receives online support for health maintenance activities, access to information on provider quality and cost histories, discount programs, and the status of his or her health care account.

Privatize Parts of Medicare, Medicaid, and Other Federal Programs

The George W. Bush administration had as one of its priorities to increase the private market approach to federal programs such as Medicaid (Texas Health and Human Services Commission, 2007). For example, private insurance companies were subsidized to undertake Medicare- and Medicaid-managed care programs. There have been a number of pros and cons raised in the debates about this policy. These programs have been fee-for-service, and there had been only limited attempts to manage care; however, the government-administered programs had very low overhead costs, and those of the insurance companies have been considerably higher. The recent profit margins and executive compensation of many health care insurers have been rising rapidly.

Implement Information and Price Transparency in Federal Programs and Promote Parallel Industrial Efforts

The letter to employer CEOs from Secretary Leavitt is an illustration of this approach. His office has been providing packets of information to the private sector. Some of this material clearly outlines the administration's vision for consumer-driven health care. In a brochure issued by the U.S. Department of Health and Human Services (Leavitt, 2006b), the Secretary envisioned the information that each purchaser of health care might need in order to support a major health care purchasing decision. This is reproduced as **Figure 5-1**. This compares five hospitals on distance, several quality-related variables, and a cost estimate for a hip replacement procedure.

Support Consumer Information Reporting and Database Availability

The combination of health information technology gathering data at the source and the reporting envisioned for individual health care purchasers will have to be based on the development of systems that aggregate data from the providers and present it as needed to the consumers. This will be an expensive proposition, and how it will be financed is uncertain.

Surgical Care Consumer Guide

Search Results: **Hip Replacement**

Summary
Average Cost in Network Facility: $11,249–$15,895
Out of Network Facility: $18,889–$23,460

Sort by: Quality ▶

What's included in the cost?

Results sorted by: Distance

Key

Quality | **** Highest | * Lowest Costs $ Least Expensive | $$$$ Most Expensive Patient Assessment **** Highest | * Lowest

Distance (miles)	Facility Name	Patients per year	Quality	Cost Estimate	Insurer pays	Patient pays	Patient Assessment of Care
6.2	Clearwater General 14280 Bay Drive Clearwater, FL 22131	400	***	$$ $15,895	85% ($13,511)	15% ($2,384)	**
13.2	All Saints Medical Center 123800 All Saintes Drive Tampa, FL 22122	86	****	$$$ $20,700	80% ($16,560)	20% ($4,140)	***
25.6	Good Samaritan Hospital 11111 E. Samaritan Drive Tampa, FL 22222	232	****	$$ $15,895	90% ($14,306)	10% ($1,590)	****
26.3	Tampa Hip Hospital 1400 East Tampa Boulevard Tampa, FL 22211	170	***	$$$ $20,700	75% ($15,525)	25% ($5,175)	***
27.3	Orthopedic Clinical Hospital 1444 Goodle Drive St. Petersburg, FL 22113	432	*	$ $11,600	70% ($8,700)	25% ($2,900)	*
33.2	Valley General Hospital 1400 Tampa Bay Way Tampa Bay, FL 22031	310	***	$$ $16,230	85% ($13,796)	15% ($2,434)	***

FIGURE 5-1

The Future

Source: M. O. Leavitt, Better Care, Lower Cost, DHHS, p. 6.

Constrain Anticompetitive Practices

The Federal Trade Commission has been active in overseeing hospital mergers and in stopping constraints on professional service advertising once deemed "unethical" by professional associations. The Food and Drug Administration also oversees the truthfulness of drug advertising claims, even those under a patent monopoly; however, much of the action to maintain or constrain the market in professional services is centered at the state level, as states make and enforce professional licensure requirements and oversee their local health insurance markets.

Insurers have tended to compete on premium levels because of payer and consumer sensitivity to those payments. They have taken a number of steps to control costs. The easy way to do this is to discourage utilization of services. Since the HMO concept became widely accepted in the 1970s, many national and state government efforts have attempted to offset the market power of dominant insurers and providers and to offset any tendency to rely on anticompetitive practices against both payers and providers.

Other Interventions

The federal government also undertakes programs that support health care effectiveness, but are not aligned with one political or economic point of view, including investments in medical research, professional education, and information technology. These tend to be individual legislative responses that fulfill generally accepted roles for government. The government at times also invests through public health education programs and screening programs. It may also choose to relax regulatory barriers that in effect reduce the investment requirements of providers, although the tendency has usually been toward more regulation, which requires more government investment and more matching efforts by providers and provider organizations. Government also may respond to crisis situations or special situations that arise and gain public support.

Supporting Research, Development, and Deployment

Health care is a service sector with few major players that have enough geographic coverage, and hence enough volume, to amortize the costs of a proprietary research program. Possible exceptions are large insurers, hospital chains, and HMOs. The industry is dependent therefore on vendors such as the pharmaceutical industry and equipment suppliers to conduct applied research and product development; however, they, in turn, tend to focus on high volume, patentable new technologies, often called *blockbusters*. Therefore, there are gaps that government research programs must address.

- Treatment methods: These are developed by private industry where patentable and by the government and universities. The U.S. government has maintained a number of world class research organizations in NIH and CDC. A newer player is AHRQ, which emphasizes research into treatments that are already in use. Much of the actual research is conducted by universities and think tanks, but the research strategy is often in the hands of the federal agencies.
- Delivery system methods: Increasingly, the government has become involved in managerial innovations pertaining to the quality and cost of health care. Examples include the National Health Information Network, where the government is also facilitating deployment, and the work of the Institute of Medicine on medical errors and subsequent research to reduce error rates.

Provider Quality and Availability

The issue of planning for the supply of health personnel has often been controversial. For example, there has been considerable political pulling and hauling about assuring residency places for U.S. citizens who are also foreign medical graduates. In many countries, the ministry of education decides how many professionals of what type will be trained, sometimes in collaboration with the ministry of health and sometimes without its input. In the United States, neither health care nor education is the responsibility of the central government, and thus, the planning is highly decentralized. Individual schools and institutions, influenced by federal, state, and local budgets and local staffing needs, decide how many persons to admit and graduate at each level. Professional associations control supply to some extent by the number of residency and training programs that they accredit, but they must be ever mindful of the possibility of antitrust actions when they try to cut back on the supply. Various nonprofit associations (boards) controlled by the professions handle postgraduate training, testing, and certification; however, the federal government plays a major role by offering grants that support training in shortage areas such as nursing and pharmacy and loan forgiveness to graduates who agree to work in underserved areas.

Health and Safety Regulation

The Food and Drug Administration is involved in many regulatory programs aimed at protecting the health and safety of the public, including drug and medical device approval, drug advertising, clinical laboratory standards and inspections, drug biologics manufacturing safety, and a host of other programs. The National Institutes of Health policy governs the use and maintenance of laboratory animals. Federal policy also supports a number of voluntary regulatory efforts such as JCAHO and various professional societies by requiring certification as a condition for payments from federal programs.

Special Situations and Opportunities

The federal government intervenes in special situations such as hurricanes by picking up the state and local shares of program funding and offering tax and investment incentives. It is also sensitive to some high-visibility public health concerns such as potential pandemics, developing and stockpiling vaccines and treatment supplies. Where the federal government sees an opportunity, such as community funding of access for the uninsured, it can allow allocation of budgeted funds to encourage experimentation and evaluation.

STATE AND LOCAL GOVERNMENT OPTIONS

In fiscal-year 2004, Medicaid spending surpassed education as the largest item in state general funds budgets (SCI, 2006, p. 28). The states have proven to be 50 distinct laboratories for developing health policy initiatives designed to increase access to care, especially for children and the uninsured. States are continuously making tradeoffs among programs and funding sources. Local governments, with encouragement from Washington, are also adding programs to ameliorate the problems of the uninsured, despite their limited and rather inflexible tax bases. Often they participate as partners with state government, Medicaid, employers and insurers. A somewhat typical model is the 2005 three-share access program of Muskegon County, MI for low-income uninsured workers (less than $11.50 per hour) not eligible for existing public programs. The employer pays about a third of the premium, and the worker and the community pay similar amounts. Local government funding comes from federal programs, and care must be delivered locally.

Table 5-3 provides a list of current and proposed state and local government policy initiatives. Again, this is not intended to be exhaustive, as many of the federal government options in **Table 5-1** also can be and are being implemented at these levels.

TABLE 5-3   Illustrations of State and Local Government Health
             Policy Options

Access to Care
- Administered system
  - Universal coverage using general revenues
  - Expanded/reduced eligibility and benefits
  - Mandated coverages and services
  - Captive providers (e.g., health department clinics)
  - Increase funding to enable full enrollment of eligible populations
- Oligopolistic competition
  - Mandate employer participation/play-or-pay
  - Impose special taxes on providers and insurers to subsidize low-income uninsured
  - Increase primary care provider supply
  - Support pooled insurance risks
  - Support cooperative buying arrangements for smaller businesses
  - Make reinsurance more widely available
- Free-market competition
  - Individual mandate for health insurance
  - Reallocate federal and state funds and blend with others sources to subsidize universal or near-universal coverage
  - Modify medical practice constraints

Quality of Care
- Administered system
  - Require participation in quality improvement programs
  - Encourage "medical home," especially for special needs enrollees
  - Use pay-for-performance approach
  - Mandate installation and use of health information technology
  - Train providers in evidence-based practices

(continues)

- Oligopolistic competition
  - Support regional consumer information reporting and databases
  - Adopt pay-for-performance in private as well as public sector
  - Support interoperability and transferability of personal health records
- Free-market competition
  - Support reporting of quality outcomes and quality survey data
  - Support training of providers in evidence-based practices

Cost of Care

- Administered system
  - Malpractice (tort law) reform
  - Negotiate program fees and discounts
  - Require disease management for special populations
  - Reduce/enhance provider payments
- Oligopolistic competition
  - Facilitate "Connector" system to enable access to more than one insurer's plans and full portability
  - Modify medical practice laws and constraints
  - Encourage managed care and disease management
  - Encourage licensure and credentialing of new providers
  - Use certificate-of-need procedures
  - Enforce antitrust laws and regulations
- Free-market competition
  - Remove insurance barriers to medical tourism
  - Remove constraints on insurance products to attempt to bring free-riders into the system

Other Interventions

- Research and development (e.g., embryonic stem cell research)
- Policy analysis advice to legislative processes
- Education of professionals
- Distribution of professionals and services
- Public health functions and departments

Access to Care—Administered System

Universal Coverage Using Tax Revenues

State governments can attempt to provide universal coverage. States are unlikely to go much further than to reallocate existing federal and state health care funds without further taxation because they have greater financial constraints than the federal government. They cannot print money. Massachusetts has been considering the following amendment to its state constitution:

> *Upon ratification of this amendment and thereafter, it shall be the obligation and duty of the Legislature and executive officials, on behalf of the Commonwealth, to enact and implement such laws, subject to approval by the voters at a statewide election, as will ensure that no Massachusetts resident lacks comprehensive, afford- able, and equitably financed health insurance coverage for all medically necessary preventive, acute and chronic health care and mental health care services, prescription drugs and devices.*

In the meantime, the Governor and the Legislature have agreed on a program intended to cover over 95% of the population by requiring most citizens to carry health insurance or pay into a pool through the state income tax system. The new approach also required employers to pay $295 per year per uncovered employee (play-or-pay). Governor Romney used his line-item veto to try to strike that provision from the law, but that veto was overridden.

Maine's Dirigo health plan intends to cover most of the state's unin- sured individuals by 2009. It will be financed through savings from a series of related cost cutting moves and will provide sliding scale subsidies to low- income families.

Expanded/Reduced Eligibility and Benefits

Just as federal agencies can modify eligibility and benefits in their programs, state and local governments can do so in the programs that they fund. They also can apply for Medicaid waivers to reallocate resources in that program toward high-priority needs.

Mandated Coverages and Services

Hawaii has come the closest to achieving universal coverage by requiring all employers except for those employing seasonal agricultural workers to provide a minimum level of group health coverage and pay at least half the premium for all workers working 20 or more hours per week after 4 weeks of employment. Its laws also specify how to meet the needs of children, the disabled, and pregnant women. Other states are not likely to follow suit because the Hawaii plan required a congressional amendment to the ERISA law, and this is unlikely to be repeated. In March 2005, Tennessee ended coverage of some 320,000 adults enrolled in the TennCare program.

Coverage for some 119,000 children continued. State and local governments can also determine what services are covered in the programs that they administer for their employees and client publics.

Captive Providers (e.g., Health Department Clinics)

A number of states and municipalities provide primary care services directly through their public health system. Many counties and municipalities also own their own local hospitals, many of which were built with federal government subsidies through the Hill-Burton legislation. Academic medical centers owned by state universities also have their own hospitals and faculty practice plans, often with some expectation of serving the state's population as well as training health personnel. State mental hospitals and other institutions for the disabled are usually the states' largest direct expenditures on health services after Medicaid.

State and local health departments and hospitals can be a source of free care for those without insurance. For example, this was proposed by Mayor Newsome of San Francisco. Often this is seen as a cost reduction measure that keeps patients from getting sicker and presenting themselves in emergency rooms where care is more expensive.

Increase Funding to Enable Full Enrollment of Eligible Populations

A number of existing programs are not fully funded by the states, and thus, some eligible children and adults cannot receive the services intended for them. Governments at all levels could appropriate sufficient monies to cover all eligible individuals and their needs under their programs.

Access to Care—Oligopolistic System

Mandate Employer Participation/Play-or-Pay

Some states have been experimenting with mandates on employers, usually the large- and medium-sized ones, to provide health insurance. Where employers choose not to pay insurance premiums, they are required to pay a set amount per employee per month to a pool that would cover health insurance purchases for their employees. These payments are seldom sufficient to cover the full premium, and thus, additional funding sources are usually needed. This "play-or-pay" requirement may be of questionable legality if imposed on self-insured firms exempted under ERISA.

Impose Special Taxes on Providers and Insurers to Subsidize Low-Income Uninsured

The initial proposal for California from Governor Schwarznegger included a 4% payroll tax that would go into a state insurance fund. Doctors and hospitals would pay 2% to 4% of their revenues into that fund to subsidize insurance for low-income individuals and increase Medicaid payments to physicians (Fuhrmans, 2007a).

Increase Primary Care Provider Supply

Many states have offices that are trying to expand primary health care services in rural areas. These often work in collaboration with the National Health Service Corps in setting up clinical services in those areas. States may also mandate coverage for alternative and complementary health services. Most every state requires the inclusion of chiropractors as providers. In the state of Washington, all health insurance programs except the self-insured must cover acupuncture.

State educational systems also play a major role in determining the supply of medical providers. When there is a shortage of professionals, state educational institutions are quick to expand their programs; however, it is much harder to get them to cut back when there appears to be an oversupply.

Support Pooled Insurance Risks

Most of us are familiar with risk pools in auto insurance where drivers with poor claims records are assigned to a risk pool and each insurance company operating in the state must take a proportionate share of those in the pool as an assigned risk at an assigned rate. The same can be done with high-risk patients, forcing the companies that want the lucrative business in a state to take a certain proportion of the chronically ill from specific categories in order to participate. That reduces the likelihood that those sicker patients will be excluded by the insurance underwriting process. In 2005, some - 31 states had pooled-risk programs.

One frequently debated option is community rating, in which the whole community is a single pool and the insurer cannot profit by excluding sicker citizens or pricing them out of the market; however, the insurance industry has strongly resisted this concept as unfair to those who take care of their health. Risk pools are therefore used as a compromise to overcome some of the inequities of the underwriting process.

States can use their powers to regulate insurance to encourage plans that pool health insurance risks. There are three ways that this can be encouraged:

- Barring discrimination through underwriting against high risk individuals under existing employer programs
- Establishing special pools of high-risk enrollees, a portion of which must be accepted by the insurance companies who want to participate in the state's markets at a special rate (perhaps with a subsidy from the state)
- Cross-subsidizing the high-risk enrollees through a special tax on all health care premiums that is used to offset their higher premiums

Support Cooperative Buying Arrangements for Small Employers

Montana and Arizona have developed buying cooperatives for small businesses seeking to provide coverage for their employees. State or local governments may or may not choose to pay part of the premium costs for those participating in their buying pools.

Make Reinsurance More Widely Available

An alternative to or a supplement to risk pools is a reinsurance program. Under that program, the risk of catastrophic cases would be borne by a master policy with other insurers or by a state-financed entity. In New York, the state has offered a reinsurance program since 2001, thereby allowing catastrophic coverage for sole proprietors, small firms, and low-income workers at more reasonable rates. Federal reinsurance legislation has also been introduced in Congress. This could address the problem of adverse section and help bring younger, healthier individuals back into the health insurance market.

Access to Care—Free-Market Competition
Modifying Medical Practice Constraints

Delivery of health care is tightly constrained in the United States by any number of laws and regulations governing medical practice. They cover both individuals and institutions. State medical practice acts and reimbursement policies can have a profound impact on the supply of potential providers. As noted in Chapter 2, there are many possible substitute workers to do specific tasks or pieces of tasks done by existing professionals: psychiatrists for psychologists, nurse practitioners and physician assistants for primary care and emergency room physicians, nurse midwives for obstetricians, nurse anesthetists for anesthesiologists, dental hygienists for dentists, pharmacy technicians for pharmacists, and so forth. State governments can step in and expand the roles allowed to the substituting professions, increasing the supply of services and potentially reducing the costs of care.

Quality of Care—Administered System
Encourage "Medical Home" for Special Needs Enrollees

The American Academy of Pediatrics (2007) has advocated that categorical plans and Medicaid plans require that each covered child with special needs have a medical home, a designated provider who would provide continuity of care, know the family and child situation, work with the family, coordinate community-based services, and follow up on the case in a timely manner. Some states are working to expand this concept beyond children.

Use Pay-for-Performance Approach in State-Purchased Plans

Each state and local government is a major regional purchaser of health care, including Medicaid and coverage for state employees and retirees and their families; therefore, these governments can insist that pay-for-performance systems be included in their purchase specifications and care contracts.

Mandate Installation and Use of Health Information Technology

State and local governments can likewise use their buying power to require the expansion and use of health information technology with their clients, including computerized physician electronic order entry and electronic medical records. They can also support economically the development of community health information networks.

Train Providers in Evidence-Based Practices

State programs can also undertake to train providers on the nature of and motivate the use of evidence-based practices. **Case 12-1** presents one such effort, supported with federal funds to implement evidence-based practices in the North Carolina mental health system. State continuing-education programs for providers, such as the Area Health Education Center programs, can also participate in such educational efforts, providing courses and academic detailing.

Quality of Care—Oligopolistic System
Support Regional Consumer Information Reporting and Databases

Many states now have their own quality data reporting requirements for hospitals similar to NCQA and JCAHO requirements. Because these inspectors are voluntary organizations representing the interests of employers, insurers, and hospitals, state programs would assure that the data on costs and outcomes are available to the general public.

Adopt Pay-for-Performance in Private as Well as Public Sector

Federal and state programs can publicize the effects of pay-for-performance plans in public pronouncements and can demand it from insurers and providers who service their employees and their dependents. This will quickly build a critical mass of activity that will pervade both private and public programs.

Support Interoperability and Transferability of Personal Health Records

Similarly, state and local governments can encourage the development of local health information networks by including such requirements in contracts for their employees and dependents, knowing that the system, once in place will be used by all parties.

Quality of Care—Free-Market System
Support Reporting of Quality Outcomes and Quality Survey Data

State and local governments can demand quality transparency for their employee and dependents programs and through funding of surveys and database systems for public use.

Support Training of Providers in Evidence-Based Practices

State institutions provide much of the training of providers through universities and continuing education systems. In overseeing and funding such programs, states can have considerable impact on the pace of adoption of evidence-based practices through continuing education courses and academic detailing.

Cost of Care—Administered System

Malpractice (Tort Law) Reform

There is a high level of dissatisfaction in the health care industry with the costs of malpractice cases and resulting premiums for malpractice insurance. A number of states have intervened to set health care apart from their usual tort law procedures and remedies. Various remedies have been proposed and many experimented with by states.

Tort law reform usually refers to legislation limiting (capping) the size of malpractice awards caused by negligence, especially the components awarded for pain and suffering and as penalties for gross negligence, and/or limiting the contingent fees paid to lawyers who win such cases. Because the cost of malpractice suits and insurance is much higher in the United States than any other country and legal fees and court costs consume close to half of the awards, a number of alternatives have been proposed, including the following:

- No-fault malpractice insurance similar to that used in some states for auto insurance
- Mandatory arbitration or mediation
- Institutional (enterprise) liability on a no-fault basis.

All of these would bypass the system of jury trials currently used to prove or disprove negligence and assume that juries and plaintiffs lawyers are responsible for the size of the awards. Proponents of enterprise liability believe that after an organization sees negligence cases as costing it directly, it will act to reduce such errors in ways that the professions have so far been unwilling or unable to adopt.

Negotiate Program Fees and Discounts

In some cases, payers may ask for bids from various providers and then select a small number who offer the lowest prices, or more often, the deepest discounts off published prices. There may also be other restrictions in the bidding process that limit the availability of suppliers, such as 24/7 services, access to hospital beds, financial strength, number of years in business, and special certification or licensure requirements.

State and local governments also can enlist suppliers and especially regulated insurers into any number of possible cost-sharing or premium-supplementing arrangements. For example, the governor of Pennsylvania negotiated a deal in 2005 with the state's four nonprofit Blue Cross insurers to contribute 1.6% of their premium revenue over six years and 1% of their Medicare and Medicaid premiums (close to a billion dollars) from retained earnings to a state fund that would pay for coverage for low-income and uninsured individuals.

Require Disease Management for Special Populations

States have adopted a wide variety of strategies for inducing their enrollees to join HMOs and accept disease-management alternatives. They have mandated these approaches in some cases and offered a number of inducements for those who elect to accept that type of coverage.

Reduce/Enhance Provider Payments

For a number of years, just about every state has been reducing or freezing payments to providers under their Medicaid programs. Despite inflation, a growing caseload and improved access have increased the costs to the states by a rate of almost 9% annually. A significant proportion of the community-based provider population does not take Medicaid patients. States also adjust payments upward where there is a shortage of providers. An example is increasing the compensation of obstetricians where increasing the availability of prenatal care is likely to offset major preventable costs later.

Cost of Care—Oligopolistic System

Facilitate the "Connector" System to Enable Access to More Than One Insurer's Plans and Full Portability

One innovation of the Massachusetts legislation to achieve near-universal coverage was the "Connector." This has attracted a great deal of attention. There has been some confusion because there are two components under that label. One is the Connector Authority, which negotiates with insurers for basic policies for the uninsured and sets the level of subsidy that the state will contribute for those between the Medicaid upper limit and 300% of the national poverty level. The other is the "Connector," which allows individuals to compare prices and coverages of all the participating insurers to determine which plan best meets their individual needs. These individuals would include the working poor and those with higher incomes whose employers do not offer insurance. This would enable them to meet the individual mandate for health insurance required under law in Massachusetts (Texas Health and Human Services Commission, 2007).

Those who favor the demise of employment-based health insurance see this as a facilitating step for a competitive individual marketplace. There is concern that some states will use the concept to replace public coverage of those under Medicaid or the State Children's Health Insurance Program with vouchers (Solomon, 2007). How this will play out is uncertain. Initial insurer bids were considerably higher than Massachusetts plan designers had anticipated and tradeoffs in coverage have been necessary.

Modify Medical Practice Laws and Constraints, as Necessary, to Encourage Licensing And Credentialing of New Providers

Most professionals are licensed by state boards, whereas most specialists are certified by national professional boards. All of these represent an opportunity for restricting entry. The Federal Trade Commission has been very much aware of this issue and has moved decisively against professional rules against advertising enforced by the professions. Any attempt to introduce a new type of provider who will perform a limited range of services at lower cost has usually been resisted by the entrenched professions. In general, legislatures have had to intervene, citing the needs of underserved areas or populations. Examples include nurse practitioners, physician assistants, and surgicenters.

Encourage Managed Care and Disease Management

The Texas Medicaid program reported that it was moving from 40% of its population under managed care toward a target of 72% in 2008. It had implemented disease managed care programs for the rest of its population targeting a number of chronic diseases. It also had implemented a preferred drug list program for Medicaid requiring a supplemental rebate or special proposal for negotiation (Texas Health and Human Services Commission, 2007).

Use Certificate-of-Need Procedures

Certificate-of-need legislation requires providers to obtain state approval of additional major capital investments in items such as imaging equipment and additional bed capacity if they are to receive reimbursement. It is an attempt to mediate arms races among provider institutions; however, it is often a highly political process that has often lacked effectiveness, and it is opposed by those who argue that it stifles competition by limiting entry into the field and can be used to stop expansion to meet demand by successful competitors (Havighurst, 2005).

Enforce Antitrust Laws and Regulations

States have their own antitrust laws and regulations that can be applied to mergers of organizations such as hospitals. States can also outlaw anticompetitive practices, which include the following:

- Attempts of licensing boards and professional societies to limit new entrants
- Colluding to set prices for services.

State antitrust laws can also be used to overcome too much concentration in specific markets, although many major health care markets are clearly multistate, especially those involving complex or specialized referrals.

Cost of Care—Free-Market System
Strengthen Antitrust Laws and Regulations

States do also legislate against specific anticompetitive practices. For example, Pennsylvania law duplicates and supplements a number of the anti-kickback and Stark amendments provisions. One section prohibits hospitals from renting clinic or office space to physicians below market, and others require disclosure to patients that their doctor has an economic interest in the facility to which they are being referred and that they are informed of their rights to choose an alternative facility.

Many HMOs require their providers to be board certified. This is a marketing decision that adds another constraint to their local supply of providers. Professional organizations must also approve residency programs in their specialties, thereby exerting some control nationally over the quantity and quality of services available. Large HMO organizations may become dominant in a region and limit the options for other would-be providers.

To offset some of these possible anticompetitive effects, states have countered with antitrust actions and with *any willing provider* legislation. Such legislation often addresses two issues, namely (1) restrictions on the panel of providers that a patient can access within a profession and (2) restrictions across professions as to who can be compensated for a service. Under such a law, for example, if one has acute low-back pain, the insurer cannot limit the individuals to seeing a small number of pain experts and clinics, and it cannot limit payment to primary care physicians and orthopedic specialists. It may also be required to include coverage for chiropractors and acupuncturists. Such laws are considered by some to be a hindrance to institutional cost control efforts.

Remove Insurance Barriers to Medical Tourism

The primary barrier to medical tourism, individuals leaving the country to seek nonemergency health care at much lower costs plus tourism inducements, is the fact that it has not been covered by one's health insurance contract. Mattoo and Rathindran (2006) suggested that failure to do so is due to the oligopoly nature of the private health insurance industry. These companies operate under the regulatory umbrella of state insurance commissioners. They argue that patients can and do move, making health care an item of international trade, and that quality need not be a problem with certifications available through the Joint Commission International and the U.S. Medical Licensing Examination. They point out that 25% of U.S. physicians, including 20% of medical school faculty, and 14% of U.S. nurses were trained abroad and that modern, well-equipped facilities are available.

They and Altman et al. (2006) provided data showing savings of 40% to 65% and more, even after travel and lodging costs, for procedures such as hip and knee replacements, cardiac and gall bladder surgery, hysterectomy, and rhinoplasty. Foreign providers are increasing represented by sales organizations in the United States that are negotiating contracts directly with self-insured employers to add foreign doctors and hospitals to their provider network. The West Virginia legislature has been considering the possibility of making this an option for its state employees and their dependents.

Other Interventions

Research and Development

Health care research and development have usually been an activity of the federal government; however, when the policies of the George W. Bush administration restricted embryonic stem cell research, California acted to set up its own funding and other states have indicated a willingness to follow suit.

Capital Investment

Although most states do not fund health care facility construction and renovation directly, many have authority to issue special purpose bonds on behalf of the state's nonprofit health care institutions. The objective of these agencies is to reduce the funding costs for each borrower by going to the market in larger amounts with a broader risk pool. In most cases, institutions receive lower rates when the states back the securities.

Education of Professionals

State-owned technical schools, colleges, and universities are major suppliers of health personnel. They are often sensitive to the personnel needs perceived by legislatures and local institutions. States frequently have offices and programs that recruit and support services in rural areas. Area Health Education Center programs are an example of an extensive support system for dispersed personnel. They provide both training and specialized services to areas of need.

Public Health Functions and Departments

States also administer the traditional public health system in conjunction with local government units. Sometimes these offer primary care to the indigent. Virtually all jurisdictions provide the basic public health services of maternal and child health clinics, infectious disease control, health education, sanitary inspections, and environmental health and safety inspections. Ten essential public health services are frequently cited. They are outlined in **Table 5-4**.

TABLE 5-4   Essential Public Health Services

1. Monitor health status to identify community problems.
2. Diagnose and investigate health problems and health hazards in the community.
3. Inform, educate, and empower people about health problems.
4. Mobilize community partnerships to identify and solve community problems.
5. Develop plans and policies that support individual and community health efforts.
6. Enforce laws and regulations that protect health and ensure safety.
7. Link people to needed personal health services and ensure provision of care.
8. Ensure a competent public and personal health care workforce.
9. Evaluate the effectiveness, accessibility, and quality of personal and population-based health care.
10. Research for new insights and innovative solutions to health problems.

Source: McLaughlin & Kaluzny, *Continuous Quality Improvement*, 3rd Ed., pp. 361–362. Jones and Bartlett, 2006.

CONCLUSION

The U.S. market for health care is very much influenced by governments in their roles as payers, insurers, employers, regulators, and providers of last resort. Much of the public debate is over the current trend toward more reliance on the marketplace. Whatever the ideology adopted, governments must deal with the following concerns:

- Information asymmetry coupled with product complexity
- The conflicting roles of providers as agents for both patients and others
- The tendency of market systems to maximize consumption.

Thus we see governments adopting a confusing and seemingly inconsistent array of measures designed to deal with these concerns at every level of government. For example, resources go out to enhance access to services, expanding the supply of providers and technology at the same time that other programs seek to constrain consumption. No wonder professionals caught up in this maelstrom sometimes appear discouraged and sullen. Still most professionals persevere and reap the intellectual and personal rewards of their craft. They continue to balance the interests of their patients and their organizations successfully.

All of this reflects the Chinese curse: "May you live in interesting times."

Case 5-1

SPECIALTY HOSPITALS AND COMMUNITY HOSPITALS

BACKGROUND

The Medicare Prescription Drug, Improvement, and Modernization Act of 2003 included an 18-month moratorium on payments to specialty hospitals (cardiac, orthopedic, and surgical) that were not operating or under development by November 2003 and in which physicians had an ownership or investment interest. This moratorium expired in June 2005. The CMS effectively extended the moratorium by continuing to review its criteria for approving or starting to pay new specialty hospitals.

Specialty hospitals have been around for a long time—children's hospitals, rehabilitation hospitals, psychiatric hospitals, eye and ear hospitals, and cancer hospitals. The Omnibus Budget Reconciliation Act of 1989 included a provision against payment for physician referrals to facilities in which they had an economic interest, but specifically exempted ambulatory surgery centers and "whole" hospitals. Thus far, specialty hospitals have qualified as whole hospitals.

A specialty hospital is defined as an inpatient hospital in which at least two thirds of the claims are in one or two major diagnostic categories or diagnosis-related groups (DRGs). In February 2003, 110 hospitals met these criteria. Of those, 92 were cardiac, orthopedic, surgical, or women's hospitals. They had tripled in number between 1990 and 2003 and were concentrated in states without certificate of need (CON) legislation. Seventy-four percent were for-profit hospitals and on average were 50 percent physician-owned. Seventy percent had some physician ownership. Their growth and that of the ambulatory surgery centers were in part attributed to the substitution of DRG-based reimbursement for fee-for-service payment in the late 1980s. DRGs are not finely calibrated to reflect the actual costs of different kinds of cases that would fall within the same grouping.

Has there been a difference between the older group of specialty hospitals and the new ones? The older ones tended to operate as nonprofits that supplemented the existing facilities in the community. The newer ones tend to be for-profit, physician owned and to duplicate the facilities and services already supplied by community hospitals. It can be argued that when community hospitals perform the kinds of profitable procedures that are attractive to for-profit specialty hospitals, they use the profits to cross-subsidize other community services (Altman et al., 2006). Vladeck (2006) suggested that they subsidize the following:

- Health professions education
- Losses in special departments (burn centers, trauma centers, neonatal intensive care units, and AIDS clinics)

- Standby (emergency and surge capacity) costs
- Uncompensated care
- Other community services.

These services accounted for 16% to 18% of a community hospital's budget. Some states compensate hospitals for some of these services. For example, New York compensates 8.95% for health professions education.

Specialty hospitals can be very attractive to physicians. They are drawn to these focused factories by the following:

- Their control over scheduling, staffing, admission, discharge, and so forth
- Added profits from ancillary services and technical component revenues
- Profits from case mix within DRGs
- Selection of the patients and their payer mix
- Reduced "on-call" responsibilities
- Avoiding participation in hospital governance and other mandated activities.

They do have to pay for additional capital facilities and equipment that would normally be supplied by the community hospital; however, the variety and scale of these investments are considerably reduced by the narrow range of services provided.

Community hospital advocates point to the fact that physicians may select only those patients with adequate insurance, can "cherry pick" the healthier patients, avoid emergency department duties, and avoid surveillance under some quality improvement and utilization review programs.

Community hospitals have responded by (Greenwald et al., 2006):

- Prohibiting physicians with a competing ownership interest from participating in governance
- Buying up the potentially referring primary care practices

- Signing exclusive service contracts with insurers
- Providing other resources, such as office space, to their competitors
- Offering inpatient specialist "management" subcontracts to offset ownership
- Advertising their own "centers of excellence"
- Making economic credentialing decisions that penalize competing physicians.

The legal status of these measures under federal and state anticompetitive statutes is likely to be in litigation for quite some time.

Results of Studies

The Medicare Prescription Drug, Improvement, and Modernization Act of 2003 required the Medicare Payment Advisory Commission (MedPAC) and the U.S. Department of Health and Human Services to study a number of related issues during the moratorium period. The MedPAC's report (Guterman, 2006; Stensland & Winter, 2006) concluded that physicians were responding to incentives built into the DRG payment rates. These incentives resulted from the wide variation in the relative costliness of cases. Cardiac hospitals seemed to treat more of the profitable cases than community hospitals. Orthopedic hospitals seemed to treat more complex cases, but in healthier patients than community hospitals. No conclusions were reached about the surgical hospitals. Patient satisfaction also seemed higher in the specialty settings.

The study also concluded that the specialty hospitals delivered less uncompensated care, but that this was offset by the payment of property and corporate income taxes and by not receiving disproportion share hospital payments. The U.S. Department of Health and Human Services study (Greenwald et al., 2006) reached similar conclusions and observed that physicians did refer to hospitals they owned, but often continued to take emergency department calls to maintain their referral base. The studies did not identify much differential impact on either quality or utilization. Their recommendation was to modify the DRG prices to reflect costs more closely and to remove the incentives they provided.

CMS Decisions

CMS ended the moratorium in August 2006 and proposed to follow the MedPAC's recommendations to revise the DRG payments so that they would be closer to hospital costs than hospital charges. It also proposed a rule that specialty hospitals would have to accept patient transfers under the Emergency Medical Treatment and Labor Act. At oversight hearings before the Senate Finance Committee, this decision was questioned sharply by ranking Senators Chuck Grassley (R-Iowa) and Max Baucus (D-Montana), who noted the negative impact on community hospitals and the apparent conflict with the intent of existing self-referral prohibitions.

The Various Points of View

The prologue to a series of articles on these issues in the January-February 2006 issue of *Health Affairs* (25:94) noted that:

> *In the larger context, though, the issues are not so simple. A decade ago, "market-driven reform" meant competition between integrated delivery organizations whose incentives for quality and efficiency derived from the capitated payments they received. Specialty competition and price transparency are fee-for-service strategies that exacerbate the distress of multi-specialty groups that thrived under capitation and were the darlings of the policy community a decade ago.*

The proponents of three economic system views have sought support in press releases, testimony, lobbying, and the published literature. All three sides used parts of the U.S. Department of Health and Human Services and MedPAC studies to support their positions.

Oligopolistic Competition

On May 30, 2006, the American Hospital Association supported the senators for continuing "to stand up for the needs of patients and the community hospitals that take care of them." Berenson et al. (2006) suggested that the specialty hospital movement and parallel physician efforts to control service lines within community hospitals may signal the restoration of the types of hospital–physician relationships that preceded managed care.

Administered System

Choudhry et al. (2005) wrote about the role of law in this situation and recommended that the issue be controlled by CON determinations to avoid duplication of resources and increased utilization. Altman et al. (2006) seemed to support the administered approach by asking, "Could U.S. Hospitals Go the Way of U.S. Airlines?" They argue that specialized competition, coupled with price transparency and consumer price sensitivity, would result in community hospital downsizing, reduced community services, reduced staffing levels, and reduced salaries.

Free-Market Competition

The American Association of Orthopedic Surgeons' December 2005 "Position Statement on Specialty Hospitals" urged the repeal of all CON laws to foster "healthy competition." Their statement also attributed that position to the Federal Trade Commission and the Department of Justice. Havighurst's (2005) commentary on Choudhry et al. (2005) took a strong position that CON inappropriately supported the oligopoly position of the community hospitals. In January 2006, the American Medical Association president-elect issued a statement continuing its strong support of specialty hospitals (Champlin, 2006). Porter and Teisberg (2006) also argued against the CON approach because it supported local monopolies, but acknowledged the risks associated with physician ownership and self-referral.

DISCUSSION QUESTIONS

1. What has happened with this debate since mid 2006?

2. How might one try to come to an objective conclusion?

3. Senator Grassley noted during the Senate Finance Committee hearings that "it appears that 40 new specialty hospitals have opened" during the moratorium and the investigation. Do some research to find out whether this is true and how it might have happened.

4. If you were a legislative decision maker, what solutions would you propose after the MedPAC proposals to reduce selected DRG payments substantially and redefine a number of groupings for orthopedic and cardiac procedures that were headed off by a campaign by lobbyists for medical device makers, hospitals, and specialist physicians?

CHAPTER 6

Alternative Responses and Initiatives of Institutions and Professions

Tardiness or refusal to pay what doctors consider legitimate medical claims may add as much as 15% to 20% in overhead costs for physicians, forcing them to pursue these claims or pass along the costs to patients, according to Jack Lewin, a family doctor who is chief executive of the California Medical Association, a professional group of 35,000 physicians (Freudenheim, 2006b, p. 1).

Nongovernmental health care organizations operate in a market system, albeit an imperfect and sometimes highly regulated one. They provide most medical services and handle the financing of much of the system. For-profit and not-for-profit institutions operate side by side, often competing for the same business from employers, insurers, governments, and other professionals.

It is useful to identify the strategies that these actors adopt in response to governmental programs and initiate on their own to influence health policy. We again start with a table outlining the actors and the alternatives for responding to government actions and the marketplace (**Table 6-1**). Where alternatives have been addressed and terms defined in earlier chapters, we try not to repeat all of that information again. Then we look at some recommended policy alternatives that potentially affect all the players.

TABLE 6-1 Responses and Initiatives of Institutions and Professions

Common Approaches
- Public relations
- Marketing and education
- Lobbying

Payers
- Employers
  - Eligibility
  - Subsidy offered
  - Plans offered
  - Relationship with insurers/self-insurance
  - Worker education and training
- Insurers
  - Method of organization
  - Method of payment
  - Plans offered
  - Case management/carve-outs
  - Utilization constraints
  - Consumer education

Providers
Professionals
- Organization of practice
- Services offered
- Incentives
- Pricing
- Patient relationship
- Primary versus specialty care
- Efficiency

Institutions
- Organizational structure
- Scope and scale of services
- Pricing/discounts
- Efficiency
- Quality improvement
- Consumer information
- Credentialing decisions
- Involving payers in change processes

Professions
- Quality improvement
- Provider education
- Consumer education

Consumers
- Plan selection
- Provider selection
- Self-help

COMMON RESPONSES

All of the players listed in the Table 6-1 employ strategies to influence the marketplace and its regulators. These can be classified into three main types of interventions:

- Public relations
- Marketing and education
- Lobbying.

Each player manages its relationships with the media and with politicians and regulators directly, and each acts indirectly through trade associations and professional groups. You will see illustrations of this throughout the cases included in this book and in subsequent chapters dealing with political feasibility and values. The focus among these three interventions changes depending on the nature of the specific market. Lobbying is particularly intense in administered markets such as Medicare and Medicaid, especially when policy changes, such as new legislation affecting one's interests, are under consideration. Public relations and education (sometimes referred to as social marketing) are used more assertively when regulators are considering changes, and marketing, especially advertising, is most intense where the market is less regulated. The term *education* can apply to the many different types of efforts to influence behavior. Government antismoking campaigns can be characterized as education, for example, but the term can also be used as one of the rationales behind highly commercial interventions like direct-to-consumer advertising of prescription drugs.

PAYERS

Customarily, the term *payers* refers to the financial entities, usually insurers, who pay the bills; however, they are only intermediaries for the true payers, those who sign the contracts for care, who are usually employers and the government. In an increasing number of cases, insurers cover individuals who purchase their policies directly.

Employers

Employment-based health care benefits have changed markedly since the 1950s. At first, employers were very passive about whether their unions took collective bargaining settlements as wages or as benefits and how those benefits were distributed. All that they cared about was the immediate cost per hour of the total contract agreement. Health care costs were low, and the workforce was young; however, these defined benefit packages took on a life of their own as costs in both pensions and health care began to rise much faster than prices or productivity. Now employers have to deal with both these rising costs and the reactions of employees, retirees, and the public when they reduce benefits. A number of U.S. steel and airline companies, for example, have gone through Chapter 11 bankruptcy proceedings to free themselves of these "legacy" liabilities for their employees, even the unionized ones.

Employers compete for the best workers, especially the highly skilled ones, in every labor market. They want their health benefits for workers and their families to be in line with competing employers. If benefits are too low, better employees will go elsewhere. If they are too high, the employer will attract those with high health care costs or health risks in their families (adverse selection) and become saddled with higher costs than their competition.

Eligibility

Employers can decide who gets health care benefits and when they start. New employees usually have a waiting period before they are eligible for health care benefits. Full coverage is typically limited to full-time, directly employed individuals and their families. This is one reason why contract employment and outsourcing have become so attractive. Contracting relieves the employer of the direct expense of health care and pension benefits, although some of those costs are probably reflected in higher wages paid to skilled contract employees and in the bids from prospective domestic suppliers.

Subsidy Offered

The proportion of employees' health insurance that the employer pays is fixed by contract in unionized settings and by company policy elsewhere. The employer negotiates for an array of plans, marketing them to employees, collecting premiums, and funding much of the cost of the basic plan. More recently, employers have moved toward promising a defined contribution (a fixed dollar amount). Coverage for dependents is usually much cheaper under the employer's plan than anything available independently. This is due to the purchasing power of the group and the reduced costs to the insurer of marketing and administering the plan. Employers may also offer additional health insurance products not normally included in health insurance, such as dental insurance, long-term care insurance, and eye care insurance. Here they most likely do not subsidize the care, but pass along the advantages of group purchasing.

Many employers offer new employees plans that do not exclude preexisting conditions, offering coverage not usually available on the open market. Some employers, however, do require a pre-employment physical. Under the Americans with Disabilities Act, the use of this information must be limited to the ability to meet specific job requirements, but it may still have a chilling effect on the job-seeking behaviors of those who have severe health problems.

Plans Offered

Most employers offer multiple plans so that they do not bear the onus of forcing their employees to participate in a specific plan. Because of the antipathy among Americans to plans that do not allow a choice of providers, most offer a point-of-service plan as well as the basic plan and plans with alternative tiers of deductibles and co-payments.

Some employers also offer *cafeteria plans* which allow employees to select customized sets of benefits that best meet their individual needs, including or excluding health care benefits. Cafeteria plans are also called flexible benefit plans or Section 125 plans after the applicable section of the Internal Revenue Code.

Relationship With Insurers/Self-Insurance

Employers have the option of bargaining with insurers or of self-insuring. A self-insured plan may be administered by the employer or by an insurance company or *third-party administrator,* but regardless of who administers it, the employer takes the risks and rewards of the resulting underwriting loss ratios. This alternative is available only to large organizations, but it offers a number of advantages, as well as the disadvantage of reducing the size of the risk pool that is covered under a single plan. Park (2000) reported that in 1994 about half of all covered U.S. employees worked for self-insured employers. This proportion reached 85% in firms with more than 1,000 employees and 75% in multistate companies.

Worker Education, Disease Management and Worksite Wellness

Increasingly, employers are providing wellness and disease management programs directly or through their insurers. Most commonly, they provide wellness promotion through Web-based portals. Some employers provide personal interventions. Rapidly growing Quantum Health Care's personnel will call an employee who makes a doctor's appointment and suggest questions to ask the physician, "help them choose the right specialist, give them advice about which tests to take, and ensure that tests are not duplicated" (Gogoi, 2006, p. 80). Quantum Health is compensated through savings and can provide employees with incentives to use preventive services. Employers can also provide incentives for healthy behaviors, such as not smoking or joining and using a health and fitness club. Some are changing the workplace environment to promote health—for example, placing parking lots away from the building, publishing walking maps and holding walking meetings, installing exercise equipment on site, and replacing high-calorie, high-fat food and drink in lunchroom vending machines with more healthy fare. The Centers for Disease Control and Prevention decorated its stairwells with art and piped in music to make them more enticing to employees who might otherwise take an elevator.

Employers have a strong interest in promoting medical savings accounts, which shift more of the costs of routine medical care to the employees while still providing catastrophic care insurance. In the future, employers are likely to add incentives for their employees to take advantage of medical tourism when the timing of treatment for major interventions can be controlled. **Case 6-1**, Global Medical Coverage, looks at the ups and downs of this phenomenon in one corporate situation.

Insurers

Insurers are intermediaries between payers and patients. Many insurers provide a wide array of insurance products and work to sell employers on the economics of one-stop shopping for all of their insurance needs. Others offer only or primarily health insurance products. Some are for-profit and some are not-for-profit. They all compete in the same market with similar products offered under the same state regulatory requirements. Insurers compete with each other based on price (driven by costs), their ability to keep enrollees happy, and their ability to come up with creative solutions to perceived problems.

Historically, insurance has been described as "driving through the rear-view mirror." Premiums were based on experience rating, namely the past claims experience of one's employees or similar employee groups. If claims were high in one year, losses could be recouped by raising premiums the next. Even when changing insurers, one cannot necessarily run away from a costly claims history. Underwriting departments examine past data and the composition of the work force and decide whether to take on a group and, if so, at what premium level. Their analyses are backed by statistical analysts, called actuaries, who estimate trends in costs and claims and forecast outcomes.

Method of Organization

The insurer can provide insurance only, or it can also provide health care services as well. Organizations that combine both insurance and care management functions tend to be called health maintenance organizations (HMOs). If the company is only an insurer, it negotiates the terms of contracts (policies) with providers and with the enrollee. It collects a premium up front and invests it in reserves until claims are filed. Corporate profits are a function of claims history, operating efficiency, and investment earnings. If the investment income is sufficient, premiums can be less than the combined costs of operating and paying claims. If a company provides coverage at sites where it does not maintain much of a presence, that company may use a third-party administrator to process claims and provide other services locally.

Reinsurance

Insurance is a business of taking risks. If the insurer decides that the risk is too great to take alone, it may purchase reinsurance against unacceptable losses (also called stop loss insurance) from one or more other insurers.

Method of Payment

The payer wants to motivate providers to look after its interests. In economics this is called an agency issue. For health care providers, agency is a major issue because the physician is already an agent for the patient, and thus, if the provider is also expected to be an agent for the payer or the insurers, this sets up a potential conflict of interest. To exert some influence over clinical decision making, insurers have experimented with a number of alternative ways of paying for care. **Table 6-2** lists various contract options used by insurers and also identifies the dominant organizational form associated with each payment method and the degree of control that each method exerts on providers.

Health insurance companies historically paid for care on a fee-for-service basis, with the provider establishing a fee schedule and billing accordingly. Then large payers, especially the Blues, began to take discounts, and Medicare and Medicaid took even greater discounts to the tune of 40% to 60%. Some payers contract with their key network providers, usually primary care gatekeepers, to assume some of the risk and allow a withhold from their payments until a certain settlement date, at which time each provider receives some or all of the withheld funds depending on their cost performance. Today, a number of payers are experimenting with pay-for-performance plans that offer additional compensation for meeting certain quality criteria, especially in the areas of prevention and following evidence-based practices. Capitation involves giving the provider so much per enrollee per time period and leaving the provider to take the profit or loss on the actual transactions for the period. For example, a primary care provider might be given a certain amount per member per month to cover primary care and diagnostics. Sometimes the costs of subspecialty referrals are included, which puts the primary care provider at even greater risk. Provider organizations may choose a staff-model HMO structure as well. Where state medical practice acts allow, physicians may be employed directly. Otherwise, they form a separate partnership entity that contracts (sometimes exclusively) with the HMO to deliver services. In such cases, the arrangement may offer additional compensation to the physician group if it meets certain targets.

HMOs

As Chapter 3 noted, HMOs started out as providers that integrated prepayment and service delivery into a managed care system, usually with a closed panel of providers. Over time, that distinction has blurred. Today HMO is virtually synonymous with a managed-care organization. It is an organization that does more than pay claims. It takes responsibility for the quality and content of care over a period of time.

TABLE 6-2 Compensation Arrangements for Physician Health Care Services

Type of Fee Arrangement	Associated MD Organization	Cost Risks Allocated to	Payer Control	Comments
FFS	Independent partnership	Insurer	Weak	Rapidly disappearing
Discounted FFS	PPO	Insurer	Relatively little, some through review process	Includes Medicaid and Medicare under assignment
Discounted FFS with withhold	PPO or IPA-type network	Mostly insurer	Relatively weak	Often associated with gatekeeper roles
Discounted FFS with performance incentives	PPO or IPA network, heavy concentration in one payer	Mixed	Some through incentive structure	Frequently related to quality and not quantify
Mixed capitation-FFS	HMO network	More to provider	Some through structure of payments	May include hospitalists and other specialists
Capitation	HMO contract	Provider	Must review quality	Few providers can tolerate risks for long, little enrollee choice
Salary and bonus	Staff model HMO	Mixed	Potentially high	Medical practice acts often limit control

FFS = fee-for-service; PPO = preferred provider organization

There are a number of ways of setting up the HMO–provider relationship:

- Staff model: Physicians are employed or in a captive group with physicians on salary, with or without profitability bonuses.
- Group model: A physician group accepts capitation from the HMO and allocates the capitation payments among its members.
- Network model: The HMO contracts with groups and individual physicians to take care of its enrollees. Providers may be paid by capitation or on a discounted fee-for-service basis.
- Individual practice association (IPA) model: A set of practices contracts as a whole for payment under either capitation or discounted fee–for–service.

Plans Offered

Insurers usually offer an array of plans to meet employer demands. Most corporate benefits managers would prefer to leave the choices up to employees rather than risk a backlash from dissatisfied employees who believe the company is forcing them to use a specific plan or specific provider. The recent trend has been toward point-of-service plans that make even more provider choices available, but at additional cost.

Case Management/Carve-Outs

Many of the problems in patient care occur because of a lack of coordination. A patient stays in the hospital extra days because the family cannot arrange care at home or no one in the area does a recognized procedure for treating a rare but costly problem. Payers have responded by employing case managers for costly cases. Where there is better expertise outside the organization, they may carve out a set of cases, such as diabetes or congestive heart failure, for a specialized contractor to manage. This is typically done where mental illness is covered (carrying the dubious name behavioral health) because the insurer's professionals may be familiar only with medical/surgical cases. In many markets, they have contracts with most established acute-care providers. Case managers often oversee services provided after hospital discharge and may act as patient advocates within the hospital. In some situations, they may recommend providers who are especially qualified to deal with rare situations; however, there are concerns about a payer representative directing someone to a provider because the dominant criterion might be cost rather than quality. In 2002, the American Case Management Association (2006), whose members are predominantly nurses and social workers, defined its field as follows:

> *Case Management in Hospital/Health Care Systems is a collaborative practice model including patients, nurses, social workers, physicians, other practitioners, caregivers, and the community. The Case Management process encompasses communication and facilitates care along a continuum through effective resource coordination. The goals of Case Management include the achievement of optimal health, access to care, and appropriate utilization of resources, balanced with the patient's right to self-determination.*

Utilization Constraints

Precertification is one device widely used to control hospital use. The provider must obtain authorization before admission for common procedures and usually is told how many inpatient days are allowed. If the admitting physician wishes to keep the patient longer, he or she must notify the insurer and get reauthorization for the additional costs if the insurance company is to pay. Certain procedures must be preauthorized because they are expensive or experimental, so the insurer's medical staff must agree beforehand that the intervention is medically necessary.

Although most providers object strongly to these measures, they are not as draconian as they appear. If the provider pushes back hard enough, the insurer usually lacks a scientific reason for rejecting the physician's definition of medical necessity and ultimately gives in. Much of the cost reduction seems to come from the sentinel effect—providers change behavior just because they know that someone is watching.

Insurers have experimented with a number of ways to reduce inappropriate utilization of health care resources. They profile providers to identify outliers in terms of costs per diagnosis, consumer satisfaction, and appropriateness of treatment, and they cancel contracts with those who appear out of line. The federal government has profiled physicians on the basis of their distribution of codes used for office visits, using the data as indicators of "fraud and abuse."

Consumer Education

Insurers have partnered with employers to provide consumer education materials, guidelines, and events. They advertise their skill at this type of information dissemination and are continuously upgrading their Internet portals for more and better customized information for each enrollee, from the worried well to the chronically ill.

PROVIDERS

Professionals

For many years, most physicians and dentists were in solo practice or a simple partnership. These have gradually been replaced by entities that mix the partnership and the corporate form under the titles of professional association (PA) or limited liability partnership or corporation (LLP or LLC). They maintain professionals' control, but offered tax advantages, greater access to capital, and/or protection from some liability claims other than malpractice. Which entities are acceptable depends on each state's corporate practice of medicine act and its medical licensing board's interpretation of that act. For example, Texas does not allow LLCs or LLPs (Texas Medical Board, 2006).

Essentially, most medical practice acts restrict the practice of medicine to an individual licensed practitioner and forbids others from exercising such privileges. The Medical Board of California states that the legislation "is intended to prevent unlicensed persons from interfering with or influencing the physician's professional judgment," and it governs the following (Medical Board of California, 2006):

- Determining what diagnostic tests are appropriate for a particular condition
- Determining the need for referrals to, or consultation with, another physician/specialist
- Responsibility for the ultimate overall care of the patient, including treatment options available to the patient
- Determining how many patients a physician must see in a given period of time or how many hours a physician must work
- Ownership is an indicator of control of a patient's medical records, including the contents thereof, and should be retained by a California-licensed physician

- Selection and hiring/firing (as it relates to clinical competency or proficiency) of physicians, allied health staff, and medical assistants
- Setting the parameters under which the physician will enter into patient care services
- Decisions regarding coding and billing procedures for patient care services
- Approving of the selection of medical equipment and medical supplies for the medical practice.

Similar boards and distinctive regulations also govern other health care providers, including nurses, pharmacists, dentists, and physical therapists.

With these restrictions, how can HMOs, hospitals, and physician practice management firms (PPMs) buy physician practices and merge them into a horizontally or vertically integrated care system? Kaiser-Permanente, a long-standing and respected integrated system with much of its operations in California, has been able to do this by separating the medical practice component from everything else. After 1955, Kaiser-Permanente split into three organizations—two nonprofits, one for the health plan (insurance and administration) and one for the owned hospitals, and a for-profit organization for the physicians. Subsequently, to meet the requirements of the medical practice acts, the physician groups have become separate entities in each state or section of a state. The Kaiser health plan contracts with the local medical group for physician services. Kaiser physicians tend to self-select on the basis of values other than income maximization, but negotiations have been contentious at times.

Emergency departments are an area where there are conflicting concepts of professional practice responsibilities. At least half the emergency rooms in the country are staffed under contracts with PPMs that specialize in staffing and operating these 24/7 activities that are not of much interest to other community physicians. The PPMs and the American Academy of Emergency Medicine have been at odds over due process for their contract physicians, proportion of professional fees going to them, job opportunities for board-certified individuals, and physician access to billing and economic data on their worksites (McNamara, 2006). Most health care professionals other than physicians can be employed directly. They sometimes require supervision by a physician and sometimes not.

These examples show the balancing act the political system goes through to maintain professional accountability for services and enforce licensure requirements, yet avoid sustaining the old professional monopolies and not interfere too much with appropriate labor substitution and the development of integrated health delivery systems.

Practice Ownership

As physician incomes dropped in the 1990s, many physicians chose to sell their practices to new organizational entities or to form associations to deal from strength with payers and the hospitals. These numerous and sometimes complex relationships led to the Alphabet Soup of the 1980s and 1990s. Alternatives have included the following:

- Selling out
  - To HMOs that were developing integrated service organizations, often without ownership of the hospital component
  - To hospitals that were attempting to develop integrated delivery systems and capture patients through their physicians
  - To academic medical centers that also were attempting to develop integrated delivery systems
  - To publicly traded PPMs, which were in vogue in the 1990s, but then ran into profitability problems due to their inability to increase physician productivity
  - To others

- Taking greater risks in return for greater rewards (ideally)
  - Accepting capitation, which involves a fixed payment for providing care to an enrolled population for a defined set of services per member per month. It has tended to be too risky for all but the largest integrated practices and IPAs.
  - Joining IPAs, which contract with the managed care organization, usually for capitation, and then allocate the work and the revenue to their members.

- Partnering with institutions
  - Physician-hospital organizations, usually formed to contract with managed-care plans
  - Medical service organizations, often owned by hospitals that provide management and support services to independent practices and may purchase certain practice assets in the process, presumably at a fair market price

- Withholds, which are usually associated with a gatekeeper role and involve the payer holding back some portion of the negotiated fee as a risk pool in case of cost overruns
- Community hospital, often by seeking more board representation in hopes of influencing the impact of cost cutting on providers
- Pricing
  - Negotiating the fees paid under managed care contracts. Practices' bargaining power varies widely. If a practice is large, provides a scarce resource, or includes a substantial number of the payer's enrollees, it can and should bargain. If the practice is small and has many competitors, it can do little more than accept the discount structure offered. In large urban areas, a practice may contract with many payers. In rural areas, options for either or both parties may be limited.
  - Refusing to accept insurance or specific plans such as Medicaid or Medicare. If a provider believes enough paying patients would be willing to pay directly, the provider may refuse to accept insurance payments. The patient can either pay directly or file directly for insurance, usually based on paperwork supplied by the physician's office. The risks of reduced payments, denials, and deductibles then rest with the patient.
  - Offering boutique or concierge medicine, in which the provider, usually a primary care provider, agrees to provide outpatient care for a fixed annual fee, taking many fewer patients and having more time to devote to the concerns of each one. Some practices meld both insurance and an annual fee for personalized service.
  - Refusing to accept assignment from Medicare, perhaps on a patient-by-patient basis. Providers who accept assignment from Medicare agree to charge patients no more than the Medicare approved amounts. This includes co-payments and unmet deductibles. Money is paid directly to the physician by the Medicare Part B intermediary. Physicians who do not accept assignment receive somewhat less (currently 5% less) from Medicare, but are allowed to bill the patient for an additional amount (called balance billing), capped at 15% above the lower schedule. The Medicare intermediary writes the check to the patient, who must then write a check for the full amount due to the nonparticipating physician.

Services Offered

Physicians can organize by specialty or join a multispecialty group. Solo practice is an option for some, but most prefer a group partnership to deal with issues of after-hours coverage, efficiency of operation, economies of scale, contract negotiation, collegiality, and intellectual stimulation. Group stability tends to vary widely depending on personalities and degree of agreement on lifestyle and work life objectives, which, of course, change over time. Academic medical centers tend to be organized along rigidly specialized lines, whereas the multispecialty group practice is more prevalent in the outside community.

Dividing lines between specialists and generalists are often fuzzy. Primary care providers may perform procedures often left to specialists. Examples include radiologic exams and sigmoidoscopy in primary care practices and automated neurologic testing in primary care offices. Some insurers offer incentives to PCPs to added outpatient services, such as sigmoidoscopy, that otherwise would require a specialist referral.

Incentives

The health policy literature devotes ample attention to the misalignment of incentives in the health care system. Providers are encouraged by fee-for-service payment systems to promote overutilization, whereas payers and HMOs might provide incentives that encourage underutilization. The issue is how to define and incentivize right-utilization based on scientific knowledge and expert assessments. Free-market capitalism is fueled by ever-increasing consumption and health care is no exception.

Pay-for-performance, also known as pay-for-quality, is a current hope of many interested in health policy. It involves providing incentive payments (usually as a percentage of the usual negotiated fees) to those provider network members who conform to certain process requirements, such as computerized prescription order entry, computerized billing, and meeting targets for preventive services. For the most part, it does not mean achieving specific clinical outcomes because of the difficulty of recording and then effectively risk-adjusting clinical outcomes. What payers do not want to do is motivate the better clinicians to avoid difficult or high-risk cases just to improve their numbers.

Plan managers who want to encourage provider participation can also enhance the rates they are paying to a desired group. Medicaid plans in a number of states, for example, have raised obstetrical fees to get more women into care earlier, even while holding down or reducing other fees.

Disincentives for utilization are numerous and varied. We all hear litanies of the numbers of calls a practice makes in a day to get prior approvals and reverse denials. Some insurers seem to use denials as a hurdle the office staff must clear in order to get paid, but paid late.

Providers also have to keep in mind that their decisions might be reviewed by the insurer's utilization review staff, by Medicare and Medicaid's data-mining fraud and abuse computers, and by the hospital's quality audit staff. Any one of these may cost future business income.

Porter and Teisberg (2006) offered an alternative view of incentives. They argued that the current competition in health care is based on an inappropriate zero-sum mentality. Providers attempt to do the following:

- Provide the broadest range of services to avoid movement to other providers or locations
- Tie patients into their system for the broadest possible range of services
- Reduce utilization through hurdles, barriers, co-payments, and deductibles.

They suggest a somewhat utopian alternative mindset in which the focus of all payer and provider decisions would be on maximizing the value of health care for the patient. We revisit some of their proposals later on.

Patient Relationships

Individual providers and provider organizations are becoming increasingly sensitive to their service reputations with patients they want to keep. This is due in part to the widespread use of consumer satisfaction surveys by payers and employers. Consistent negative evaluations can affect their access to patient revenues, but an even more important reason is the increasing competition for the patient's attention, especially as more and more commercial entities try to disintermediate traditional patient–provider relationships. For example, emergency room waiting time increased from 38 minutes in 1997 to 47 minutes in 2004 (National Center for Health

Statistics, 2006). This has prompted development of alternative systems for delivering acute care on a low-cost, rapid-access basis, especially as insurers take measures to discourage using hospital emergency rooms as dispensaries. Urgent care centers and clinics staffed by nurse practitioners and physician assistants are appearing in chain stores such as Wal-Mart and Target. They charge less and offer shorter waiting times and their longer hours help patients and family members avoid lost wages. Their efforts seem focused on the needs of uninsured families. It is interesting to speculate how this system might develop as the number of individuals without insurance increases. Another example is Wal-Mart offering a low fixed price for a month's supply of a broad array of generic prescriptions.

Primary care practices have responded by setting aside a larger portion of their day for same-day acute care visits. This has meant longer waits for those needing routine physicals and checkups. Available software has enabled practices to handle more prescription renewals and patient inquiries without telephone calls and visits and to schedule same-day visits effectively. Some insurers also compensate physicians for responding to patients via the Internet.

Primary Versus Specialty Care

In most countries, the gatekeeper role of the primary care physician is critical to the efficient functioning of the health care system. In the United States there is considerable confusion, much of it purposely created, about the role of primary care and how it is delivered. Most U.S. patients do not hesitate to self-refer to a specialist based on their personal assessment of the problem. Specialists encourage this by advertising themselves as primary care providers for specific populations. An example would be a sports medicine clinic. It would likely be part of a specialized orthopedic practice.

A male patient who uses an academic medical center and has a chronic heart problem might select as a primary care physician, someone who is in the

- Family medicine department
- General internal medicine division of the internal medicine department, or
- Cardiology division of the internal medicine department.

His children could go to either pediatrics or family medicine and their mother to either OB/GYN or the practices listed above. For eye care, the family could go to an ophthalmologist or an optometrist, unless tertiary care is required. The family also has similarly confusing choices among physicians in the community, not to mention additional choices among chiropractors, urgent care centers, and community health centers.

There was once great hope for integrated health systems built around multispecialty groups linked to one or more community hospitals; however, that has not proved as successful as hoped for and is threatened by the development of specialty hospitals and ambulatory surgery centers.

Efficiency

Providers work hard to increase the number of patients seen. Visits have been continually shortened. More and more practices have added not only nurses and nursing assistants, but also nurse practitioners, physician assistants, and certified nurse midwives. Physicians have resisted computerized systems that fail to speed up their work processes, but have added computer systems where they anticipate improved efficiency and embraced electronic claims filing. One of the drivers for same-day appointment systems is that they tend to eliminate no-shows and increase practice throughput.

Distribution of Specialties

Over time, the availability of physicians in specific fields reflects perceptions of income potential. Average physician income in constant dollar terms has fallen 7% over the most recent 8 years for which data are available. The income of primary care providers fell 10% during the same period. Increasingly, medical students have chosen to avoid primary care training (family medicine, pediatrics, and general internal medicine) and have chosen instead specialties that produce fees for performing procedures. An orthopedic surgeon could expect to earn roughly twice the income of a primary care physician after expenses (Abelson, 2006c). As the experience of other countries and studies of small area differences in practice patterns indicate, the prevalence of specialists and other resources often seems to influence the amount of care delivered, some of which is of questionable value to patients, even at the medical centers with the most prestigious reputations (Fisher et al., 2004).

Institutions

The dominant actor among health care institutions has been the general hospital, especially community hospitals and academic medical centers. The array of institutions delivering care, however, includes community health centers, specialty hospitals, large integrated systems, large multisite practices, state and local government hospitals, pharmaceutical companies, and other vendors.

Relationship to Providers

Much of the time, a key institutional objective is to capture a large population for its services. If one accepts the primary care provider as a gatekeeper, the way to increase activity is to capture referrals from local gatekeepers, especially if insurers constrain self-referral. This has been why hospitals, academic medical centers, and others have bought so many primary care practices and have worked to put satellite centers in shopping centers and continuing care retirement communities. They want the referrals, together with the ancillary revenues in their laboratories, operating rooms, and imaging centers. Their behaviors epitomize the zero-sum mentality Porter and Teisberg (2006) cited as a core problem behind the growth in health care costs.

Despite extensive regulations designed to prevent institutions from buying referrals, there is a continuous effort to bind referring providers to the institution. Hospitals build office buildings on site or in high traffic areas, offer physicians seats on hospital boards, and give them influence over the capital investments the hospital makes.

Pharmaceutical companies donate samples, provide educational lunches and speakers, and support technical society meetings. Some even make large donations to charities controlled by private-practice physicians that fund research and medical residency programs (Abelson, 2006b).

Efficiency

Institutions, including large medical practices, have to decide how to configure their staff and facilities for the efficient use of all their resources. They must conform to all sorts of regulations and restrictions and still come up with an efficient and effective delivery system. Especially sensitive areas include staffing and labor substitution. Because these institutions are loosely coupled organizations, most departments try to operate as independently as possible and tend to emphasize growth over reduced use of resources. Interest in saving resources tends to focus on scarcity situations. For example, a Leapfrog Group standard calling for the use of intensive-care hospitalists in every intensive care unit would have required a fourfold increase in the number of these specialists; however, telemedicine capabilities have enabled these specialists to cover the intensive care units of a number of hospitals at once. Initial results shows that this system still yields significant results in lives saved and costs avoided (Mullaney, 2006).

Staffing

Perhaps no debate rages as long or as loudly as whether an institution is staffed adequately. Health professionals usually see themselves as over-worked because there is always more that could be done for the patient. The demand for their services is highly variable, and thus, there are peak periods when they are under pressure to go faster. That is not without risks, but staffing only for peak demand results in considerable lost value the rest of the time. There is usually a dynamic tension, therefore, between professional leadership and institutional management over whether more staff is warranted.

There are areas where staffing shortages are critical, such as nursing and child psychiatry. There is an increasing body of evidence that adverse hospital events, such as hospital-acquired pneumonias and urinary tract infections, are associated with low levels of nurse staffing and nursing staff education (Stanton, 2004). The market response is to raise wages, and most institutions try that. It does work over time. Nursing education programs are expanding as potential students are increasingly attracted by rising wages and plentiful employment opportunities; however, institutions are also sensitive to the increased salary costs. The pressure to develop and license substitutes is great.

Labor Substitution

Current areas of contention related to labor substitution include the educational requirements for registered nurses, substitution of other nursing staff for registered nurses, the degree of independent practice allowed nurse practitioners and physician assistants, substitution of anesthesiologist assistants for nurse anesthesiologists, and granting prescribing authority to psychologists. These battles differ from state to state, but it is not unusual for the health committees of state legislatures to devote a significant amount of their time to scope of practice issues. The currently dominant professional group usually objects strongly to substitution. The training and licensure of substitutes are usually justified at first on the basis of work-force shortages. After a new group gains a foothold in some states and establishes an acceptable safety record, its members push for privileges in other states as well.

Institutions see these substitutions as having potential for leveraging expensive staff members and for allowing flexibility in work team composition. A secondary issue is sometimes control. In a hospital, for example, nurse practitioners usually report to the director of nursing, whereas physician assistants report to a different administrative unit or to the medical staff directly. Medical staffs often prefer the latter.

Scope and Scale of Services

Institutions can add or drop programs. Many hospitals are dropping services that do not appear to pay for themselves. The risk is patients and providers will go somewhere else to access a missing service and not come back.

Pricing/Discounts

California hospitals received only 38% of what they "charged" in 2004. As noted, they do not offer meaningful price lists and try to deal with payers individually. Monopsonistic federal and state programs arbitrarily set their own payment levels, but there is room to negotiate with large insurers. The individual consumer usually lacks reliable information on which to compare costs or quality, the cornerstone comparisons of any consumer-driven health care system.

Quality Improvement

Institutions are the key to quality improvement. They have the data and operate on a corporate model that can support improvement and change. Accreditation requires that they show that quality-improvement efforts are under way. The main problem remains provider involvement. Institutions that have effective programs, however, have achieved major outcome improvements. As quality is increasingly reported, these programs should begin to pay off in improvements in patient volumes and increased reimbursements under pay-for-performance initiatives.

Consumer Information

Institutions, just like insurers, woo consumers with Web portals and informational advertising. They advertise "ask–a–nurse" lines to capture self-referrals and increase patient loyalty. They work with primary care providers to stimulate referrals and set up centers of excellence to enhance visibility in the marketplace for profitable procedures.

Credentialing Decisions

Many physicians cannot serve Medicare and Medicaid patients without hospital privileges, even if they have predominantly outpatient practices. Hospitals can award or withhold these privileges through their credentialing processes. Credentialing is intended to assure quality of care and patient safety, but there are also opportunities for *economic credentialing*— rewarding physicians who bring in profitable patients and penalizing those who own competing organizations.

Involving Payers in Change Decisions

The impact of changes may benefit others rather than the institution. One strategy is to involve the payers in the change process so that they can explain to staff where the costs of the institution are out of line with competing providers and also see how the bottom line of the provider is affected by process changes. For example, Virginia Mason Medical Center in Seattle teamed up with Aetna and Starbucks to look at the cost of treating back pain cases. It found that it was not responding rapidly enough and that many cases could be referred directly to physical therapy without expensive magnetic resonance imaging. Those cases that appeared complicated were sent to specialists for workups, but those that were acute without sciatica were treated promptly at much lower cost. After a review of the finances by Aetna and Starbucks, Aetna agreed to increase the payments for physical therapy to offset some of the lost income (Fuhrmans, 2007b).

Professions

Professional societies and their representatives can have a major influence on the cost, quality, and access dimensions of health care. Starr (1982) documented the American Medical Association's long and strong opposition to universal health insurance as a primary reason we do not have it today. Because the societies test and credential their members, they also have a major potential to influence the quality of the care provided.

Quality Improvement

Two physician leaders of the quality movement, Lucian Leape and Donald Berwick (2005), point to their profession's need for autonomy and authority as a major barrier to the implementation of many quality improvement measures. They argue that a climate devoted to safety would require acknowledgment of errors and additional teamwork to reduce them. They suggest a number of interventions that include parallel and coordinated enforcement of standards by the Joint Commission, Medicare and Medicaid, the American Medical Association, and a system of incentives for implementing safe practices and disincentives for the continuation of unsafe ones. In 2003, JCAHO began to require hospitals to implement 11 safety practices and added more in 2005. The error rate reductions reported at specific institutions are quite impressive:

- 62% reduction in ventilator-associated pneumonias
- 81% and 90% reductions in medication errors
- 15% reduction in cardiac arrests
- 66% and 78% reductions in preventable adverse drug reactions (Leape and Berwick, 2005).

Their efforts have been expanded into the 100,000 Lives program discussed in Case 11-1, which appears to have saved over 122,000 lives already and will continue to expand. With medical error frequently cited as the eighth largest cause of death in the United States, continued research and system improvement efforts seem to have a momentum of their own.

Provider Education

Most professions have continuing education requirements linked to certification and licensure. Providers must maintain proficiency in their field and retake professional examinations at prescribed intervals. Given the data on regional variability in care, one must question how up-to-date and evidence-driven these courses tend to be. Some subspecialty groups are also considering requirements for participation in quality improvement programs as part of their recertification process (Solliceto et al., 2006).

Consumer Education

Professional societies also undertake consumer education programs designed to persuade potential patients to use their members. Often it is hard to differentiate between consumer education and advertising in defense of professional turf. Societies often lend their names and data to other advertising campaigns acceptable to their professional ethics. There is considerable risk in doing this because new data might show that they supported a policy or product that later turns out to be counterproductive.

CONSUMERS

The choices consumers make involve their preferences and the options available. Until recently, most viable options have been related to employment and public assistance, but options are increasing.

Plan Selection

During the managed care revolution of the 1980s and 1990s, plans were quite restrictive in their efforts to keep members within their provider networks. After consumers rebelled, insurers expanded their networks and offered point-of-service options. Users also had to decide what gambles to take in terms of deductibles and co-payments, balancing premium costs above the basic employer plan against anticipated out-of-pocket costs during each enrollment period.

Retirement Planning

Middle- and upper-income families also have to plan for their health care needs during retirement, especially given the increasingly shaky status of employment-based coverage for retirees. They must make decisions about coverage during retirement, long-term care insurance, specialized insurance, and income needs.

Provider Selection

Individuals want to continue their provider relationships if they are satisfactory. They have made their preference for not changing providers clear. Most of those forced to change providers have been members of Medicaid managed care or retiree benefit programs with restricted choices. This is why patients' quality concerns seem to center on the affective relationships with their providers, and that is the focus of most consumer quality assessment questionnaires. Technical proficiency or outcome measures may be available, but where they exist, consumers have to be alerted to their availability and shown how to interpret them. Bedside manner still is important, especially when interactions with providers have been shortened by productivity and income pressures.

Self-Help

Increasingly plan members are steered to Internet self-help sites. Many large insurers, including HMOs, provide customized Web portals for their insured, which build on diagnoses reported by network providers. These portals provide information on treatment and prevention as well as links to lower cost providers of complementary services and supplies. Experiences with these sites may encourage enrollees to search further on their own and study available quality information on potential providers.

Insured With Low Likelihood of Use

Many of the insured have little likelihood of using services during a particular time period. Some 20% of the population under 65 accounts for 80% of that group's expenses. Given the recent imposition of increased deductibles and co-payments in many plans, even those seeking acute, episodic care may not file claims except to build their deductibles just in case. Members of this group would be the candidates for medical savings accounts and high deductibles, that is, consumer-driven health care. If they remain healthy, there are no claims and their premiums go down further, but if they have major claims, they are covered for amounts for catastrophic events above the large deductible.

This is a group where the important arena is prevention. If their insurer, their employer, or the media keep them informed of risks of chronic and acute disease and they follow valid advice, they should benefit like everyone else. The question still to be answered is whether they will behave differently from the untreated population in general and whether efforts to reach them will induce changes. There are factors pushing in both directions. Physicians are known to be a strong force for change when they have a bond with the patient. Yet these individuals might not visit a primary care practice regularly nor form a bond with the provider staff. On the other hand, they will have some financial motivation to stay healthy.

FOR-PROFIT VERSUS NOT-FOR-PROFIT

We noted at the start of this chapter that for-profit and not-for-profit firms operate side by side in many sectors of health care. One policy decision is whether to encourage one form or the other in the private sector or to ignore the issue. Hansmann (1996) noted that the not-for-profit portion of the economy has grown steadily.

> *Nonprofit firms commonly arise where customers are in a peculiarly poor position to determine, with reasonable cost or effort, the quantity or quality of the services they receive from a firm. As a*

consequence, assigning ownership to anyone other than these customers would create both the incentive and the opportunity for the customers to be severely exploited. At the same time, the customers are so situated that the costs to them of exercising effective control over the firm are unacceptably large relative to the value of their transactions with the firm. The solution is to create a firm without owners—or, more accurately, to create a firm whose managers hold it in trust for its customers. In essence, the nonprofit form abandons any benefits of full ownership in favor of stricter fiduciary constraints on management (Hansmann 1996, p. 228).

Many of the same issues get cited as the sociological grounding of professional status and autonomy for health care providers. Somehow, accountability must be established to protect the interests of the patients when only highly imperfect information is available to the individual at risk.

THE VALUE-DRIVEN CARE INITIATIVE

What if we were to make the value offered to the patient the basis of competition in the health care marketplace? This is the objective suggested by Porter and Teisberg (2006). To achieve this focus they recommend the following:

- Mandating participation in health insurance by all, with subsidies for low-income participants
- Focusing on the complete disease management process at the level of specific medical conditions (such as coronary artery blockage) to optimize process coordination and efficiency and information flow
- Providing reliable and relevant information at the medical condition level on total cost and outcome
- Organizing systems of care to compete on the basis of maximum patient value, which they believe would result in narrower product lines in community hospitals, more referrals of complex and rare cases to centers of excellence, and more organization into multisite (horizontally integrated) systems
- Reporting all process steps electronically, producing reports that give bundled costs of care across providers and institutions, and providing more extensive follow-up and reporting of outcomes

- Creating extensive incentives to reduce duplication and waste and improve quality for each medical condition at all process stages.

Figure 6-1 revises Figure 3-2 to include this alternative along a continuum of market power. Despite its emphasis on competition, we have put it under an administered system because it is going to have to be buyer-driven at the onset.

Their analysis has attracted considerable interest among employers because it is easy to understand in terms of the industrial model for marketing and operational improvement, appears likely to support new forms of oligopolistic competition, and draws parallels from consumer experiences with the rationalization of other professional services where the consumer was once considered unable to make decisions (such as travel, insurance, and financial services). The impact on the professions and health care delivery institutions of such a major shift in emphasis would be profound. Just what would kick-start it and drive it over the opposition of entrenched interests is hard to contemplate. That is why we referred to it above as somewhat utopian. On the other hand, it would make great sense if we were building our health system from scratch.

CONCLUSION

The health care marketplace is very complex. Many actors and many alternatives merit consideration as the system tries to strike a balance between overutilization and underutilization and as the commercial aspects of health care become increasingly apparent. We will develop an approach to the evaluation of these alternatives in subsequent chapters, recognizing that there is unlikely that any one approach could keep everyone happy.

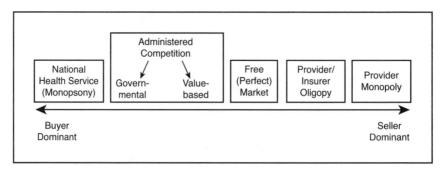

FIGURE 6-1   Modified Stages of Health Care Market Power

Case 6-1

GLOBAL MEDICAL COVERAGE

BACKGROUND

Blue Ridge Paper Products, Inc. (BRPP) in Canton, NC is a paper company making predominantly food and beverage packaging. It was the largest employer left in Western North Carolina in 2006, with 1,300 covered employees in the state and 800 elsewhere. Started as a Champion Paper plant in 1908, it was purchased by the employees and their union (a United Steelworkers local) in May 1999 with the assistance of a venture capital firm and operates with an Employee Stock Ownership Plan (ESOP). To purchase it, the employees agreed to a 15% wage cut and frozen wages and benefits for seven years. From the buyout through the end of 2005, the company lost $92 million and paid out $107 million in health care claims. It became profitable in 2006. Maintaining health benefits for members and retirees is a very high priority item with the employees and the union, although retiree medical benefits have been eliminated for salaried employees hired after March 1, 2005.

BRPP employees are "predominantly male, over 48, with decades of services and several health risk factors. They work 12-hour, rotating shifts, making it extremely difficult to manage health conditions or improve lifestyle" (Blackley, 2006). The ESOP has worked hard to reduce its self-insured health care costs. Health insurance claims for 2006 had been estimated at $36 million, but appeared likely to hold near $24 million, which is still 75% above the 2000 experience. A volunteer Benefits Task Force of union and nonunion employees worked to redesign a complex benefit system. After two years of 18% health care cost increases, the rate of growth dropped to 2% in 2003. It was 5% in 2004 and a negative 3% in 2005.

Programs initiated in 2001 included a plan offering free diabetic medications and supplies in return for compliance and a tobacco cessation plan with cash rewards. In 2004, the company opened a full-service pharmacy and medical center with a pharmacist, internist, and nurses. In 2005, it began a Population Health Management program. Covered employees and spouses who completed a health risk assessment were rewarded with $100 and assigned a "personal nurse coach." The nurse coach assists those who are ready to change to set individual health goals and choose from among one or more of 14 available health programs, which may include "cash rewards, waived or reduced co-pays on over 100 medications, free self-help medical aids/equipment, educational materials, etc."

Where BRPP could not seem to make headway was with the prices paid to local providers. Community physicians refused deeper discounts. Even banding together in a buying cooperative with other companies could not move the local tertiary hospital to match discounts offered to regionally dominant insurers. This hospital was not distressed and had above-average operating margins.

Articles on "medical tourism" in the press and on television attracted the attention of benefits management. Reports were of high quality care at 80% or less of U.S. prices with good outcomes. BRPP contacted a company offering services at hospitals in India, IndUShealth in Raleigh, NC, and began working on a plan to make its services available to BRPP employees.

IndUShealth

IndUShealth provides a complete package to its U.S. and Canadian clients, including access to Indian superspecialty hospitals that are Joint Commission International accredited and to specialists and supporting physicians with U.S. or U.K. board certification. It arranges for postoperative care in India and for travel, lodging, and meals for the patient and an accompanying family member—all for a single package price. For example, it represents the Wockhardt hospitals in India, which are Joint Commission International accredited and affiliated with Harvard Medical International. Other Indian hospitals boast affiliations with the Johns Hopkins Medical Center and the Cleveland Clinics.

Mitral Valve Replacement

One of the first cases considered was a mitral valve replacement. IndUShealth and BRPP sought package quotes from a number of domestic medical centers and could get only one estimate. That quote, from the University of Iowa academic medical center, was in the $68,000 to $98,000 range. The quote from India was for $18,000 including travel, food, and lodging for the patient and one companion. Testifying before the U.S. Senate Special Committee on Aging, Mr. Rajesh Rao, IndUShealth CEO, (2006) cited the following costs.

Procedure	Typical U.S. Cost	India Cost
Heart bypass surgery	$55,000 to $86,000	$6,000
Angioplasty	$33,000 to $49,000	$6,000
Hip replacement	$31,000 to $44,000	$5,000
Spinal fusion	$42,000 to $76,000	$8,000

EMPLOYEE PARTICIPATION

To encourage employee participation, BRPP prepared a DVD on its medical tourism initiative, which it called Global Health Coverage. It outlined the opportunities and described the Indian facilities and credentials. The next step was to be a trip by an employee "due diligence" committee to India to inspect facilities and talk with doctors. Then they would discuss how to handle the option in the next set of union negotiations.

SENATE HEARINGS

On June 27, 2006, the U.S. Senate Special Committee on Aging held hearings entitled "The Globalization of Health Care: Can Medical Tourism Reduce Health Care Costs?" Both BRPP and IndUShealth presented together with others.

When testifying to the Senate subcommittee, Bonnie Grissom Blackley, benefits director for BRPP, concluded:

Should I need a surgical procedure, provide me and my spouse with an all expense-paid trip to a Joint Commission International-approved hospital, that compares to a 5-star hotel, a surgeon educated and credentialed in the U.S., no hospital staff infections, a registered nurse around the clock, no one pushing me out of the hospital after 2 or 3 days, a several-day recovery period at a beach resort, email access, cell phone, great food, touring, etc., etc. for 25% of the savings up to $10,000 and I won't be able to get out my passport fast enough.

BLUE RIDGE PAPER PRODUCT'S TEST CASE

The test case under the new arrangement was a volunteer, Carl Garrett, a 60-year-old BRPP paper-making technician who needed a gall bladder removal and a shoulder repair. He reportedly was looking forward to the trip in September 2006, accompanied by his fiancée. A 40-year employee approaching retirement, he would be the first company-sponsored U.S. worker to receive health care in India. The two operations would have cost $100,000 in the United States but only $20,000 in India. The arrangement was that the company would pay for the entire thing, waive the 20% co-payment, give Garrett about a $10,000 incentive, and still save $50,000.

The United Steel Workers Union national office objected strongly to the whole idea, however, and threatened to file for an injunction. The local district representative commented, "We made it clear that if healthcare was going to be resolved, it would be resolved by modifying the system in the U.S., not by offshoring or exporting our own people." USW President Leo Gerard said, "No U.S. citizen should be exposed to the risk involved in travel internationally for health care services" and sent a letter to members of Congress that included the following (Parks 2006):

> *Our members, along with thousands of unrepresented workers, are now being confronted with proposals to literally export themselves to have certain "expensive" medical procedures provided in India.*
>
> *With companies now proposing to send their own American employees abroad for less expensive health care services, there can be no doubt that the U.S. health care system is in immediate need of massive reform*
>
> *The right to safe, secure, and dependable health care in one's own country should not be surrendered for any reason, certainly not to fatten the profit margins of corporate investors.*

The union also cited the lack of comparable malpractice coverage in other countries. The company agreed to find a domestic source of care for Mr. Garrett, but may continue the experiment with its salaried, nonunion employees. Carl Garrett responded unhappily, "The company dropped the ball.... people have given me so much encouragement," he said, "so much positive response, and they're devastated. A lot of people were waiting for me to report back on how it went and perhaps go themselves. This leaves them in limbo too" (Jonsson, 2006, p. 2).

DISCUSSION QUESTIONS

1. What difference did it probably make that BRPP is an ESOP owned by the union members or that the union nationally is busy recruiting health care workers as members?

2. What are the ethical implications of a reward of up to $10,000 for the employee to go to India for a major procedure?

3. If you were a hospital administrator, how would you react when a number of patients and companies began to ask to bargain about prices, including presenting quotations from companies like IndUShealth?

4. What would be the difference in the bargaining position of an academic medical center and a large tertiary community hospital system?

5. How might state and national governments respond to this expanding phenomenon?

PART II

The Policy Analysis Process

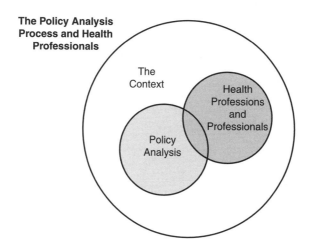

The Policy Analysis Process and Health Professionals

The Context

Health Professions and Professionals

Policy Analysis

This section describes policy analysis processes applicable to health care. It begins in Chapter 7 with the need to develop an appropriate definition of the issues to be analyzed and then presents three major areas of analysis: technology (Chapter 8), political feasibility (Chapter 9), and economic viability (Chapter 10). This is followed in Chapter 11 by a review of values issues that impact many analyses and the presentation process and in Chapter 12 by consideration of implementation issues. Although each chapter covers a discrete topic, in the real world, these are usually intertwined and are often addressed iteratively or in parallel. The interrelatedness of these topics is illustrated by the five cases included with these chapters.

CHAPTER 7

The Policy Analysis Process — Identification and Definition

In a December 1, 2005 talk at Duke University, Dr. Julie Gerberding, director of the Centers for Disease Control and Prevention (CDC), suggested three important concepts to consider when looking at the occurrence of recent public health crises (epidemics, terrorist attacks, and natural disasters) and preparing for future threats:

- Imagination
- Connectivity
- Scale.

She argued that we have to do a better job of imagining problems if we are to prepare for them. The connectivity issues are widely known—the ease and speed with which information, people, and diseases move around the world bringing clusters of individuals into contact. These issues are often cited in descriptions of globalization (Friedman, 2005; Naim, 2005). Scale relates to the fact that when critical events happen, they happen on a scale of considerable magnitude. Citing the response to Hurricane Katrina in New Orleans, Dr. Gerberding noted that the lack of preparedness was not due to a failure of imagination. The tragedy was widely forecast. Connectivity worked favorably, as rescuers and support resources were quickly assembled from all over the United States and Mexico. To her, much of the problem was one of scale. The governments involved were not prepared to deal with events of that scale; however, Admiral Thad W. Allen, the U.S. Coast Guard commandant who took over the federal response, reported at least one failure of imagination. There were procedures to deal with a hurricane and its storm surge, and there were procedures to deal with a flood; however, there were not procedures to deal with both occurring in the same place only a day apart.

When it comes to preparing for or responding effectively and imaginatively to any major health care event or pressing health policy issue, defining the problem is critical. Imagination involves calling on more than what is already known and experienced. There are a number of adages about how well generals are prepared to fight the last war. Learning from experience is a good thing, but only when it is relevant experience.

Identifying and defining the problem may be only the first steps. When experienced individuals who deal regularly with an issue are unable to resolve it, one or more of the following conditions likely pertain:

1. There is not a shared understanding of the nature of the problem.
2. There is a shared understanding, but it is not appropriate to the situation.
3. There is a realistic and relevant understanding, but it is not in some people's interest to resolve it.
4. There is an appropriate understanding and a shared desire for a solution, but there are not sufficient resources to implement the solution:
    a. There are inadequate facilitation and leadership skills to reach the necessary compromises.
    b. There are inadequate levels of skilled personnel to implement the preferred solution.
    c. There are insufficient financial resources to implement the preferred solution.
    d. The implementers cannot focus the political process on the problem or the solution sufficiently to move ahead.
    e. Some combination of the above.

In this chapter, we deal primarily with the first two conditions—making sure that there is an accurate and appropriate definition of the problem that is understood by all involved. The other conditions relate to political feasibility, economic feasibility, implementation, and leadership—factors to be addressed in subsequent chapters.

GETTING THE SCENARIO RIGHT

Assessing the Impact of a Health Policy

A World Health Organization (1999) report, known as the *Gothenberg Consensus Paper,* defines a health impact assessment as:

> *A combination of procedures, methods, and tools by which a policy, programme or project may be judged as to its potential effects on the health of a population and the distribution of those effects within the population.*

As we see later, the distributional effects may take these studies well beyond the population at immediate risk, especially in a market system like the United States. The World Health Organization report notes that there are three possible stages of such assessments:

- Prospective
- Concurrent (also called evaluation)
- Retrospective (also called evaluation).

This text refers primarily to prospective assessments of proposed policies, although much of the information may originate from evaluations of ongoing or completed program efforts.

If we are to reach agreement about the scope of potential and existing problems, possible alternatives, and desired outcomes, we have to reach some agreement on several key areas (University of Birmingham, 2003):

1. The relevant definition of health
2. Identifying the target population
3. The current or likely future status of the health of a targeted population
4. The factors that determine the health status of concern with that population
5. The methods realistically available to change that health status
6. The responsibilities of the various actors in dealing with the identified issues
7. The societal values that are to govern the selection of alternatives and the acceptability of alternative outcomes.

A health policy analysis seldom starts with a clean slate. Complex systems are full of not only of problems in search of solutions, but also solutions in search of problems. A policy proposal is often put forward by someone with a specific solution already in mind. It is important, however, to ask whether a broader range of alternative solutions should be considered. One Secretary of Defense used to complain that the Joint Chiefs sent up the requisite three alternatives, two of which did not count. It is a waste of scarce resources to evaluate fully alternatives that do not count. Screening for additional alternatives, however, can be enlightening. The box below describes an actual situation in which this occurred.

Finding an Alternative Definition

The administrators and the board of trustees of a large academic medical center were at an impasse over the design of their new facility. At issue was whether to purchase a new and relatively untried monorail system for the distribution of supplies, laboratory samples, paperwork, and so forth. The investment would be large, and the risk was relatively high. Finally, one of the senior medical staff asked a consultant to meet with them. After listening to the arguments on both sides, the consultant asked, "Why are you in a hurry to make a decision now?" They replied, "The architect for the first building needs to know how big to make the passageways and utility channels in the plans which are nearly complete." After listening to the various concerns, the consultant asked, "How much additional would it cost to design the building to take either the new or the old technology?" It turned out not much when compared with the uncertain gamble on the new technology. Both sides quickly agreed on that new alternative.

Defining Health

Table 7-1 presents the view of health and health care espoused in the Constitution of the World Health Organization. Although the U.S. is a member state, one would be hard put to find consensus here on a number of the points that it cites as basic principles.

What are the points in contention in both values and behaviors in and by the United States?

TABLE 7-1   Excerpts from the Preamble of the Constitution of the World Health Organization

...the following principles are basic...

- Health is a state of complete physical, mental, and social well-being and not merely the absence of disease or infirmity.
- The enjoyment of the highest attainable standard of health is one of the fundamental rights of every human being without distinction of race, religion, political belief, or economic or social condition.
- The health of all peoples is fundamental to the attainment of peace and security and is dependent on the fullest cooperation of individuals and member states.
- The achievement of any state in the promotion and protection of health is of value to all.
- Unequal development in different countries in the promotion of health and control of disease, especially communicable disease, is a common danger.
- Healthy development of the child is of basic importance, and the ability to live harmoniously in a changing total environment is essential to such development.
- The extension to all people of the benefits of medical, psychological, and related knowledge is essential to the fullest attainment of health.
- Informed opinion and active co-operation on the part of the public are of the utmost importance in the improvement of the health of the people.

Governments have a responsibility for the health of their peoples which can be fulfilled only by the provision of adequate health and social measures.

Source: WHO, http://policy.who.int/cg-binom_isapi.dll?.

- Is health more than the absence of illness or infirmity? Some might come down on the side of physical and mental well-being, but have a problem with social well-being, citing our norm of "pursuit of happiness." The fact that we have millions of uninsured and do not provide mental health care to much of the population would seem to indicate lack of commitment to even that principle.
- The notion that health care is a governmental responsibility would probably trigger the most intense debate, even though the U.S. government has become the funder of more than 45% of the health care in the country and more than 60% if one includes the income tax breaks for health insurance premiums and other medical expenses. There are some who would like to expand that role and some who would contract it.

Those analyzing or deciding on a policy need to understand the differences in the operational definitions of health that are represented around the table. In the best of all possible worlds, they would agree on that definition and move on, but as Chapter 9 points out, sometimes the art of politics depends in part on knowing when to try to agree on principles, or on actions, or on both, and whether to use limited political capital to try to bring them into alignment publicly.

Defining the Target Population

Just whom are we talking about? The history of the community mental health centers illustrates how difficult this can be. The system to help the severely and persistently developmentally disabled and mentally ill migrated into a general mental health treatment system in which many practitioners avoided the original target group and concentrated on the more rewarding (professionally and financially) cases (Torrey, 1997). As more and more states now focus more intently on the original target population, many of those previously served must rely more on private payment or insurance or go without.

It is important that any policy analysis strives for clarity about the target population and then moves on to looking at its health status. For example, if one was thinking about a maternal health program policy, one might want to start looking at the health of all females of childbearing age. We know that we would have to put both an upper and a lower limit on that range in order to get a count. The CDC reported in 2000 on changes in serum foliate levels in noninstitutionalized women ages 15 to 44 participating in the National Health and Nutrition Examination Surveys from 1991 to 1994 and in 1999 (CDC, 2000). It did not do a special study of pregnant women or women of child-bearing age, the recommended target group. They segmented the data in the existing surveys and analyzed that. There certainly are women bearing children above age 44, below age 15, and in institutions; however, the age range covered most of the potential recipients, and the differences were so great that the analysts did not feel the need for further refinements. For more about this program, see Case 10-1, Folic Acid Supplementation.

Identifying the Health Status of the Target Population

One frequently hears about the 47 million people in the United States without health insurance. Are they in trouble without it? Some are. Some are not. Many are young people who are making a calculated tradeoff between the cost of health insurance and the fact that they are young and healthy (a group sometimes referred to as "the young immortals"). Yes, they are more likely to have severe auto accidents than an older population, but until one happens, they are not part of the 20% of the non-aged population who account for 80% of the health care costs. They are transferring the risk of low probability events to the public at large because they would probably receive care anyway. Others may want insurance and need it, but are excluded by the underwriting policies of insurers because of pre-existing conditions; however, income seems to have an awful lot to do with it. The Kaiser Commission on Medicaid and the Uninsured (2006) reported that 81% of the uninsured were in working families with at least one full-time worker in 69% of them. One could further segment this population, isolating the children, the 23% who were without children and not low income, those who were temporarily uninsured because they were between jobs, the wealthy self-insured, and so forth. The point is that there is plenty of room to talk at each other rather than problem solve.

Identifying the Factors Determining the Health Status of Concern With That Population

Causation is the bane of the policy world. Politicians and polemicists would have us think that the right policy is certainly this or definitely that. If it were that simple, however, there would be little need for analysis. The results of studies seeking causation are seldom as clear as taking the handle off the local water pump and watching the cholera epidemic stop. Most policy problems fit among those characterized by the Danish mathematician and poet Piet Hein, who wrote, "Problems worthy of attack prove their worth by hitting back." Inference is one thing, and causation is another. **Case 7-1**, on small area variations in cardiac treatments, illustrates this point.

If we return to our uninsured population as a target, we find that they have poorer health than the average population, and data shows that they are more likely to postpone care and not fill a prescription because of cost and have an avoidable hospitalization One might counter that some of them lack coverage because they are in poor health and cannot find employment. Also, when one deals with a policy issue of uninsured populations, one probably needs to address issues of the underinsured as well and take on even thornier problems of definition and causation because so many available studies rely on claims data.

Identifying Methods Realistically Available to Change Health Status

With all the alternative solutions being offered for health policy challenges, the analyst would be advised to identify the few that are most realistic economically and politically. By politically realistic, we mean acceptable to those who are likely to fund and use the analysis and implement its findings. Many potential actors may express a preference for specific alternatives a priori. The analyst must respect these preferences and still keep the process simple enough that decision makers are not likely to ignore the work or be confused by it.

HIDDEN ASSUMPTIONS

There can also be an entire series of other assumptions, often dealing with values, impinging on an analysis. They may get addressed, or they may be left implicit or tacit to maintain organizational civility. They include professional perspectives and personal conceptions of equity, due process, decision-making methods, and rights. This is not an exhaustive list and does not include many value issues, such as the value of a human life.

If the group doing the analysis seems to be stuck and seems to be agreeing but cannot reach closure, it is wise to look for hidden assumptions that might be holding up the process. If the problem persists, it may be necessary to bring in a skilled process observer who will listen carefully to what people are saying and identify the stumbling blocks. It is unlikely that the team's leadership can push successfully on toward closure until the hidden assumptions issues have been addressed.

Professional Perspectives

Social science disciplines seem to have built-in assumptions about how societal and personal decisions are made, and these underlie known differences between each discipline's jargon, research methods, and notions of cognitive processes, equity, appropriate governance, and so forth. These assumptions also support aggregate assumptions (sometimes called visions) of institutional roles and how effective change takes place in a society.

Each discipline appears to redefine issues in its own terms and research approaches. MacRae (1976, pp. 109–110) used his background in public policy research to characterize how social science disciplines approached decision making. He noted that disciplines talk to themselves, try to emulate the physical sciences, like to believe that they engage in "value free" activities, and reward research that conforms to existing theory. He characterized four policy-related disciplines as follows:

- "Economics deals with the satisfaction of existing individual preferences."
- "Psychology—especially in its relations with education and psychotherapy—is concerned with the changes that may be produced in preferences and their structures in individual personalities."
- "Sociology is concerned with social norms, and a related emphasis is on joint action undertaken to change them."
- "Political science, insofar as it escapes from the economic perspective, deals with those roles and institutions in which responsible citizens and public officials may be expected to consider the general welfare."

In business education, most decisions are assumed to be individual rather than social outcomes. Marketers usually see preferences as malleable. Decision theorists usually assume that they are a given. The assumptions cited by MacRae, although subject to challenge, still seem to dominate today and the disciplines differ in their approaches to common issues of our society involved with ethics, markets, social change programs, political regimes, and social norms.

Implications for Problem Solving

Think about a meeting called to consider chronic local underemployment and homelessness. One participant cites educational differences, whereas another mentions disparities in educational opportunities. Then another speaks of imperfections in the local labor market. Oops! By now, the meeting is ready to derail. The term labor market is seen by some as dehumanizing. Others see it as jargon. What is a concrete, defined concept to one discipline may have a strong negative valence for another.

Such attempts at multidisciplinary work might come closer to cooperative problem solving if instead of defending concepts the group could deal early on with the following:

1. How we express our personal assumptions and vision and incorporate them into intellectual discourse that respects others' points of view. This includes acceptance of the sensitivities of those with other approaches.

2. What notions of social equity and social change processes we hold.
3. What is a reasonable social change objective?
4. If we cannot agree on those assumptions and visions, how can we best cooperate on limited objectives compatible with our disparate viewpoints?

Is it unrealistic to expect any ad hoc group of busy professionals to spend the time necessary to achieve that level of trust and understanding? Yes, but without that level of investment, the group may be wasting its time by convening in the first place. Without that trust and understanding, participants are unlikely to respond effectively. At a minimum, thinking about one's own assumptions and visions and their topic-specific and temporal inconsistencies is a prerequisite for a personal commitment and contribution to interdisciplinary work. Sowell (2002, p. 254) suggested that "an analysis of the implications and dynamics of visions can clarify issues without reducing dedication to one's own vision, even when it is understood to be a vision, not an incontrovertible fact, an iron law, or an opaque moral imperative." All too often they are unexamined after years of immersion in one's profession, and awareness of them in one's self and in others is probably half of the uphill battle toward successful interdisciplinary problem solving.

Professional Conflicts

Similar problems are of concern among the physical and medical sciences, according to the National Academy of Sciences and the Institute of Medicine (IOM, 2000a). Working with a multidisciplinary group, you have to be sensitive to these professional visions. If you are including health professionals in the group, you also have to deal with the animosities between professions that have existed for years, especially those relating either to status differentials (such as nurses' anger at their treatment by physicians) or conflicting economic interests (such as between academic- and community-based physicians). People will bring those experiences and attitudes into the meeting room.

Equity

Discussion aimed at defining a situation may stall because individuals have not reached consensus about the definition of equity to be applied. People's assumptions about equity are seldom out on the table unless the group is very homogeneous in their value structures. If they are that homogeneous, they face the problems of all seeing things the same way, sometimes called group think. In almost any health care policy analysis, the issue arises of how the costs and benefits are distributed. Then follows the issue of what is fair. Individuals in a policy group can define equity at least five ways: (1) equal payment, (2) equal inputs, (3) equal risk, (4) equal satisfaction of demand, or (5) equal process (McLaughlin, 1984).

Equal Payment

In legal terms, equity requires equal payment for equal services. This concept is written into a number of requirements of the Medicare and Medicaid programs; however, that notion of equity omits two important conditions: externalities and ability to pay. Externalities can be illustrated by the fact that you cannot go to school with a case of measles even though you are not going to catch measles again. In other words, the costs of your actions are external to your frame of reference. A neighbor may not inoculate her children because she cannot pay for the vaccine. The county health department may provide the service free because it is in the public interest to avoid the spread of the disease and the permanent injury that might result from additional cases. The health department has a number of policy choices in providing the vaccine from tax revenues. It could provide it to all comers as a free *public good.* It could subsidize the process and charge less than private sector providers to encourage participation, or it could use a sliding-fee scale based on ability to pay.

Equal Inputs

A communicable disease program might choose to allocate its resources to provide so many service resources per capita throughout the counties of a state. That way there would not be hassles over whether any one section of the state is being short changed.

Equal Risk

If illegal drug use is high in a particular section of a city, prevention programs are likely to be concentrated in that area. This will likely increase productivity, but one might object to some versions of that approach as trying to equalize risk across the whole community. If I live in a neighborhood that has a relatively low incidence of crack cocaine use, I still may want it stopped in my neighborhood. Residents of upscale neighborhoods might be arguing that they are entitled to less risk because they are paying more in taxes.

Equal Satisfaction of Demand (or Need)

Many health care organizations start out allocating resources on the basis of need, as professionally determined. After a while, need may or may not turn into consumer demand, even when the resources available are adequate. Staff will ultimately be assigned to clinics in proportion to the number of patient visits and ambulances will be assigned to various sections of town based on the frequency of emergency calls (Savas, 1978).

Equal (Due) Process

People want the same access to health care, regardless of whether or not they use it. They want to be treated with the same respect regardless of ability to pay, and they do not want unreasonable waiting times. All of these are relatively independent of the equality of inputs, risks, and so forth. They are what one would call equal process (Drucker, 1974).

Decision Making

A team also has to address the members' hidden assumptions about how the group reaches decisions. It is unlikely in policy analysis that decisions would be reached by majority vote; however, the group does need to think about the concept of consensus and how to determine when and whether it has been reached. The group also has to decide how to handle dissent. In some settings, a dissenting report or note is appropriate and in others it would not be acceptable. In others, the approach of sensitivity analysis can be used to deal with disagreement over numerical values.

Rights

Paradoxically, no hidden assumption gets more attention than whether health care is a right. A yes or no answer gets us nowhere. Is one talking about antibiotics for a serious illness, cosmetic surgery, or in vitro fertilization? Again, there is a need to try to define what one is arguing about rather than repeating assertions based on undefined assumptions. Most health care professionals can agree in the abstract on the patient's right to privacy; however, there are always gray areas. When does a college student deserve privacy, especially from parents? What if the student is no longer a minor, but the parents are still supporting them? Fifty years ago, colleges functioned *in loco parentis* (acting parent), but that principle has been abandoned by most schools. What about the patient's right to see their medical record? What if there are comments on it about the patient or the patient's family being uncooperative. To what extent is the health record a business asset of the physician, the hospital, or the health maintenance organization? Again, state laws may differ on this, but increasingly, the patient is gaining more access, a symptom of the waning dominance of the medical professions.

In some cases, issues of rights may be extremely contentious, but those situations are usually politicized well beyond the domain of the policy analysis team. Certainly, this has been the case with Levitt and Dubner (2005) and their assertion that the passage of abortion rights laws by the states and then the Rowe vs. Wade decision are closely associated with a decline in serious crime rates some 20 years later. Both liberals and conservatives have been left unhappy by that finding.

DEFINING WHAT IS A MEDICAL PROBLEM

One current medical care debate concerns the medicalization of so much of human experience. How much is this improving the quality of life, and is it worth paying for individually or collectively? Increasingly, we are expanding the conditions that can be treated, especially with biochemical treatments, yet all of these treatments have negative impacts beyond costs. They introduce side effects, some hazardous, especially when combined with other treatments. Because their manifestation varies from individual to individual, what is the dividing line between:

- Those who would benefit from treatment and those who would not?
- Those who need treatment and those who do not?
- Those whose treatment should be covered by a society and those for whom treatment is a "lifestyle" choice?

Increasingly, the debates over where these limits should be are moving into the realm of debates about permissible marketing, advertising, and commercialization, and charges of outright disease mongering. Much of this debate centers on the role of direct-to-consumer advertising and other marketing efforts, particularly by the pharmaceutical industry. **Table 7-2** outlines promotional steps that seem to lead to the development of new, highly advertised treatments or screening policies. One example is the recommendation that all pregnant women be screened for herpes, which is not supported by CDC or the American College of Obstetricians and Gynecologists, but has been advocated by continuing medical education instructors in programs supported by the suppliers of screening tests and

---

TABLE 7-2   Strategies Attributed to Disease Mongering Campaigns

- Develop a drug effective with a small segment of the population that is heavily impacted by the symptoms.
- Redefine the disease in terms of the symptoms that the drug treats.
- Inflate disease prevalence rates.
- Encourage academic specialists to promote new disease definitions in seminars and articles.
- Advertise to create anxiety about the symptoms which may be quite normal.
- Promote the drug as an aggressive, first-line treatment for the symptoms.
- Promote treatment of risk factors, especially if their status is measurable.
- Promote the drug widely to all physicians rather than specialists handling problematic cases.

---

treatment drugs. A very small portion of children born to infected mothers will experience blindness, cerebral palsy, and/or death, but there is inadequate evidence of the extent to which screening and subsequent treatment for asymptomatic women whose sexual partners do not have the disease would avoid these adverse outcomes and there are risks of significant side effects. Cost-effectiveness study results range widely as well (Armstrong, 2006), yet providers of tests and treatments are free to go ahead paying for presentations that support their positions.

CONCLUSION

Defining the problem and the process appropriately is critical to effective analysis. That is not to say that there will not be learning along the way. Policy analysis is a learning process, and there must be sufficient cognitive flexibility among the actors to allow learning. At the same time, it is a step in a political process. There are some who see its rationale as political and may object to the notion of analysis in the first place. The policy process must be open to inputs from a variety of viewpoints and attempt to deal with objections as they arise, even going so far as to open up hidden assumptions among the participants where that seems essential to achieving a product that is acceptable to the working group and, hopefully, to the users of the analysis.

Key issues that are likely to arise include the operational definition of health to be used, the definition of the problem, and the hidden professional and personal values and assumptions of those participating in the policy process. Key decisions relate to how much time, effort, and political capital to expend in attempting to bring recommendations and values into alignment.

Case 7-1
SMALL AREA VARIATIONS
BACKGROUND

The study of small area variations has provided a number of useful comparisons for looking at the efficiency and effectiveness of alternative methods of delivering care. Researchers at Dartmouth Medical School (including Jack Wennberg and Elliott Fisher) have applied this approach to the Medicare data base.

Reporting in August 2006, for example, they cited the example of cardiac revascularization in Elyria, Ohio. Medicare patients in this city of 55,953 (2000 Census), the county seat of Lorain County, received angioplasty at a rate nearly four times the national average. Thirty one of the area's 33 cardiologists belonged to the North Ohio Heart Center and performed 3,400 angioplasties in 2004. The Elyria rate in 2003 was 42 angioplasties per 1,000 Medicare enrollees versus 13.5 for all of Ohio and 11.3 nationwide (Abelson, 2006d).

All three treatment approaches to blocked coronary arteries are used there—drugs, bypass surgery, and unblocking procedures such as angioplasty with or without stents. In Elyria, however, the cardiologists rely heavily on angioplasty. There is open debate on where and when to use which procedure— "some experts say that they are concerned that Elyria is an example, albeit an extreme one, of how medical decisions in this country can be influenced by financial incentives and professional training more than by solid evidence of what works best for a particular patient" (Abelson, 2006d, p. 1). Both angioplasties and bypass surgery are considered to be highly profitable procedures, so profitable that Medicare has been trying to lower payment rates markedly, but has been forced through lobbying to accept only a very small cut. At Elyria's community hospital, Medicare pays the hospital about $11,000 for an angioplasty with a coated stent and up $25,000 for bypass operations. The cardiologist receives about $800 for the angioplasty and the surgeon up to $2,200 for bypass surgery. The bypass surgery in Elyria is done by surgeons from the Cleveland Clinic who have privileges at the community hospital.

Outcomes

The founder and president of the North Ohio Heart Center responded to the reported data by noting that the clinic had good results and outcomes with its patients and attributed the high use of angioplasty to early diagnostic interventions and aggressive treatment of the coronary artery disease and to concern about patient safety, which led them to practice staging of their patients, doing more than one admission and procedure on many patients whereas other cardiologists might do multiple arteries at the same time. Thirty-one percent of the patients underwent multiple admissions and procedures, about three times the rate in Cleveland. Insurers reported that the hospital's results were good, and United-Health had designated it a center of excellence for heart care.

DISCUSSION QUESTIONS

1. What do you think using small area studies based on large Medicare data bases to identify outliers like cardiology treatment in Elyria, Ohio?

2. Salaried cardiologists at Kaiser Permanente in northern Ohio tended to use drugs more and cardiac procedures at a rate slightly below the national average. Analyze the role that differing financial incentives might be playing here.

3. If you were Anthem Blue Cross and Blue Shield in Ohio, what studies would you conduct to attempt to explain and/or deal with these striking local differences in treatments and costs

CHAPTER 8

The Policy Analysis Process — Evaluation — Technology Assessment

Technology assessment is already an important aspect of health care planning, and the accelerating rate of technological change in health care will make it even more important to the future. This is due to the following:

- Increasing investments in medical research at the molecular level, leading toward breakthroughs in molecular biology and genetics
- Applications of information technology to medical research and epidemiology
- Globalization of health research and health delivery, reducing costs and increasing market competition
- Increased will to enhance dissemination and application of new knowledge and acknowledged evidence-based practices

Advances in technology, its adoption, and its implementation are a mixed blessing to policy planners. They present new possibilities for intervention and improvement, but with each new possibility comes new issues and uncertainties of future cost, efficacy, financing, and ethical decision making. Reliable technological forecasts are important in health care because of (McLaughlin & Sheldon, 1974).

- Long lead times for testing and approval of new technology
- Slowness of adoption of new technology due to bureaucracy, decentralized decision making, and diffusion of power
- Impact of new technology on delivery and costs of health care

TERMINOLOGY

When the Washington State Legislature established a Health Technology Clinical Committee to review the evidence basis for up to eight medical technologies a year, the authorizing legislation, House Bill 2575, defined health technology as "medical and surgical devices and procedures, medical equipment, and diagnostic tests." The definition specifically excluded pharmaceuticals, but the state already had established a separate process for evaluating pharmaceuticals and establishing a preferred drug list. For most of us, when we use the word technology these days, we are often referring to highly sophisticated machines, computers, and networks such as the Internet. In the context of health care, however, we should think about the term more broadly. In this chapter, for instance, we include pharmaceuticals and medical procedures within the definition of health and medical technologies, regardless of whether they are considered high tech.

At the same time, issues related to computerized storing, processing, and exchanging of information—in other words, information technology—play a major role in the current evolution of health and health care. Many would argue, in fact, that it is critical that they play a greater and greater role in the immediate future. In the application of information technology, the health care sector lags behind other industries, and there are several reasons why the rate of deployment should be accelerated.

Key terms related to the discussion of health information technology (HIT) include the following:

- Health information network (HIN): A way of connecting provider offices, hospitals, and other places where health care information is generated or used in order to allow the secure exchange of electronic information.
- Electronic medical records or electronic health record (EMR or EHR): A database or other software application used for electronically storing and retrieving family histories, diagnosis, treatment records, laboratory results, prescriptions, and other elements of a patient's medical record.
- Personal health record: A Web portal or other technologically assisted way patients can gain access to their own medical records. A robust person health record would include health information other than just medical treatment records, would be interactive, could be added to or even be owned and maintained by the patient, and could be shared

with the patient's care team, which may include family members and other sources of support in addition to medical providers.

- Regional health information organization (RHIO): An organization, often a nonprofit, that promotes and coordinates the use of HIT within a given region.

This chapter looks concurrently at medical technology used to provide care and information technology used to document and coordinate care.

TECHNOLOGICAL FORECASTING

Some new health care technologies were immediate successes. Others failed at first and then succeeded or succeeded and then failed. There are even cases of technologies that succeeded, failed, and then succeeded again. Our ability to forecast adoption rates and outcomes with new technology is limited at best; however, we have no choice but to try because it is an important input to rational decision making. Many of our recent health crises are described by able thinkers as failures of vision. We cannot be prepared, given the scale of many events, unless we have predictive scenarios with which to work.

Aiming at a Moving Target

One problem with technological forecasting is that we are always moving ahead with limited knowledge, despite our admittedly cumbersome systems to avoid unnecessary uncertainty, such as the Food and Drug Administration's (FDA) new drug clinical trail and licensing procedures. There are always differences among forecasters based on their visions of how societies work. Other differences may be driven by tunnel vision, self-interest, or by one's general outlook on life (e.g., optimistic or pessimistic). The forecasting process has to accept the context of the analysis, and yet avoid being biased completely by that context.

Forecasting Costs

Forecasting costs is important. The 10-year forecast made by the actuaries for Medicare and Medicaid was cited earlier. Some trends like inflation rates are relatively well behaved. Many critical cost estimates, however, require assumptions about where our technology is headed. Around 1990 when the Oregon Health Services Commission was attempting to set up a utility ranking for medical conditions and treatments, it gave a very low utility to the treatment for AIDS because at that time there was a very low chance of survival. Any replication of that citizen response today would likely provide very different ranking as we try to get our much more effective treatment resources to AIDS cases all over the world; however, the drug costs of treating those AIDS survivors have now become a significant component of any state's current and future health costs and have to be addressed in planning.

Forecasting Efficacy

One important component of most health care forecasts is how well an alternative will treat a given medical problem. Is it safe and is it effective? That is why many new drugs and devices undergo FDA safety approval before they enter the market. The effectiveness of most surgical procedures seems to be improving as less invasive methods are developed. In 1932, a member of our family required a subtotal thyroidectomy. The survival of the patient was doubtful; the patient was laid up so long he lost his job and the long-term prognosis was not encouraging. Some 50 years later another family member born in 1932 needed a subtotal thyroidectomy (for a different diagnosis). He was hospitalized a couple of days, was back in the office within a few more days with the sutures still in his neck, and his prognosis was excellent; however, contemporary experience with infectious diseases is less consistent. Antibiotics have worked wonders, but we face a continuing battle over whether we will stay even with microbes' ability to develop resistance. Serious diseases such as HIV, hepatitis, and influenza evolve, and unknown ones may cross species to create new diseases and potential pandemics just as SARS did a few years ago. These kinds of shifts in efficacy complicate the forecasting steps that provide key data for technology assessments.

LEVELS OF TECHNOLOGICAL FORECASTING

Sometimes it is important to forecast the effect of a given technology; at other times, it is adequate to forecast a specific system variable and at other times to forecast an effect. Gilfillan (1952) visualized six systematic levels of "future causality." They were as follows:

1. A specific invention
2. Alternative inventions for the same purpose

3. Technical accomplishment
4. Social and economic effects possible with a set of technical accomplishments
5. Social and economic effects predicted to flow from a set of accomplishments
6. Secondary and indirect effects of the predicted technology.

All too often we focus on the invention or the technical accomplishment and not on the latter three levels of prediction. Consequently, we face surprises and unintended consequences.

Sterman (2006) referred to these unintended consequences as policy resistance. He argues that many complex systems cannot be understood without some modeling of their behavior, including feedback loops that allow simulated system adaptation to the planned intervention. He suggests that this is true when the systems are as follows:

- Constantly changing, adapting and evolving
- Tightly coupled
- Governed by feedback
- Nonlinear
- History dependent
- Characterized by tradeoffs
- Counterintuitive.

Tight coupling implies that one actor reacts strongly in response to the actions of another actor. Weick (1976), however, suggested that it is also difficult to predict the behavior of systems when the actors are loosely coupled. History-dependent processes are ones that are very slow to change in response to the forecast interventions. Coye and Kell (2006) noted that barriers to adopting new technology are built into hospital budgeting processes. They classify them as fragmentation barriers and funding barriers. They also argue that there is a need for an umbrella organization in the United States to evaluate the evidence base behind new technology and advise hospital decision makers. One concern they express is the resistance in the fragmented system to any disruptive technology, especially technology that physician groups find threatening. On the funding side, they argue for revolving loan funds and other new financing vehicles to support the adoption of new technology.

Selecting the Right Level

Addressing technological forecasting at the right level is important. All too often we are overly focused on the first and second levels of Gilfillan's typology when others are the really critical ones. Two historical examples are Moore's Law and the Polaris missile program. In 1965, Gordon Moore, cofounder of Intel, observed that the number of transistors per square inch on integrated circuits had doubled every year since the integrated circuit was invented. He predicted that this trend would continue for the foreseeable future. Although the technology has changed, data density has doubled approximately every 18 months. This is the current definition of Moore's Law, which is forecast to hold for at least another decade. This has been a useful predictor at the third level, which is not tied to any specific invention. At the time of the Russian space launch called Sputnik, President Eisenhower called on the armed services to develop the capability for a deterrent nuclear ballistic missile. Admiral William Radford analyzed the trend in the size and weight of atomic warheads developed by Atomic Energy Commission contractors. He decided that over the period of time given for the task, the Navy could not develop a missile to lift existing warheads, but could develop one that would lift a warhead of the size that he forecast would be available by the end of that period. He proposed the Polaris program on this basis and the gamble paid off. He did not have to know which technical breakthroughs would be achieved by the contractors. He looked at the overall trends in the specific design parameters that affected his forecast and his planning. Often this result can be conceived of as an envelope of the results of a succession of innovations over time as illustrated in **Figure 8-1**.

NOT JUST *WHAT*, BUT ALSO *WHEN*

To forecast the flow rates implied at the fifth level of Gilfillan's typology, one has to understand the influence of several interacting processes that may affect the timing of the predicted outcome, including the following:

- Regulation (in many cases)
- Dissemination
- Adoption/compliance

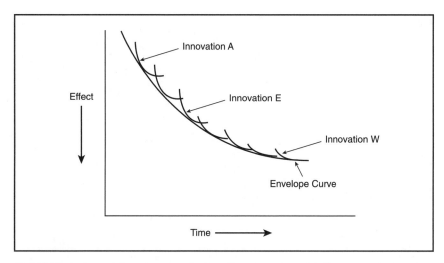

FIGURE 8-1   Using An Envelope of Innovations' Effects to Estimate a Technology Trend Over Time

It is not enough for the technology to be effective or even cost-effective. It must also be pushed and guided through these additional processes, and policy analysts must be aware of their importance and how they can be characterized.

Regulation

Health care is one of the more heavily regulated sectors of our society. Proponents of a new technology must often prove to both regulators and potential users that it is safe and cost-effective. The FDA process for dealing with potential new prescription drugs is a well-known example. It is outlined in **Table 8-1**. There are really two submission processes, one for an Investigational New Drug and after the clinical trials one for the New Drug Approval. These processes can be very slow and costly, but are in place to protect the populace against unsafe drugs.

Health care is also governed by many voluntary regulatory bodies that set standards and then administer professional licensure and certification, inspect and certify facilities, and test and certify products and equipment. These are both collaborative and competitive settings where interest groups are represented and present their points of view, and where most of the time compromise solutions are reached.

TABLE 8-1   The Drug Discovery, Development, and Approval Process

The Drug Discovery, Development and Approval Process

It takes 12–15 years on average for an experimental drug to travel from the lab to U.S. patients. Only five in 5,000 compounds that enter preclinical testing make it to human testing. One of these five tested in people is approved.

	Discovery/Preclinical Testing	Phase I	Phase II	Phase III	FDA	Phase IV	Total
Years	6.5	1.5	2	3.5	1.5		15 Total
Test Population	Laboratory and animal studies	20 to 100 healthy volunteers	100 to 500 patient volunteers	1000 to 5000 patient volunteers			
Purpose	Access, safety, biological activity and formulations	Determine safety and dosage	Evaluate effectiveness; look for side effects	Confirm effectiveness, monitor adverse reactions from long-term use	Review and approval process	Additional post-marketing testing required by FDA	
Success Rate	5,000 compounds evaluated	5 enter trials			1 approved		

File IND at FDA

File INDA at FDA

Source: Pharamaceutical Research and Manufacturers of American, www.pharma.org. Used with permission.

Dissemination and Adoption/Compliance

After a product or process is deemed effective by regulators and evaluators, it is available for use, but that does not mean that it will be used. News about the safety and effectiveness of the new technology has to reach potential adopters. Many experiments have been conducted to determine how to introduce change into clinical practice. Our experience is that, when asked about adoption rates, clinical experts vastly overestimate the speed with which the change will take place. Adoption depends on the impact of experience building up perceptions of technology's utility and ease of use, especially where the users are unfamiliar with the technology (Davis, 1989; Tornatzky & Klein, 1982). Even when the criteria for use are met, it still takes a great deal of time to work through the various groups of potential adopters, starting with the risk takers and then the early adopters and then the late adopters and so forth (Rogers, 1983).

Where patients are concerned, the adoption issue often centers on compliance, the use of a prescription or a routine as directed. Compliance often starts high but then slacks off, particularly with chronically ill patients.

The Interactive Adoption and Startup Processes—An Example

The much anticipated introduction of interoperable HIT systems is an example of the complexity of introducing new technology into the ongoing health care system. Despite the highly favorable cost-effectiveness estimates and the vast transformations that information technology has produced in other professional services, the adoption of HIT has been agonizingly slow in health care.

Development and implementation of interconnected health care networks and EMRs requires a process characterized by six basic steps (Kibbe & McLaughlin, 2004):

- Acceptance of the need for the technical capability
- Alignment of interests and actions
- Feasibility demonstrations
- System blueprints—standards, protocols, and specifications
- Configuration of operating systems including certification of components
- Capital availability and financing.

Acceptance of the need for interoperable health information capability is virtually universal now that more and more organizations are demanding computerized physician order entry (CPOE) as a safety measure and look to EMR systems to reduce waste and improve care. In addition, backers of consumer-driven health care and pay-for-quality see the availability of EMRs as a key to ongoing quality-of-care reporting and evaluation. In April 2004, the White House issued a policy paper on technology that included the objective of a computerized personal health record system for all U.S. citizenry within 10 years. One of its components was to be the development of a National Health Information Network (NHIN) under the oversight of the Office of the National Coordinator of Health Information Technology (ONCHIT), which was then under the direction of David Brailer, MD. The NHIN initiative is discussed in the case study following this chapter.

Alignment and Demonstrations of Feasibility

Providers and vendors have been busy aligning their efforts to produce systems that have considerably more interoperability and integration than ever before; however, two competing alignments arose, leading to multiple sets of standards. The vendors of large, complex, legacy systems have recommended expanding their systems as intranet-based community networks. Advocates of Internet-based systems, such as the American Academy of Family Physicians, have launched several demonstration projects involving implementation of an Internet-based application service provider system and an open standards technology infrastructure.

System Blueprints—Standards, Protocols, Specifications

In May 2003, the Massachusetts Medical Society asked ASTM International (formerly American Society for Testing Materials) to develop a standard for a clinical care record. There were many additional sponsors, including the American Academy of Family Physicians. The initial approach was to use XML (EXtensible Markup Language), a Web authoring language that readily allows for secure transactions, to digitize and expand the Patient Care Referral Form that the Massachusetts Department of Public Health designed and mandated by for use in patient transfers, primarily from the inpatient setting to nursing or long-term care facilities. At the same time, Health Level Seven, Inc., the nonprofit standards development organization associated with hospital information systems using the HL7 language, worked to develop a competing standard.

In February 2004, at the Health Information Management Systems Society meetings, the two standards organizations developed a memorandum of understanding to "harmonize" the two standards. Amid an acrimonious war of words, memoranda, press releases, and changing alliances, balloting continued, and two standards slowly moved ahead. On July 22, 2004, 14 medical organizations formed the Physicians Electronic Health Record Coalition to speak for the doctors. "While physicians are adopting information technology in large numbers, there remain substantial economic and technical barriers to the full-scale deployment of EHRs, especially in small- and medium-size medical practices" (American Academy of Family Physicians, 2004).

The New York Times reported on the HIMSS meeting in "Health Industry Under Pressure to Computerize":

> *Dr. Brailer in meetings with health care and technology executives here at their industry's big annual convention has told them to come up with a single set of technical standards for EHRs. The approach, he said, must include a method to certify that the records can be opened and read by doctors and specialists, as authorized by the patient, even when different clinics and hospitals have different computer systems. If the industry cannot agree on such standards by this summer, then government will probably do what it does best— put out a mandate.*

Capital Availability and Financing
Planned exemptions to the antikickback and Stark Amendment regulations to allow hospitals and health care systems to supply EHR systems to affiliated practices were widely recognized as a first step in solving the problems of financing the needed capital investment; however, lowering system complexity and capital and operating costs was a parallel alternative.

Competing Approaches Continue
Case 8-1 illustrates two approaches to the development of community-centered HIT networks. The federal government's program includes four independent vendor and hospital-centered approaches with RHIOs embedded in each one. The Whatcom Health Information Network represents a pragmatic, bottom-up, Web-based system similar to that espoused by the physician-centric groups. The NHIN approach would build off of

mature technological platforms. The Web-based alternatives probably meet the Christensen et al. (2000) description of a disruptive technology— simple, inexpensive, but capable of expanding across a boarder range of applications once it enters the marketplace.

They observed, "Health care may be the most entrenched, change-averse industry in the United States. The innovations that will eventually turn it around are ready, in cases—but they cannot find backers." HIT was one of their primary examples, an area where this industry has lagged behind virtually all other information-intensive service sectors. Now there is agreement that its time has come.

Christensen et al. (2000) made a number of recommendations that would support disruptive innovations in health care, including the following:

- Less investment in high-end technology and simplification of complex problems
- Creation of new organizations to do the disrupting
- Overcoming regulatory barriers
- Leadership favorable to change.

You can observe whether and how these recommendations play out in **Case 8-1**. **Figure 8-2** shows how the HIT development process might be characterized if one views it as an adoption process involving competition and collaboration between two contending technologies—a slowly developing mature technology and a potentially disruptive new technology.

FORECASTING METHODS

Methods of forecasting include the following:

- Gathering expert opinion
- Time series analysis
- Surveying and sampling
- Correlational and causal modeling
- Simulation and system modeling.

Gathering Expert Opinion

When a technology is new, few individuals have sufficient experience to estimate trends or identify causal relationships. In such cases, one is likely to assemble a panel of experts in the field who venture their best estimates of likely events and outcomes. If one is concerned about the dominance of one

Stage	Mature IT Systems	Shared	Potentially Disruptive New Technology
Awareness		CPOE as a safety measure EHR for all in ten years	
Alignment	Hospitals HL-7		Mass. Medical Soc. AAFP
	HIMSS		Web-based vendors
Feasibility Demonstration	Intranets		CCR demos
System Blueprints	Health Level Seven, Inc. standard		ASTM standard
		"Harmonization" agreement effective Dr. Brailer threatens "mandate" and calls for level playing field, low cost and information sharing	
Certification		CCHIT established	
Capital availability		New Stark amendment exemptions proposed	

FIGURE 8-2   Coalitions and Compromises in the Regulatory and Adoption Process for HIT

or two individuals in the forecasting process, there are a number of approaches, such as the nominal group or Delphi techniques, that gather and feed back information while avoiding the undue influence of any one person. One major Delphi study of the future of health care consisted of three rounds of questionnaires. The first round asked the experts to suggest significant medical events that were likely to occur in the time period 1969 to 1999. These suggestions were then edited by the researchers to define 62 specific events. They were both technological and societal. For example, one event was defined as follows: "Solution of the histocompatability problem in transplantation, or the means around it." Another was, "We now have a legal precedent for the right of the terminally ill patient to determine his (or her) own time and method of death." A second questionnaire asked respondents to estimate for these 62 events a date of occurrence (in 5-year periods), a priority classification (high, low, or none), a current level of action category (much, little, or none), and the respondent's own level of expertise on this item (some or none). The third round reported back on 33 items where there was lack of agreement and asked the experts to refine their date estimates in the light of the feedback. They were also asked to comment on why they selected a specific alternative. The third questionnaire also included scenarios that indicated interactions among them and their overall impact, and the respondents were asked to give their feelings about the acceptability of that overall possible outcome (McLaughlin & Sheldon, 1974).

Another example of the use of experts is the RAND study of the adoption of EMRs published in 2005. It estimated safety and efficiency savings of $142 to $371 billion per year. Although there were many vendors of EMR systems, they were still in their infancy in terms of interoperability and over-all potential impact, and thus, the RAND study team (Hillestad et al., 2005) pulled together estimates of the potential impact from surveys, studies in the literature, and opinions of experts. You can tell from the range of the poten-tial savings that there was a great deal of uncertainty in that analysis. Commentaries in the same issue of *Health Affairs* ranged from "RAND's vision of 'gold in them thar hills' owes more to Merlin than metallurgy" (Himmelstein & Woolhandler, 2005, p. 1123) to "We have enough esti-mates. They suggest, as persuasively as such estimates can, that well-implemented electronic medical records have the potential to improve medical records at reasonable cost" (Walker, 2005, p. 1120). Ironically, both observers were in agreement that the next step would be a demonstration project using prototype systems under realistic field conditions to test the technology, determine the acceptability to providers, and refine the estimates of benefits and costs. Walker et al. (2005), authors of a similar study, see the choice as a binary one, proceed or not proceed with the demonstration.

Time-Series Analysis

If data are available, one can plot a trend line and extrapolate it to estimate a value in the future. This can be done visually or by using regression analy-sis to fit a trend line. The model can weigh the more recent data more heav-ily using one or another form of exponential smoothing. If there are multiple variables in the estimating equation, these can be adjusted for time lags where applicable (Gardner & McLaughlin, 1980). The examples of Moore's Law and Polaris system both involved identifying and extrapolating technology trends over time. Software is readily available for applying alternative models to time series analysis and selecting the one that fits the historical data most closely.

Surveying and Sampling

One can also ask the affected individuals about their anticipated behavior in response to a forecast scenario or analyze their past and current behavior by gathering survey data. Unfortunately, such surveys are useful only if the participants already have experience with the same or similar technology. A clinical trial is one form of surveying and sampling. A set of patients receives the new technology, and the results are observed and compared to the results from those who did not experience the change. This approach is likely to provide good forecasting information, but it is very expensive to develop and administer and is applied only if the stakes are very high. In the corporate world, this is called market research, and many consultative resources are available to help with these predictions.

Correlation and Causal Modeling

Life is simplest when we know how a given action causes a reaction. To do that, we often turn to regression analysis with time series data, which tells us over time what is likely to happen to the dependent variable as independent variables change over time. One example is the assessment of survival rates for surgical procedures at an institution over time as experience mounts. For open heart surgery, survival rates increase with reduced pump time. Pump time decreases with experience, and experience usually increases more rapidly with greater volumes of procedures. In industry, this is called the learning curve or progress function. It has been shown to apply in health care, as well; however, one should be aware that most statistical models only show relationships that may or may not indicate a cause. Sometimes the relationships are temporally related so cause and effect are evident, but most of the time one can only say the degree to which two effects are correlated, leaving the issue of causation open to argument.

Simulation and System Modeling

As the picture of relationships becomes clearer, it does not necessarily become less complex. The complexity often calls for computer modeling of the system to see how the variables interact with each other. Four approaches to modeling seem to be in general use for prospective studies of technology (Homer & Hirsch, 2006; Jones et al., 2006):

- Spreadsheet models (including those derived from regression models)—these involve the simple mathematical manipulation of estimates to provide projected results into the future.
- Probabilitistic (Monte Carlo) simulations—these add uncertainty to the model by including the distributions of random variables in the process and then projecting out the results of a large set of runs of the model that include both deterministic and stochastic elements. This approach has been used to support sensitivity analysis in a wide variety of analyses.
- Feedback models (also known as systems dynamics models)—these are based on causal analysis and use an interlocking set of differential and algebraic equations to model complex systems, which may combine physical and societal elements.
- Markov models—these add one or more elements in which there are time-dependent transitions from one state (e.g., getting better, staying the same, or dying) built into the model, which may tend to reach some calculable end state distributions over time. Many Markov models can be solved analytically.
- Scenarios—taking individual predictions and putting them into a story that assumes their coexistence and their interaction, the kinds of interactions that so often lead to unintended negative consequences of otherwise desirable plans.

Integrated Approaches

A major study can combine a number of these techniques. For example, a RAND study of the health status and medical treatment of the future elderly for CMS used the following:

- Expert panels to identify key technologies, their time of availability and their impact (Shekelle et al., 2005)
- A representative sample of 100,000 Medicare beneficiaries drawn from the Medicare Current Benefit Surveys and also forecast the health of future entrants based on the National Health Information Survey
- A demographic and economic probabilistic simulation model that moves the participants ahead through time, changing their health

status and estimating their survival patterns and adding a new cohort each year. This digital simulation was used to ask "what if" questions about the cost of Medicare under varying conditions of health status, medical innovation, and changes in chronic disease patterns (Goldman et al., 2004, 2005)

This model showed that future costs would be quite sensitive to the implementation of certain new technologies and to the health status of the incoming cohorts, especially if obesity trends continue.

Appropriate Skill Sets

Technology assessment for health policy analysis relies on a combination of clinical assessment skills, data analysis skills, and technology evaluation skills to assess and implement medical technology, including the following:

1. Identifying populations affected by the technology: As the preceding chapter noted, this population must be very carefully defined so that data on it can be mined from available databases or collected appropriately. It must be the population specifically affected by the technology under consideration. After the affected population is identified, it must be segmented for measurement purposes. An example is segmentation of HIV/AIDS cases by ranges of T-cell counts to estimate the resources necessary to treat that population.

2. Identifying the impact of the technology on the treatment of those populations: This usually requires a detailed process analysis, including the identification of the process changes induced by the new technology. This may or may not require developing detailed protocols for the application of that technology. These details may be needed to estimate the impact of an innovation on the relevant costs. These costs are not only monetary but also convenience costs of use by providers and patients.

3. Projecting clinical outcomes under a representative cross section of payment and reward systems: Because we have a mixed payment system, we are likely to see mixed effects from adopting a new technology unless it clearly dominates existing technology on the dimensions of cost, convenience, and health outcomes. Currently, improved costs are a hurdle any technology must pass unless there is a significant and obvious improvement in outcomes and/or quality of life. Adoption

rules for new technologies are likely to differ considerably, depending on whether providers are compensated via capitation (cost minimization) or fee-for-services (revenue maximization).

4. Projecting degree of adoption and/or compliance with the proposed innovation: Projections should take into account the motivation for adoption in both the provider and patient communities. Health professionals can help by identifying the drivers that will lead to adoption of a specific protocol by the relevant provider community.

5. Comparing results with existing methods of delivery and competing new alternatives: If the multidimensional results are mixed, as they often are, determine the tradeoffs between cost, convenience, and outcome quality.

6. Recommending whether to adopt a proposed technology, how best to implement it and how best to arrange for its adoption and diffusion: Making a recommendation is only the start of the process of technological change. Health care organizations are notoriously slow to change. Given the risks to patients of any change, this resistance is not irrational. There has to be either a significant improvement in cost or outcome and/or a strong understanding of the scientific causation behind the change if the technology is going to be adopted quickly or on a wide scale.

Segmentation

Health care practices and institutions provide a wide variety of products. Current practice using diagnosis-related groups (DRG) categories identifies almost 500 products, and that differentiation is often too coarse for effective technological planning. This leads to two requirements for technology management: (1) methods to identify the affected population segments and (2) simplicity in approach to allow application to multiple product lines. Not only does one need to have large clinical databases to identify enough cases affected by a specific technology, but one must also deal with ever-shifting definitions of disease states as medical knowledge accumulates and the technology itself affects the nature and distribution of what is to be treated. An example was the treatment of AIDS. The usual classification schemes differentiated between patients with T-cell counts of 200 or more and those with 100 or fewer; however, Portela (1995) found the economic impact of AIDS to be greatest in the population with T-cell counts below 50 and recommended a different segmentation for treatment planning and costing. Since then, the success of the drug "cocktails" involving expensive prophylactic treatment for the much larger population with T-cell counts less than 400 has changed the approach to fighting the disease from one of avoiding overwhelming infections to one of fighting drug toxicity and drug resistance. This new approach brings much different technical requirements, morbidity patterns, and survival rates.

CHANGING BUSINESS MODELS

The management of technology in health care has a number of requirements that make it different from most industrial decision making. It does not just deal with dollars and cents but with a number of aspects of well-being and occasionally with matters of life and death. Furthermore, health care is an industry undergoing a rapid transition, one in which the basic units for analysis have been shifting from the cost of a visit or a day in the hospital toward the cost of an episode of care or cost per person per period of time, either generally or in population segments or in high-risk groups. McLaughlin and Simpson (1998) discussed new realities in terms of technology assessment as analysis has shifted from being demand driven to being concerned with cost minimization, consumer satisfaction, and adequacy of care and outcomes. One such comparison focusing on hospitals is presented in **Table 8-2**.

ORGANIZATIONS DEVOTED TO HEALTH CARE TECHNOLOGY ASSESSMENT

We have already mentioned the important, albeit fragmented, roles of federal agencies such as the Centers for Disease Control (CDC), AHRQ, FDA, and the National Institutes of Health (NIH) in technology assessment. They are not the only actors to pay attention to. There have been numerous organizations engaged in health care technology analysis and assessment in other government entities and especially the private sector.

The Role of States in Technology Assessment

From 1972 to 1995, the focus for technology assessment in the United States was the Office of Technology Assessment (OTA), an arm of the U.S. Congress that was overseen by six senators and six representatives equally representing both political parties. It was a small agency with a professional staff of about 140, and it provided reports on a number of scientific areas,

TABLE 8-2 Two Approaches to Technology Assessment

	Revenue Enhancement Emphasis	Expense Control Emphasis
Examples	Build cancer center Buy latest imaging technology	Adopt new clinical guidelines Add a new drug to the formulary
Financial risk	Usually increases billings more than costs	Hopefully decreases costs more than billings
Technical risk	Demand forecasting	Epidemiological impact
Accounting focus	Marginal revenue estimates dominate	Marginal cost estimates dominate
Organizational locus	Often involves capital budget loop	Clinical decision making and governance (e.g., QA and P&T)
External political concerns	Certificate of need HMO contracts	Quality reporting Marketing possibilities
Internal political focus	Service chiefs Clinicians	Clinical experts Quality assurance

including health care, global warming, telecommunications policy, nuclear defense, and transportation (Houghton, 1995; Leary, 1995; Morgan, 1995). It published a 1980 study of how benefit/cost analysis should be applied to health that is still widely cited (OTA, 1980):

> *Between 1997 and 1980, another OTA group set the stage for today's booming industry in the technology assessment of health care by demonstrating the inadequacy of information on which decisions about technology were made; laying out the strengths and weaknesses of methods to evaluate technology; and crystallizing the process by which economic tradeoffs could be incorporated into decisions* (Houghton, 1995, p. E1968).

The booming industry that Representative Houghton describes includes what is referred to today as pharmacoeconomics. The OTA had a reputation for being professional and balanced in its reports, even though that meant that many of its reports were not conclusive and were cited in debate by both sides addressing an issue (Morgan, 1995). For a while, there was a hope that state agencies such as the Oregon Health Resource Commission would take over much of that effort (Mendelson et al., 1995). The charge of the Oregon Health Resource Commission is outlined in **Table 8-3**.

What has happened is that we have a patchwork of federal agencies (the FDA, the AHRQ, CDC, NIH and others)—state agencies (such as Oregon's commission and Washington's Health Technology Clinical Committee), and private industry (to justify inclusion in formularies and health plan reimbursement) that tend to focus on new technology rather than on existing treatment practices. AHRQ does, however, support considerable evaluative effort on high-volume, high-cost problems such as acute low-back pain where new technology may not be involved.

Technology Assessment in the Private Sector

Developers of new technologies understand that they cannot get their products approved and sold until the professionals consider them safe and effective, and the payers deem them cost-effective. This trend accelerated as HMOs began to enter into disease management and hospitals became more aggressive in limiting drug formularies. Private sector activity has grown to the point where most pharmacy schools now have departments, professorships, or centers with the word *pharmacoeconomics* in their titles, often together with the terms *disease management* and *outcome studies*. Houghton's forecast of a boom has not come true in government, but it has in the private sector.

Technology Assessment Internationally

Because of their more centralized health systems, a number of countries have their own government units responsible for technology assessment. The United Kingdom requires rigorous cost–benefit analysis for new technologies and drugs prepared by its National Institute for Clinical Excellence (NICE). It also offers advice about the use and safety of existing technology. It has been known to recommend very expensive but effective procedures despite the budgetary limitations of the National Health Service (Bradshaw & Bradshaw, 2004). It is supported by the National Coordinating Center for Health Technology Assessment at the University of Southampton, which commissions and supervises needed studies at independent academic centers.

TABLE 8-3   Charge to the Oregon Health Resources Commission

The Health Resources Commission was created as part of the Oregon Health Plan to help it achieve its goal of assuring all Oregonians access to high quality, effective health care at an affordable cost, whether that care is purchased by the state or by the private sector. Its role is to encourage the rational and appropriate allocation and use of medical technology in Oregon by informing and influencing health care decision makers through its analysis and dissemination of information concerning the effectiveness and cost of medical technologies and their impact on the health and health care of Oregonians. Through its activities, the commission can contribute to reducing the cost and improving the effectiveness of health care, thereby increasing the ability of public and private sources to provide more Oregonians with financial access to that care.

The Health Resources Commission is directed to:
- Conduct the medical technology assessment program (MedTAP) that it has developed, which performs assessments of selected technologies, develops advisory health resources, plans that address the introduction, diffusion, distribution, and use of assessed technologies, and disseminates the assessments and associated plans to public and private health care decision makers and policy makers
- Serve as a statewide clearinghouse for medical technology information
- Monitor the use, costs, and outcomes associated with selected medical technologies in Oregon, using available data
- Identify information that is needed but lacking for informed decision making regarding medical technology and fostering mechanisms to address such deficiencies
- Provide a public forum for discussion and development of consensus regarding significant emerging issues related to medical technology
- Inform health care decision makers, including consumers, of its findings and recommendations regarding trends, developments, and issues related to medical technology.

In carrying out this program, the commission is encouraged to:
- Seek the advice of the Health Services Commission, medical directors of health plans, and practicing physicians in identifying for assessment those technologies with the highest likely impact on the health and health care of Oregonians, particularly on the cost of that care
- Achieve an appropriate balance between the cost, access, and quality of the medical technology available in Oregon, containing its costs while enhancing its quality and accessibility
- Develop cooperative public–private partnerships with health care providers, payers/health plans, purchasers, manufacturers, and suppliers, consumer and community groups, and academic research centers, as well as with other government agencies

(continues)

- Solicit the cooperation of health care providers and payers in the appropriate allocation and use of medical technology
- Strive for scientific credibility, timeliness and responsiveness, public accountability, and independence from but collaboration with health care stakeholders and constituencies.

Source: Oregon Health Resources Commission. Accessed March 4, 2006, at http://www.oregon.gov.DHS/OHPPR/HRC/about_us.shtml.

The Canadian Coordinating Office for Health Technology Assessment publishes brief reports on new drugs and technologies that include references about them and comments on their use, cost, and evidence of effectiveness. Its *Health Technology Update* also identifies recent assessments by other agencies in Canada and in other countries. There is at least one international journal and an international association of health technology assessment centers.

Technology Assessment and Staffing Requirements

Knowing where technology is going could also help us in developing the workforce that will be needed in the future. Although the United States lacks a central policy on the supply of professional personnel, there is concern about potential shortages and surpluses of trained personnel in the job market and in the educational pipeline. The most widely publicized effort to address this was the Graduate Medical Education National Advisory Committee report of 1980, which predicted a major physician surplus by 2000. It forecast a surplus of 70,000 physicians and recommended reducing the number of trainees in residency programs in a number of areas. That forecast seems to have been very wide of the mark. Still other reports suggested a shortage of physicians as the population has aged and new technologies have been added. They have been closer to accurate, but the shortage has not materialized because of in-migration of large numbers of foreign-born physicians, the return of Americans in foreign medical schools, and the growth of trained nurse practitioners and physician assistants to carry much of the primary care caseload. In 2005, the Association of American Medical Colleges (AAMC) announced that it was moving from a neutral position to one favoring expanding medical school enrollment based on the Council on Graduate Medical Education's estimates of a shortage of 90,000 physicians by 2020; however, the AAMC website noted that "there are many unknowns that make forecasting future supply and demand very difficult such as medical advances and changes in organization and financing" (AAMC, 2005, p. 2).

Yes, it is difficult, but we certainly need to try and especially we need to factor in the impact of medical advances and possible changes in organization and financing.

CONCLUSION

Calculating the benefits of a technology starts with the science, with the measurement of its effect on the health of a population. Usually that involves a comparison between an existing technology and a new approach about which much less is known. We have rules and regulations that force a trial of the new technology to determine its safety and its efficacy. Although these trials are often conducted under ideal conditions and on limited populations, they are usually enough to provide an estimate of the benefits in nonmonetary terms—their impact on quality of life and patient survival. Because the results are so important for the developers of the technology, a great deal of money and effort goes into those trials and into measuring the technology's effects at each stage of development; however, there is still a great deal that is not known about treatments that have been around a long time. Even with the results of the trials in hand, it is necessary to estimate the impact on the health care system of the new technology when used under field conditions.

Several techniques are available to forecast the progress of technology and the overall effects of technology for the purpose of health planning. Some, like expert opinion, are necessary when the general public has no experience with the technology. As experience develops, users and consumer opinion can be consulted and surveyed. Where experience is extensive, time series and causal modeling methods can be applied. It is important to recognize, however, that in the real world there is a great deal of interaction among factors and it is important to estimate systemic effects in the complex physical and social systems applicable to health care; therefore, more complex modeling techniques are often necessary to estimate the adaptation of the system to multiple factors and to assess whether resulting adaptations are acceptable or must be forestalled. That is why relatively sophisticated organizations are needed to conduct health care technology assessment and advise decision makers and the public on what measures to choose. Before the investment is made, society should be thinking about not only the direct effects, but also the indirect effects of major technology decisions.

Case 8-1

REGIONAL HEALTH INFORMATION ORGANIZATIONS (RHIOs): DISRUPTIVE TECHNOLOGY OR BUSINESS AS USUAL?

HIT provides an opportunity for insights into why and how the health industry remains so far behind others in the adoption of new information technologies, despite leadership and motivation for change. Entrepreneurial vendors abound. Influential politicians and professionals call for change, and the public wants it; however, this potentially disruptive set of innovations continues to sputter and lurch forward, often threatening to stall. This case contrasts two approaches to community-wide health information and communication networks.

- The first approach is the Whatcom Health Information Network (HINET), a grassroots, community-based, community-initiated, distributed model that links physician practices, the local hospital, and other providers of health-related services. This network dates to the early 1990s.
- The other approach is the NHIN—the federal government's recent attempt to exert market-oriented technological leadership, including the encouragement of demonstration projects of RHIOs. This national strategy seems to favor a more top-down, centralized model and has tended to emphasize extending the reach of complex, large-scale, dedicated systems used by large hospitals and integrated health care systems.

These two approaches are not mutually exclusive and, indeed, have significant overlap. Much of the value of the Whatcom Health Information Network stems from the fact that it gives providers online access to EMRs stored at the local hospital. HINET is an example of a RHIO, and the federal NHIN strategy is designed to support RHIOs. Community networks similar to HINET participate in the four teams the Office of the National Coordinator for Health Information Technology (ONCHIT) assembled to develop regional models that might serves as models for a national system.

The approaches are, nonetheless, different in several ways. One attempts to deploy emerging products from a wide set of vendors in a manner that is responsive to the capacity and cost requirements of smaller practices and the local community. The other represents an attempt to speed up the agonizingly slow and often disappointing development process for large-scale technologies first attempted with time-shared systems in the late 1960s.

DEFINITION OF TERMS

Narrowly defined, a HIN is a web of hardware (desktop computers, imagers, wires, fiber optic cables, servers, etc.) and basic communications software that allows the exchange of documents (e-mails, image files, database records, and other items) between providers, but the term can also encompass the software (databases and other programs) that allow for maintenance of EMRs, also called EHRs.

The highest form of HIN is achieved when EMR programs are compatible, can contribute to personal health records that are accessible to or controlled by consumers, allow for CPOE, and are able to exchange patient information across a network or through other media.

BACKGROUND

The Stakes Are High

The impetus for promoting EMRs that can be exchanged across HINs is fourfold—cost containment, quality, patient empowerment, and data.

- Cost containment: Interoperable EMR systems have the potential to eliminate waste and duplication of effort, streamline workflow, increase productivity, and slow health care inflation.

- Quality: The 2001 Institute of Medicine Report *Crossing the Quality Chasm* identified five activities in which the use of health IT has been demonstrated to improve the quality of patient care: (1) researching treatment alternatives or recommended guidelines; (2) sharing clinical data and images; (3) reviewing patient notes, lists of medications, and lists of problems; (4) creating reminders for preventive care; and (5) writing legible prescriptions.

- Patient empowerment: Medical practice is moving toward patient-centered care. When knowledgeable patients are actively involved in self-management and decision making, outcomes can improve along with patient satisfaction. Many cost-containment strategies also rely on patient involvement, which is enhanced by access to one's own EHR.

- Data: The fourth argument for EMRs is simply to improve the quality and quantity of data that can then be used for a variety of purposes. "Trying to create an accountable system or a well-functioning health care marketplace without accurate, accessible, meaningful, and timely date is an exercise in futility" (Halvorson, 2005, p. 1266).

Forecasting the Impact

The RAND HIT team began a study in 2003 to better understand the impacts of HIT (Hillestad et al., 2005). The researchers, after reviewing the literature on HIT and developing an economic model, made the following findings:

- If the adoption rate of HIT reached 90% between 2002 and 2016 and the resulting productivity gains were on the order of 4% per year, efficiency savings for inpatient and outpatient care could reach $77 billion per year.

- After concluding that "improved patient safety from EMR use in hospitals and ambulatory care largely focus on alerts, reminders, and other components of CPOE," the researchers estimated that EMRs could prevent 2 million adverse drug events annually, at a savings of $3.5 billion.

- Health IT could result in improved care and better outcomes by increasing the delivery of proven preventive services, improving chronic diseases management in the near term, and preventing and managing chronic diseases in the long-term. Some $40 billion in net savings could be realized there each year.

- The cost of implementing HIT is significant, but would not outstrip savings. Reaching a 90% adoption rate by 2016 would require an average annual investment for hospitals of $6.5 billion and for physicians of $1.1 billion.

- Net cumulative savings over the 15-year implementation period from 2002 through 2015 from greater efficiency and safety savings would be $513 billion—$371 billion from hospital systems and $142 million from provider systems.

The RAND team concluded, "Given our analysis, we believe there is substantial rationale for government policy to facilitate widespread diffusion of interoperable HIT....It is not known what changes should or will take place after widespread EMR system adoption—for example, increased consumer-directed care, new methods of organizing care delivery, and new approaches to financing. It is increasingly clear, however, that a lengthy uneven adoption of nonstandardized, noninteroperable EMR systems will only delay the chance to move closer to a transformed health care system" (p. 1115). Such fragmented adoption will also cost significantly more than a strategic, standards-based approach.

Most observers would agree that the state of affairs the RAND researchers warn against—an attenuated period of adoption with fragmented networks, no clear standards, and the proliferation of systems with limited or no interoperability—is where the United States finds itself. Roughly 1 in 4 or 1 in

5 hospitals have EMR systems, whereas the number for ambulatory care practices in probably closer to 1 in 10 (Taylor et al., 2005). The rate of IT investment per employee per year is around 5%—relatively low compared with other successful industries (Bower, 2005).

The situation is changing, however slowly. The Center for Health Systems Change compared data from the 2000 to 2001 and 2004 to 2005 HSC Community Tracking Study Physician Survey (Reed & Grossman, 2006). It found that significant improvements (5% or more) had been made in the number of physicians using information technology to obtain guidelines, exchange clinical data, access patient notes, generate reminders, and write prescriptions (see **Figure 8-3**).

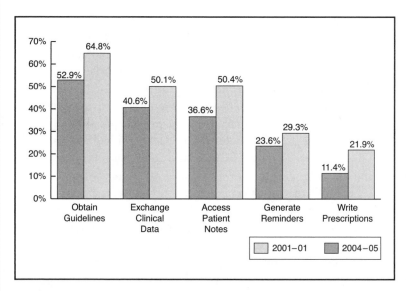

FIGURE 8-3   Percent of Physicians in Practice with IT for Specific Clinical Activities, 2000–01 and 2004–05

Changes from 2000-2001 to 2004-2005 are statistically significant to P < .0001 for all activities.

Source: Community Tracking Study 2004-2005 Physician Survey, © Center for Studying Health System Change, from Grossman and Reed (2006).

Barriers to Adoption

In an April 24, 2006, column in the online version of *Time,* pediatrician Donald Berwick, president of the Institute for Healthcare Improvement, lamented, "My pizza parlor is more thoroughly computerized than most of health care."

There are several explanations for slow adoption of HIT. One is the initial cost of purchasing EMR systems, which are expensive, complex, and disruptive. Initial costs for a system to serve a provider office are in range of $25,000 to $50,000 per full-time equivalent (FTE). Miller et al. (2005) put initial costs to solo or primary care small-group practices at $44,000 per FTE and estimated ongoing costs of about $8,500 per year.

A major barrier to health IT adoption is that costs are generally paid by hospitals and providers, but providers only see about 11% of the benefits; the bulk of the benefits accrue to payers and consumers (Bates, 2005). Miller et al. (2005), however, reported that small practices generally recouped expenses in 2.5 years and profited thereafter, largely because they increased their reimbursements through more aggressive coding (a finding that will be of concern to many). Despite some evidence health IT will pay for itself, Hackbarth and Milgate (2005) are among many observers who argue that government should make a bigger investment. This is in contrast to ONCHIT's market-based approach. Former national coordinator David Brailer said he supports pay-for-performance but not pay-for-health IT use. "I think that it [EMR adoption] becomes incredibly hard for a provider to resist because the evidence is so overwhelming that care is better whenever it is done" (Cunningham, 2005, p. 1153).

Middleton (2005) argued that health IT in the Unites States provides a classic example of market failure. He urges that it be seen as a public good, saying that "a Third Hand is needed to address the failure of the Invisible Hand." Kleinke (2005) bluntly explained why the market has not produced a viable health information system and articulated the case for more direct government intervention. He maintained that rather than searching out the business case for health IT, we should recognize that many players in the health care industry have a strong business case for not implementing IT (and many of those players, interestingly enough, are in leadership positions on the national organizations charged with rationalizing health IT and promoting a NHIN). Insurers, he pointed out, are judged by their "medical loss ratio" and are rewarded for slowing down or preventing transactions. Faster, better, more transparent claims-processing is not in their interest. Similarly, hospitals get reimbursed according to the number of services they provide, even if they are necessary because of medical errors. Reducing duplication, eliminating unnecessary procedures, and avoiding errors are not outcomes from which they benefit. It is not in the interest of any provider or facility to have a sick patient empowered to transfer to another facility or practice with his or her medical records in hand. EMRs and e-mail could reduce the number of billable office visits per patient, which would be economically detrimental to many practices. Few players would actually benefit from transparency in pricing, detailed billings, and more consumer choice. "It is noteworthy not that so few practices computerize their clinical activities," he wrote, "but that so many of them actually do" (p. 1252).

WHATCOM HEALTH INFORMATION NETWORK

In 1990, St. Joseph Hospital in Bellingham, Washington convened a 2-day retreat with 84 area physicians to develop a vision for seamless care in Whatcom County. A group convened later included technology experts. As an outgrowth of that discussion, the hospital knew when it began looking into EMRs in 1994 that what it wanted to create was not merely a hospital records system, but what it called a "community health record"—a common electronic record that would promote an integrated delivery system and ensure area providers had access to the right information in the right place at the right time (Nichols, 2006).

St. Joseph is the only hospital in Whatcom County, which has about 175,000 residents. Of those residents who had health insurance in 1994, about two thirds were covered through the local Blue Shield licensee, the Whatcom Medical Bureau. While the hospital was looking to computerize its records, the bureau was looking to share eligibility and benefits information electronically. It already processed 68% of claims electronically. The two organizations agreed to put $1.7 million each into startup costs for the Whatcom Health Information Network—a way for providers to communicate with one another, link up with the hospital records system, and submit claims. The system would be free to providers for the first few years and for at least 3 years after that the monthly fees for physician offices would not exceed $70 per month per physician.

HINET launched in 1995. Two technicians working with the hospital technical staff designed and built the system, supplying each provider office with three computer lines per physician. They supplied one computer and one printer per practice. The network itself began as a frame relay system. Users could access a bulletin board system and send and receive files using FTP (file transfer protocol) software.

HINET had to come up with a sustainable business model for when the $3.4 million in seed money ran out. It did not want to create disincentives for using the system, and that meant no transaction costs. It decided to apportion costs to each sector of the industry based on the share of the health care dollars it received. Using federal data, it decided the hospital should carry 40% of the costs, and 22% should be distributed across the doctors. Under the first year of this scheme, medical practices paid $45.88 per doctor per month—far less than the pledged $70 ceiling. Costs were similarly distributed among other users—long-term care facilities, pharmacies, and "others." In 2006, HINET spun off from the hospital. A limited liability corporation with an annual budget of about $1 million, it maintains the network and the servers and provides a help desk, Internet, e-mail, security, and spam protection. It links 2,400 personal computers in health care providers' offices, as well as the county jail, mental health service organizations, skilled nursing facilities, and even the fire department. The network itself is a private intranet built with a mix of fiber and cable. In the spring of 2006, the cost per physician was $74.95 a month. For that fee, providers can not only communicate better and access online information sources, but they can also call up hospital emergency room reports on their patients, receive laboratory results, and view x-rays and other digital medical images. A coalition of independent community organizations, funded through a Robert Wood Johnson Foundation Pursuing Perfection grant, developed a personal health information Web application called Shared Care Plan. The network also participates in the county's e-Prescribing Project, which will provide electronic prescription software.

NATIONAL HEALTH INFORMATION NETWORK

As national coordinator for HIT, David Brailer saw the need for a government policy to promote HIN development on a national scale. He argued for using a market-based approach to achieve that end. Government's role would be to facilitate the development of leadership structures. ONCHIT laid out a three-pronged strategy: (1) support and promote RHIOs, (2) encourage development of a NHIN "to exchange patient health information accurately and in a timely manner under stringent security, privacy, and other protections," and (3) drive EMR deployment by reducing the costs and risks to physicians. To implement this voluntary, nonregulatory strategy:

- ONCHIT issued a request for information on November 15, 2004, asking what an NHIN might look like. Two months later, it received nearly 5,000 pages of responses from 512 organizations. It issued a summary report in June 2005.

- It chartered the American Health Information Community, a federal advisory commission, on September 13, 2005. Health and Human Services Secretary Michael O. Leavitt chairs "the community" and the rest of its membership comprises 16 health care, government, consumer, and business leaders.

- It established the Healthcare IT Standards Panel (HITSP) under a $3.3 million contract awarded to the American National Standards Institute on October 6, 2005. The panel's charge was to harmonize standards. On June 29, 2006, HITSP recommended selected standards for EHRs, biosurveillance, and consumer empowerment.

- At the same time, ONCHIT awarded $11.5 million to RTI International to oversee the Health Information Security and Privacy Collaboration (HISPC), a multidisciplinary team that was to work with state and territorial governments to develop baseline requirements for security and privacy protections. State and territorial groups that received HISPC contracts were to report their assessments, proposals, and plans to RTI by June 9, 2006.

- The third contract awarded that same day was for $2.7 million and went to the nonprofit Certification Commission for Health Information Technology (CCHIT). The commission was charged with figuring out criteria for evaluating and certifying HIT products and solutions that comply with recommendations of HITSP and HISPC. In phase 1, CCHIT looked at inspection and certification of ambulatory EMRs, issuing commercial criteria on May 3, 2006. CCHIT issued its first certifications in July 2006. They seemed to be tailored for a variety of systems and vendors; however, at CCHIT's May 2006 conference in Baltimore, a "town hall" meeting elicited serious concerns from small vendors. Later phases will examine inpatient EMRs and HIT networks.

- On November 10, 2005, ONCHIT announced that it was providing $18.6 million to four teams that would develop regional HINs (see **Table 8-4**). Although they would serve specific markets, they would be prototypes for a NHIN. Existing community RHIOS were key players on each team. "We called for regional organizations as business conveners," said Brailer (Cunningham, 2005, p. 1154). Eventually, these regional systems would have to speak seamlessly to one another to begin to create a nationwide network.

- The four regional consortia reported on their efforts in Fall 2006. In June 2007 ONCHIT issued a request for proposals to fund an additional ten state, regional and non-geographic consortia.

TABLE 8-4 The Four RHIO Partnerships Selected

The four regional teams supported by the Office of the National Coordinator for Health Information Technology are:

- Accenture, with partners Apelon, Cisco, CGI-AMS, Creative Computing Solutions, eTech Security Pro, Intellithought, Lucent Glow, Oakland Consulting Group, Oracle, and Quovadx, which is working regionally with the Eastern Kentucky Regional Health Community, CareSpark (Tennessee), and the West Virginia eHealth Initiative

- CSC, with partners Browsersoft, Business Networks International, Center for Information Technology Leadership, Connecting for Health, DB Consulting Group, eHealth Initiative, Electronic Health Record Vendors Association, Microsoft, Regenstrief Institute, SiloSmashers, and Sun Microsystems, which is working regionally with the Indiana Health Information Exchange, MA-SHARE (Massachusetts), and Mendocino HRE (California)

- IBM, with partners Argosy Omnimedia, Business Innovation, Cisco, HMS Technologies, IDL Solutions, Ingenium, and VICCS, which is working regionally with Taconic Health Information Network and Community (New York); North Carolina Healthcare Information and Communications Alliance (Research Triangle and Rockingham County)

- Northrop Grumman, with partners Air Commander, Axolotl, Client/Server Software Solutions, First Consulting Group, SphereCom Enterprises, and WebMD, which is working regionally with Santa Cruz RHIO (California); and HealthBridge (Cincinnati, Ohio) and University Hospitals Health System (Cleveland, Ohio).

Source: Office of the National Coordinator for Health Information Technology.

INHERENT CONFLICTS

A community-based RHIO such as HINET that is developed with participation from the entire local medical community can employ a variety of solutions geared to the needs of small practices—an important consideration since nearly a third of all physicians work in solo or two-physician practices and more than half work in practices with fewer than 10 physicians (Grossman & Reed, 2006) and small practices lag behind large ones in their use of health IT (see **Figure 8-4**). A HINET-type network could easily incorporate an ASP (application service provider) Internet system and open standards technology, which would reduce the investment required by a practice. Groups such the American Academy of Family Physicians have launched demonstration projects aimed at developing Internet-based EMR systems costing about $100 per physician per month to maintain.

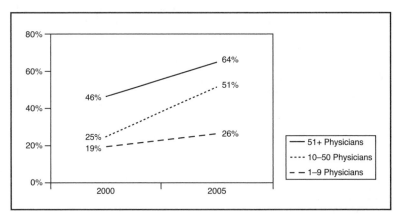

FIGURE 8-4   Physicians in practices with IT for at least three of five clinical activities in 2000–2001 and 2004–2005 by practice size

Changes between 2000–2001 and 2004–2005 in the gaps between group practices with 1–9 physicians and group practices with 10–50 physicians and 51+ physicians were statistically significant at P < .05.

Source: Community Tracking Study 2004-2005 Physician Survey, © Center for Studying Health System Change, from Grossman and Reed (2006).

Such approaches, however, also reduce the market for proprietary systems and standalone hardware and software, setting up a conflict with hospitals and large practices that use systems built around the HL7 language developed by Health Level Seven, Inc., a nonprofit standards development organization, and with technology companies intent on developing and marketing systems they control. Low-costs systems also reduce the competitive advantage of larger practices that can afford high-cost systems.

The federal NHIN approach, by comparison, has the potential to favor large-scale systems that would benefit the technology companies and large health care companies that sit on the four regional development teams and other leadership groups that are part of the NHIN effort. The tendency will be to try to extend the reach of HL7-based, hospital-type systems into the offices of smaller provides. This could help promote interoperability by discouraging the proliferation of many potentially incompatible systems, but it also has the potential to drive up costs and complexity and to delay uptake by solo providers and small group practices.

While delivering the keynote address at the Health Information and Management Systems Society (HIMSS) meetings in February 2005, Brailer spoke openly of the inherent conflicts. Health Data Management reported him saying the following:

> *The electronic records investment by large group practices is strategic, intended to shift the market toward them. They should be recognized for their leadership and not faulted for their inventiveness. However, if we believe electronic records improve health status, then we have an obligation to level the playing field. We can't allow one part of the physician community to have the technology and another unable to afford it.*

Brailer also took aim at the mindset in the health care industry that patient data is a proprietary strategic asset, a concept that could undermine regional networks. "Interoperability is not just an IT issue. We need guidelines on how to share and access data between competitive organizations," he said. "Data sharing is a precursor to widespread use of electronic records. Proprietary boundaries are growing around health information at the same time that talk about interoperability has become commonplace."

He also noted that in comments ONCHIT received in response to the Request for Information on RHIOs, "Many respondents recommended that the NHIN be a virtual network that leverages the public Internet."

According to a New York Times report on the HIMSS meeting, Brailer asked technology executives in small group meetings to put aside their narrow corporate interests and give up some of their proprietary lock on customers in order to open up a larger market opportunity to everyone. "Each company cannot get all it wants," he said. "The elephant in the room in what we are trying to do is the small physician practices.... That's the hardest problem, and it will bring this effort to its knees if we fail" (Lohr, 2005).

DISCUSSION QUESTIONS

1. What do you think of the NHIN as an illustration of "disruptive technology"?

2. Why has the concept of a networked health care information system been so slow to take hold in the United States? Why has it moved ahead faster in other countries?

3. What are likely to be the "unintended consequences" of implementing such a national network?

4. Where does the government's NHIN strategy fall on the political and economic spectrum of alternative approaches to health care policy?

5. Which of the two alternative approaches to developing an RHIO outlined in the case is more likely to have an EMR in the hands of all Americans by 2016?

CHAPTER 9

The Policy Analysis Process — Evaluation — Political Feasibility

Since Progressives first introduced national health insurance proposals to the United States in 1912, countless health care reform proposals have been funded, developed, modeled, modified, and debated. Ultimately, however, all have been rejected.... Unfortunately, the U.S. political system has not been impressed, and despite the best-laid plans of advocates and analysts, universal coverage has consistently been felled by one opponent: political feasibility (Oberlander 2003, W3–394).

Assessing political feasibility can be one of the most challenging steps in the policy development process. Policy choices are proposed, considered, adopted, and implemented in sociopolitical contexts that are complex, subjective, and dynamic. They are difficult to quantify or to analyze within a structured, rational framework. Indeed, politics can be quite irrational when factors such as emotions, ambitions, egos, disputes, personalities, allegiances, relationships, and deeply held value systems come into play.

This makes reliable prediction of whether policies have a realistic chance of being adopted and successfully implemented virtually impossible (Dror, 1969). It also helps explain why explicit discussions about political feasibility are often absent from policy debates and why literature specific to political feasibility is sparse. Oberlander (2003, p. 392) observed that "political calculations are often a footnote in health care reform proposals." Dror (1969, p. 3) remarked, "In view of the importance of political feasibility for policy making, it is quite surprising that it is neglected and even ignored in the policy sciences literature, including most prediction studies. Main reasons for this neglect seem to include the general tendency in much of normative policy sciences, including prediction studies, to exclude political phenomena as either too difficult and/or too 'mundane.'" In addition, some analysts and politicians may be reluctant to discuss politics and health care in the same breath. Yet no policy analysis is complete if it avoids the issue of political feasibility, and systematic techniques can help predict political feasibility.

TERMINOLOGY

Brown (2006) described *political feasibility* as "the right fit between bright ideas and the values and interests that animate stakeholders with crucial pieces of power" (p. W163). Oberlander (2003) noted, "Feasibility analysis deals not with policy ideals but with what is more or less adoptable given policy constraints" (p. W3–392).

Dror (1969) identified three characterizations of political feasibility:

1. For a political actor, political feasibility is a measure of the actor's ability, within a given period of time, to influence various activities, specifically policy adoption and implementation. He used the term *political leverage* to describe the actor's influence and *political leverage domain* to describe the setting or range of activities within which an actor can exercise political leverage effectively.

2. For a specific policy alternative, political feasibility is a measure of the likelihood that an alternative will be adopted and implemented within a specific time period.

3. For an issue area, political feasibility is a measure of the range of policy alternatives that could potentially be adopted and implemented within a specific time period. Dror referred to the range of politically viable alternatives as the *political feasibility domain.*

He also described four sets of "variables" for thinking about political feasibility:

1. The main actors—who they are and what they intend.
2. Other inputs into the policy arena—the political climate, the state of the economy, public opinion, technological capabilities, and so forth.

3. The interplay of the first two—how actors come together and interact, taking the other inputs into account. Those interactions are governed by laws and informal "rules of the game." Some actors may join to form a *required coalition* with enough combined political leverage to move a policy forward.

4. The threshold for adoption—in Congress, for example, the threshold for passage is a simple majority, but the threshold changes if Congress has to override a presidential veto, which requires a two-thirds majority. An actor or a coalition may have considerable aggregated policy leverage, but whether it has enough will depends on the threshold that has to be met.

In Dror's model, the actors, influenced and informed by various inputs, interact with other actors and seek to combine political leverage to achieve *critical leverage mass.*

Another set of variables involves factors that induce actors to become concerned about a particular issue or attracted to a particular policy strategy or solution in the first place. If an issue is not on anybody's radar, there are no actors and no *actor-interactions.* In the fields of political science and public affairs, the process by which government entities decide to try to address a particular problem or consider a particular policy approach is called *agenda setting.* A prerequisite, of course, is that a set of circumstances be identified as a problem. A number of factors influence when a problem is identified, how it is defined, and whether politicians choose to address it. These including public opinion, the national political mood, media coverage, emerging social movements, interest group mobilization, voter attitudes, arising risks and threats (real or perceived), new research findings, critical evaluations of program performance, economic changes, the level of sympathy for the affected populations, and the availability of potential policy solutions (Hacker, 1997; Oliver, 2006). Action on an agenda item may be either *ceremonial* or *intentional.* Ceremonial action means going through the motions for public relations reasons or political leverage, but does not imply a strong will to address the underlying issues. For example, Congress may wish to appear to have done something about health care access to avoid a "do-nothing" label in a forthcoming election but lack a true commitment to improving the system.

OVERVIEW

To assess political feasibility, one needs to turn to the field of political science. This chapter focuses on the *authorizing environments* in which policy is made. By mapping an authorizing environment, we identify the major actors that populate the political stage. These are all policy makers to some extent, even if they are not elected officials, bureaucrats, or judges, because they all can influence political feasibility. Next we discuss the players' roles and briefly describe some inputs they typically take into account, some factors that influence what gets onto their agendas, some formal and informal rules they operate under, and some ways they push a policy toward adoption. The oft-repeated word in the preceding sentence is *some*.

Although this chapter focuses primarily on government policy making—the adoption and implementation of policies through legislation, budgets, executive orders, rules, or court decisions—many other channels for implementing policy exist. Organized community-based activities that are designed to change attitudes, beliefs, and individual norms also can be considered policies (Lamson & Colman, 2005). The 100,000 Lives Campaign case study that follows Chapter 11 explores voluntary regulation, which can occur in partnership with or independent of government. Individual private not-for-profit and for-profit organizations are also political environments in which policy alternatives have to be evaluated for political feasibility (Hansmann, 1996).

AUTHORIZING ENVIRONMENTS

The term *authorizing environment* comes from the field of public administration and refers to a list of the actors from whom a public manager must receive authorization in order to survive and be effective. It applies equally well to an institution, and in a pluralistic, nontotalitarian society, it is relevant to the development, adoption, and successful implementation of a policy.

Consider the authorizing environment experienced by one of the authors while employed by the Washington State Board of Health. The board's authorities include the ability to make rules for the environmental health and safety of public buildings, including schools. When the board decided to update its school environmental health rules, it had to operate in a very complex authorizing environment.

From statehood, Washington has valued local autonomy and the state's laws grant local jurisdictions considerable authority. The primary authority for schools rests with the local school district, and school board members' primary accountability is at the ballot box. The state, however, mandates that students spend most days in school. The state pays 69% of operating costs and most construction costs. The Washington State Constitution says that education is the "paramount duty" of the state, and the Legislature imposes many mandates on districts, such as requiring schools to administer the Washington Assessment of Student Learning.

School health and safety inspection programs, where they exist, generally reside with local public health jurisdictions governed by local boards of health comprised wholly or in part of county commissioners. They work closely with the state Department of Health, but they, too, have considerable local autonomy. Local governments and local boards of health can enact their own ordinances, as long as they are not less stringent than state statutes and rules. They have limited authority over school districts; however, they can adopt and enforce building codes. Nine of 35 local health jurisdictions have school inspection programs and typically charge schools a fee for each inspection.

The governor appoints nine of the board's 10 members to three-year terms. She is the supervisor of the 10th member, the Secretary of Health. Governor Christine Gregoire has made education and health top issues for her administration. Geographically, her political base is Seattle and the urban communities that ring Puget Sound. School health is a high-profile issue in Seattle because its school district failed to disclose or act quickly on tests that showed that lead was leaching into school drinking water. There also were local concerns about other drinking water contaminants, indoor air quality, and mold. These issues were the subject of extensive media coverage. Governor Gregoire had already demonstrated her willingness to intervene in the affairs of boards and commission when she objected to a Board of Pharmacy rule that would have allowed pharmacists to refuse to dispense Plan B, the morning-after pill. When she was attorney general, Governor Gregoire issued an investigative report on school construction.

A majority of state legislators are from the Seattle metropolitan area (one senator's wife teaches in a Seattle school that had contaminated water). Legislators from outside of the Seattle area have also had to deal with school health issues in their communities. The Legislature held hearings on bills related to school drinking water and mold, but did not enact them, in part because of the cost and in part because the state Board of Health planned to address the issue in a rule. It granted the board its regulatory powers and could repeal them or cut the board's budget. It also could overrule board action through legislation, and it operates a Joint Administrative Rule Review Committee that investigates whether an agency's rules exceed its authority.

Other agencies have authorities and programs related to health and safety.

- The Office of the Superintendent of Public Instruction operates a "coordinated school health" program funded by the Centers for Disease Control and Prevention (CDC) and has sustainability standards for school construction.
- The Department of Health is a partner on the coordinated school health project, provides technical assistance to schools and local public health, regulates drinking water systems, and administer one-time money for schools to test for lead.
- The Department of Labor and Industries protects employees' workplace safety.
- The Department of Ecology addresses contaminated soils on school grounds.
- The Department of Agriculture regulates pesticide use on school grounds.
- The Building Code Council establishes the statewide building code.

The U.S. Environmental Protection Agency regulates drinking water, although a standard for lead in school drinking water has been invalidated by the courts. It also runs a voluntary program to help schools assure a healthy environment and provides an online software tool called the Healthy School Environments Assessment Tool (HealthySEAT).

In Seattle and other communities, parents are active and organized. Many tell tragic stories about severe illness leading to disability and academic decline that they associate with mold, heavy metals, and other exposures in school. They complain that no single agency is accountable for school safety at the state level and that rules are unenforceable. The Washington State PTA is an influential political player in the state.

Joining with parents were teachers and the Washington Education Association (WEA). School employees attribute many ailments to school environmental conditions. Although Labor & Industries regulates workplace health and safety, school employees looked to the board's rules to create better protections. The WEA is also a major actor in state politics, and members voted to raise their dues to push for improved school environmental health.

The board is committed to basing decisions on science, but the science is incomplete, inconsistent, inconclusive, and evolving. Many studies document the health impacts of environmental contaminants, including lead and mold, but many peer-reviewed articles argue that most cases of multiple chemical sensitivity and sick building syndrome are psychosomatic. Academics and scientific experts who testified to the board expressed a variety of sometimes contradictory viewpoints.

The state, the schools, and the WEA all consulted with lawyers during rule making. School districts could challenge an overly broad rule in court by arguing that they have primary authority over school facilities; however, advocates theoretically could sue the board for failing to fulfill its statutory duties if it did too little.

On this one rule alone then, the board's authorizing environment included schools, school boards, local government, local public health jurisdictions, the governor, the Legislature, several state agencies, two federal agencies, parents, students, teachers, researchers, the courts, labor, the media, and the general public (see **Figure 9-1**).

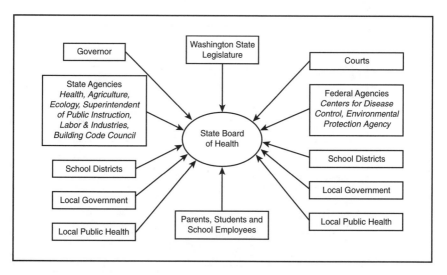

FIGURE 9-1   Washington State Board of Health Authorizing Environment for School Health and Safety Rules

Nearly all policy making operates in similar authorizing environments. Even a simplified, generic map of the policy making environment (see **Figure 9-2**) can be quite complex given the number and variety of actors. Each has its own agenda, its own constituencies, its own set of inputs to consider, and its own idiosyncrasies. That complexity is one of the main reasons that political feasibility is so difficult to predict.

KEY GOVERNMENT ACTORS

There are many important governmental actors at the federal level, and in this section, we consider factors that determine how they behave within their niches. That will be followed by a discussion of key actors at the state and local level and the ways they may differ from their federal counterparts.

Federal Government Actors

The drafters of the U.S. Constitution were wary of a government that put unrestrained power in the hands of one individual or institution. The Constitution that took effect in 1789 created a stronger national government, but it established a three-headed state with legislative, executive, and judicial branches and a system of checks and balances to ensure that no one branch would dominate. This basic framework also exists down through lower levels of government. At the federal level, the strengths of

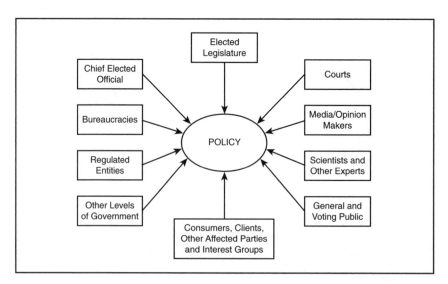

FIGURE 9-2 General Authorizing Environment for Policy Making

these branches relative to one another have waxed and waned over the years, but the separation of powers envisioned by the drafters of the Constitution has survived intact.

Congress: The Legislative Body

Assessments of the relative power of the three branches of government in the modern era tend to conclude that Congress is the most powerful. That is largely because only Congress has the power to make laws and create budgets, whereas bureaucracies implement them and courts interpret them. The relative power of Congress has grown over the past few decades as its members have expanded their capacity to act as policy entrepreneurs. In this, they are supported by personal and committee staffs that grew after World War II and expanded dramatically in the 1960s and 1970s. The larger staffs have freed Congress from reliance on the executive branch to generate major policy proposals. According to Oberlander (2003, p. W3–394), "Congress, measured in terms of its political independence, administrative capacity, and ability to pursue policies that diverge from the executive, may be the most powerful legislature in the world."

The Senate and the House of Representatives have different makeups and personalities. Each plays by its own rules. Senators are elected by a statewide vote—two from each state—which means that the least populous states have the same representation as the most populous. House members represent congressional districts that are roughly equal in population and are redrawn after every census. The leader of the House, the Speaker, is typically the spokesperson for the majority party in that body, assigns members to committees, refers bills to committees, and calendars bills on the floor. Both the House and the Senate have majority and minority leaders that also serve as spokespeople for their respective parties and help develop and promote their party's policy agenda.

Committees are where the bulk of the work in Congress gets done. When legislation is introduced, it is referred to one or more policy committees. Policy committees consider authorizing legislation that would set up a new program or policy. They may hold hearings, mark up a bill, and refer it to the floor for action. Committees have subcommittees with policy expertise in certain areas. Major policy subcommittees for health care issues are the Subcommittee on Public Health of the Senate Committee on Health, Education, Labor, and Pensions and the Subcommittee on Health of the House Energy and Commerce Committee. If the policy has budgetary implications, it will also have to go through one or more of the six powerful fiscal committees—Appropriations and Budget committees in both houses, House Ways and Means, and Senate Finance. These focus on appropriations, and two of them, the House Ways and Means and the Senate Finance, tend to be bottlenecks for major health care legislation. In the House, another powerful committee, the Rules Committee, directs the progress of legislation and establishes the rules of debate, which can be very restrictive.

Another form of committee sometimes comes into play if related but different legislation passes both houses. One house may ask the other to reconsider, or leadership from both houses may appoint a joint conference committee that will develop compromise legislation and send the new iteration back to both houses for adoption. Legislation can perish from neglect in a conference committee. Committee members can also add major policy changes with little fanfare. Just 10 days before the 1974 passage of the Employment Retirement and Income Security Act (ERISA), conferees slipped in language that restricted states from regulating the health benefit plans of self-insured companies. As discussed earlier, this so-called "ERISA exemption" severely limits the ability of states to enact significant health care reforms such as play-or-pay laws.

Congress will sometimes authorize a new program but not provide an appropriation. In 1998, for example, Congress passed the Ricky Ray Hemophilia Relief Fund Act, which authorized payments of up to $100,000 to hemophiliacs and their partners infected with the human immunodeficiency virus or their survivors. Congress, however, did not appropriate money for the payments until 2001. This is discussed further in Chapter 12.

Another part of the budget process that can undermine policy committees, and one that has had a profound impact on health policy, is the reconciliation bill. The old way of tying policy to budget was to adopt a law and then appropriate the funding to implement it, but that was before the Congressional Budget Act of 1974. Congress can now adopt a budget, and then committees can go back and recommend changes to existing laws to conform to the budget instructions. These recommendations are compiled into a reconciliation bill that requires no hearing and often passes with little scrutiny. Anything vaguely related to the budget can be thrown in. Most major health legislation during the 1980s took this route to passage, including mandates for state's to provide coverage to women and children with incomes above the federal poverty level (Weissert & Weissert, 2002).

Bill Clinton worked hard to convince Senate Robert C. Byrd, who chaired the Senate Appropriations Committee, to include the Health Security Act in a budget reconciliation act, but Byrd refused (Clinton, 2003).

Before major legislation can take effect then, it may have to wind its way through a maze of committees and subcommittees, be scheduled for a floor vote, receive a majority vote in both houses (and perhaps 60 votes in the Senate to withstand a filibuster), survive a conference committee, have a budget appropriation, and be signed by the president or have enough votes for a veto override. It is hardly surprisingly that major reform initiatives are easy to derail. Oberlander (2003) identified this fragmented structure of Congress as a significant barrier to health care reform.

The President: Chief Executive Officer

The U.S. president is often referred to as "the leader of the free world." The phrase perhaps overstates the importance of the office, given the relative strength of Congress. The day after the 2006 midterm elections, Representative John P. Murtha told National Public Radio, "The president has no power. The president has perception of power." The phrase, however, is very apt in some ways because although a president has limited authority to *make* policy, he or she has tremendous ability to *influence* policy. A president is more likely to become a policy maker because of leadership than any direct authority.

The president can and does craft major legislative initiatives—the annual State of the Union address is often full of new policy initiatives—but only Congress can introduce them. The president must find a sponsor to introduce legislation, and after a bill is in the hands of Congress, there is no guarantee it will pass or if it does pass that it will resemble the original proposal. In health care, perhaps the greatest single example of the limits on a president's ability to assure a bill's passage is the 1993 Health Security Act proposed by Bill Clinton, which is the subject of **Case 9-1**.

The president initiates the budget process. The federal government passes a new budget for each fiscal year, which begins on October 1. The president transmits the first iteration to Congress between the first Monday in January and the first Monday in February. The budget that emerges from Congress, however, may be significantly different. In 2006, George W. Bush proposed a fiscal year 2007 budget that would have eliminated the Urban Indian Health Program. Legislative committees marking up the

Department of the Interior, Environment, and Related Agencies Appropriation Bill quickly restored the funding and even proposed an increase in the program's budget.

A president's ability to push a measure through Congress depends in large part on his or her *political capital.* For presidents, political capital primarily comes down to two things—their popularity and their party's strength in Congress. For a recently elected president, popularity can be judged by the electoral margin of victory. For a president well into her or his term, popularity can be assessed by opinion polls. George W. Bush, for example, took office after losing the popular vote. He had no claim to a mandate, and his approval rating was an unremarkable 57 percent in February 2001, according to the Gallup poll. Even though his party was only one vote shy of a majority in the Senate and held a clear majority in the House, he enjoyed little success with Congress in the early days. His political capital increased after the attacks of September 11, 2001, because his public approval rating as a wartime president hit an astounding 90%. Public approval tanked as dissatisfaction with the war in Iraq grew. After the 2006 election, he was a lame duck facing Democratic majorities in Congress—his political capital was negligible.

The 1965 passage of Medicaid and Medicare has been attributed to Lyndon Johnson's phenomenal political capital. He clearly had a mandate, as he was elected with more than 61% of the popular vote, a feat unsurpassed since. The first Gallup poll of his term showed an 80% approval rating. He was a Democrat, and his party had a two-thirds majority in both houses. This gave him authority to push the agenda that had gotten him elected and a Congress unified enough, despite a North/South split in the Democratic Party, to tackle even the most divisive issues.

In a sense, the president is a stand-in for the body politic, the most visible official in the country and the one with the greatest access to the media. Presidential words can carry considerable moral authority. Presidential messages reach the public through numerous vehicles—the State of the Union address, press conferences, speeches, fireside chats, photo opportunities, public appearances, and more. This gives the president unparalleled ability to elevate issues onto the national agenda, propose strategies, and bring public pressure to bear. The president's leadership role involves working to build coalitions, broker negotiations, and develop compromises. When Congress balks at a presidential proposal, the president can engage in education, persuasion, and horse trading. Extreme arm-twisting by a president, however, is rare.

Presidents do have authorities they can use to leverage policy. One is veto power. The president has 10 days after enactment to sign or veto legislation. Congress can override a veto by a two-thirds vote in both houses. Presidents have used this power 2,550 times since 1789, and Congress has overridden only 106 (4.2%) of those. Presidents exhibit vastly different propensities to exercise this power. Eight presidents never used their veto power (Kosar, 2006). George H.W. Bush initiated 29 regular vetoes and 15 pocket vetoes during his term, but his son was a year and a half into his second term before he used his first veto to kill funding for embryonic stem cell research.

Another policy tool at the president's disposal is the ability to issue executive memoranda, which provided direction to executive branch agencies. If they are published in the *Federal Register* and not challenged by Congress, they become executive orders. Executive orders have the force of law. Because they can address almost any policy area provided that they are supported by some constitutional administrative authority or congressional directive, they can be legislative in nature. Bill Clinton published more than 50,000 pages of executive memoranda and issued 364 executive orders. A 1999 executive memorandum required the Federal Employee Health Benefits Board to provide mental health parity (coverage for mental illnesses equivalent to that for physical ailments) by 2001. **Table 9-1** lists health-related executive orders Clinton issued. Executive orders are an example of the authority a president exerts over federal agencies, which are major players when it comes to implementing—even creating—health policy.

Bureaucracies: Administrators and Regulators

In theory, most bureaucracies are line agencies under the control of the executive, but the truth, as usual, is more complicated. For one thing, the president's reach is limited. Although a president fills some 2,400 positions, appointees occupy only the top layers of a bureaucracy's management ranks. It is not unusual for career bureaucrats further down in the organization to try to subvert a president's agenda. How much attention a given president pays to the management of executive agencies varies.

Bureaucracies serve two masters. Senior appointments may require congressional confirmation. Congress establishes the agencies' budgets, authorizes their programs, and enacts the laws under which they must act.

TABLE 9-1　Examples of Health-Related Executive Orders Issued by Bill Clinton

13181	Protecting the privacy of protected health information in oversight investigations
13155	Promoting access to HIV/AIDS pharmaceuticals in sub-Saharan Africa
13147	Establishing the White House Commission on Complementary and Alternative Medicine Policy
13145	Prohibit discrimination in federal employment based on genetic information
13124	Amending federal civil service rules to increase opportunities for people with psychiatric disabilities
13017	Establishing the Advisory Commission on Consumer Protection and Quality in the Health Care Industry
12963	Establishing the Presidential Advisory Council on HIV/AIDS
12961	Establishing the Presidential Advisory Committee on Gulf War Veterans' Illnesses
12898	Addressing environmental justice in minority and low-income populations
12878	Establishing the Bipartisan Commission on Entitlement Reform

Source: The National Archives, Executive Orders Disposition Tables.

Congressional committees and subcommittees spend a large amount of their time overseeing agencies under their purview. The House Energy and Commerce Committee, which oversees the Department of Health and Human Services agencies, including the CDC, as part of its health-related responsibilities, provided an example of this on October 23, 2006. Representative Joe Burton, the committee's chair, and Representative Ed Whitfield, chair of its Subcommittee on Oversight & Investigations, sent a letter to CDC Director Dr. Julie Gerberding requesting a briefing on the agency's reorganization plan, a copy of a consultant report critical of the agency's financial management office, an explanation of the how human tissue samples are handled, and agency regulations related to property management and laboratory equipment.

Bureaucracies and bureaucrats can draft legislation, and their expertise may be called on to craft amendments at various stages of policy deliberations. Weisert and Weisert (2002, p. 154) described the role that Wilbur

Cohen, a longtime federal bureaucrat, then Assistant Secretary of Health, Education, and Welfare and the leading expert on Social Security, played in the 1965 passage of Medicare and Medicaid: "Cohen helped draft the administration bill on Medicare, consulted with members on proposed bills, and was asked to summarize various proposals to the key committees. When Wilbur Mills decided to combine several proposals into a 'three-layer cake' (the layers were later known as Medicare Parts A and B and Medicaid), he asked Cohen to draw up legislative language to pull the pieces together, along with an analysis of the costs, within 12 hours."

Many bureaucracies generate data, information, and research as part of their regular activities, and these work products can inform the policy development process. Examples in health care include the research produced by the 25 centers and institutions that make up the National Institutes of Health and the data on the cost and quality of personal health services generated by the Agency for Healthcare Research and Quality.

Bureaucracies have their own networks and constituencies. They can mobilize outside groups to support or oppose legislations, work with them to try to convince them of the merits of a particular proposal or to at least minimize resistance, or pull together stakeholders early in the policy-making process to craft a policy alternative that has broad support. They can also use their outside contacts to try to assess political feasibility.

Finally, bureaucracies with regulatory authority are policy makers in their own right. While legislatures make law, regulatory agencies make administrative law in the form of rules and regulations. The case study on folic acid fortification that follows Chapter 10 is an example of the policy-making power of government agencies.

At the federal level, most agencies with health-related portfolios are part of the Department of Health and Human Services (DHHS). A list of such agencies appears in **Table 9-2**, whereas **Table 9-3** lists some of the agencies that operate health-related programs but are not part of DHHS.

The Judiciary: The Federal Courts

When Maryland enacted a law requiring that any company with more than 10,000 employees spend at least 8% of its payroll on employee health care or pay into a state fund for covering the uninsured, the Retail Industry Leaders Association filed suit in federal court. U.S. District Court Judge Frederick Motz overturned the law on July 19, 2006, finding that ERISA preempted state authority.

TABLE 9-2   U.S. Department of Health and Human Services
Program Divisions

Administration for Children and Families
Administration on Aging
Centers for Medicare & Medicaid Services
Agency for Healthcare Research and Quality
Center for Disease Control and Prevention
Substance Abuse and Mental Health Services Administration
Agency for Toxic Substances and Disease Registry
Food and Drug Administration
Health Resources and Services Administration
Indian Health Service
National Institutes of Health
Office of Civil Rights
Office of the National Coordinator for Health Information Technology
Office of Global Health Affairs

Source: U.S. Department of Health and Human Services organizational chart. Accessed October 20, 2006, at http://www.hhs.gov/about/orgchart.html.

The federal courts most often play a critical role when it comes to issues of federal preemption, constitutional protections, and interstate commerce. In the federal system, the 94 district courts are the trial courts for most civil and criminal matters, although there are separate court systems for bankruptcy, international trade and customs issues, and claims for monetary damages against the federal government. All districts belong to one of 12 regional circuits, each of which has its own U.S. Court of Appeals. The federal appeals courts hear appeals to decisions reached by district courts, the Court of International Trade, the Court of Federal Claims, and federal agencies. The U.S. Supreme Court picks from among the cases brought before it and chooses which it will hear. It seeks out cases involving important issues related to the Constitution or federal laws and hears cases where the rulings of the district courts appear to be in conflict.

One of the most profound policy changes in terms of health outcomes for this country came through the courts. Attorneys general from several states agreed in 1994 to sue tobacco companies to recover the costs of caring for publicly insured individuals with smoking-related illnesses. In 1998, the five largest tobacco companies and 46 states, plus six common-

TABLE 9-3 Federal Agencies with Health-Related Duties (Excludes HHS Divisions)

Department of Agriculture
- Animal and Plant Health Inspection Service
- Cooperative State Research, Education, and Extension Service

Department of Defense
- TRICARE
- Army Medicine Department
- Navy Medicine
- Air Force Medical Service

Department of Homeland Security

Department of Labor
- Mine Safety and Health Administration
- Occupational Safety and Health Administration
- Employee Benefits Security Administration
- Benefits Review Board

Department of Veterans Affairs, Veterans Health Administration

Environmental Protection Agency

Federal Bureau of Prisons, Health Services Division

Federal Mine Safety and Health Review Commission

Nuclear Regulatory Commission

Occupational Safety and Health Review Commission

Uniformed Services University of the Health Sciences

wealths and protectorates, signed the Master Settlement Agreement (four states settled previously). The agreement called for payments of $206 billion over five years. Several of the states have used the money to fund antitobacco programs that have contributed to lower smoking rates. The settlement also imposed restrictions on marketing of tobacco to youth. Although the states filed the suits in state courts, the cases might have been consolidated in federal court eventually if the parties had not settled.

State Governments

States play a leading-edge role in formulating health policy and are major purchasers of heath insurance and health care. Health care is the most critical cost driver for state government. Medicaid spending alone accounts for 22% of spending across all states. In 2004, it surpassed elementary and secondary education to become the largest component of state budgets. All of health care accounts for 32% of total state spending (National Associaiton of State Budget Officers & National Governors Association, 2006). States also manage and fund public health and mental health services, authorize public hospital districts, regulate health insurance, license and discipline health care providers, and oversee health care facilities. They also serve as test markets for reform efforts.

States are organized on the surface as smaller versions of the federal government. The governor corresponds to the president. All have legislative bodies that correspond to Congress, and all but Nebraska have a bicameral legislature. At the state level, legislative seats in both houses are apportioned based on population—the result of Supreme Court decisions in the early 1960s affirming the "one man, one vote" doctrine. States also have their own state courts system, including their own supreme courts, but to describe states as miniature replicas of the national government would not do them justice. Their different powers, authorities, and organizational structures need to be taken into account.

There are a number of ways that states' political processes are distinct from those of the federal government and from one another. For example, most states allow the governor to veto line items in the major budget bills or sections of legislation (to which legislators can respond by carefully crafting legislation to make it hard to excise a single section). The President does not have line-item veto authority. Six states, however, restrict the governor to vetoing a major budget bill in its entirety. Fifteen states also have term limits. The only federal term limit is Article 22, ratified in 1951, which restricts presidential terms. State legislatures have their own rules and customs, as well. The Washington State Legislature, like the federal government, has separate tracks for budget appropriations and for policy and programmatic bills, but it will sometimes include a "null and void" clause that invalidates any unfunded bill.

Bureaucracies are also organized differently from state to state. Some states have combined public health, social services, and health care purchasing into a single huge agency. Some have split off public health into a separate department so that it does not get overshadowed. Some states have health care purchasing agencies that may or may not include federal entitlement programs. Washington, for example, has a Department of Health that focuses on public health and professional and facilities licensing, a Department of Social and Health Services that includes a division that manages Medicaid and SCHIP, and a Health Care Authority that runs the Basic Health Plan and the Uniform Medical Plan and purchases health-related benefits for government employees. Something as simple as state boards of health provides an example of the high variability in organizational structure among states. The Washington State Board of Health (2003) identified entities fitting the definition of a state board of health in 30 of the 50 states. Eight were advisory only, whereas 22 made policy in addition to providing advice. Eight of the 22 policy-making boards had direct oversight of the state health agency.

The judiciary, too, can be very different on the state level. In Washington, State Supreme Court justices are elected to 6-year terms and must retire when they turn 75 years old, whereas justices to the U.S. Supreme Court receive lifetime presidential appointments that must be confirmed by the Senate.

Weissert and Weissert (2002) have identified three key differences between states and the federal government that directly affect health care policy making:

- Budget limitations: States are not able to run at a deficit (although technically, Vermont is not prohibited from doing so), and they are generally prohibited from borrowing to cover operating expenses.
- Direct democracy: Twenty-four states allow initiatives—voters can pass statutes directly by voting on them on the ballot or indirectly by submitting them to the legislature. Twenty-four states (mostly the same 24) allow referendums. A legislative referendum is when the legislature puts something to public vote. A popular referendum is when, as a result of a petition, voters can confirm or repeal a legislative action. Eighteen states allow voters to recall officials.
- Media coverage: State governments receive less news coverage. Fewer reporters cover the state houses, and legislators are less adept at generating media attention.

Local Government

Local government bodies can be even more diverse. General speaking, each state has two levels of local governments: counties (parishes in Louisiana and boroughs in Alaska) and municipalities (cities, town, villages, and boroughs).

Typically these exist side by side, but there are examples of combined cities and counties (San Francisco is one), and in Virginia, some large cities operated outside of the county structure. Hawaii has four counties and no municipalities, except that Honolulu is a consolidated city–county.

There is typically a chief executive, a legislative body, and a court system. Depending on the level of government, the state constitution, state statutes, and the charter for the political subdivision, office holders may have different titles, and institutions may have different names. Municipalities typically use one of two basic structures:

- The council–manager system: A city council, board of alderman, city commission, or other legislative body handles policy. The mayor (who may be a member of the council) is largely ceremonial, and a city manager hired by the council performs most day-to-day administrative functions.
- The mayor–council system: A legislative body works with a separately elected mayor. How much executive authority the mayor has depends on whether the municipality has a "strong mayor" or "weak mayor" system.

County government is typically equivalent to the council–manager system. Counties generally are run by a legislative body, most often called the board of commissioners, which hires a county administrator, manager, or executive. Counties are typically responsible for providing services such as fire, police, public health, criminal justice, garbage and recycling, and roads in unincorporated areas.

Just as states have despaired at looking to the federal government to address access to care issues and other problems linked to the nation's system of health care finance and delivery and tried to find solutions on their own, so too have local governments and local communities. Some local community efforts have experienced significant government involvement, whereas others have relied on grassroots efforts. An example of a government-driven effort began in the early 1990s in Hillsborough County, Florida, in response to the strain on the local budget due to the rising costs of providing services to the disadvantaged at the local public hospital. Voters approved a half-cent increase to the county property tax. The money went to purchase health coverage for low-income residents ineligible for other public health insurance programs. Through a network of local hospitals, clinics, and providers, the Hillsborough County Health

Care Plan would provide case-managed care to an initial 30,000 beneficiaries. Part of what made the plan politically feasible was a commitment that the plan would in time lead to a reduction in property tax levies.

The plan garnered national accolades, but within a few years after its February 1993 launch, it was in political trouble. Over time, some of the plan's earlier champions became less involved, and conservative businessmen arguing against public sector insurance programs pointed to the plan's $154 million reserves as evidence that the initial need was overstated. The Republican ascendancy in 1994 worsened the plan's political woes. Brown (2006) documented how the plan survived a series of challenges and reforms over a decade and how its advocates worked successfully to "institutionalize" it. According to local officials, the plan annually saved taxpayers $44 million per year, generated $15 million in economic benefits by helping people continue to work, and brought $16 to $18 million in federal and state funds into the county.

POLITICAL INPUTS

Being able to identify the actors and describe their interactions is only part of the challenge of assessing political feasibility. It is also important to understand another set of variables—the inputs that influence the actor interactions. There are many such inputs, but key ones include elections, constituent relations, campaign fundraising, party agendas, the economy and its impact on government budgets, political trading, and idiosyncratic personal factors.

The Election Cycle

Elected officials, unless they are planning to retire or face term limits, must be concerned with re-election. The timing of elections can have a profound impact on their willingness to take on controversial issues. If an issue is likely to interest the electorate favorably, it might rise to the top of a politician's or party's agenda preceding an election. Such instances often provide examples of ceremonial agenda setting. If an issue or policy is likely to alienate or confuse voters, politicians might put the issue off until after the election. Policy makers, for example, are reluctant to raise taxes during an election year. Presidents typically focus on re-election throughout most of their first term, but tend to demonstrate more independence during their second. When assessing political feasibility, it is important to consider the timing of the next election and the mood of the electorate.

Constituent Relations

For politicians concerned about reelection, one of their top two concerns is likely to be constituent relations. The nature of constituent relations activities will differ depending on the geographic area and population represented. Generally, the smaller the direct constituency, the greater the importance given to grassroots activities such as addressing service clubs and attending pig pickings at the local firehouse. When politicians represent an entire state as senators do, they tend to rely less on direct personal contact and more on using the media as an intermediary. This means that they are apt to focus more on big picture issues likely to gain them statewide or nationwide coverage.

One of the jobs of a politician is to bring home benefits, such as state and federal funding for roads and other capital improvement projects. A member's focus on these activities could make it difficult to get other issues onto their agendas. In Washington State, supporters of more spending for public health hoped for support from a key member of one of the budget committees but understood that most of her energies and political capital would have to go to securing funding to open up a branch campus for the region's medical and dental schools in her home town. A policy proposal may conflict with the interests of folks back home. Efforts to ban tobacco sampling in the Washington state were tied up for years in the House Rules Committee by Majority Caucus Chair Bill Grant. Grant said he opposed sampling bans because giving tobacco to kids was already illegal, and for adults, tobacco is a legal product; however, Grant also represented a rural Eastern Washington district that is home to many small rodeos that are supported by tobacco companies and are major sites for tobacco giveaways (Callaghan, 2006).

Campaign Fundraising

The second major concern for politicians looking to be re-elected is campaign fundraising. Like constituent relations, fundraising can vary in scope depending on the office. The bigger the constituency, the more it costs to campaign. An average race for the House of Representatives in 2004 cost $1 million to $2 million (Birnbaum, 2004). A Senate race cost more than $8 million, and a challenger typically had to outspend an incumbent by 2-to-1 to win an occupied seat (Causin et al., 2005). Presidential candidates in 2008 are projected to spend $500 million each (Kuhnhenn, 2006).

The need to raise money continually influences the behavior of elected officials in many ways. When one of the authors covered politics as a reporter in California during the 1980s, legislators jockeyed aggressively for appointments to so-called juice committees—those that regulated industries and professions where a lot of money was involved, such as horse racing. These regulated entities could be counted on to make generous campaign contributions to assure their access to committee members.

Discussions of the role of money in U.S. politics tend to focus on campaign fundraising and often begin with the axiom that money buys access, not votes. That can be said of various gifts and junkets, as well as cash campaign contributions. Jesse "Big Daddy" Unruh, the powerful speaker of the California Assembly in the 1960s, once said of lobbyists, "If you can't take their money, drink their booze, eat their food, screw their women, and still look them in the eye and vote against them, you don't belong here." While the axiom may be true in general, there are numerous examples, some recent, of contributions and gifts, as well as outright bribes, influencing government decisions or creating conflicts of interest. North Carolina's Speaker of the House, Jim Black, helped push through a bill in 2005 requiring comprehensive eye exams for children during the first six months of kindergarten. These exams would earn optometrists $75 to $100 per exam. Black is an optometrist and accepted $59,750 in campaign money from his professional peers that year.

Party Agendas

Candidates' ability to bring their own money to the table or to raise funds independent of the political party they represent has weakened party control in U.S. politics. Oberlander (2003) argued that the weakness of political parties in the United States is one of the political obstacles to health reform in this country. Weisert and Weisert (2002) agreed that U.S. political parties are relatively weak, but party loyalty increased for both parties from 1965 through 2000 as partisan conflicts increased. Other factors contributing to relatively weak political parties are the capacity of candidates to organize a campaign without party support and the ability of office holders to vote in opposition to the party's position with few repercussions. Their primary allegiance is to their constituencies, not their parties. Nonetheless, parties are influential as organizing networks that facilitate communication between members. They can provide a setting to air issues, work to achieve critical leverage mass, and broker compromises.

Members who are unable to track every bill on every issue can turn to the party for direction on how to vote (Weissert & Weissert, 2002). Parties still manage to exert influence through fundraising. Another way parties try to exert control—with mixed success—is through leadership and caucuses. Plum committee assignments, favored consideration of certain bills, peer acceptance, and other perks can reward party loyalty.

The Economy and the Budget

The state of the economy and the revenues flowing into government coffers can greatly impact politicians' willingness to create new programs or retain or expand existing ones. When Washington's Governor Gregoire took office in 2005, one of her first acts was to roll back health care-related changes instituted under her predecessor that had reduced the number of children enrolled in government health insurance programs. The state budget called for a Medicaid eligibility review every 6 months, rather than every 12, as had been the case. It also called for Medicaid and SCHIP premium shares of $15 per month and eliminated the Children's Health Program, which provided state coverage for noncitizen children. Advocates for children argued that these changes had driven some 39,000 children off the Medicaid rolls. Gregoire reinstituted 12-month continuous eligibility and eliminated premium shares for families below 200% of the federal poverty level. She also put money into her supplemental budget request to re-establish the Children's Health Program. Although these actions reflected the fact that Gregoire had made health care, particularly coverage for children, a priority for her administration, they also reflected a change in the state's economy. After the September 11, 2001, attacks and the economic downturn that followed, the previous administration and the legislature had needed to cut $1 to $2 billion a year from the state budget for a few years running. By 2005, the state economy had begun to rebound, which left Gregoire with a projected surplus and allowed her to allocate an additional $140 million to provide coverage to an estimated 70,000 more children.

Political Trading

Lawmakers will not infrequently leverage their votes, pledging to vote a certain way in return for obtaining something else they are interested in. Leadership and committee chairs can also hold a bill hostage until some kind of quid pro quo is negotiated. In Washington, one Senate committee chair refused to release a bill to reduce commercial sources of environmental mercury, including methylmercury which is found in fish, unless an agency withdrew its opposition to her bill banning vaccines for children and pregnant woman that have more than trace amounts of thimerosal, a preservative that contains ethylmercury. Methylmercury is a persistent toxin that accumulates in the environment and is extremely harmful to humans, while ethylmercury appears to be metabolized quickly and cleared by the body. Yet the committee chair saw the two mercury bills as linked. Public health advocates had to weigh their concerns that the thimerosal bill, which was largely symbolic, would reinforce unsubstantiated fears about vaccine safety against the very real threat to human health posed by environmental releases of elemental mercury from sources such as thermometers, motion switches, and fluorescent light ballasts.

Adjournment

In states whose legislatures do not meet year-round, the end game can become very important. Bills can languish and appear to be dead, when in fact they may be being saved for the wheeling and dealing that invariably happens as the end of session approaches. On the other hand, a bill may pass in one chamber and be kept bottled up in another until the session ends, thwarting its passage. Sometimes a bill passes both houses quickly; however, the money to implement it may not be appropriated before the session ends, and it effectively dies, although the legislators can claim credit for having voted for it.

Personal Issues

In the fields of public administration and public policy, rational decision making is held out as the ideal. Decision makers are expected to weigh the costs and benefits of various policy options and make reasoned choices that maximize the gains to themselves, their constituents, or society as a whole, but personal preferences, relationships, irrational behaviors, and unanticipated events often influence political feasibility. In the case of the thimerosal legislation, for example, the chair of the Senate committee who sponsored the bill was the grandmother of a child with autism, and family members believed the autism was linked to an immunization the mother received when pregnant. Few analysts trying to assess the political feasibility of the environmental mercury legislation would have anticipated that its fate might be tied to a controversy around vaccine preservatives. In the case of the tobacco sampling bill, it was rumored that Representative

Grant's personal dislike of the bill's sponsor, Senator Oke, was one reason the bill never moved. Sympathy for Oke, who was terminally ill and wheelchair bound, may have contributed to the bill's eventual passage.

Sometimes a bill does not move because one party does not want the other to get the credit or because one house does not want the other house to have credit or because one member does not want another member to have credit. Committee chairs have been known to bottle up legislation in response to a sponsor's behavior before their committee.

Unexpected Events

An unanticipated event that many believe influenced the outcome of health legislation occurred in Washington State during the 2004 legislative session. Senator Rosa Franklin, an African-American Democrat, sponsored Senate Concurrent Resolution 8419, which established the Joint Select Committee on Health Disparities. Many observers doubted the resolution would pass because of a lack of enthusiasm among Republicans who held a majority in the Senate. As part of an unrelated discussion of health policy, however, the chair of the Senate Health and Long-Term Care Committee called the minority leader of the House Health Care Committee a "nigger in the woodpile." Both men are white Republicans. Franklin defended the Senate committee chair (although not his choice of words) and tearfully accepted his apology on the floor of the Senate. There was never any public discussion of a deal, but few political observers in the state capital were surprised when Franklin's resolution passed unanimously.

NONGOVERNMENTAL ACTORS

The Public

Politicians are constantly attempting to read the prevailing winds of public sentiment as they chart their policy courses. This is commendable up to a point. In a representative democracy such as the Unites States, elected officials presumably have some autonomy to pursue the policies and advance the values that got them elected without polling the electorate before every vote, but there is also an expectation that their actions will reflect the views of the majority of their constituents. At a baser level, focusing on public opinion can be about winning the next election, and subservience to public opinion polls can work against elected officials providing leadership, consistently pursuing long-term strategies, or taking necessary risks. It is telling that politicians often focus on determining and responding to the opinions of likely voters more than those of their entire constituency. This is relevant in the context of health care reform, where a significant number of the uninsured are socially disenfranchised and generally not a powerful voting bloc. Regardless, the opinion of the public as a whole can be highly influential in setting the policy agenda and determining outcomes.

Individuals can also make a difference. Politicians can be very sensitive to a small number of contacts from constituents expressing an opinion on an issue (they are less influenced by individuals they do not represent). The type of contact also matters. Elected officials are more likely to be influenced by a unique, personalized visit, telephone call, letter, or e-mail than by something obviously generated by an organized letter-writing or e-mail campaign. Furthermore, efforts to sway public opinion are often targeted to sets of individuals who are well informed and engaged in public issues. These are people who have a "big picture" view of the world and help form other peoples' opinions and can bring issues to the attention of the media and policy makers (Goddard, 1998).

Public opinion polls consistently show that at most points in time a majority of people in the United State favor health care reform. Historically, however, public support for major reforms has been "soft." The public can easily be talked out of supporting a reform through the use of carefully crafted messages. In 1993 and 1994, polls repeatedly showed that Americans supported universal access to health care. While the Clinton administration was working on its Health Security proposal, 79% of the country supported what it knew of the plan. In September, when Bill Clinton gave a televised speech formally unveiling the plan, support was at 59% (Blendon et al., 1995).

The Clinton team was well aware of the influence of public opinion. It organized a public relations campaign designed to carry a few clear messages directly to the public and bypass established Washington elites (Hacker, 1997). Public support continued, and even seemed to be growing as the Clinton plan moved forward, even though people seemed confused about exactly how the plan would work or what it would do. That supportive trend began to reverse itself in late 1993, about the same time that the Health Insurance Association of America begin running its famous Harry and Louise advertising campaign (Goldsteen et al., 2001). These ads were targeted at informed members of the public that could serve as opinion leaders (Goddard, 1998). By April 1994, only 43% of the country supported the proposal (Blendon et al., 1995). Schick (1995) argued that support was weak because most Americans already had health insurance they considered satisfactory, and they had concerns about the Clinton plan—that it might limit their choices, that it might increase costs of medical care, that it might limit the availability of some expensive services, and so forth.

One useful construct for understanding the vulnerability of public support for health reform is the notion of frames. The FrameWorks Institute defines a frame as, "The way a story is told—its selective use of particular values, symbols, metaphors, and messengers—which, in turn, triggers the shared and durable cultural models that people use to make sense of their world" (Gilliam, 2005). Essentially, people use predictable story elements to help them sort information; they respond to metaphors, plots, and values and other familiar aspects of the story. When communication is inadequate, says Gilliam, people rely on the pictures and stories already in their heads, but effective communication can allow them to see things from new and different perspectives. Health care reform efforts, if not understood, are subject to attack by arguing within certain frames and appealing to certain closely held values. For example, many Americans are skeptical about government and opposed to too much direct government involvement in their lives. Designers of the Harry and Louise ads conducted research that told them the public did not want a massive government program and tailored their campaign accordingly (Goddard, 1998). In other words, they told a story within a "big government" frame. According to Gilliam (2005), frames, or value-based messages, that move people toward supporting health care reform (i.e., increase political feasibility) include interdependence, the need for practical management, and the importance of prevention. They suggest that advocates of health reform promote the need for a health coverage infrastructure akin to a utility or transportation infrastructure. **Table 9-4** provides an example of the kind of language that might have framed the issue effectively.

Interest Groups

When individuals and corporations with common social and political goals join together in an organized way to try to influence policy in support of those goals, they compose an interest group. Weissert and Weissert (2002, p. 117) argued, "Next to Congress, interest groups may well be the most important actors in health policy." The use of the term *the third house* to refer collectively to the lobbyists that represent interest groups before the legislative branch is no misnomer.

TABLE 9-4   Sample Frame for Promoting a Health Coverage
Infrastructure

In the last 50 years, the United States has built a series of modern networks that are essential to our economy and our quality of life—our power grid, phone systems, water systems, interstate highways, and the Internet; however, with health coverage we are stuck in the 1940s because we never built a modern Health Coverage Infrastructure. Instead, we still have job-based insurance, which has become an increasingly hit-or-miss, inefficient, and unreliable approach. What we have is the equivalent of scattered wells, individual generators, and county roads but no Health Coverage Infrastructure we can rely on, no system for making sure that people have health coverage.

Source: © 2006 Frameworks Institute—Susan Bates and Frank Gilliam.

Interests groups do more than just attempt to sway votes in their favor; they can be critical partners with government actors in policy development from inception to implementation. They generate proposals, provide expertise that can improve others' proposals, offer channels for testing the feasibility of policy proposals with their members, broker deals, and help mobilize public opinion. After a policy is adopted, their support, apathy, or opposition can determine whether it succeeds or fails. Much of the legislation introduced by lawmakers is initially drafted by interest groups.

Interest groups also lobby the executive branch and may resort to lawsuits to assert their policies. Some narrowly focused industry or consumer groups work almost exclusively with regulatory agencies. Others, such as the Sierra Club Legal Defense Fund in the environmental policy arena, work almost exclusively through the courts.

Hundreds of interest groups are involved in health care issues. A majority of them represent either occupations or health-related companies. Major, long-standing examples of these, respectively, would include the American Medical Association (AMA) representing physicians and the American Hospital Association (AHA) representing health care facilities. The last few decades have witnessed a splintering and proliferation of these groups. Each medical specialty, for example, is likely to have its own professional association that engages in some form of political lobbying. Nurses, midlevel professionals, home health aides, and providers of alternative and complementary medicines also have their own groups. In addition to the AHA, there are associations representing smaller, more specific groupings of health care facilities, such as specialty hospitals, rural hospitals, and public hospitals, as well as associations of other types of facilities that provide care, such as long-term care facilities and adult family homes. Then there are the insurance companies and their associations and the manufacturers of pharmaceuticals, other health care technologies, and durable medical equipment. Because of our employer-based system for health insurance, associations of businesses and labor unions also lobby on health care. There are also several interest groups organized to represent consumers, specific subsets of consumers, and the uninsured. These include groups formed to combat a certain disease or class of diseases and to represent the interests of those afflicted. One of the most powerful consumer groups in the country, the AARP, represents people over 50 years of age and is a major player in discussions related to Medicare, retiree health benefits, and other health policy issues. Oliver (2006) stated that the proliferation of groups "has led scholars to conclude that political influence is more generally dispersed across loosely organized 'issue networks' or 'policy communities'" (p. 209).

For many years, a useful model for describing politics has been the *iron triangle,* involving congressional committees, interest groups, and bureaucrats. Together they shape policy. The iron triangle is still relevant today, but it is very limited in its ability to capture the evolving complexity of interest group politics. Interest groups now have multiple tools at their disposal for influencing policy, including the following:

- Political action committees: Fundraising committees that can make contributions to candidates, parties, or issue campaigns.
- Direct democracy: Sponsoring voter initiatives and referendums, hiring signature gatherers, and funding campaigns.
- Grassroots lobbying: Organizing the general public (or voters) to appeal directly to lawmakers or to make their positions known at the ballot box.
- Cross-lobbying: Convincing other groups to support a particular policy or change an existing position that runs counter to that policy.
- Coalition-building: Increasing political leverage by forming coalitions to work on a specific issues or policy, often for a limited time.
- Research: Conducting studies, compiling data, and producing reports that influence policy choices, often focusing on the evidence basis and economic and technological feasibility of policy options.
- Framing: Using public opinion research, message development and other communications techniques to "tell the story" about a policy in a way that changes the public discourse.

This modern era of lobbying, where interest groups are equipped with phone banks, voter rolls, and carefully honed messages, as well as lobbyists, prompted West and Francis (1995) to postulate a new kind of triangle— the *electronic triangle.* In this triangle, the three points represent legislators, lobbyists, and communications consultants.

The Media

The news media play a critical role in shaping policy debates and outcomes in this country. There are three principle ways media outlets exert their influence:

- Setting the frame: The news media tell stories to interest their readers and viewers, and the way those stories are organized helps to establish the frames that people use to interpret both the coverage and the underlying social issue. Media provide the context people use to help form opinions on an issue, and even a set of often subtle cues to guide them to their decision.
- Sorting and delivering data and information: Decision makers rely on data and information; however, their time is limited, and we live in an era of information overload. They are not able to sort and process all of the relevant information that emerges in a constant stream of studies, reports, and journal articles, and thus, they tend to rely on media to sort information and identify what is relevant. Opinion makers tend to rely on facts to shape their opinions or buttress them—facts they often gather as news media consumers. "You do not tell these people, 'Here's how you should think about an issue.' If you do, they'll turn you off," said Goddard (1998). "What you do is you give 'informed Americans' a set of facts."
- Setting the agenda: The role of the New York Times in promoting the Jackson Hole Group's managed competition model, which is described in **Case 9-1**, provides one of the clearest examples of how the media can set the political agenda.

Here is how Goddard (1998) explained the role the media plays in U.S. public opinion formation and agenda setting:

The media communicates with opinion leaders...about an issue. "Hey! Here's something that's important." So the opinion leaders pay attention and their opinion sort of filters down to the public.

Now this happens, but actually... it is the least important step in the process. What's really critical is that the opinions that "informed" Americans form after exposure to them are then communicated to policy makers. And all of a sudden the policy makers say, "Wait a minute! All these people out there who I count on for support are concerned about this issue." So then the policy makers tell the media, "Hey, there's an important issue here. Here's something that people are really concerned about." So the media communicates that to opinion leaders, who then express a stronger opinion to policy makers, who then tell them what their constituents are telling them, and the communication loop continues to cycle.

Scientists and Other Experts

The notion of rationality in decision making presupposes that there is sufficient information and resources to understand fully the implications of each policy alternative. Although this rarely occurs in practice, most policy makers try to understand what the research tells them about the value of various policy proposals. This gives researchers who generate data and informed analysis considerable influence over political feasibility.

Research and data can come from a variety of sources. Generally, the most credible sources are academic researchers who publish their findings in peer-reviewed journals. Policy makers also turn to raw data from primary sources (especially from government agencies) and to reports and studies from think tanks, advocacy groups, pharmaceutical firms, university centers with narrowly defined missions, and a variety of others sources whose work may reflect an ideological or financial bias.

The push toward evidence-based medicine has heightened the focus on making policy based on data, as government policy makers have realized that much of what they spend goes to pay for ineffective, unnecessary, or even dangerous care. The case study that follows Chapter 12 illustrates how North Carolina has refocused its mental health system on the delivery of evidenced-based interventions. It is becoming increasingly common for state governments to fund research centers that evaluate the comparative evidence basis for certain drugs and other medical technologies. Oliver and Singer (2006) found that research conducted by the California Health Benefits Review Program, which relies on university-based researchers to analyze the evidence-basis for requiring that health insurance plans cover certain types of care, has played a significant role in shaping legislative decision making around mandated benefits in that state.

METHODS FOR ANALYZING POLITICAL FEASIBILITY

Dror (1988) confessed that he has become skeptical about formal modeling. Almost by default, political feasibility prediction tends to rely on seeking out expert informants and asking them how key players are likely to respond to the policy or policy alternatives.

Identifying the actors by mapping the authorizing environment, as we did in the example earlier in this chapter, is often a key early step. A subsequent step would likely involve determining the amount of support or opposition that each actor is likely to generate, either by soliciting information from the actors themselves or from some other set of experts. One could also solicit the experts' opinion on how much influence each actor is likely to have over the outcome. It is important, as well, to identify other inputs likely to influence the outcome of a specific policy debate. This would involve asking a variety of questions, such as the following:

- Is the economy expanding or contracting? What is that likely to mean for government revenues? How expensive is the policy alternative?
- What other focusing events are likely to demand the attention of the public and decision makers?

It may be useful to tease apart the different factors that contribute to political feasibility. Kingdon (1984) has suggested that there are three streams to the policy process. He argued that change will be incremental unless these three streams converge favorably, typically as a result of a crisis that redefines a problem or a change in who controls the government, creating a window of opportunity. The three streams are:

- The problem stream: People need to agree there is a problem, their understanding needs to be supported by basic science, and they need to share a common definition of what the problem is.
- The policy stream: There need to be credible scientific, technological and/or policy solutions available.
- The political stream: The problem needs to be on the agenda and there needs to be political will to address it.

Another useful concept for thinking about political feasibility is force field analysis, a decision-making tool developed by psychologist Kurt Lewin that provides a way of examining the forces working for or against a particular decision. Lewin argued that issues were held in balance by driving forces (those promoting change) and restraining forces (those favoring the status quo). These included both strong and weak forces, as represented in **Figure 9-3**. As a decision-making tool, force field analysis is often represented with a chart. In a box in the middle is the decision, or in our case, the policy. On the left side is a set of arrows representing the forces for change, and on the right side is a set of arrows representing forces against change. In political feasibility analysis, those arrows would represent actors and inputs.

After you have identified the forces bearing on the policy, you can assign them a score from 1 (weak) to 5 (strong) and tally to create a combined score for the forces for and against.

In their analysis of the political feasibility of mandated health insurance benefits, Oliver and Singer (2006) used a framework that examines whether the costs and the benefits are concentrated among a few or diffused among many (see **Figure 9-4**).

The most politically feasible solutions are those involving "client politics" where there are strong advocates who would reap the concentrated benefits but little opposition because the costs are minor or are spread broadly among many interests or individuals. The least politically feasible

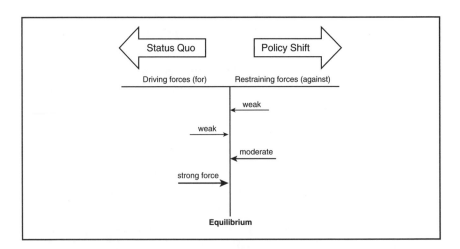

FIGURE 9-3   Force field analysis diagram.

Source: Based on Lewin (1951).

are those involving "entrepreneurial politics" where the benefits are shared so broadly that there are no impassioned, self-interested advocates and yet there is great opposition from interests that would bear the concentrated costs. Incrementalism, says Singer, is a natural byproduct of "interest group politics" that occurs when both benefits and costs are concentrated. "With clear winners and losers, the level of conflict is high and the outcome of any single proposal is highly unpredictable (2006, p. 211).

Dror proposed a framework for political feasibility analysis that relies on the Delphi method, which is described in Chapter 8. He recommended that prediction panels consist of senior executives, politicians, and political observers. "While politicians are the ideal panel members for political feasibility prediction studies, this itself may be politically and personally nonfeasible, especially if such studies become widespread. Therefore, main reliance may have to be put on politics-observing persons, such as political aides, political correspondents, political science scholars, senior civil servants, etc." (1969, pp. 12–13).

Dror suggested that panelists be asked to complete three different types of questionnaires. One form would ask the panelists to rate the probability

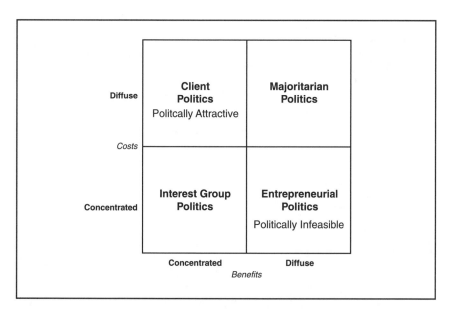

FIGURE 9-4   Framework for analysis of policy design and political feasibility.

that specific policy alternatives might be adopted across different timeframes (**Table 9-5**). Another would ask whether various alternatives were feasible within a specific timeframe and solicit information about barriers to adoption and what conditions would have to change to make adoption possible (**Table 9-6**). The third one would solicit opinions about the various actors— how much leverage they have, what are their intentions, and what actions they are likely to take alone or in combination with other actors. He also recommended that the informants be divided into three panels that get the surveys at different times. This would allow the coordinator to test for consistency. A number of researchers and analysts over the years have proposed or employed numerous variations on both the Delphi technique in general, and the framework proposed by Dror. Turoff (1970), for example, has proposed a variant technique call the Policy Delphi that can be used to identify the universe of policy options, estimate the impact and consequences of those options, and assess their acceptability.

The highly qualitative nature of such techniques makes their results subject to human error. Dror (1988) cautioned that "experts may easily be emotionally biased when hot political issues are touched upon and may be

TABLE 9-5   Scheme 1: Direct Political Feasibility Estimation

Policy Alternatives	Political Feasibility Estimate			
	Next X Years	Next Y Years	. . . .	Next N Years
Alternative 1				
Alternative 2				
. . . .				
Alternative N				

Each cell to be filled out with a probability, or probability distribution, or alternative probabilities with explicit assumptions—depending on the capacities of the predictor.

Source: Dror (1969). Used with permission.

overconservative in underestimating possibilities of changes and jumps in political situations" (p. 273). Oberlander (2003) pointed out that the headlines about health reform in 2003 were reminiscent of those that appeared in 1993 and 1973. The disturbing statistics and the comprehensive reform proposals designed to address them were eerily similar. The problem, he argued, is not a lack of good ideas but a consistent failure to realistically assess political feasibility. People confuse feasibility with desirability and tend to argue that their favorite solution is the most feasible, he stated, or they can be predisposed to accept a flawed feasibility analysis that supports their position. He added that a "beltway mentality" leads people to assume that whatever appears in the *Washington Post* or has caught the imagination of Washington insiders is most politically feasible.

Both Dror and Oberlander raised concerns about the use of political feasibility predictions. Dror pointed out that such predictions assume that no unexpected occurrences would take place—and they often do. Bill Clinton ran for president on a campaign built around a central premise: "It's the economy, stupid." The economic downturn that hit at the end of George H.W. Bush's term not only doomed his re-election bid, but it also produced

TABLE 9-6   Scheme 2: Political Feasibility Conditions

Policy Alternatives	Is politically feasible during next X years?	If not, what changes in conditions are required to make it politically feasible?
Alternative 1		
Alternative 2		
. . . .		
Alternative N		

Depending on interest and on capacities of the predictor, the scheme can deal with various time spans, different feasibility probabilities and probability changes, and various combinations of conditions and assumptions.

Source: Dror (1969). Used with permission.

a great deal of public anxiety about people losing their health insurance. That was in 1992, however. By the time Congress was seriously considering the Clinton Health Security Plan in late 1993 and early 1994, the economy had greatly improved, and the public was less inclined to see health insurance as an immediate crisis.

Something akin to the Heisenberg uncertainty principle of quantum physics also operates in the realm of feasibility prediction. Efforts to measure something can influence the thing being measured and change the measured result. Feasibility analyses can actively influence the outcome of a political debate—they can be self-fulfilling or conflicting analyses can cancel each other out. Oberlander (2003) stated that "feasibility analysis does not merely play a passive role in the political process as an objective judge of what will or can happen. Rather, policy analysis itself can influence the course of events and is often deployed as a political weapon." As an example, he pointed to the number of policy analysts that opponents of the Clinton health plan brought forward to explain why the plan was irredeemably flawed.

Dror (1969) cautioned that "care must be taken to avoid a mistake widespread in practice and sometimes supported by theory, that 'feasibility' becomes a dominant criterion of a preferable alternative, in the sense of 'the more feasible the better.'" He suggested that political feasibility analyses should be seen as challenges, not constraints. He writes that "every political feasibility prediction tends to ignore the capacities of human devotion and human efforts to overcome apparently insurmountable barriers and to achieve not only the improbable but the apparently impossible. A good policy may be worth fighting for, even if its political feasibility seems to be nill (sic), as devotion and skillful efforts may well overcome political barriers and snatch victory out of the mouth of political infeasibility" (pp. 18–19).

CONCLUSION

Policy analysts may tend to avoid political feasibility assessments because they are highly qualitative in nature and subject to a great deal of uncertainly. We have discussed how medicine has become increasingly industrialized, but politics will likely remain more of an art than an industry. To address political feasibility at all, an analyst must understand the authorizing environment, the key political actors, the various inputs into the political process, and how they are likely to interact. Techniques such as force field analysis, independent looks at the three streams of policy that can create windows of opportunity, and whether the benefits or costs of a policy are concentrated or diffuse can be useful. Systematic approaches to assessing political feasibility typically rely on surveys of experts. The Delphi technique provides a structure for such inquires. It is important, however, to select the right experts and to be aware of their biases and limitations. Finally, political feasibility analyses can become self-fulfilling prophecies if not used wisely. Analysts should be wary of abandoning good policy ideas because they seem unfeasible or settling on a poor idea because it would be an easy sell.

Case 9-1

THE POLITICS OF THE CLINTON HEALTH PLAN

BACKGROUND

A premature death helped set in motion the events that ultimately pushed health care reform to the fore of the U.S. political agenda in 1993, but it was not the early demise of a child whose insurance company refused life-saving treatment or the death of a heart attack victim turned away from the closest emergency room because of lack of insurance. The precipitating event was the April 4, 1991, plane cash that killed Henry John Heinz III, a Republican Senator from Pennsylvania. On November 5, Harris Wofford, the Democrat appointed to replace Heinz, won a special election to complete the term by upsetting frontrunner Richard Thornburgh with a campaign built almost entirely around health care reform. Politicians and pundits of all stripes quickly agreed: Major health care reform was just a matter of time.

Bill Clinton's election to the White House a year later reinforced that belief. Clinton recruited many of the campaign consultants who had advised Wofford, and he pledged during the campaign to reform health care reform. He set about delivering on his pledge within days of taking office.

On September 22, 1993, before Congress and a national TV audience, he outlined his plan to "fix a health care system that is badly broken." A little more than a year later, however, another unexpected death occurred. The deceased was President Clinton's plan for "Health Security." The plan's collapse doomed any hopes advocates had of passing significant health care reforms in 1990s and was credited by some with inducing the electoral tsunami that gave Republicans control of both houses of Congress in the 1994 elections.

BUILDING TOWARD REFORM

A confluence of events put health reform on the top of the agenda in the early 1990s, not just the bellwether Senate race. The Clinton-era reform effort was not a unique event but rather part of a chain of efforts that spanned much of the century. These efforts are described in Chapter 3. What seemed to set the 1990s apart, however, was the variety of stakeholders prepared to support some kind of reform. Most came to the table because of spiraling cost of health insurance and the growing number of uninsured.

- Businesses that covered their workers were spending as much as 25% of their earnings on health insurance.
- Organized labor was seeing business shift more and more of the costs of health care onto workers.
- Providers were frustrated by insurance companies managing their professional decisions and losses when patients did not pay up.
- Hospitals were concerned about the increases in uncompensated care.
- State governments had watched the share of their budgets going to health climb from 9% to 14% in the 1990s.
- Large insurers were concerned about small insurers siphoning off younger and healthier customers, leaving them to cover more high-risk populations.

Less certain going into the 1991 election was where the electorate, particularly the middle class, stood. As the sign at Clinton's campaign headquarters noted, "It's the economy, stupid." The United State was in the grips of a recession, and the middle class was worried—about unemployment, about medical bankruptcy, about jobs that offered no health insurance, or about insurance that required high out-of-pocket expenses or covered only catastrophic events. Wofford's and Clinton's elections had seemed to settle the issue—it seemed the electorate was prepared to support a major overhaul of the health care system.

THE MENU OF OPTIONS

Even before the 1991 and 1992 elections, several health care proposals were in the hopper. There were basically three concepts under consideration:

- Many congressional Democrats were pushing play-or-pay. Businesses that did not provide employee insurance would pay more in taxes, and government would use that money to provide health care to uncovered employees. There was concern that this strategy would lead businesses to decide to pay, not play, effectively creating a government health care system.
- Progressive Democrats were pushing for a single-payer system modeled on Canada's. Government would replace insurance companies, but would not run the health care delivery system itself. Under a variant, which Hacker (1997) referred to as "the liberal synthesis," the government would purchase universal capitated coverage from a mix of competing public and private insurance plans.
- Many congressional Republicans and President Bush supported various packages of market-oriented reforms that would regulate insurance company practices, provide tax credits or subsidies for people unable to afford insurance, offer tax incentives for business to cover

employees, establish industry-wide insurance purchasing pools, reform malpractice, and support expansion of managed care.

In the late 1980s, Alain Enthoven and Richard Kronick began developing their "managed competition" approach. Their first proposal included a pay-or-play system. People who could not obtain employer coverage could acquire coverage through a "public sponsor." Plans would have to offer standardized types of coverage and set premiums based on risk. Employers and the public sponsor would only pay a fixed percentage (they initially proposed 80%) of the cost of a plan that provided a basic set of standardized benefits. If employers or individuals wanted to purchase more comprehensive coverage, it would come out of their pockets. Tax reform would ensure that this additional money was not tax-exempt.

Enthoven and Kronick believed health care inflation was driven mostly by the fee-for-service system, which provided no incentive for providers to provide better health outcomes at lower costs. They were also concerned about the effects of risk selection on the health insurance affordability. They believed their plan would encourage people to purchase basic, lower cost plans appropriate to their level of actuarial risk and priced accordingly. They also believed it would drive people toward managed care plans.

Enthoven and Paul Ellwood invited health policy experts, government officials, and reform-minded executives of health care organizations and large health insurance companies to a meeting in Jackson Hole in February 1990. The group anticipated that government would play a greater role in regulating health care unless someone put forward a successful market-oriented proposal. They sought to reform the system while minimizing government regulation and used managed competition as a starting point.

The group met throughout 1990 and 1991 to refine ideas and seek consensus. Ellwood and health policy consultant

Lynn Etheridge drafted four papers that collectively articulated the Jackson Hole proposal. Much of the Enthoven-Kronick framework remained. An independent health board would certify health insurance plans and established the basic services those plans would cover. Employers would be required to provide coverage to their full-time employees. They would also pay a business tax to fund coverage for part-time employees. The public sponsor notion evolved into something called "health insurance purchasing cooperatives" (HIPCs)—regional organizations that would contract with certified insurance plans to purchase coverage for the employees of businesses with fewer than 100 employees and for people not covered through work or federal entitlement programs. HIPCs would subsidize coverage up to the cost of the least expensive plan. People who chose more expensive plans (or businesses that provided employees with additional coverage) would make up the difference. Only the cost of the least expensive plan would be tax deductible.

Although the Jackson Hole Group considered the proposal to be an academic exercise initially, Michael Weinstein at the *New York Times* picked up on the plan. The paper ran dozens of articles that mentioned "managed competition" and endorsed the Jackson Hole Group framework on its editorial page. Thus, when Wofford won his election in November, the idea had public legitimacy and was known to members of Congress and congressional staffers as a policy to champion. In particular, the idea attracted considerable interest from the conservative wing of the Democratic Party, although the Conservative Democratic Forum rejected the idea of an employer mandate.

During the 1992 presidential primary campaigns, many health care reform proposals emerged, including one by Paul Tsongas that emphasized managed competition. Clinton, a centrist with ties to the conservative wing of his party, promoted a play-or-pay strategy, but after winning the nomination began moving toward a plan that combined managed competition with regulatory reforms designed to drive down costs. He formally unveiled this plan at a September 24 speech delivered at the headquarters of Merck & Co., a major pharmaceutical company.

DEVELOPING THE CLINTON PROPOSAL

Clinton took office in January 1993, and for about the first eight months, his administration focused primarily on developing a budget that might grow the economy and reduce the deficit; however, he did try to deliver early on his promise to reform health care. Within days of his taking office, Ira Magaziner, an old family friend and business consultant, completed a work plan for an interagency health care task force that would oversee working groups charged with conducting analyses related to topics such as financing, economic impacts, controlling costs, and delivering preventive care. Acting on Magaziner's framework, Clinton established the President's Task Force on Health Care Reform, made up mostly of Cabinet members. Magaziner would coordinate the effort, but the chair would be the First Lady, Hillary Rodham Clinton.

A ballooning number of working groups set about defining their respective pieces of the elephant. Participants, mostly executive agency employees, numbered more than 500. As they identified preferred policy options, they then took them to the task force leaders for a protracted, sometimes days-long vetting process called "tollgates." The task force also held hearings to solicit input from stakeholder groups.

The task force's initial meetings were not open to the public or the press—a fact that prompted a *Washington Post* story saying that the private meetings violated the Federal Advisory Committee Act. The act is meant to prohibit committee members who are not part of the government from having undue and undisclosed influence over government policy making. It technically applied because Hillary Rodham Clinton did not draw a paycheck and was not a "government employee." On March 10, a judge ordered that all task force meetings be public. Critics of health care reform exploited the brouhaha. "It was a deft political move," Hillary Clinton wrote in her autobiography, "designed to disrupt our work on health care and to foster an impression with the public and the news media that we were conducting 'secret' meetings" (2003, p. 154).

In May, the task force handed a thick set of recommendations to the White House and disbanded. Work continued as small White House teams began the next phase, which included tasks such as converting the task force output into legislative language, working up budget projections, and developing political and communication strategies. Most of this work was done behind the scenes while the president focused his efforts, and the public's attention, on the budget. Very few decisions were put on paper and high-level meetings were avoided from the end of May through August.

It wasn't until September 7 that copies of a "Working Group Draft" went to key members of Congress and from there leaked to the public. Full bill language was not available until October—after Clinton's September 22 televised address to Congress.

THE HEALTH SECURITY PROPOSAL

Clinton's Health Security proposal owed a lot to the Jackson Hole Group, but also borrowed from existing proposals on both sides of the aisle. It relied on the employer-based system by mandating employer coverage. To help small businesses and those with low-wage employees, the government would offer subsidies. It would also provide payments to help the poor cover the costs of premiums and out-of-pocket expenses. The self-employed would be able to deduct their premium costs fully. Annual premium increases would be capped, but as a cost-control measure, this was a backup to the core of the Clintons' plan—the creation of regional "health alliances" much like the Jackson Hole Group's HIPCs. Under the oversight of a national health board, they would pool individual and business premiums and collectively bargain with insurance companies.

The proposal had to be revenue neutral, and thus, there had to be a way to offset the estimated $331 billion cost. Some of that money, according to the administration, could come from a cigarette tax and a 1% tax on corporations with more than 5,000 employees that did not participate in the regional alliances. Because health care costs would presumably go down, tax revenues would increase. Nearly $200 billion could be trimmed from Medicare and Medicaid budgets because of cost savings and decreasing caseload. Critics scoffed at the savings potential, pointing out that cutting Medicare and Medicaid would be politically difficult and arguing that increased coverage would lead to greater utilization of health care services, driving costs up, not down.

THE BEGINNING OF THE END

On October 27, the Clintons handed off their brainchild to the U.S. Congress. It suddenly had to compete for attention with more than twenty cousins. These included a single-payer bill supported by more than 200 liberal House Democrats, another version of managed competition supported by centrist Democrats that stopped short of an employer mandate and would not have limited premium increases, a Republican proposal that would have required individuals to purchase insurance and used resulting Medicaid savings to help low-income individuals and families pay their premiums, and another Republican proposal to introduce insurance industry reforms that would help chronically ill people obtain and retain health insurance and allow for the creation of health savings accounts (called *medisave* accounts).

Not only were there competing proposals, but there were competing fiefs. Health care as an issue did not belong exclusively to any one committee in either house. Arguably, five different committees had jurisdiction. Each committee and its chair had its own personality and its own perspective on the issue. The Clintons' plan quickly bogged down in jurisdictional disputes. Congress was becoming increasingly polarized and partisan, making it difficult to move any kind of major initiative. Breaking this gridlock would have required a coordinated, unified approach from the party leadership, but many Democrats were still drawn to the simplicity of a single payer. Many Republicans, meanwhile, were drawn to a strategy advanced most strongly by the Project for a Republican Future—refuse any temptation to compromise and defeat any Clinton proposal outright, at any costs. Democrats did not seem to have a clear strategy for moving the bill through the various committees without Republican cooperation.

As the Health Security proposal took a tedious, contentious, and messy path through committee hearings and markups, external stakeholder support, which had seemed so solid at the start, began to crumble. The plan's greatest nemeses proved to be the Health Insurance Association of America and the National Federation of Independent Business (NFIB), which vehemently opposed any employer mandate. In addition to lobbying policy makers, NFIB engaged in what Michael Weisskopf, a *Washington Post* reporter, labeled "cross lobbying"—targeting other stakeholder groups to change their positions. One of the first targets of cross lobbying was the AMA. The AMA had expressed several reservations about the Clinton plan, but had reversed its decades-long opposition to any employer mandate and was on record as supporting health system reform. At the urging of NFIB, the AMA House of Delegates voted December 7, 1993, to rescind its support for an employer mandate.

Big business also broke ranks. Medical inflation seemed to be slowing in late 1993, and President Clinton had failed to deliver on his promise to reduce domestic spending. In February 1994, the Business Roundtable endorsed a competing plan and the National Association of Manufacturers and the U.S. Chamber of Commerce followed quickly by repudiating the Clinton proposal.

That same month, the Congressional Budget Office announced that it could not support many of the budget assumptions the Clinton working groups had used to argue that the plan would help reduce the deficit. It would not even agree the plan was budget neutral. Instead, it argued the plan would add $74 billion to the deficit.

The White House, meanwhile, was losing ground in the court of public opinion. Polling immediately after the proposal went public was strongly favorable. A Harris Poll conducted in March 1993 found strong support for short-term price controls (76%), caps on premium increases (78%), an employer mandate (82%), and regional purchasing cooperatives (86%), but early polling also disclosed that people did not understand these concepts. Early response to the Clinton proposal released later that year was also favorable according to the polls, but some of the same surveys demonstrated that the public did not really understand what was being proposed in the highly complex 1,342-page draft legislation. The public also had some major concerns.

An ABC News/*Washington Post* poll conducted in early October 1993 found that 51% supported the Clinton Plan, and 59% thought that it was better than the current system; however, 57% opposed new taxes to pay for it. More people thought health care would get worse under the plan (34%) than thought health care would improve (19%). Many were worried about having less choice in providers (72%), increasing costs (70%), a loss of access to expensive services (69%), and a host of other issues.

These concerns gave the plan's opponents very effective points of leverage. In particular, HIAA focused in on them with its Harry and Louise campaign, which featured a worried couple discussing concerns about the plan. These campaigns made good use of polling information. The first advertisement focused on worries that health insurance plans would be less comprehensive and there would be fewer types of plans from which to choose. The couple concluded its conversation with the exchange, "They choose. We lose."

Congress struggled with the proposal through the first half of 1994, trying different solutions and searching for some kind of compromise that had a chance of success on the floor; however, none of the proposals appeared to have enough support to survive a filibuster. At one point, Republican Senator Phil Gramm announced that Congress needed to "stop carrying around this corpse, changing its clothes, and putting more powder on its face."

When Congress returned from summer recess, it was prepared to consider less-ambitious reforms. By this time, 57% of the public favored more incremental steps according to a *New York Times* poll published September 13, although 50% said the president should veto anything that did not cover everyone. Even modest reform bills were considered too risky by this point, as they could serve as stealth vehicles for comprehensive reforms, expanding at the last minute into some kind of universal coverage legislation. In late September, congressional leaders delivered a demand to President Clinton—if the president expected action on the General Tariffs and Trade Treaty, there could be no more discussion of health care legislation. On September 26, a year after Clinton said he would fix a broken system, Senate Majority Leader George Mitchell took health care reform off life support. The "corpse" was now officially dead.

DISCUSSION QUESTIONS

1. Theda Skocpol (1996) described two approaches that critics argue Bill Clinton should have used to develop his proposal: (1) Ask a small group to develop broad outlines for reform and then ask Congress to work out the details and (2) establish a prestigious blue-ribbon commission that might have achieved buy-in from business groups, congressional leaders and other policy makers, and stakeholders. What might be some of the pros and cons of the three different approaches? (The third was the Clinton approach.)

2. What would a map of Bill Clinton's authorizing environment for health care reform look like?

3. Discuss how the three streams of policy making identified by John Kingdon—policies, politics, and problems—opened a window of opportunity for health care reform in 1993 and what had changed in those streams by the time that window had closed in 1994.

4. What would a force field analysis of the Health Security plan look like?

5. Where would the Health Security proposal fall on the grid in Figure 9-4? What were some of the concentrated costs and benefits and to whom did they accrue? Now answer the same question of diffuse costs and benefits.

6. Who would you have surveyed if you were using the Delphi technique to analyze the political feasibility of the Clinton proposal at the time?

CHAPTER 10

The Policy Analysis Process — Evaluation — Economic Viability

The kinds of problems for which cost-effectiveness/cost–benefit analysis are needed are far too complicated to be solved in someone's head (Sloan 1995, p. 6).

Policy analysis usually involves the allocation of scarce resources, and thus, economic issues almost always enter into the decision process. This is true in both the public and private sectors. This chapter focuses on economic and financial aspects of health policy analysis. Together, these determine the economic viability of a proposed policy alternative, which likely turns on the following questions:

- How much will it cost?
- What value will we be getting for the money?
- How does that value compare with other alternatives under consideration?
- If it is something we want to do, how will we pay for it?

To address these questions, the analysis team needs to undertake the tasks outlined in **Figure 10-1**. The team also needs to consider the points of view or interests that the study must deal with in the analysis and in its report. This can be a tricky business because there is a fine line to walk between pleasing the "customer" and compromising the group's professional integrity. One

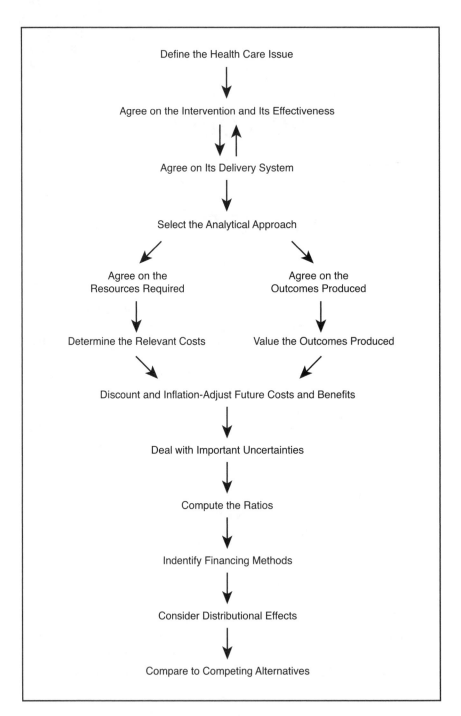

FIGURE 10-1   Steps in the CBA/CEA Process

way to address this is by "changing hats." The analysis can say, "When we put on Hat A, we get X, but we put on Hat B, we get Y." All of us wear many hats, including patient, payer, parent, spouse, professional, and citizen.

The team can then proceed to subsequent steps, the first of which is to define the health issue that is to be addressed, including population, diagnosis, incidence, and impact, and study the relevant intervention technologies. Then the group must agree on the effectiveness of the current and/or proposed interventions and, if necessary, conduct research to establish an acceptable range of effectiveness values for the analysis. These three steps have been discussed in earlier chapters.

DEFINING THE HEALTH CARE PROCESS INVOLVED

The team should follow a detailed process analysis to assure agreement on how the intervention is delivered. It is not always easy to define the process involved, especially if the intervention has not been implemented yet, but it is well worth the effort to visualize how the process will work and how the detailed implementation of the process will go forward. Otherwise, the team will be making a stab in the dark about the resources required.

The feedback arrow in Figure 10-1 indicates that sometimes the process analysis produces a revised estimate of the expected effectiveness as the team learns in more detail how the intervention is to be implemented. Many more feedback loops could be added to Figure 10-1 because at any point in time the team can uncover a need to go back and revise earlier estimates.

Agreeing on Its Effectiveness

Clear evidence on the effectiveness of a proposed policy is a rarity. Most evidence is contestable even as to its science. Clinical trials may be limited or in a few cases not even feasible. The populations involved in trials and demonstrations may have been small or somewhat different from the ones that will be affected by the policy. Often different professional groups, having differing interests, cite those studies that support their viewpoint and ignore those that do not. In the analysis of folic acid supplementation, reported in **Case 10-1**, those who favored it cited its effects on neural tube defects (NTDs), whereas those opposed cited its ability to mask other metabolic deficiencies. Where the evidence is unclear or disputed, one way to proceed is through sensitivity analysis. After an analysis is done using the efficacy estimate that the analysis team thinks most valid, the calculations are repeated with alternative efficacy values to determine the range of values over which the conclusion holds. Many times the conclusion is not affected despite the heat generated by the differing estimates, but where the solution is sensitive to the choice of high-end or low-end parameter values, it is necessary to make the decision makers aware of the applicable range. Perhaps they will authorize a study to narrow that range further. Sensitivity analysis is relevant to other variables besides efficacy, including costs, population affected, and inflation rates.

The relevant change in effectiveness associated with an intervention is the marginal change. For example, in 2005, the Washington State Legislature directed the Washington State Institute for Public Policy to report on the benefits and costs of "evidence-based" approaches to alcohol, drug, and mental illness treatment. The Institute performed a meta-analysis based on a review of 206 studies in the literature that met a specific set of criteria for quality of experimental design and measurement, such as use of a control group. This was an unusually complex analysis because the Legislature specifically mandated the study of the effects of treating individuals with substance abuse disorders and/or mental illness disorders in terms of their fiscal impact and "the long-run effects on statewide education, crime, child abuse and neglect, substance abuse, and economic outcomes." There were already systems in place for dealing with these disorders, and thus, the researchers calculated the benefits based on marginal changes in costs and outcomes from expanding the existing services to provide evidence-based and consensus-based services to those not yet served. Few mental illnesses are currently cured, and substance abusers have a high reoccurrence rate over time. The study team had to estimate the reduced incidence or severity from implementing best practices. They estimated the number in the state's population with each disorder and subtracted out the number already receiving services. Then they assumed that about 50% of the untreated populations would accept services, if they were made available. The analysts did not try to estimate the impact of having existing services move from their current modes of operation to the evidence-based approaches. Because the available studies were all short-term studies, the institute's staff estimated a "decay rate" for each disorder to represent the loss of participants and program impact over time and also included a factor in the modeling for those individuals who would recover on their own without treatment.

The institute's meta-analysis of the suitable studies concluded that the expansion of services would achieve a 15% to 22% reduction in incidence or severity of these disorders, resulting in a savings of $3.77 for each additional $1 invested. Taxpayers would see direct savings of $2.05 per additional $1 invested or $416 million per year in net payer benefits, if fully implemented (Aos et al., 2006).

AGREEING IN DETAIL ON THE DELIVERY SYSTEM INVOLVED

Analysis team members may have differing assumptions about how the intervention is to be delivered in the field. Reaching a common description of that process is often an important early team task. Discussing the process and drawing up a detailed process map are ways to get at that reality. It leads directly to a description of the resources required. It may be that after the process is better defined the team will have to revise their estimated effectiveness as they better understand the problems of implementing the process in the field.

SELECTING THE ANALYTICAL APPROACH

There are a number of types of economic analysis that can be performed (Rychlik, 2002; Max, 2004; Walley et al., 2004). Anyone who has had an economics course knows that an estimate is needed of the impact any proposal will have on the supply and demand for services, as payment, access, and quality issues affect the perceived price and demand for services as well as their costs. After the analysis of changing demand and supply is completed, then the team must decide whether to proceed to analyze the current proposal and/or the status quo ante or find another approach. Rychlik (2002) suggested a hierarchy of analytical approaches for comparison and decision making:

- Establish the cost (burden) of the illness usually including quality-of-life impacts of the problem.
- If the assessment shows little difference in impact from the relevant interventions or between the intervention and the status quo ante, conduct a cost-minimization study.
- If the comparison is among similar types of outcomes but there are significant differences in benefits and costs, conduct a cost-effectiveness study.

- If there are significant differences among the programs being considered, such that a common metric is necessary for benefits and costs, do a cost–benefit study.
- If quality of life after survival is an important parameter, then consider a cost utility study, in which differing quality measures are compared using market research techniques such as conjoint analysis.

Public agencies tend to focus on whether a proposed outlay is cost neutral or cost-effective. To be cost-neutral, the proposal must not increase the overall costs to the agency. To be cost-effective, the proposal must be the least costly method for reaching a predetermined level of total benefits to the public. In the medical literature, however, the term cost-effectiveness analysis (CEA) has acquired its own specialized meaning of an analysis in which the benefits are measured in nonmonetary units, such as lives saved or quality-adjusted life years (QALYs). Such economic approaches, however, do not allow for comparisons of proposals that express outcomes in different units. At higher policy levels, health care investments must be compared with other public investments, including those outside the health sector. When a common metric must be used to value both costs and benefits of the full set of proposals being analyzed, it almost always turns out to be dollars. This is known as cost–benefit analysis (CBA). Private sector organizations use the same techniques but often with a different set of terminology, using terms such as return on investment (ROI) and internal rate of return (IRR) to evaluate and compare investment opportunities.

Hacker (1997) suggested that concerns about health care as an economic marketplace emerged forcefully in the 1970s. This concern followed the introduction of Medicare and Medicaid and the resulting cost inflation. With the nation's access problems seemingly addressed, government and industry turned toward issues of efficiency and effectiveness. This concern for efficiency and effectiveness in the federal government went well beyond the health sector. The Bureau of Management and Budget issued Circular A-94, currently entitled Guidelines and Discount Rates for Benefit-Cost Analysis of Federal Programs, in 1972. It was and still is intended for use across most federal government agencies and programs.

BASIC TOOLS

The basic tools of economic analysis, including supply and demand analysis and benefit and cost analysis, are frequently bypassed by health care professionals because of measurement difficulties. These measurement problems pertain primarily to demand and benefit estimation, but also apply to costs. Analysts crossing over from other sectors will find some very specific problems in applying these methods in health care. They can expect to encounter lack of cooperation because of fear of loss of autonomy, accounting systems biased toward revenue rather than cost finding, high levels of inherent variability, compartmentalization of information systems, and poorly aligned reward systems. Effective cost analysis in health care also requires understanding the nomenclature and coding systems used in this sector. Furthermore, market failure in this industry makes it necessary to measure separately the consumer satisfaction and benefit/cost impacts of specific technological alternatives.

The role of benefit and cost analysis in health care was investigated thoroughly in the 1960s and 1970s (Baker et al., 1970; Bunker et al., 1979; Office of Technology Assessment, 1980; Weinstein & Stason, 1977). During that period, the problems of benefit measurement seemed so insurmountable that most health care professionals doing analysis have preferred to rely on CEA. Weinstein and Stason (1977) described the difference as follows:

> *The key distinction is that a benefit–cost analysis must value all outcomes in economic (e.g., dollar) terms, including lives or years of life and morbidity, whereas a cost-effectiveness analysis serves to place priorities on alternative expenditures without requiring that the dollar value of life and health be presented.*

The underlying premise of cost-effectiveness analysis in health problems is that, for any given level resources available, society (or the jurisdiction involved) wishes to maximize the total aggregate health benefits conferred. Alternatively, for a given health-benefit goal, the objective is to minimize the cost of achieving it. In either formulation, the analytical methodology is the same (p. 717).

The basic problem is not one of using dollars, however, but one of expressing all of the relevant factors in any single metric. The alternative approach is to express the outcomes as a vector, but because one alternative vector seldom dominates the others, one must still deal with tradeoffs among variables. Discussion of the vector representation is well beyond the scope of this book.

Further problems arise from the following:

- Determining the relevant costs, especially supply and demand estimation and resulting price levels

- Incorporating nonmonetary values
- Analyzing the way in which benefits and costs are distributed

Pauly (1995) suggested that CBA and CEA are used because the better normative measure, willingness to pay, is hard to assess in the real world. He defines a personal benefit as an informed individual's willingness to pay for a program, whereas a programmatic benefit is the sum of the willingness to pay of all informed persons affected by the program, including those making altruistic contributions but not directly affected by the service process. Willingness to pay can be imputed from what individuals are paying for insurance against an event or to mitigate the risk of an event, such as installing seat belts or highway crash barriers. "Such concepts as addition to measured gross national product associated with a health program, the additional wages to beneficiaries and providers, or additions from investment now and in the future have validity only to the extent that they proxy willingness to pay" (p. 103).

Whose Willingness to Pay?

A study to determine the need for a third London airport, as well as its location, found that a preferred location would displace a 12th Century Norman church that was still in use. One group contended that the willingness to pay valuation of the church should be based on the value the current parishioners were insuring the building for against fire. A second group, however, argued that the Normans had incurred an opportunity cost for the last eight centuries for the 100 pounds that they invested to build it. They had foregone the opportunity to loan the money to the local usurers at a reasonable rate of interest; therefore, the church should be valued at the willingness-to-pay of the original parishioners, which would lead to a valuation of 100 pounds plus compound interest for over 800 years. Using this calculation, it would be worth more than the construction cost of the entire new airport.

A proxy is something that stands in for the real thing. For example, in one analysis, the costs of the early loss of a mother because of breast cancer were estimated by the value of replacement family care services plus a proxy for the emotional losses. The proxy chosen for the latter was the estimated cost of the amount of psychotherapy used by those who lost a mother early in life (Bunker et al., 1979).

Pauly opposes two other approaches often cited in the literature: (1) the human capital approach, which emphasizes the economic cost to society, such as a worker's daily wage times the number of work days lost, or some other measure of lost productivity (assuming full employment), or (2) the friction cost approach, which measures the loss in productivity until the system resumes full productivity with a trained and experience new worker or the ill worker restored to full capacity.

Supply and Demand Concepts

Much of the health policy literature is concerned with how to align incentives properly through payment mechanisms, such as co-payments, withholds, discounts, and reimbursement rates. All of these really refer to changes in perceived prices and the effects these perceptions will have on the supply and demand for services. What really complicates health care is that some demand is generated by the consumer and some by the consumer's agents, especially health professionals.

The policy analysis team will have to estimate the impact of those perceived price changes on the activity levels that they can expect to see in the service system. These estimates are not easy, even where a program is budget constrained. Take, for example, the situation in which a program is budget constrained and a budget increase is proposed. **Figure 10-2** illustrates a simple demand analysis relating to a budget constraint.

Given: Initial Budget $= B_0 = C_0 \times Q_0$

Where initial cost $= C_0$, clients served $= Q_0$

Increased Budget $= B_1$, where $Q_1 > Q_0$ and $B_1 > B_0$

In **Figure 10-2A**, the new larger budget is fully consumed, but no cost change is assumed ($B_1 = C_0 \times Q_1$, where Demand $= D_0$ still is $> Q_1$).

In **Figure 10-2B**, the budget is increased to B_2, but this enhanced availability of services exceeds the demand (D_2) at the current perceived cost ($Q_1 > D_1 > Q_0$) and the budget is underexpended ($C_0 \times D_2 < B_2$).

In **Figure 10-2C**, the program management proposes responding by making the services more accessible (available more conveniently at more sites). This reduces the perceived cost of the service to the clients and the demand increases ($D_3 > D_2$), but at an added cost, which increases the average cost ($C_2 > C_0$). Given this situation, the program management and the policy analysts must make new estimates (C_2, D_3) and see whether the demand will be greater than, less than, or approximately equal to the new budgeted level of activity, which is B_3 divided by C_2. This will again determine the programmatic resources required.

Yes, this is complicated, but this is the way life goes.

If the prices charged are modified by a proposal, then the analyst must investigate supply and demand relationships further, including the following:

- The rate of change in demand with a given change in price (price elasticity)
- The rate of change in supply with a given change in price

Where data are available, these relationships can be estimated through regression analysis.

Benefit/Cost Concepts

Rational people do not spend resources voluntarily unless they are satisfied with the results. Where there are multiple choices, rational people will select one or more alternatives that maximize their satisfaction, or what economists would call their utility; however, our utilities are specific, if not unique, to each of us. Although individual utilities are cumbersome to capture, aggregating the utilities of a population presents far greater problems. Thus decisions that involve more than one person usually require a common measure. Most analyses are based on aggregating all of the costs and benefits to individuals regardless of what their utilities are and to whom or from whom they accrue. That is why so many studies end up choosing dollars, however, not all agree on that. Whatever the metric chosen, one ends up with a ratio of benefits to costs and the higher that ratio the better an alternative. In health care, however, we must also consider to whom these benefits and costs accrue.

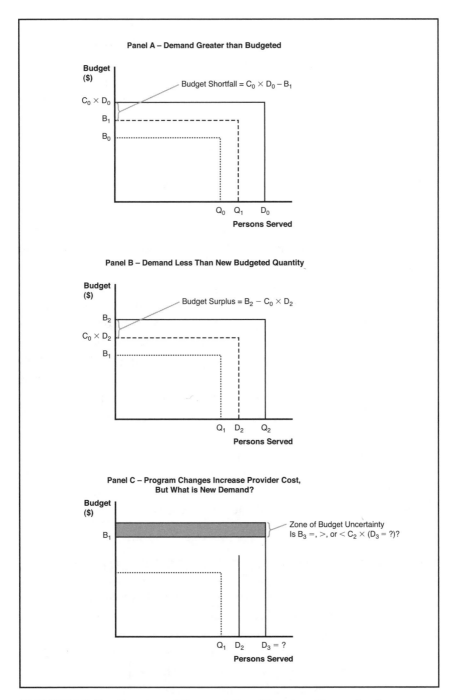

FIGURE 10-2   Supply and Demand Over Time in a Constrained
Budget Setting

Circular No. A-94 defines cost-effectiveness as "a systematic quantitative method for comparing costs of alternative means of achieving the same stream of benefits or a given objective."

In other words, the economist would say no to the request to "get me the most for the least money" because it is a mathematical impossibility. The two feasible formulations are as follows:

- Get me the most benefit for a given sum of money (i.e., maximize my benefit–cost ratio).
- Get me a given benefit package at least cost (i.e., minimize my cost-effectiveness ratio).

Analysts often retreat to the previously prepared position of trying to produce a set of benefits defined by the politicians at the least possible cost and labeling the results cost-effectiveness. That leaves the hardest part, the valuation of benefits, up to the political process. At higher government levels where the tradeoffs are between noncomparable benefits such as health care, highways, police protection, and recreational services, the only comparable means of comparison usually turns out to be money. The analyst has to be clear which is called for and be consistent in reporting the results. Pauly (1995) suggested that where money is used to measure benefits and (1) there is a fixed budget and (2) there is little variation in the preferences for outcomes, then use cost-effectiveness analysis, but where there is a variable budget and varying utilities of outcomes, cost-effectiveness is "much less suitable, in theory than cost-benefit analysis" (p. 111).

At this point, the analysis splits into two streams, as illustrated in Figure 10-1. One stream estimates the costs, whereas the other values the outcome. This chapter proceeds next with the cost side, simply because that is the easier path to consider.

AGREEING ON THE RESOURCES REQUIRED

All too often the analysis team starts by talking about monetary costs. This is the wrong place to start in a cost analysis. If one were trying to compute the costs of a wedding reception, one would not start with a dollar figure per guest, but with estimates of the number of guests, the menu for food and drink, the portions offered, the number of helpings per person, and the staffing needed. After these are defined, it is a simple matter to determine the costs by multiplying these resources by their market prices and totaling them up. That gives us an estimate of the total variable cost of the reception. Then there are the fixed costs of the reception such as the chef and hiring the hall; however, the kitchen staff only has a certain capacity, and if the guest list exceeds a certain number, the staff would have to be augmented; therefore, many fixed costs apply only over a specific program volume range. These are sometimes called step-variable costs or semifixed costs.

After we have the cost of our ideal menu and level of hospitality, it is time to figure out whether it falls within the acceptable budget range. Chances are it does not, and we would have to agree to spend more on the wedding than we had planned, cut some costs out of the reception, or cut down on some other aspect of the ceremony.

DETERMINING RELEVANT COSTS

Relevant costs are those affected by the decision being considered. There are two methods of estimating costs: aggregate costs and marginal costs. One arrives at aggregated costs by taking the total costs of an organizational unit and dividing it by the number of units produced. This figure is usually relatively easy to produce from existing departmental cost data, but using this method is not recommended. It does not take into account how processes and hence costs change with volume, nor does it include those relevant costs that occur outside of the given organizational unit. Relevant costing ignores those costs that are not affected by a decision, including those that are real but fixed. Relevant costs are referred to as incremental or marginal costs in the economics literature. For example, the comparison of two treatments for pneumonia would not include the costs of diagnostic tests unless different tests were to be ordered as part of each treatment regimen.

Relevant costs for the two treatments are likely to include the following:

- Changes in costs of medicines, consumable supplies, and tests caused by the introduction of the alternative method
- Changed labor costs, including physicians, nurses, and pharmacists and ancillary services
- Costs altered by the changes in length of stay or location of treatment
- Changes in costs incurred by the patient and the patient's family, including access costs and lost income, if any
- Changes in overhead costs associated with the new alternative including amortization of new specialized equipment and space requirements

Hospital costs represent an especially difficult problem because so many costs are lumped into the overhead cost categories and then allocated to the various operating departments. It is also hard to know what true costs are because published charges are so heavily discounted for federal and state governments, insurers, HMOs, and large employers.

A process-based cost study is usually a must in the hospital setting. Usual hospital cost reports are so loaded with fixed costs that it is necessary to map out the process and identify directly the resource inputs required and then price them.

AGREEING ON THE OUTCOMES PRODUCED

Earlier chapters dealt with the technological and political uncertainties of producing a desired outcome. The analysis team must decide how to deal with those uncertainties in its economic and financial analysis. Sometimes the uncertainty is handled with multiple analyses up front, a sort of branching in the analysis; however, the usual way of handling uncertainties is through sensitivity analysis in which the inputs of uncertain parameters are allowed to take on a realistic range of values to see whether the analysis is sensitive to that parameter and over what range. Where the value of the outcome is very sensitive to the value of a variable, the analyst is likely to show the outcome at both extremes of the range (and some values in between) and report those multiple values in the final staff report. Hopefully, the analysis staff will at last be able to agree on the range of effects that are realistic.

For example, in the Washington State study of evidence-based treatment of substance abuse and mental illness disorders, the Washington State Institute for Public Policy conducted a sensitivity analysis with many different parameters using a Monte Carlo simulation technique, in which a probability distribution was assigned to each range of values and the simulation model run 10,000 times with the values of each variable sampled randomly from its distribution. This process indicated that there was only a 1% probability that the investment would provide a negative return to the taxpayers. This was very important to the credibility of the analysis because so many of the measures and variables were so difficult to define and to measure (Aos et al., 2006).

Much of the value of a simulation would be to identify the interaction of various factors as a policy is implemented. For example, we have seen a number of governors prepared to assure access to health care for virtually all their state's population; however, very little has been said about what will happen to health care demand and supply and the resulting prices. Given what happened in 1965, this might well be a matter for concern. **Figure 10-3** illustrates one model that might be used to simulate the effects of increased access. As the demand increases so do the direct costs of services and the capital costs of providing the necessary delivery infrastructure, especially supplying sufficient primary care providers (PCPs), nurses, and community-based services; however, these changes will not take place in a vacuum. There are policy variables that can be manipulated to affect those costs, including the new covered service definitions, the management and organization of the new efforts, the amount of waste and medical error experienced, the financing and incentives of the program, and whether middlemen are used and what their margins will be. This again would seem to call for a simulation model to assess the overall impact of the planned interventions. The model is not revenue nor budget constrained, but that component could also be added. This model might start as a spreadsheet

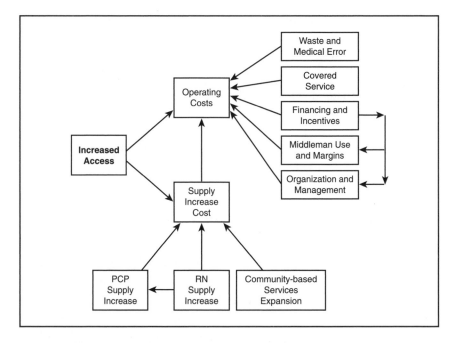

FIGURE 10-3   What Happens to Cost, If We Resolve the General
Access Problem

model, but be converted to a Monte Carlo simulation if one wanted to see how sensitive the model would be to uncertain values. What additional variables and/or feedback loops would you like to add? If there were many loops, a feedback type of model might be used. Certainly, the organization and management of services and the financing and incentives available would affect the capacity changes that might be needed.

VALUING THE OUTCOMES PRODUCED

One of the hard parts of health care policy analysis is valuing the benefits. We have already addressed the willingness-to-pay argument versus the use of utility metrics such as QALYs saved or deaths avoided. Most utility comparisons are based on psychometric instruments that can be used to compare and rank order alternative outcomes. QALY is one example of a utility measure. The quality of a life year is rated on a 0 to 1 scale, on which 0 is complete health and 1 is death. The attributes recognized in the comparisons included physical function limitations, social function limitations, emotional well-being, pain levels, and limitations on cognitive ability. Many intermediate states have been identified from wearing glasses to acute pain to physical incapacitation. Any one individual may have a quirky utility curve, such as "I would rather be dead than a vegetable," but the scale is based on the aggregate values of a representative population and not the individual. That is why people are urged to think about their own utilities and express them in a living will. There are many other scales for specific diseases and disease states, as the QALY may not be sensitive enough over the range experienced by that specialized population. The monetary value of a QALY varies considerably among medical interventions, as illustrated by **Table 10-1**.

Determining the Present Value of Costs and Outcomes

If we asked you for a $10 bill and paid it back tomorrow, you probably would be okay with that. If we requested $10 and said we will return it in five years, you probably would decline the honor. The value of money has a time dimension with two components: (1) will it have as much utility in the future or will inflation reduce its purchasing power and (2) there is a lost opportunity to create utility with it in the interim which is adjusted for by applying a discount rate. The discount rate may represent interest income forgone or what one would have to pay to borrow the money at

TABLE 10-1   Examples of Costs per Quality Adjusted Life Year Saved in Then-Current U.S. Dollars

Flu vaccine for the elderly[*]	< $0 (saves money)
Antihypertensive therapy (ages 45–64 years)[**]	$1,297
Hip replacement[**]	$1,628
Valve replacement for aortic stenosis[**]	$1,673
Cholesterol testing and treatment[**]	$2,042
Kidney transplant[**]	$6,500
Combination antiretroviral therapy for certain patients infection with HIV[*]	$10–20,000
Home hemodialysis[**]	$23,819
Varicella zoster vaccination against shingles for 60+[#]	$35,000
Maintaining hemoglobin targets of 11.0 to 12.0 g/Dl with intravenous erythropoietin in hemodialysis patients[##]	$50–60,000

Sources:

[*] Kiewra. K. (2004, Fall). "What price health?" *Harvard Public Health Review*. Retrieved April 30,2007 at http://www. hsph.harvard.edu/review/review_fall_04/risk_whatprice.html.

[**] Schechter, M. (2001) Retrieved May 10, 2006, from http://www.fda.gov/OHRMS/DOCKETS/AC/01/slides3678sl_03-schechter.ppt

[#] Messonnier, M.L. & Zhou, F. (n.d., 2006 or later). Review of economic studies of varicella zoster vaccine. Retrieved April 30, 2007 at http://www.cdc.gov/nip/ACIP/slides/Oct6/01_Herpes_Zoster/zoster_3-messonnier.pdf

[##] Tonelli, M., Winkelmayer, W.C., Jindal, K.K., Owen, W.F., Jr. & Manns, B.J. (2003). The cost-effectiveness of maintaining higher hemoglobin targets with erythropoietin in hemodialysis patients. *Kidney International*, 64, 295–304.

interest to operate until the payoff takes place. Economists argue not over whether the time value of money should be recognized, but over the appropriate rates to use; however, there are legitimate concerns about how inflation adjusting and discounting tends to devalue programs such as preventive care that pay off a ways into the future.

Inflation Adjusting

A constant inflation rate produces a cumulative geometric increase in costs. Over time, analyses can be very sensitive to the inflation effect, especially in health care, where overall inflation rates are high; however, the inflation rate in health care costs reported in the popular literature is the result of a number of factors, including the following:

- Input prices for labor and purchased goods
- Increasing technological opportunities, including pharmaceuticals
- Aging of the population

The costs of a given program, however, are not necessarily subject to all of these factors, and thus, one has to be careful in the selection of an appropriate rate. Because the population is defined and the technology is assumed to be fixed for comparative purposes, the appropriate inflation rate for an analysis is usually the first item, the input prices for labor, and purchased goods. A reasonable lower bound on this rate is the consumer price index (CPI), but because health care is a labor-intensive professional service that does not usually exhibit the same productivity improvements as much of the rest of the economy, the appropriate rate is somewhat higher than the CPI. Available indices applicable to components of an analysis include Producer Price Indices for specific segments and medical care CPI price deflators. Newhouse (2001) estimated that historically the inflation in health care costs as has been about 2% above the overall CPI. He also noted that the available indices may be biased on the high side, in part because of the lack of reliable data on real transaction prices rather than charge data. For example, the Producer Price Index for pharmaceutical preparation manufacturing was as follows:

1995	253.9	2001	314.5
1996	259.1	2002	326.7
1997	290.1	2003	343.3
1998	298.5	2004	360.1
1999	306.6	2005	378.7

To determine a rate of change from raw data use this formula:

1. Decide on the number of years in the interval (try 5 and 10).
2. Divide the ending index by the initial one.
   5 years $378.7 \div 306.6 = 1.235$
   10 years $378.7 \div 253.9 = 1.492$
3. Set the number of years equal to N, and take the Nth root of the appropriate value above.
   5 years $(1.235)^{(1/5)} = 1.0431$ meaning a 4.3% inflation rate
   10 years $(1.492)^{(1/10)} = 1.0408$ meaning a 4.1% inflation rate

If one were looking at the prices charged by pharmaceutical manufacturers, the forecast of prices would grow at whatever rate you thought appropriate. If you chose 4.2% over a 5-year period, then the price of drugs now at $200 would be calculated in the fifth year to be $200 times 1.042^5 or $245.68. This is based on a mixture of products, some of which might be going up rapidly, whereas others become generic and go down markedly.

Discounting

The same mathematics applies to discounting, except that the values of future benefits and costs are reduced to a net present value (NPV). Each stream of both costs and benefits needs to be brought back to a current value using the formula:

$$\text{NPV } (V_t, N, r) = V_0 + \frac{V}{(1+r)} + \frac{V_2}{(1+r)^2} + \frac{V_3}{(1+r)^3} + \ldots + \frac{V_N}{(1+r)^N}$$

where V_t = the value of the cost or benefit in time period t, N = the number of periods in the series, and r = the discount rate to be used.

These values can be calculated directly using a spreadsheet model or function or calculated using the discount factors from a NPV table similar to the one in **Table 10-2**. For example, if the annual benefit received from a program is $10,000 and the discount rate chosen is 6%, then the NPV of benefits received over five years would be worth $42,124 (NPV = $10,000 × 4.2124).

An Example

If a proposed program were to cost $100,000, but yield a stream of benefits annually starting at the end of five years for five more years, we have the following calculations to make to arrive at a NPV using a 4% discount rate.

Investment at the beginning of Year 1 of $100,000.

Benefits

Year 6	$40,000	NPV = (40000) ÷ $[1 + .04]^6$	=	$31,612.58
Year 7	$40,000	NPV = (40000) ÷ $[1 + .04]^7$	=	$30,396.71
Year 8	$40,000	NPV = (40000) ÷ $[1 + .04]^8$	=	$29,227.61
Year 9	$40,000	NPV = (40000) ÷ $[1 + .04]^9$	=	$28,103.47
Year 10	$40,000	NPV = (40000) ÷ $[1 + .04]^{10}$	=	$27,022.57

Total Benefit $146,362.97

The same result can also be calculated assuming a 10-year stream of benefits from which the initial five years of the stream has been subtracted. Using **Table 10-2**, we would then calculate the following:

$$
\begin{aligned}
\text{NPV} &= 10 \text{ year stream} - 5 \text{ year stream} \\
&= \$40{,}000 \times (8.1109 - 4.4518) \\
&= \$146{,}363
\end{aligned}
$$

Computing Ratios

Ratios are easy to compute. In the previous example, the NPV of the investment is $100,000, and of the benefits it is $146,363; thus, the benefit–cost ratio is (146363 ÷ 100000) or 1.46. This would be a comparison figure to rank order with other social or corporate investments. Each investment would then be subjected to other comparative evaluations or perhaps a minimum target IRR. IRR is the discount rate at which the benefits and the costs equal each other (i.e., the rate that brings the NPV to 0). In the previous example, the IRR is 9.155%. This rate can then be compared with the cost of capital and/or financing the investment. It must also be evaluated in terms of the uncertainty of the values used, the distributional impact on various actors and bystanders, the impact on other programs, especially in terms of budgets available, and financial viability.

DEALING WITH IMPORTANT UNCERTAINTIES

There are three approaches one might use to deal with important uncertainties in the financial analysis:

- Adding a risk premium to the discount rates used for uncertain parts of the calculations. This means that different streams of costs and benefits will be adjusted at different rates because they will have different uncertainties associated with them.
- Developing a subjective probability distribution for those values and applying that distribution to the modeling process. If there is a 60% chance that a program will cost $100,000, a 30% change that it will

TABLE 10-2   Present Value of a Dollar Received in Year N
at Discount Rate r

N r = 0.03	0.04	0.05	0.06	0.07	0.08	0.09	0.10
1 0.97087	0.96154	0.95238	0.9434	0.93458	0.92593	0.91743	0.90909
2 0.9426	0.92456	0.90703	0.89	0.87344	0.85734	0.84168	0.82645
3 0.91514	0.889	0.86384	0.83962	0.8163	0.79383	0.77218	0.75131
4 0.88849	0.8548	0.8227	0.79209	0.7629	0.73503	0.70843	0.68301
5 0.86261	0.82193	0.78353	0.74726	0.71299	0.68058	0.64993	0.62092
6 0.83748	0.79031	0.74622	0.70496	0.66634	0.63017	0.59627	0.56447
7 0.81309	0.75992	0.71068	0.66506	0.62275	0.58349	0.54703	0.51316
8 0.78941	0.73069	0.67684	0.62741	0.58201	0.54027	0.50187	0.46651
9 0.76642	0.70259	0.64461	0.5919	0.54393	0.50025	0.46043	0.4241
10 0.74409	0.67556	0.61391	0.55839	0.50835	0.46319	0.42241	0.38554
11 0.72242	0.64958	0.58468	0.52679	0.47509	0.42888	0.38753	0.35049
12 0.70138	0.6246	0.55684	0.49697	0.44401	0.39711	0.35553	0.31863
13 0.68095	0.60057	0.53032	0.46884	0.41496	0.3677	0.32618	0.28966
14 0.66112	0.57748	0.50507	0.4423	0.38782	0.34046	0.29925	0.26333
15 0.64186	0.55526	0.48102	0.41727	0.36245	0.31524	0.27454	0.23939

Cumulative Present Value of a Dollar Received Annually for N Years
Discounted at Rate r

N r = 0.03	0.04	0.05	0.06	0.07	0.08	0.09	0.10
1 0.97087	0.96154	0.95238	0.9434	0.93458	0.92593	0.91743	0.90909
2 1.91347	1.88609	1.85941	1.83339	1.80802	1.78326	1.75911	1.73554
3 2.82861	2.77509	2.72325	2.67301	2.62432	2.5771	2.53129	2.48685
4 3.7171	3.6299	3.54595	3.46511	3.38721	3.31213	3.23972	3.16987
5 4.57971	4.45182	4.32948	4.21236	4.1002	3.99271	3.88965	3.79079
6 5.41719	5.24214	5.07569	4.91732	4.76654	4.62288	4.48592	4.35526
7 6.23028	6.00205	5.78637	5.58238	5.38929	5.20637	5.03295	4.86842
8 7.01969	6.73274	6.46321	6.20979	5.9713	5.74664	5.53482	5.33493
9 7.78611	7.43533	7.10782	6.80169	6.51523	6.24689	5.99525	5.75902
10 8.5302	8.1109	7.72173	7.36009	7.02358	6.71008	6.41766	6.14457
11 9.25262	8.76048	8.30641	7.88687	7.49867	7.13896	6.80519	6.49506
12 9.954	9.38507	8.86325	8.38384	7.94269	7.53608	7.16073	6.81369
13 10.635	9.98565	9.39357	8.85268	8.35765	7.90378	7.4869	7.10336
14 11.2961	10.5631	9.89864	9.29498	8.74547	8.24424	7.78615	7.36669
15 11.9379	11.1184	10.3797	9.71225	9.10791	8.55948	8.06069	7.60608

cost $110,000, and a 10% chance that it will cost $90,000, the expected value would be:

([100,000 × 0.6] + [110,000 × 0.3] + [90,000 × 0.1]) = $102,000
and could be substituted for the $100,000 value to adjust for uncertainty in costs

• Investing in further research to reduce the uncertainty. For example, one could refine the cost estimate until one was relatively certain that $100,000 was the proper mean estimate of the cost and then use that.

IDENTIFYING FINANCING METHODS

One has to consider where the money for the investment is coming from, even if it is offset later by benefits. Those benefits may or may not result in offsetting cash flows into the organization. For example, money spent on smoking cessation programs by a state government would ultimately reduce the costs of its Medicaid program, but much of the benefit accrues to the federal government, to insurers, and to individual citizens; thus, there must be a budgetary source of funding specifically for the advertising campaign. For this reason, one is unlikely to spend most of the available budget on one program with a highly favorable ratio because it would crowd out other meritorious programs and threaten the organizational and political coalitions that make a budget viable. To match the acceptable share of available funds better, any very large program investment is likely to seek multiple sources of funding or spread out the investment over multiple budget cycles.

CONSIDERING DISTRIBUTIONAL EFFECTS

One of the major problems in evaluating health policies is that financial decisions affect both actors and nonactors. There are issues of free riders and moral hazards associated with some alternatives. There also are impacts on provider income, payer cash flows, and patient cash flows. In a financial sense, every proposal can be considered a zero-sum game in which there are winners and losers under our current set of incentive systems. Professionals are usually paid more for doing more. Vulnerable patients often end up paying more than those strong enough to monitor their own care. The health policy analyst must be very astute about how to "follow the money" without being too cynical and attributing all motivation to greed. We will revisit distributional issues in later chapters.

COMPARING WITH COMPETING ALTERNATIVES

The ratios that we have been studying (benefit–cost and cost-effectiveness) have little meaning in and of themselves. They are useful only in comparison with either a minimum standard value or in terms of rank ordering a set of alternatives. Sometimes a set of subcategories are used, such as these:

- Absolutely necessary because of the regulation or risk to the patients
- High priority in terms of meeting overall organizational goals
- Medium priority
- Low priority.

Where there are subcategories, the ratios may be used to rank order the alternative investments within each category. The priorities may be one way to work in some of the political pressures in what would otherwise be a relatively robotic ranking system.

FINANCIAL FEASIBILITY

An organization's financial system must be up to the tasks of evaluating an alternative's costs and forecasting the financial implications of various funding alternatives. Cleverley and Cameron (2003) suggested three major target areas of financial strategic planning for health organizations:

1. Revenue estimation
2. Capital budgeting (more of a concern for organizations that pay income tax)
3. Financing of operations and capital investments

To this we would add cash flow estimation.

They expand on these by suggesting that the underlying financial systems must:

- Provide data on revenue, costs, and capital requirements according to program or product lines
- Adjust these estimates for inflation and increasing technology requirements

- Supply ROI or IRR estimates for decision making. (The mathematics of these calculations is identical with the discounted cash flow calculations discussed previously here.)
- Estimate working capital and cash reserve requirements under expected operating conditions
- Establish the desired capital structure and the resulting debt capacity of the organization
- Provide procedures for the allocation of capital among competing internal programs and facilities

The first three steps are the same in both the public and private sectors. The last two are especially important to organizations and companies operating in the private sector. Even governmental programs that are separately funded like Medicare have to estimate flows and reserves. The actuaries at the Center for Medicare and Medicaid Services are the ones who keep telling us when the Medicare trust funds will run out.

It is important to recognize that different parts of the organization may disagree on the value of an activity, such as reducing the length of stay, depending on whether they are looking at full costs or marginal costs, whether they consider the organization to be at capacity or below it, and how the reimbursement system operates (Ward et al., 2006). In response to this concern, Voluntary Hospitals of America has developed a template for evaluating the cost, revenue, and cash flow impacts of various proposals. It is illustrated in **Figure 10-4**, which analyzes a proposal to improve hospital laboratory turnaround times, thus reducing the overall average length of stay by 0.1 days. It then proceeds to evaluate three types of costs. The costs of the project, the cash flow impacts of the cost reduction, and the cash flow impacts of the new patients that can be accommodated in the freed-up beds (called backfill).

Capital Allocation Processes

The last item, capital allocations, is one place were it is likely that facilities and services available to the poor and the uninsured are likely to be short-changed over time as large multisite health care organizations seek to maintain reasonable payer mixes and returns on their investments (Hurley et al., 2005; Robinson & Dratler, 2006). The use of analytical techniques to estimate rates of return over time is unlikely to lead to expansion of services for those who can pay little or nothing.

Costs of Process Improvement		
Salaries	$	(100,000)
Fringe Benefits	$	(100,000)
Supplies & Services	$	(20,000)
Other	$	-
Costs of Process Improvement	$	(220,000)

Cash Flow Impact of the Improvement				
Changes in Net Revenue Associated with				
Case based reimbursement	$	-		
Per Diem reimbursement	$	(96,000)		
Percentage of Charges reimbursement	$	-		
Medical Device Revenue	$	-		
(Revenue = device cost and markup)				
Drug Revenue	$	(10,000)	$	(106,000)
(Revenue = drug cost and markup)				
Changes in Operating Cost Associated with				
Supply costs driven by changes in patient days	$	15,000		
Medical device changes	$	-		
Medication substitution	$	25,000	$	40,000
The Cash Flow Impact of the Improvement			$	(66,000)

Backfill Cash Flow Estimate				
Incremental Net Revenue Associated with Backfill				
Case based reimbursement	$	243,902		
Per Diem reimbursement	$	96,000		
Percentage of Charges reimbursement	$	48,780	$	388,683
Medical Device Revenue	$	-		
(Revenue = device cost and markup)				
Drug Revenue	$	10,000	$	398,683
(Revenue = drug cost and markup)				
Incremental Operating Costs Associated with Backfill				
Incremental supplies	$	(15,000)		
Medications	$	(25,000)		
Medical Devices	$	-	$	(40,000)
The Cash Flow Impact of Potential Case Backfill			$	348,683

Backfill Cash Flow Estimate				
Cost of Process Improvement	$	(220,000)		
Cash Flow Impact of the Improvement	$	(66,000)		
Net Cash Flow Improvement Exclusive of Potential Case Backfill			$	(286,000)
Cash Flow Impact of Potential Case Backfill			$	348,683
Total Cash Flow Impact from Process Improvement Initiative			$	62,683

FIGURE 10-4   VHA Cash Flow Analysis Template

Source: "Faster Labs: Process Improvement Initiative Cash Flow" spreadsheet from the Financial tab of "Building the Business Case for Clinical Quality". © 2006 VHA. All rights reserved.

CONCLUSION

Decision makers need to know what a program will cost, what revenue, if any, it will generate, and how and by whom the balance will be financed. Cash flow management is also important, even if it is not usually considered part of health policy analysis. Comparative tools such as benefit–cost analysis and CEA are basic tools of policy analysis, but they present a number of ethical and value-based concerns that also have to be considered. They are critical to the budget approval process and to gaining top level support of one's proposals. Smaller organizations also have to worry about the sources of working capital necessary to undertake and sustain both current and higher levels of activity. Although some may see financial viability analysis as "the dark side" of policy analysis, competency in that area is a must.

Case 10-1

THE FOLIC ACID FORTIFICATION DECISION: BEFORE AND AFTER

BEFORE

At 5 PM on July 20, 1991, Dr. Godfrey P. Oakley, Jr., head of the Division of Birth Defects and Developmental Disabilities at the Centers for Disease Control and Prevention (CDC), took a phone call that, he says, "forever changed my life." On the phone was a member of the British Medical Research Council (MRC) Vitamin Study Group, calling to share study results that would be published the following month in *The Lancet* (SerVaas & Perry, 1999).

The MRC study, as it became known, focused on women who had previously had a pregnancy in which the fetus or child had a neural tube defect (NTD), a birth defect of the spinal cord or brain. In April 1991, the MRC halted its study after almost eight years because the data indicated that daily folic acid supplementation before pregnancy and during early pregnancy resulted in a 71% reduction in the recurrence of NTDs (CDC, 1991). It was no longer ethical not to provide folic acid to all of the women.

"Until that time," Dr. Oakley told the Saturday Evening Post Society in 1999, "I thought that prevention of neural tube defects by taking folic acid supplementation was certainly no better than 50–50. If you really pressed me on what I would have thought the likelihood that a vitamin would have prevented neural tube defects, I would have said no more than 10% or 20%. But this was the first randomized, controlled trial designed and executed in a way that it proved folic acid would prevent spina bifida—not all of it but most of it. You could bet the farm that folic acid prevents neural tube defects" (SerVaas & Perry, 1999, p. 3).

The study ignited a policy debate that would continue for several years. In the United States, the question of how to increase folic acid consumption in woman of child-bearing years was contentious in itself, but the issue was complicated further by the controversy that surrounded implementation of the Nutrition Labeling and Education Act (NLEA) of 1990, which required the Food and Drug Administration (FDA) to regulate the health claims of food manufacturers.

Among the tools policy makers had to help them sift through their options were three economic analyses: two cost–benefit analyses produced in 1993 and 1995 and a CEA completed in 1996. All three predicted positive net economic benefits from fortifying foods with folic acid.

TECHNICAL BACKGROUND

NTDs are a class of birth defects that involve the brain and spinal cord. The most extreme form is anencephaly, in which all or part of the brain is missing. Another form is spina bifida, in which the spinal cord is not fully encased in the spine. In the early 1990s, there were typically about 4,000 NTD-associated pregnancies per year in the United States.

Folates are a form of B vitamin that occurs naturally in leafy vegetable, legumes, nuts, and other foods. Folic acid is its synthetic form. Folates help cells replicate quickly.

Reports that increased folic acid intake could help prevent birth defects date back to 1965 (Hibbard & Smithells, 1965). Vitamin manufacturers learned how to add it to their supplements in the 1970s. The Saturday Evening Post Society launched its campaign to promote folic acid supplementation in October 1982 in the wake of a report that women who took a vitamin supplement with 400 mg of folic acid experience fewer NTD-affected pregnancies. In the late 1980s, the CDC held a workshop to discuss emerging research linking folic acids to reductions in the numbers of NTDs which renewed interest among supplement manufacturers.

Support for folic acid was limited, however; Post writers Cory SerVaas and Pat Perry (1999) reported that they were ridiculed for their efforts. Scientific evidence was sparse, inconclusive, and based on observational epidemiological studies. Around the time of the CDC workshop, in fact, the National Research Council advised the U.S. FDA that it should lower the recommended daily allowance. A 1990 report by the Institute of Medicine's Food and Nutrition Board called taking vitamin supplements to prevent NTDs "unjustified." The National Academy of Sciences also discounted the link between NTDs and folic acid in its 1990 *Report on Nutrition and Pregnancy.*

In the midst of this debate, the NLEA skated through Congress and was signed by President Bush. The act directed the FDA to establish standards for nutrition labels and define how certain terms such as "low fat" and "low cholesterol" could be used on food packaging. Congress also directed the FDA to investigate 10 specific health claims and develop language food manufacturers could use to convey any valid claims on their packaging. One of those claims, to the surprise of many, was that folic acid reduced the risk of neural tube defects. The FDA was hard at work on its proposed rules when *The Lancet* published the MRC study (MRC Vitamin Study Research Group, 1991).

The MRC study involved more than a thousand women in 33 centers across 17 countries. Researchers divided the subjects into four groups. Those in the first group received 400 mg of folic acid. Those in the second group received the same amount of folic acid plus a multivitamin supplement. Those in the third group received neither the multivitamin supplement nor folic acid, and those in the final group received only the multivitamins. NTDs recurred 1% of the time when mothers received folic acid, with or without other vitamins, and 3.5% of the time when they received nothing or only the multivitamin supplement.

The MRC study did not settle the debate. It studied women who had already had an NTD-associated pregnancy and therefore might be predisposed to having another, and thus, the results were not necessarily applicable to the general population. An FDA-contracted study released in November 1991 said that it was not possible to positively conclude that folic acid prevented NTDs, but it criticized the Institute of Medicine and National Academy of Sciences reports. The FDA draft rules issued later that month rejected claims that high-folate foods prevented NTDs, but it called its conclusion "tentative" and left open the possibility of further review.

The CDC, however, was less equivocal. At a conference on "Vitamins, Spina bifida, and Anencephaly" that same year, participants had generally accepted the notion that women who were pregnant or might become pregnant required more folic acid. They began to wrestle with what FDA Commissioner David Kessler would call "one of the most difficult issues" of his tenure—exactly how to go about providing that folic acid.

ALTERNATIVES

There were only a few ways to ingest more folic acid at the time: consume more foods naturally high in folates, take vitamin supplements, take folic acid pills, or eat fortified foods. Each option brought its own challenges. Working against the natural nutritionists was the fact that natural folates have lower bioavailability than folic acid and break down during cooking. A typical U.S. woman ingests only 25 mg of naturally occurring folates daily, and thus, it was hard to envision women ingesting 400 mg through dietary changes.

Folic acid by itself was only available in a 100-mg prescription formulation. The level of folic acid in most multivitamin supplements was so low that a woman trying to hit the 400-mg target would have to ingest toxic levels of other vitamins. One option was to make folic acid more readily available in larger doses. Another was to reformulate multivitamins. Both of these options suffered from the same problem. To be effective, folic acid had to be taken before pregnancy and during the first few weeks after conception. Yet roughly half of all pregnancies occur without early prenatal care. You would have to convince all women to take pills to supplement their folic acid intake throughout their childbearing years or risk missing more than half the pregnancies.

That left the possibility of fortification (adding a nutrient to food that does not otherwise contain it). This approach would reach everyone, including all women who are or might soon become pregnant. Food fortification and enrichment (increasing the levels of a nutrient already in a food) has a long history in the United States, beginning in 1924 with the decision to add iodine to salt to prevent goiter and other iodine-deficiency disorders. Vitamin D was added to milk in the 1930s (much later, Vitamin A was added to low-fat dairy products). Flours and bread have been enriched with various nutrients—1938 through 1942 saw the addition of thiamine, niacin, riboflavin, and iron.

Four hundred micrograms of folic acid, however, struck many as a pharmacological dose. Best-selling longevity authors Durk Pearson and Sandy Shaw called it unethical and equivalent to medicating competent adults without informed consent (Junod, 2006). Scientists worried about adverse reactions. One known issue was that folic acid at daily doses of a milligram or more could mask vitamin B_{12} deficiency, particularly among the older population, prompting some scientists to worry that fortification would simply shift risks from developing embryos to adults with pernicious anemia (Gaull et al., 1996).

SUPPORT BUILDS

Fortification gained more adherents after the MRC study appeared, however, and supporters' ranks swelled as people became aware of two studies, as yet unpublished, conducted on women with no previous history of NTD-affected births. One, conducted in Hungary by Andrew Czeizel and his colleagues, showed benefits in the general population from consuming 800 mg per day. Another, the "Werler study," studied women in Boston, Philadelphia, and Toronto. Although Werler and her colleagues recommended 400 mg daily, they found that even 250 mg offered some protection. In May 1992, Dr. Walter C. Willet argued in an *American Journal of Public Health* editorial that "fortification should be the long term goal" and criticized the tendency to disregard observational epidemiological studies (Junod, 2006).

PUBLIC RECOMMENDATION CHANGES

In September 1992, the Public Health Service announced that women of child-bearing age should get 400 mg of folic acid every day, a decision touted by the CDC but soft-pedaled by the FDA and the National Institutes of Health (Palca, 1992). The announcement did nothing to satisfy the two policy questions in the FDA's lap: whether to allow food products to promote their folic acid levels on their labels and whether to require that certain foods be fortified with folic acid.

Amid safety concerns, the FDA's folic acid advisory committee recommended against a folic acid health claim after a November 1992 meeting. In early 1993, the FDA, working under tight deadlines, adopted an NLEA rule that reflected this position and disallowed a health claim; however, the committee expressed an interest in fortification, and it reconvened in April 1993 to look at a variety of unresolved issues, including fortification. By October, the FDA had reversed its position, publishing a draft rule that would allow health claims for foods containing folic acid. There were many aspects of the rule, but its core was a provision that would allow health claims for foods that contained 40 mg or more of folic acid per serving. On December 31, 1993, the rule became final.

The October 1993 draft rule contained provisions about fortification, but fortification was not mandated as part of the New Year's Eve ruling. The FDA and its folic acid advisory committee continued to struggle with a variety of implementation questions.

CBA

Federal agencies are required to conduct regulatory impact analyses as part of rule making and starting in 1993 were required to assess expected costs and benefits of significant rules. FDA staff conducted a CBA and estimated that fortification with 140 mg of folic acid per hundred grams of cereal grain products would prevent 116 NTD-affected births per year. This analysis tallied direct savings, notably medical care avoided, and estimated a savings of $5 million for each case averted, resulting in economic benefits of $651 million to $786 million annually. The annual cost of fortification would be $27 million, and thus, the annual net economic benefit would be $624 million to $750 million (FDA, 1993).

In 1995, University of California researchers published a second CBA. They estimated that 304 NTD-associated births would be avoided through fortification. Using a different method that looked at lost productivity, they put the value of a case avoided at $342,500. The economic benefit came in at $121.5 million. From this, the researchers deducted not only the cost of fortification, which they put at $11 million, but the cost of adverse events—namely 500 cases of neurological damage annually at a cost of $16.4 million. Their calculations resulted in an estimated net benefit from fortification of $93.6 million (Romano et al., 1995).

These two studies were before the advisory committee as it debated folic acid implementation and played a role in the shaping the draft folic acid fortification rule published on March 5, 1996. A third analysis, published by the CDC that same year, was not influential. The CDC estimated 89 averted NTDs at a total benefit of $16.1 million annually. That was largely offset by the $11 million cost of fortification and an estimated $350,000 in health costs related to 89 cases of neurological damage. That left a net benefit of $4.7 million.

The FDA ultimately adopted a rule requiring fortification of cereal grain products with 140 mg of folic acid for every 100 g of grain. The rule went into effect in January 1, 1998. Between October 1998 and December 1999, the prevalence of reported cases of spina bifida declined 31%. Anencephaly declined 16%. Various studies over the years have put the total reduction of cases of spina bifida and anencephaly at 20% to 30%, much more than were reflected in the three *ex ante* economic analyses. (Not all of the improvement can be attributed to fortification, as women of childbearing age can expect to get only about a quarter of their recommended intake of 400 mg through fortified grains, and public education campaigns continue to promote consumption of folic acid through vitamin pills.) **Figure 10-5** shows the type of product labeling allowed with folate-fortified products.

THE RESULTS COME IN

Studies in Chile and Canada also reported the effectiveness of folate fortification programs. Three Canadian population-based studies showed reductions in the incidence of NTD-related births of 50%, 54%, and 43%, respectively. The Chilean study included measures of increased folate blood levels from fortification and reported a 43% reduction in the NTD rate within 6 months. Differences among these studies included differences in fortification levels and differences in measurement and reporting regarding the inclusion or exclusion of stillbirths and terminated pregnancies.

For Foods	For Vitamin Supplements

Nutrition Facts

Serving Size 1 cup (228g)
Servings Per Container 2

Amount Per Serving

Calories 250   Calories from Fat 110

	% Daily Value*
Total Fat 12g	18%
Saturated Fat 3g	15%
Cholesterol 30mg	10%
Sodium 470mg	20%
Total Carbohydrate 31g	10%
Dietary Fiber 0g	0%
Sugar 5g	
Protein 5g	
Vitamin A	4%
Vitamin C	2%
Calcium	20%
Iron	4%
Folate	30%

* Percent Daily Values are based on a 2,000 calorie diet.
Your Daily Values may be higher or lower depending on
your calorie needs:

	Calories:	2,000	2,500
Total Fat	Less than	65g	80g
Sat Fat	Less than	20g	25g
Cholesterol	Less than	30mg	300mg
Sodium	Less than	2,400mg	2,400mg
Total Carbohydrates		300g	375g
Dietary Fiber		25g	30g

Supplement Facts

Serving Size: 1 tablet

Amount Per Serving		% Daily Value
Vitamin A	5000IU	100
Vitamin C	60mg	100
Vitamin D	400 IU	100
Vitamin E	30 IU	100
Thiamin	1.5mg	100
Riboflavin	1.7mg	100
Niacin	20mg	100
Vitamin B6	2mg	100
Folic Acid	400mcg	100
Vitamin B12	6mcg	100
Biotin	30mcg	10
Pantothenic Acid	10mg	100
Calcium	162mg	16
Iron	18mg	100
Iodine	150mcg	100
Magnesium	100mg	25
Zinc	15mg	100
Selenium	20mcg	100
Copper	2mg	100
Manganese	3.5mg	175
Chromium	65mcg	54
Molybdenum	150mcg	200
Chloride	72mg	2
Potassium	80mg	2

FIGURE 10-5   Two Labels Showing How Regulations Allow Display
of Folate Content

Source: National Women's Health Information Center.

The CDC published a before- and after- epidemiological study in 2004, which reported that between 1995 and 1996 (prefortification) and 1999 and 2000 surveillance-based population studies showed a reduction in the estimated number of NTD-affected pregnancies from 4,000 to 3,000. These results are summarized in **Table 10-3**. An editorial note in the *Morbidity and Mortality MMWR Weekly* noted that a 26% reduction was somewhat less than earlier studies had indicated and short of the national goal of a reduction of 50% (CDC, 2004).

TABLE 10-3 Estimated Average Annual Numbers of Spina Bifida and Anencephaly Cases Based on Prevalence Per 10,000 Live Births from Surveillance Systems— United States 1995–1996 and 1999–2000

	Systems With Prenatal Ascertainment		Systems Without Prenatal Ascertainment		Fetal Deaths and Elective Terminations
Prefortification	*Prevalence*	*No.*	*Prevalence*	*No.*	*No.*
Spina bifida	6.4	2,490	5.1	1,980	
Anencephaly	4.2	1,640	2.5	970	
Total		**4,130**		**2,950**	**1,180**
Postfortification	*Prevalence*	*No.*	*Prevalence*	*No.*	*No.*
Spina bifida	4.1	1,640	3.4	1,340	
Anencephaly	3.5	1,380	2.1	840	
Total		**3,020**		**2,180**	**840**

Source: CDC (2004, p. 364).

For systems with prenatal ascertainment, estimated total pregnancies included live births, stillbirths, prenatally diagnosed cases, and elective terminations. For systems without prenatal ascertainment[1], estimates included live births, stillbirths, and fetal deaths through 20 weeks. Fetal deaths and elective terminations were calculated as difference between systems with and without prenatal ascertainment. The numbers of NTD-affected pregnancies and births were determined as prevalence multiplied by the average total number of U.S. births during the respective periods, as derived from the U.S National Vital Statistics System.

[1] Programs with prenatal ascertainment use specific case-finding techniques to indentify prenatally-diagnosed and electively-terminated cases.

THE NEW U.S. ECONOMIC STUDY

In 2005, Grosse et al. published an ex-post economic study. It estimated 520 averted cases of spina bifida and 92 cases of averted anencephaly annually, which led to economic benefits per case of $636,000 and $1,020,000, respectively. That translated into $425 million in economic benefits ($146 million in direct costs, mostly medical) against an annual cost of fortification of $3 million. There have been no documented adverse health effects from fortification.

This study used a 3% discount rate but noted that the new Office of Management and Budget guidelines called for comparisons using both 3% and 7% discount rates. At least one ex-ante study had used a 5% rate. Of the $636,000 savings per spina bifida case avoided, the study reported, $279,000 was direct costs, mostly medical, with the rest apparently indirect costs for nonmedical caregiving. For the anencephaly cases, almost all of the $1,020,000 in costs were indirect. In addition to the required 3% and 7% discount rate comparisons, the authors performed sensitivity analyses with only 80% of the cases avoided attributed to folate fortification and with a doubling of the fortification costs. Then they developed a worst-case scenario that assumed only 80% of the observed benefits attributed to the intervention, a doubling of the cost of fortification, and a $25 million allowance for the potential effects of neurological damage secondary to untreated anemia. This worst-case scenario still yielded annual net direct benefits of $88 million after expenditures of $6 million on fortification and an overall benefit of $312 million. The authors observed that the benefits were exceptionally large and noted that "few public health interventions beyond immunization and injury prevention are cost saving" (p. 1921).

Hertkampf (2004) estimated that in Chile the fortification process costs approximately U.S. $280,000 annually. For spina bifida, she estimated the cost of surgery and rehabilitation for each of the 110 cases avoided annually at U.S. $100,000. She noted that bread is more of a staple of the Chilean diet. Commenting on the low priority given to folate fortification in most developing countries, she noted that prevalence data are lacking and that NTDs are not recognized as an important cause of morbidity and mortality.

MEANWHILE BACK IN THE UNITED KINGDOM

On April 6, 2006, the U.K. Food Standards Agency Board "agreed to consult on options for improving the folate status of young women." When the board first discussed the issue in 2002, concerns were raised about possible risks to the health of older people. Then the Scientific Advisory Committee on Nutrition (SACN), an independent expert panel, reviewed the evidence and tracked the emerging science. A SACN report issued in draft form in November 2005 and released as a final report in December 2006 recommended mandatory fortification of flour.

The Food Standards Agency Board (2006) agreed that it would consider four options:

- Doing nothing
- Increasing efforts to encourage young women to change their diets and take supplements
- Further encourage voluntary fortification of foods
- Implement mandatory fortification of "the most appropriate food vehicle"

The board announced December 12, 2006 that it would consult with consumers, stakeholders, and industry over a 13-week period. On May 17, 2007 it voted to recommend fortification of regular, white, and brown bread (but not wholemeal) at a level of 300 micrograms per 100 grams of flour, which it estimated would add 78 micrograms to the average person's daily intake. The recommendation still needed ministerial-level approval.

DISCUSSION QUESTIONS

1. Describe the authorizing environment for folic acid fortification in the United States.

2. Why would a decision based on strong British studies influence the U.S. decision to fortify cereal products but yield a delayed response in the United Kingdom?

3. Contrast and compare the variables and their values used in the before and after CBA studies. What conclusions would you draw from them about that approach in this case? In general?

CHAPTER 11

The Policy Process—
Analysis of Values—
Last But Not Least

A policy analysis that considers technological capabilities, economic outcomes, and political support will usually point toward a single health policy recommendation. Yet any recommendation still has to take into account issues of values, especially where there are competing tradeoffs. You might ask this: Does not the political process, which a recommendation must often go through before it can be adopted and implemented, take care of those value concerns? Do not decision makers reflect their personal values and those of their constituencies in the positions they take during a policy debate and in their votes? Yes, the political process will reflect the current wider conflicts in American society over social mores, the nature of human life, the role of government, and collective versus individual rights. In this chapter, however, we consider some value issues relating specifically to health care and the health care professions. These values may or may not be considered in the political process and should be assessed as part of any robust analysis.

Value issues that we discuss briefly in this chapter include the following:

- Fair access
- Efficiency
- Patient privacy and confidentiality
- Informed consent

- Personal responsibility
- Malpractice reform
- Professional ethics
- Consumer sovereignty
- Social welfare
- Rationing
- Process equity.

Undoubtedly, you could think of others that you might want to add.

This chapter also discusses the broader question of how a wide range of social institutions might be influenced by the growth of the medical sector of the economy and a suggestion that all proposals to transform the health system undergo a formal ethics review.

FAIR ACCESS

Priester (1992) suggested that the United States should reorder its values to give the greatest emphasis to fair equity, which he defined as giving each individual access to an "adequate level of care." Skipping over issues of residency and eligibility, he argued, "Assuring access to health care, regardless of cause or source of need, is society's responsibility"; however, he added that "this does not require access to all potentially beneficial care" (p. 92). He maintained that this is the only approach that would not exceed the available resources or deprive some segments of society of their opportunity for a reasonably full life. He saw this as a floor, not a ceiling; someone with more personal resources could choose to consume more health services. He saw the U.S. system as overemphasizing provider autonomy, individualism, and assumed abundance. He felt that we have too often let economic considerations outweigh ethical ones.

EFFICIENCY

If lack of resources leads society to overlook some populations or to restrict necessary services to them, then efficiency should be an important value. As we have noted in earlier chapters, "Waste not, want not"; this is not always a fundamental value in a system in which one person's waste is another person's enhanced income. Porter and Teisberg (2006) argued against a "zero-sum" mentality that attempts to maximize each individual provider's share of the existing pie in favor of reduced waste to enhance the value received by individual consumers. One could also promote the collective view that the services available to consumers collectively form a "zero-sum" game in which all will get more if the collective waste is minimized. One way or another, waste has to be viewed negatively, rather than as enhanced income.

PATIENT PRIVACY AND CONFIDENTIALITY

Stolen laptops with personal data are frequently in the news. Increasingly, however, the potential content of electronic patient records, digitized information already collected for billing and claims, and specialized databases offer the potential for finding out more about disease processes and care outcomes. At the same time, they offer possibilities for excluding individuals from care or for breaches of the confidentiality that one expects when encountering the health care system. This is an area where tradeoffs will continue to be difficult and frustrating and will continue to be important in policy analysis and decision making.

INFORMED CONSENT

Requirements for informed consent for patients and human subjects in research represent a constraint on provider autonomy. They added to the staff burden, but are a regulatory requirement. **Table 11-1** illustrates part of the federal regulations governing informed consent by research subjects in federally funded research. You might ask yourself this: What values are represented here, and why were they made an added requirement of all research in the first place?

PERSONAL RESPONSIBILITY

A significant portion of the cost of health care can be attributed to patient lifestyle choices, such as smoking, lack of exercise, overeating or poor nutrition, not wearing seat belts and cycling helmets, and overuse of drugs and alcohol. Many policy proposals seek to change the behaviors that put one at risk or to shift those costs to the individuals at risk. Smokers pay higher insurance premiums for long-term care, for example. Analysts suggest that those involved in risky behaviors, such as not wearing motorcycle helmets, post a bond to cover their incremental medical care costs in case of an accident. The discussion of health care insurance is full of references to moral

TABLE 11-1   45 Code of Federal Regulations §46.116: General
Requirements for Informed Consent

Except as provided elsewhere in this policy, no investigator may involve a human being as a subject in research covered by this policy unless the investigator has obtained the legally effective informed consent of the subject or the subject's legally authorized representative. An investigator shall seek such consent only under circumstances that provide the prospective subject or the representative sufficient opportunity to consider whether or not to participate and that minimize the possibility of coercion or undue influence. The information is given to the subject or the representative shall be in language understandable to the subject or the representative. No informed consent, whether oral or written, may include any exculpatory language through which the subject or the representative is made to waive or appear to waive any of the subject's legal rights, or releases or appears to release the investigator, the sponsor, the institution or its agents from liability for negligence.

(a) Basic elements of informed consent. Except as provided in paragraph (c) or (d) of this section, in seeking informed consent the following information shall be provided to each subject:

(1) A statement that the study involves research, an explanation of the purposes of the research and the expected duration of the subject's participation, a description of the procedures to be followed, and identification of any procedures which are experimental;

(2) A description of any reasonably foreseeable risks or discomforts to the subject;

(3) A description of any benefits to the subject or to others which may reasonably be expected from the research;

(4) A disclosure of appropriate alternative procedures or courses of treatment, if any, that might be advantageous to the subject;

(5) A statement describing the extent, if any, to which confidentiality of records identifying the subject will be maintained;

(6) For research involving more than minimal risk, an explanation as to whether any compensation and an explanation as to whether any medical treatments are available if injury occurs and, if so, what they consist of, or where further information may be obtained;

(7) An explanation of whom to contact for answers to pertinent questions about the research and research subjects' rights, and whom to contact in the event of a research-related injury to the subject; and

(8) A statement that participation is voluntary, refusal to participate will involve no penalty or loss of benefits to which the subject is otherwise entitled, and the subject may discontinue participation at any time without penalty or loss of benefits to which the subject is otherwise entitled.

(continues)

(b) Additional elements of informed consent. When appropriate, one or more of the following elements of information shall also be provided to each subject:

(1) A statement that the particular treatment or procedure may involve risks to the subject (or to the embryo or fetus, if the subject is or may become pregnant) which are currently unforeseeable;

(2) Anticipated circumstances under which the subject's participation may be terminated by the investigator without regard to the subject's consent;

(3) Any additional costs to the subject that may result from participation in the research;

(4) The consequences of a subject's decision to withdraw from the research and procedures for orderly termination of participation by the subject;

(5) A statement that significant new findings developed during the course of the research which may relate to the subject's willingness to continue participation will be provided to the subject; and

(6) The approximate number of subjects involved in the study.

(c) An IRB may approve a consent procedure which does not include, or which alters, some or all of the elements of informed consent set forth above, or waive the requirement to obtain informed consent provided the IRB finds and documents that:

(1) The research or demonstration project is to be conducted by or subject to the approval of state or local government officials and is designed to study, evaluate, or otherwise examine: (i) public benefit or service programs; (ii) procedures for obtaining benefits or services under those programs; (iii) possible changes in or alternatives to those programs or procedures; or (iv) possible changes in methods or levels of payment for benefits or services under those programs; and

(2) The research could not practicably be carried out without the waiver or alteration.

Other sections allow further exemptions where this procedure might interfere with state and local requirements or with emergency medical treatment.

hazard and the free-rider problem. Most people would agree that individuals should take more responsibility for their behavior rather than have it borne as a collective risk, but there is less agreement on the effort society should expend to make healthy choices more attractive. There is considerable evidence, for example, that the development choices we make—our *built environment*—can encourage or discourage physical activity. A politician asked to support a bill to encourage "walkability" or "multimodal transportation hubs," however, may be inclined to attribute lack of exercise solely to, as one state legislator once put it, "a lack of personal fortitude."

MALPRACTICE REFORM

We hear a lot about malpractice reform and about frivolous lawsuits and unreasonable awards for pain and suffering. We see advertisements on our cable stations by law firms seeking to represent clients "wronged" by providers and insurers. State and federal legislatures and courts debate whether to cap the size of awards or when they are excessive. Putting political posturing aside, however, several values-related policy issues recur in the debates on this area, including the following:

- The value of a human life lost and of other negative consequences suffered unnecessarily
- The allocation of the responsibility of error between the individual provider and the overall care system
- The amount of variability in outcomes and events that is unavoidable and how much is unacceptable
- The appropriate way to compensate advocates for patient rights and to overcome inappropriate provider behavior
- How much to let the provider community police itself and how much and when to intervene in the public interest.

PROFESSIONAL ETHICS

Many of the topics in this chapter could be subsumed under the topic of professional ethics. Access and rationing are aspects of distributive justice. Confidentiality, truthfulness, informed consent, respect for patient and professional autonomy, and the safety of the patient are all topics cited in discussions of professional ethics and in professional codes of ethics. Most professionals have had some indoctrination in biomedical ethics and are aware of key issues. Most professions have an ethical code or statement. Most such statements have become more general over time as patient autonomy has become more respected and monopolistic practices have come under government scrutiny. At the same time, professional societies may take strong positions without incorporating them into a code. For example, the American Nurses Association has long supported health care as a basic right delivered through a single-payer system.

CONSUMER SOVEREIGNTY

Those who want a highly competitive marketplace want the consumer to make decisions rather than the government. The example in the box below illustrates views of health policy analysts on both sides of this economic and political ideological divide. The typical health professional is in a bit of a straddle here. Most believe in patient autonomy but also recognize that consumer sovereignty often comes at the expense of professional power and influence, which some would call paternalism, but may affect patient compliance and clinical outcomes as well.

SOCIAL WELFARE

Interest groups at the table during policy formulation may or may not adequately represent the public's social welfare. There are a number of ways of evaluating outcomes in terms of social welfare. Several are economic;

Contrasts in Economic and Political Ideology

Cannon and Tanner (2005) conclude that they

share one view held by many proponents of government activism in the health care sector: health is a special area of the economy. Unlike software, wireless communications, or banking, health care involves very emotional decisions, which often entail matters of human dignity, life, and death. However, we do not see the gravity of these matters as a reason to divert power away from individuals and toward government. Rather we see the special nature of health care as all the more reason to increase each consumer's sphere of autonomy. The nature of health care makes it all the more important that we use the competitive process to make health care available to more consumers—and makes it all the more important to get started now (pp. 146–147).

Richmond and Fein (2005) conclude otherwise:

We are confident that through effective public policy we can build a more equitable community in which many more of our neighbors would be able, not only to dream the American dream, but to fulfill it. . . . Health and health care are vitally important in influencing life's chances and one's income and wealth should not determine the amount and quality of care one receives. We seek a system in which the financing and distribution of health services reflect our image of a just society, a society in which economic arrangements reflect a moral dimension (p. 4).

several are not. We have already presented the economic models that would base decisions on benefit–cost or cost-effectiveness criteria. These raise issues of valuation, such as:

- Willingness to pay
- Contribution to gross domestic product
- Social costs avoided as in the case of support of a family when the breadwinner dies.

At the same time there are other considerations, such as:

- Lives saved
- Quality-adjusted life years (QALYs)
- Longevity
- Pain and suffering avoided.

In this arena, there are counterattacks to the economic arguments (Ackerman & Heinzerling, 2004):

> *There are fundamental values at stake—and at risk—in the debates over economic analysis of health and environmental protection. Cost–benefit analysis of health and environmental policies trivializes the very values that gave rise to these policies in the first place. Moreover, through opaque and intimidating concepts like willingness to pay, quality-adjusted life-years, and discounting, economic analysts have managed to hide the moral and political questions lying just under the surface of their precise and scientific-looking numbers. It is time to blow their cover. . . .*
>
> *[W]e offer an attitude rather than an algorithm: one that trusts collective, commonsense judgments, and is humble in the face of uncertainty, steadfast in confronting urgent problems, and committed to fairness within and beyond the generation (p. 234).*

Discounting is easy to do mathematically but difficult to interpret practically, politically, and ethically. The problem is in the tradeoff between the present and the future, a difficult problem in all policy making. The standard economists' approach of bringing the costs and benefits back to a net present value explicitly biases the analysis against future events.

Ackerman and Heinzerling also questioned the use of QALY metrics because they discriminate against the older population, who will naturally have fewer years ahead of them. The same can be said of any analysis dealing with contribution to gross domestic product, as the older population generate little output or will soon stop generating it and the output of children is so far into the future that any reasonable discount rate obliterates the benefits. That is why some suggest that the economic analysis is useful for payers and for comparing treatment alternatives of a specific illness, but really does not work well when comparing an array of different alternative public investments.

RATIONING

Bodenheimer and Grumbach (2005) suggested a precise definition of rationing, namely that it have two components: (1) limiting care that is likely to be beneficial due to scarce resources, including money, and (2) a method of fairly distributing the resources that are available. To this we would add a third condition: (3) that the decision-making method is determined by society rather than a corporation or an individual. Bodenheimer and Grumbach noted that popular use of the term rationing tends to equate it with withholding of care and ignores the second necessary condition. That distinction separates arbitrary actions to decrease the cost of care from situations in which the system attempts to distribute its limited resources in a systematic and equitable way. As we noted earlier, there are a variety of notions of equity, and thus, a rationing system may be designed to:

- Reduce overall costs to a targeted level
- Maximize access
- Maximize the social welfare based on the contributions of the individuals within the population
- Maximize medical effectiveness
    - Subject to a cost constraint
    - Subject to some other resource limitation
- Combinations of the above.

For example, the attempt of the British health service to limit the costs of care has led to at least one charge of rationing when a woman with breast cancer was denied the drug Herceptin by a local health authority on the basis of cost. An account of this has been included as **Table 11-2**.

TABLE 11-2   Rationing and the Courts

Ann Marie Rogers, 54, sued the Swindon Primary Care Trust after it refused treatment for her HER2 early-stage breast cancer with the drug, Herceptin, even after her doctor prescribed it. The Roche drug is licensed for late-stage breast cancer, but some studies showed it to be effective for early-stage cancer as well. Ms. Hewitt, the Health Secretary, had praised the efforts of other women to get the treatment, and the Health Department had ordered the local health services "not to withhold it solely on the grounds of cost," even while a government-appointed review panel was in the process of setting new guidelines for the use of the drug. Treatment with Herceptin costs $36,000 to $47,000 a year for each patient and was supplied under very different circumstances by the local health trusts. The Swindon trust had a policy of supplying Herceptin for early-stage breast cancer only in "exceptional circumstances." Ms. Rogers had pointed to her cancer being of the type responsive to the drug and to the risk factors of the death of her mother and a cousin from cancer.

When treatment was denied, Ms. Rogers started paying for the drug on her own, but had to stop when her own resources were used up. Thus, she sued the authority, citing the "postal code lottery," which determined who got treated and who did not. A lower court judge ruled in February 2006 that the Swindon health service's denial was lawful. In April, however, a three-judge appeals court overturned that verdict and said the local health service had acted unlawfully, noting that "once the Primary Care Health Trust decided, as it did, that it would fund Herceptin for some patients and that the cost was irrelevant, the only reasonable approach was to focus on the patient's clinical needs and fund patients within the eligible group who were properly prescribed by their physician." It observed that there had been "no rational basis for distinguishing between patients within the eligible group on the basis of exceptional clinical circumstances any more than on the basis for personal, let alone, social circumstances" (Lyall, 2006).

The National Institute for Clinical Excellence (NICE) issued a press release on April 12, 2006, in which NICE Chief Executive Andrew Dillon reaffirmed the importance of ensuring that new drugs are both safe to use, by having an effective system for licensing, and used in the right way through the work that NICE does. "Without these things, we risk exposing patients to risks and the health service to using its money unwisely," he said.

NICE was expected to issue guidance to the National Health Service (NHS) on the use of Herceptin in July 2006, providing the drug receives a license from the European licensing authority. NICE's guidance will make it clear who might potentially benefit from the drug, irrespective of where they live in England and Wales. "It's only in this way that consistent decisions can be taken to bring an end to the uncertainty that faces both patients and the NHS," commented Andrew Dillon (NICE, 2006).

Reduce Overall Health Care Costs to a Target Level

An effective rationing system is not aimed at minimizing health care costs. They cannot be driven to zero; however, when there is a budgetary limitation or a fixed revenue situation, there must be some system to decide which services will not be provided to which individuals. In many cases, this is done by limiting the population served and limiting the services offered.

Maximize Access

The rationing system may have as its objective the maximization of access (i.e., serving the largest number of people). For example, one of the largest Medicaid expenses is paying long-term care for older people, a service not covered by Medicare. States have quietly limited the amount they pay by limiting the number of new nursing home beds they license. They know that there is a strong linear relationship between the number of beds available and the amount of Medicare claims received. Sometimes that is cloaked behind discussions about unnecessary use because of an oversupply of beds, but in reality, it is often driven by budget considerations. The money saved might be applied to increases in fees paid to obstetricians to try to get them to take on more prenatal care for Medicaid patients, a service known to have a positive payoff.

Maximize the Social Welfare

When transplanted organs first became available, it was clear that there were not enough to go around. Institutions doing transplants set up committees of individuals concerned with medical effectiveness and medical ethics to determine who would get the next available organ. The committees examined a mixture of personal, family, and medical data to determine literally who should live and who would in all probability die. Considerations included family status, work status, medical factors such as alcoholism and co-morbidities, and psychiatric factors. Outside observers were also suspicious that ability to pay might be creeping into the decision making.

One problem with the social welfare criterion is that it goes well beyond issues that health professionals are comfortable with. Issues might include citizenship status, economic contribution, utility of one's work, and emotional impact on others. Reaching some agreement on the importance of each of these is unlikely given current value conflicts in our society. That does not mean that we cannot reach a social consensus, but rather, that it would be very difficult to justify after we have reached it.

Maximize Medical Effectiveness

"The providing or withholding of care is ideally determined by the probability that the treatment will maximize benefits and minimize harm, i.e. by the criterion of medical effectiveness" (Bodenheimer & Grumbach, 2005). This concept was operationalized in the Oregon Basic Health Services Act of 1989, which tried to guarantee health care for all and still control health care costs through an open, publicly accountable rationing process. At that time, one had to be at or below 58% of the federal poverty level to receive Medicaid benefits in Oregon, and this bill was intended to open that up to those below the 100% level. The state Health Services Commission was created to recommend the prioritization of health services. The 11-member body was to report its priorities to the governor and the Joint Legislative Committee on Health Care. An actuarial contractor would then estimate the cost of each of the prioritized services for the Joint Committee. After the Medicaid budget for services was set, the package of services offered to the Medicaid population would be developed using the priority lists. Essentially, the process would be to go down the list taking the next highest priority coverage until the estimated budget package was exhausted. Other services then would be outside this basic coverage. If the demand exceeded the funding provided, Oregon was prepared to reduce the benefit package rather than ration through eligibility thresholds or Medicaid reimbursement levels as so many other states were doing (Calkthan, 1991).

The commission used three techniques to develop the prioritization of some 800 services. It held 11 open public hearings around the state. It also had Oregon Health Decisions, a respected advocacy group, conduct 47 community forums, including one in every county. Each forum featured a slide presentation, group discussions, and a questionnaire on the participants' opinions about the relative importance of specific health situations and categories. About 70% of the more than 1,000 individuals attending these forums were health care workers. The commission also supported a state-wide random-digit dialing survey asking 1,000 individuals to rate 31 health care situations on a modified Quality-of-Well-Being Scale that had been validated elsewhere. That information was used to build a cost/utility scale called a "net benefit value" scale. That study produced a listing of 1,600 medical condition/treatment pairs. The orderings produced by the telephone survey were highly debatable. Fox and Leichter (1991) reported that "crooked teeth received a higher ranking than early treatment for Hodgkin's disease, and dealing with thumb sucking was ranked higher than hospitalization for a child for starvation" (p. 22). Because it was clear that the derived utilities were not workable in terms of overall values, commission members negotiated among themselves for an acceptable ordering. For example, the four consumer representatives on the panel argued for higher rankings for preventive services because that is what the public seemed to have been saying during this process. Rather than a continuous ranking, they came up with 709 pairs grouped according to three basic categories: essential, very important, and valuable to some individuals (Kaplan, 1995) and then under 17 subcategories of outcomes, using descriptors such as survival, degree of recovery, and degree of improvement on the Quality-of-Well-Being Scale (Fox & Leichter, 1991).

To implement this process required a federal Medicaid waiver, which was denied on the grounds that the assessments of quality of life by healthy individuals tended to stereotype and discount the value of quality for the disabled, and the process, therefore, violated the Americans with Disabilities Act. Kaplan (1995) argued that this finding was in error and offered counterevidence.

Instead of debating these issues, Oregon chose to resubmit its application with the utility portion of the model excluded. Its revised waiver application considered probability of death and probability of moving up from a symptomatic to an asymptomatic state. By giving up the utility component of the model, Oregon ignored the fact that health states are valued (Kaplan, 1995). Priester (1992) argued that the plan had been flawed because it denied access to a reasonable level of care to some, but not to others. In 1993, the Clinton administration approved the revised Medicaid waiver.

Combinations of One or More

Table 11-3 contains a description of how the United Network for Organ Sharing (UNOS) allocates available organs (not including related donors). This contractor was set up after passage of the National Organ Transplantation Act of 1984. It emphasizes the medical outcome and then pays attention to one's length of time on the waiting list; however, the issue of whether

TABLE 11-3   How the Transplant System Works: Matching Donors and Recipients

Under contract with the U.S. Department of Health and Human Services' Health Services & Resources Administration, the UNOS maintains a centralized computer network linking all organ procurement organizations and transplant centers. This computer network is accessible 24 hours a day, 7 days a week, with organ placement specialists in the UNOS Organ Center always available to answer questions.

After being referred by a doctor, a transplant center evaluates the possible transplant. The transplant center runs a number of tests and considers the patient's mental and physical health, as well as his or her social support system. If the center determines that the patient is a transplant candidate, it will add the patient's medical profile to the national patient waiting list for organ transplant. The patient is **not** placed on a ranked list at that time. Rather, the patient's name is added to the pool of patients waiting.

When a deceased organ donor is identified, a transplant coordinator from an organ procurement organization accesses the UNOS computer. Each patient in the pool is matched by the computer against the donor's characteristics. The computer then generates a ranked list of patients for each organ that is procured from that donor in ranked order according to organ allocation policies. Factors affecting ranking may include tissue match, blood type, length of time on the waiting list, immune status, and the distance between the potential recipient and the donor. For heart, liver, and intestines, the potential recipient's degree of medical urgency is also considered; therefore, the computer generates a differently ranked list of patients for each donor organ matched.

The organ is offered to the transplant team of the first person on the list. Often, the top patient will **not** get the organ for one of several reasons. When a patient is selected, he or she must be available, healthy enough to undergo major surgery, and willing to be transplanted immediately. Also, a laboratory test to measure compatibility between the donor and recipient may be necessary. For example, patients with high antibody levels often prove incompatible to the donor organ and **cannot** receive the organ because the patient's immune system would reject it.

After a patient is selected and contacted and all testing is complete, surgery is scheduled and the transplant takes place.

Source: United Network for Organ Sharing Fact Sheet. Retrieved 01/28/07 at http://www.unos.org.

the transplant takes place is also contingent on the availability of private insurance or Medicare or Medicaid funds to pay for it. By now you should be aware that trying to maximize one thing while trying to minimize or maximize another is often a mathematical impossibility. It is legitimate, however, to have a system in which one objective is traded off against another. The problem is that most attempts to do so never specify what the tradeoff ratios are because arriving at a consensus ratio is likely to generate conflict over the weightings of the competing criteria that cannot be resolved without considerable loss of momentum and goodwill. Allocation rules, therefore, tend to remain fuzzy. You can see this even in the UNOS description in **Table 11-3**. It is clear that the concept of a social welfare criterion is not really operative there.

PROCESS EQUITY

Not only must the outcome be perceived as fair, but so should the process that produced it. For example, the policy analysis group must ask itself whether all interested parties participated. If not, have the underrepresented or disenfranchised had their issues addressed by the analysts? This was a relevant concern in the Oregon process, which, although highly rational, seemed dominated by health professionals and by more educated and civically involved individuals. It is not unusual for opponents of a policy to argue against the inclusiveness or integrity of the policy development. Many governments have requirements for public hearings that are regionally representative in hopes that their process would thus appear fairer to those concerned and to protect themselves against complaints about the process.

INFLUENCE ON SOCIETY: A BROADER QUESTION

With the medical care sector headed for 20% or more of the economy, we have to wonder about the long-term effects of this much emphasis on health in our society. These might include the following:

- Focus on illness and a possible loss of a sense of well-being
- Commercial pressure to overemphasize medical problems
- The power of the medical–industrial–university complex.

Is it healthy to be so conscious of our health? Is it healthy to be so stressed about our medical bills? Just about every sector of our society adds a health concern to its primary and previous missions. Churches add a health ministry committee and/or a health-trained staff member. Schools take on more responsibility in terms of children's medications and their special needs. Tax revenues previously devoted to education and infrastructure get diverted to health care. All of these individual decisions may be virtuous, but they also signal a changing societal focus from toughing it out to getting it fixed through health care, whether that works or not.

Because health care represents an opportunity for growth, we see more and more commercial pressure to expand its markets—and its "top of mind" awareness for the public. In a way, this is good because it creates more innovation. On the other hand, it can create demand for which there is not a significant need and siphon resources away from areas of true need. Two issues that illustrate this are the explosive growth in direct-to-consumer advertising, especially on television, and the creation of new syndromes, such as the hotly debated emergence of prehypertension.

Prehypertension

Many older doctors report that they were trained that the normal upper limit for systolic blood pressure was your age (at least up to 55 years) plus 100 millimeters of mercury over 90 (diastolic). Then, in 1977, the Joint National Committee on Prevention, Detection, Evaluation, and Treatment of High Blood Pressure issued it first report establishing the guideline of 120-80 as optimal, 120-129/80-84 as within the normal range and 130-139/85-89 as high normal. Then in May 2003, its issued a new guideline stating that levels above 120/80 constituted prehypertension and indicated increased risk for heart attack, stroke, or kidney disease. This new diagnostic entity was to be treated with the same methods as before—diet, exercise, and other lifestyle changes and, if these fail to do the trick, a diuretic. Critics argue that there is no randomized clinical trial evidence below 140 mm and suggest that the pharmaceutical industry, which might double its number of treatable patients, not only approved of the decision, but may have influenced it. They note that reducing salt intake will help some, but hinder others, and that treating blood pressure "by the numbers" is not good medicine, although it is tempting when a provider is pressed for time and faced with patients who expect a prescription. They point out that hypertension can have a number of causes and that it should be viewed as part of a "mosaic" of risk factors associated with cardiovascular care. A good classroom exercise would be to search out other newly emphasized conditions and track down their medical and commercial origins. You can start by turning on your television to all of the ads for drugs that one must take regularly to suppress some distress such as acid reflux, restless legs, erectile dysfunction, or insomnia.

In the United States, much debate centers on the pharmaceutical industry's advertising aimed directly at consumers, the cost of which ranges between $3 billion and $5 billion annually. Health care advertising, especially for prescription drugs, seem to have replaced all of the air time and billboard space that had been taken up by cigarette and tobacco ads before they were banned. Are we that much better off from stopping the one set of ads and substituting the other? Other countries, including New Zealand, have barred this type of commercial activity.

Cyberpunk author Bruce Sterling offers a vision of a medically obsessed future in his novel *Holy Fire* (1996). In it, protagonist Mia Ziemann is 94 years old and still professionally active as a medical economist. In her world, wealth is all about how many medical procedures one can afford to extend one's longevity. The medical–industrial–academic complex clearly dominates the entire economy, and young people are disenfranchised because older persons rarely have the courtesy to open up employment opportunities by either retiring or dying. It is a disturbing vision, and yet one that is strangely familiar and highly plausible because Sterling draws on existing trends to shape his view of the late 21st century.

ETHICAL REVIEW

Daniels (2006) raised an interesting question: What if we required that health system transformations had to undergo an ethical review process similar to that required of medical research experiments? He noted that these social experiments can put significant populations at risk. He did not suggest what the mechanism for such reviews might be; however, he raised the issues of balancing the social value of the experiment with the risks to which those affected are exposed and how we might go about conducting such a review. He suggested three levels of analysis:

1. Select benchmarks for the ethical analysis in terms of their effect on
   a. Equity
   b. Efficiency
   c. Accountability
2. Conduct an ethical evaluation of how well the design of the proposed reform meets its goals.
   a. How good is the evidence used to justify the intervention?
   b. Is the implementation planned adequate to test the results?

    c. Will the intervention measure the effect with sufficient sensitivity to evaluate the results?

    d. Are the key implementers involved in the planning and committed to an unbiased evaluation?

3. Determine whether there is sufficient oversight to protect the rights of those involved in the experiment (in clinical settings, we have informed consent processes).

He mostly offered examples of international situations, but overall, he noted, "Unfortunately, there is little experience in measuring how systems establish transparency, accountability, and fair process in decisions involving resource allocation" (p. 450).

CONCLUSION

Values are the fourth leg of the analyst's desk, working alongside technology, politics, and economics to support recommendations. This chapter outlines a number of concerns that a policy analysis group must consider in addition to the other three as they factor in concern for the general welfare of our society and our democratic traditions. The issues of ethics and values are not just limited to professional decisions, but also play an important role in all analyses of policy alternatives.

Case 11-1

THE 100K LIVES CAMPAIGN: A VOLUNTARY CODE IN ACTION

BACKGROUND

In 2004, the Institute for Healthcare Improvement (IHI) put out a call for hospitals willing to participate in its 100,000 Lives Campaign. Its goal was to prevent 100,000 deaths in U.S. hospitals during an 18-month period (January 2005 through June 2006) by having hospitals implement some or all of six quality-improvement changes that the IHI and its campaign partners identified as evidence-based and potentially lifesaving.

The IHI developed the campaign in response to a 2001 Institute of Medicine report, *Crossing the Quality Chasm: A New Health System for the 21st Century*, that concluded that 44,000 to 98,000 Americans die each year because of medical errors and adverse events (injuries caused by medical management). This campaign provides an example of noncoercive alternatives to command-and-control regulation—referred to by some as "voluntary codes." To illustrate how the campaign worked, this case discusses one of the six changes that the IHI put forward—establishing a Medical Emergency Team (MET), also referred to a Rapid Response Team—and describes one participating hospital's efforts to implement that change.

THE 100K LIVES CAMPAIGN

The original campaign goal was to recruit 2,000 hospitals to implement at least one of the six quality-improvement changes (see **Table 11-4**). The final number recruited exceeded 3,000, representing about 75% of the nation's hospital beds and 30 million discharges annually. Because most hospitals chose to implement multiple changes—many implemented all six—the campaign inspired 12,294 new quality-improvement efforts.

Each hospital had to set a target for the number of lives it would save. It had two options for how to do this. The simplest way was to set a goal based on the campaign's target of saving 100,000 lives. To do that, participating hospitals and hospital systems would have to avoid slightly less than two deaths per thousand discharges per year. Thus, the calculation for arriving at a hospital's target for lives that would need to be saved would be as follows (IHI, n.d.):

(Number of discharges per year) $\times$ (18 months $\div$ 12 months) $\times$ (2 lives saved $\div$ 1,000 discharges)

The alternative was to look at what the literature suggested was the lifesaving potential of each change and identify the population of patients whose care would be improved. From

---

TABLE 11-4   Quality Improvement Changes,
100,000 Lives Campaign

The Institute for Healthcare Improvement and its partners identified six quality-improvement changes to promote through the 100K Lives Campaign. They were as follows:

- Activate a Rapid Response Team at the first sign that a patient's condition is worsening and may lead to a more serious medical emergency (1,781 hospitals participating).
- Prevent patients from dying of heart attacks by delivering evidence-based care, such as appropriate administration of aspirin and beta-blockers to prevent further heart muscle damage (2,288 hospitals participating).
- Prevent medication errors by ensuring that accurate and continually updated lists of patients' medications are reviewed and reconciled during their hospital stay, particularly at transition points (2,185 hospitals participating).
- Prevent patients who are receiving medicines and fluids through central lines from developing infections by following five steps, including proper hand washing and cleaning the patient's skin with "chlorhexidine" (a type of antiseptic) (1,925 hospitals participating).
- Prevent patients undergoing surgery from developing infections by following a series of steps, including the timely administration of antibiotics (2,133 hospitals participating).
- Prevent patients on ventilators from developing pneumonia by following four steps, including raising the head of the patient's bed between 30 and 45 degrees (1,982 hospitals participating).

Source: Institute for Healthcare Improvement, press release, June 14, 2006.

---

that, a hospital could estimate the number of lives that would be saved if the program was fully implemented for 18 months and then adjust that downward to account for months when the program was not operational or in a "ramp up" phase.

Participating hospitals had to agree to submit monthly raw mortality data for January 2005 through June 2006 and baseline data for the 18 months preceding the campaign (July 2003 through December 2004). To account for variations in the acuity of the patient load, the IHI calculated the "case mix ratio" (CMR) using national acuity data. The ratio compared expected deaths per discharge for each month during the campaign period with expected deaths per discharge for the comparable month in 2004. Thus, for February 2006, the formula for calculating the case mix would be as follows:

(February 2006 CMR) = (February 2006 expected
    deaths per discharge) ÷ (February 2004 expected
    deaths per month)

The IHI then calculated the expected deaths per month if there had not been any quality improvements by multiplying the number of discharges each month by the mortality rate for the same month during 2004 and then adjusting for acuity by multiplying the anticipated number of mortalities by the CMR. It then arrived at the number of lives saved by subtracting the actual number of deaths from the expected number of deaths. The formula for calculating lives saved in February 2006, therefore, would look like this:

(February 2006 lives saved) = ([February 2006 CMR]
    × [February 2004 mortality rate]
    × [February 2006 number of discharges])
    − (February 2006 number of deaths)

These calculations were made using national numbers and aggregated data from all of the reporting hospitals. Confounding factors would make it difficult for most hospitals to calculate their individual lives saved with much accuracy.

VOLUNTARY CODES

There was no immediate financial return or other significant direct benefit to participating hospitals and no monetary reward for reaching their goals, although some participants issued press releases touting their involvement and put information about the campaign on their Web sites. No law— either administrative rule or statute—was forcing them to participate. Indeed, the campaign fits the model referred to as a "voluntary code." Webb (2004, p.11) defined voluntary codes as follows:

- Commitments not required by legislation or regulations
- Agreed to by one or more individuals or organizations
- Intended to influence or control behavior
- To be applied in a consistent manner or to reach in a consistent outcome

"Unlike conventional command and control regulatory approaches," wrote Webb, "voluntary codes harness market, peer and community energies to influence behaviour, and draw on the infrastructure of intermediaries such as industry associations, standards organizations and nongovernmental organizations for rule development and implementation" (p. 11). Webb considered voluntary codes to be part of a concept called *private governance*, a term "intended to encompass the full range of ways that organizations not directly affiliated with the State attempt to organize their affairs" (p. 12). Other terms used to describe private governance include informal regulation, private regulation, voluntary regulation, self-regulation, co-regulation, and communitarian regulation, as well as soft law, self-management, and corporate social responsibility.

The 100,000 Lives Campaign seems to fit Webb's definition of a voluntary code. The intermediaries in this case are the IHI and its partners, including the Joint Commission on Accreditation of Health Care Organizations (JCAHO), the American Medical Association, the American Nurses Association, the National Patient Safety Foundation, the Leapfrog Group, the U.S. Center for Disease Control and Prevention, and the U.S. Centers for Medicare & Medicaid Services.

Perhaps the best known types of voluntary codes are principles for responsible corporate behavior promoted by nongovernmental, environmental, health and welfare, and social justice organizations and adopted by corporations. There are many examples of such campaigns, one of which is the

"No Dirty Gold" campaign started by Earthworks, with industry leadership from Mike Kowalski, Chairman and CEO of Tiffany & Company, which encourages the gold mining industry to adopt sustainable practices and the jewelry industry to use "clean" gold.

Voluntary codes are not new, and they may or may not be in the public interest. In the Middle Ages, guilds controlled almost every aspect of commercial activities. The Better Business Bureau grew out of "vigilance committees" formed in the late 1800s, and the National Consumer's League inspected working conditions at apparel factories as early as 1899, authorizing those that met its standard to use its white label.

Webb (2004) suggested that the current interest in voluntary codes may be due in part to the limitations of traditional government regulations:

> *Regulatory regimes pertaining to consumer, environmental, worker, and health and safety protection, and many other areas, have made considerable progress in improving the lives of millions. But for all their strengths, the command-and-control regulatory approach is not without its limitations, including expensive and protracted development and enforcement processes; jurisdictional constraints on subject matter, approach and scope; vulnerability to inconsistent and inadequate enforcement, due to staff resources and cutbacks, and associated downturns in government and public attention; and a tendency toward inflexibility and overformality* (p. 4).

Webb and other authors, however, are quick to acknowledge the limitations of voluntary codes—for example, a "free rider" who chooses not to participate may gain a cost advantage over competitors who are "doing the right thing." Voluntary codes and conventional government regulations are not mutually exclusive. In Canada, the use of bicycle helmets is required by law, but safety standards for their manufacture are voluntary; meanwhile, hockey helmets manufacturing standards are federally mandated, but the use of helmets during hockey games is discretionary in most of the country (Morrison & Webb, 2004).

When JCAHO, an independent, nonprofit organization, sets a standard for health care organizations and then evaluates and accredits them, it is engaging in a form of private governance. State agencies that regulate hospitals may grant "deemed status" to hospitals that meet JCAHO's standards, accepting accreditation in lieu of a visit by state inspectors or requiring less frequent state inspections.

State regulations and voluntary efforts to reduce medical errors may co-exist. As of September 2005, 23 states had passed legislation or regulations requiring adverse event reporting for hospitals (Rosenthal & Booth, 2005).

THE CASE FOR METS

Cardiac arrest teams that respond to the bedside of a patient who suddenly has no palpable pulse or detectible blood pressure, is unresponsive, or requires the initiation of life support are common features in hospitals. These teams, despite access to increasingly sophisticated technology and increasingly refined protocols, have had limited impact on survival. In the United States, the percentage of patients who suffer in-hospital cardiac arrest and survive long enough to be discharged has remained at around 15% for almost 3 decades.

The IHI has noted that there is wide variability in hospital survival rates. The IHI attribute this variability to three factors: (1) failures in planning, (2) failures in communication, and (3) failure to recognize deteriorating conditions. Cardiac arrest teams appear to illustrate the third factor. In the hours preceding arrest, patients typically show signs of distress. If those signs are recognized and appropriate steps taken, the arrest can often be prevented. One study found that 76% of patients who unexpectedly coded or had to be admitted to intensive care showed symptoms of respiratory, airway, or circulatory deterioration an hour or more before-hand (Buist et al., 2002). Patients may be dying from respiratory or cardiac failure and related complications, but hospitals' "failure to rescue" may be a contributing factor.

In February 1990, Liverpool Hospital in Sydney, Australia introduced a variation on the cardiac arrest team, something it called the MET. The difference between the cardiac arrest team and a MET was that hospital staff could summon the MET to treat anyone who was noticeably deteriorating or acutely unwell. Initial results, published in the mid 1990s, were highly favorable. In 2002, a team of Australian researchers published a study that found that establishing a MET in their hospital resulted in a 50% decrease in the incidence of unanticipated cardiac arrests, even after making adjustments for variations in case mix (the acuity of its patient population). Mortality declined from 76% to 55% (Buist et al., 2002).

Although there was broad agreement that METs made intuitive clinical sense, appeared to work, were relatively simple and inexpensive to implement, and did not seem to produce any clinical adverse outcomes, hospitals were slow to deploy them. Kerridge and Saul (2003) suggested that this "institutional inertia" might be traced to a continuing quest for data that would meet the "gold standard" of evidence-based medicine, and Buist et al., many argued, had not met that standard.

Then Bellomo et al. (2003) published more robust results. They studied a MET team established at a major Melbourne, Australia teaching hospital. The relative risk of experiencing a cardiac arrest, while a patient, declined 65% during the 4-month study period when compared with a 4-month period before the MET began operating. The relative risk of dying from an in-hospital cardiac arrest declined 56%. The number of days survivors spent in the intensive care unit declined 80%, and the total days they spent in the hospital declined 88%. Strikingly, the hospital's overall mortality rate dropped 25%. The IHI cited this experience as evidence when it put Rapid Response Teams on its menu of quality-improvement changes. To meet its goal of 100,000 lives saved, the campaign estimated that it would need to prevent about two deaths per 1,000 discharges. The data out of Australia suggested that METs alone could prevent three deaths per 1,000 discharges.

VIRGINIA MASON'S EXPERIENCE

Virginia Mason Medical Center, a 100,000 Lives Campaign participant situated in Seattle, launched its MET in July 2005 (Virginia Mason Medical Center, 2006). The goal was to prevent avoidable codes by intervening before patients developed cardiopulmonary arrest or other adverse events. Each specially trained team included a critical care charge registered nurse, a respiratory therapist, and a hospitalist. To manage the program, Virginia Mason established a team made up of a project manager, the medical director for the critical care unit and respiratory therapy, the hospitalist service director, a respiratory therapy manager, a preceptor coordinator, the chief of nursing services for the intensive care unit, an administrative director, and a communications consultant.

The hospital nursing staff was instructed to call immediately both the MET (by dialing a special phone number) and the managing physician whenever any of the following occurred:

- Care providers were worried about the patient
- The patient's heart rate suddenly went below 40 or above 130 beats per second
- The patient's systolic blood pressure suddenly dropped below 90
- The patient's respiratory rate suddenly dropped below eight or climbed above 30 breaths per minute
- The pulse oximetry saturation rate of a patient receiving oxygen dropped below 90%

- There was an acute change in the patient's state of consciousness
- The patient's urine output suddenly dropped to less than 50 ml during a 4-hour period

For outcome measurement, the team chose to monitor the number of MET calls per week, the number of cardiopulmonary resuscitation or intubation events inside and outside the intensive care unit each month, and the rate of potentially preventable codes. Initially, calls for the MET were fewer than hoped for. The project team then undertook a series of steps to increase utilization:

- It improved its communications tools and its documentation.
- It had the operator convert all STAT (immediate response) calls that were still coming in to MET calls.
- It partnered with the STROKE team, conducting another round of education and focusing more on at-risk populations.
- It "advertised" the MET's existence by paging the team through the overhead intercom in addition to personal pagers.
- It required all registered nurses to sign a form documenting that they knew when and how to call the MET.
- It audited high-volume units and provided feedback on how the MET could be better used.
- It looked for opportunities to celebrate the program and recognize nurses who made use of it.

Over time, the number of MET calls increased, averaging 70 per month (55/1,000 discharges). The hospital observed a decline in the number of cardiopulmonary and respiratory arrests occurring outside of the critical care unit, although given the hospital's low mortality rate, the numbers are too small to determine whether the intervention had a significant impact on mortality (Westley, 2007).

OVERALL 100K LIVES CAMPAIGN RESULTS

On June 14, 2006, the IHI released the results of the 100,000 Lives Campaign at its 2nd Annual International Summit on Redesigning Hospital Care. Across 18 months, the participating hospitals combined prevented an estimated 122,300 avoidable deaths. Perhaps more important, said IHI President and CEO Donald Berwick, is the fact that so many hospitals had institutionalized new standards of care as a result of the campaign. He noted that more than 20 hospitals have reported no deaths from ventilator-assisted pneumonia over an entire year. This form of pneumonia is the leading cause of deaths from hospital-acquired infections.

"When we decided to launch the campaign we didn't know if hospitals could take on another challenge," Dr. Berwick said. "But the campaign has exceeded our highest expectations. The participating hospitals have not only prevented an estimated 122,300 unnecessary deaths, but they've also proven that it's possible for the health care community to come together voluntarily to make significant changes in patient care. I have never before witnessed such widespread collaboration and commitment on the part of health care leaders and front-line staff to move the system giant steps forward" (Berwick et al., 2006).

DISCUSSION QUESTIONS

1. Purchase (2004) argued that industry groups develop voluntary codes to enhance their commercial interests, typically:

   a. To gain consumer confidence and trust
   b. To forestall collective actions by consumers
   c. To forestall adverse political interventions
   d. To promote desire of political interventions
   e. To restrain trade.

   How does well does the 100,000 Lives Campaign fit with those constructs?

2. What does the experience of Virginia Mason Medical Center say about the implementation of voluntary codes in health care?

3. If you wanted to conduct future policy research based on the experiences of the 100,000 Lives Campaign hospitals, what would you measure and why?

4. What are other examples of voluntary codes used in the health care environment? Why are they so prevalent in this industry? What seems to determine the mix of voluntary and government regulations in health care settings?

CHAPTER 12

Implementation Strategy and Planning

Health care delivery, like politics, is all local. No matter how good the policy analysis is, the selected strategy will fail unless it adapted for and elicits the support of its local implementers. Health care exhibits deep contrasts in the adoption of new ideas. It is notoriously slow to change in some areas, yet adopts technology very rapidly in others. Some argue that the adoption of new technologies is driving up costs, whereas others argue that failure to adopt new technology is partly responsible. Christensen et al. (2000) used the health care industry as an example of the need for disruptive technology to come in and overcome inertia. Their model applies very well in some areas, such as health information technology, but not in others, such as noninvasive surgery.

Dopson and Fitzgerald (2005) have published a very interesting book about the "implementation gap" for evidence-based health care in Britain's National Health Service, where centralization of management and financing would seem to create a more hospitable setting for change than the decentralized U.S. system. They point out that this failure to achieve what has been carefully planned "has a long-standing place in the analysis of public policy" (p. 36). Some would argue that failure to implement is merely political bargaining as usual at the microlevel; however, empirical studies suggest that implementation is a separate stage of the change process (Torenvlied & Thomson, 2003).

The policy process must both include consideration of how to implement the decision and be designed to promote that implementation. The Australian government considers implementation so important that it established a Cabinet Implementation Unit in late 2003 within the Department of the Prime Minister and Cabinet.

LEVELS OF IMPLEMENTATION FAILURE

Sometimes plans are unrealistic. Sometimes there is a failure to execute critical elements of certain plans, whereas other plans are foiled by much more subtle (all too human) innovation adoption problems. Still others are simply overtaken by events—wars, budget crises, changes of government, competing technologies or ideologies. Many social programs started at the federal level with great effort failed in the field over time.

> *Our legislators develop and adopt certain social programs that so often seem to miss their intended objectives. It is sometimes tragicomic to read the laws of entitlement, such as the one guaranteeing equality of education for the handicapped and exceptional children, and then see how they work out in group homes, classrooms, and clinics. Some have blamed public parsimony. Others would cite professional narrowness, individual insensitivity, and bureaucratic myopia. But much of the blame falls on the haste with which public policy is adopted, implemented, and then displaced by new policy* (McLaughlin, 1984, p. 83).

The "deinstitutionalization" effort of the 1970s is a good example of failure to execute. After early antipsychotic drugs became available, the inpatient populations of psychiatric hospitals began to decline. The community mental health centers that were to serve those released from mental institutions were up and running in many areas and Medicaid and Medicare provided some funding, but the promised resources that had been put into psychiatric hospitals never arrived in the community in sufficient quantity to provide both direct care and supportive services such as housing and employment training. An entire new population of homeless individuals appeared in our cities, and the terms *revolving door* and *bag lady* entered the public vocabulary. Hospitals and community centers were not coordinated, but were separate systems that often competed for the same resources. Furthermore, many Community Mental Health Centers drifted away from the goal of supporting deinstitutionalization of the mentally ill and began serving a much broader spectrum of patients. "Once trained, however, the vast majority of these professionals decide to provide psychotherapy for people with mental health problems rather than treat people who were mentally ill" (Torrey, 1997, p. 185). It is not easy to keep well-intentioned policies from going off the tracks. As the saying goes, "The devil is in the details." One attempt to turn that mental health system around and focus it on the target population of the persistently and severely mentally ill is the effort to introduce evidence-based medicine reported in **Case 12-1** later in this chapter.

IMPLEMENTATION PLANNING

Implementation planning arrives early and stays late. The chapter on political feasibility emphasized the importance of involving all stakeholders, including implementers. An Australian Cabinet Implementation Unit (2005) process guide referred to two implementation processes: (1) implementation assessment, which contributes to the documentation that accompanies the submission of a proposal to the cabinet, and (2) implementation planning, which continues that process in much greater detail once the decision is final. **Figure 12-1** shows the stages of the implementation planning process. Several of these topics—scope, funding, risk management, and schedule—may also be inputs, alongside program objectives, outcomes, and governance considerations, to the strategic decision-making process.

Scope of Work

This is a major consideration during the proposal and decision-making stages, but it should also be reviewed after the decision. Policy making is an art, and the "who, what, where, when, and how" may have changed either subtly or substantially. Implementers must be made aware of what was actually approved. There is a saying that the camel was intended to be a horse, but it was designed by a committee. Note the result: The camel is highly adapted to its environment, but it is something quite different from a horse. Consequently, it needs a very different management approach to operate it and evaluate its ultimate performance. In the latter stages of implementation, one needs to establish lines of authority and accountability for implementation and consider how the effort interacts with other initiatives and programs already under way. It is also important to consider

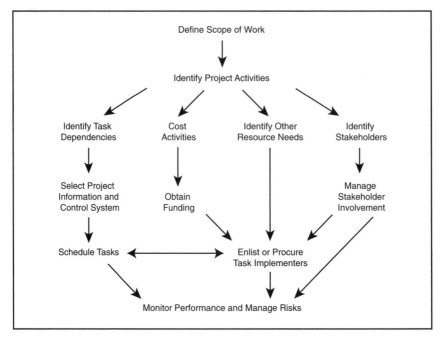

FIGURE 12-1 Guide to Preparing Implementation Plans

whether the new policy can be effectively implemented using existing organizational structures, management systems, and funding approaches or whether it is necessary to innovate in these areas as well.

Defining Project Activities

This stage is a detailed analysis of the tasks generated by the implementation requirements of the policy. Political decision makers are likely to establish some important dates (milestones) for implementation, dates that may or may not be achievable. Then the implementing organization must get to work:

- Identifying the tasks that must be performed to implement the effort, such as submitting a detailed budget, hiring personnel, finding office space, issuing rules and regulations, establishing advisory committees, and specifying information reporting requirements. This is something called developing a Work Breakdown Structure

- Identifying the units and individuals responsible for each task and gaining their commitment to complete the task within a specific time period
- Establishing reporting responsibilities for the status of each task
- Including coordination tasks as well as intradepartmental tasks
- Developing a master schedule and an estimated time of completion for the project and mechanisms for monitoring progress.

Depending on the complexity and urgency of the project, the project implementation staff may choose to use any one of a number of project management techniques and their accompanying software to show what the resulting project schedule would be and whether this is likely to meet the original target. If that is not the case, then the implementation planners may decide to undertake a number of efforts to "crash" the project and remain on schedule. This process works best when the estimate of the duration of each activity comes from its responsible implementer, building further commitment to estimate realistically and to then meet one's own estimates.

There are many systems for project planning and scheduling, often using the acronyms CPM (critical path method) and PERT (program evaluation and review technique), that enable the staff to build a feasible schedule and to track performance, updating that schedule as the effort moves along. Microsoft Project is one such program that is usually readily available.

Funding

Few proposals get considered without a cost figure attached; however, there are a number of steps to be taken once that figure is approved. Congress authorizes much more initiatives than it funds. For example, in 1998, Congress passed, and President Clinton signed, the Ricky Ray Hemophilia Relief Act, which authorized a compassionate payment of $100,000 to each hemophiliac infected between 1982 and 1987 from contaminated blood products, or to their families if they had died. This was to compensate for lax government control of the blood supply. The authorization bill did not include the funding required, estimated to be $750 million, but only after considerable effort by advocacy groups was $75 million appropriated in fiscal year 2000, $100 million in fiscal 2002, and $475 million in other bills. By the time the program terminated in 2005, $559 million had been dispersed.

Stakeholder Engagement

Implementation must include a review of who the stakeholders are, including the following:

- Who needs to be kept informed?
- Who needs to participate in what detailed planning activities?
- Who can be an opinion leader or champion of the program?
- Who needs further training and motivation?
- Who can be an enabler?
- Who can be a blocker and needs to be co-opted?

The implementation planners must identify what messages to send to whom from whom, their frequency, and their content (see **Table 12-1**). Should it be delivered personally, by e-mail, through the media, through a representative, etc.? After those coordination and communication tasks are identified, they must also be scheduled either as discrete events or on an ongoing basis.

TABLE 12-1   Communications Strategy Tool

Key stakeholder	Desired commitment and strategy for securing commitment	Key messages that need to be delivered	Responsible officer

Source: Cabinet Implementation Unit, Dept. of Prime Minister and Cabinet, Canberra, Australia Commonwealth © 2005.

Enlist or Procure Task Implementers

Key resource needs should have been identified by this point in time, especially because the funding requirements have to be based on a schedule of the resources needed, especially personnel, equipment, and support systems. There may also be other less tangible resources that are mission critical, such as office space, computers and communication equipment, loaned personnel, and contractor personnel with special skills. For example, it is a frequent practice for contractors to assign their most competent personnel to preparing and marketing the proposal, but then substitute less experienced, less skilled, and less costly personnel as the work gets under way. Implementation managers must then fight to get the quality people and services that they expected originally.

Monitor Performance

The policy proposal usually specifies the quality and quantity of outcomes anticipated and may refer to the process and outcome measures to be used; however, the implementation planners may still have to develop, validate, and install measures and measurement systems to monitor progress and suggest improvements as the implementation proceeds. When planning for quality assurance measures, implementers should also keep in mind the kind of data, information, and documentation that will be needed to conduct an evaluation after the policy has been implemented.

When it comes to sequencing these implementation activities, there is no magic order. Many have to go forward in parallel from the proposal stage, with adjustments being made to each as problems and opportunities are encountered. New technology or results from ongoing studies may lead to program changes after the policy makers have completed their work. If so, the implementation team should then adopt them, but inform the policy makers of the change so that there will be no big surprises when the effort is being reviewed (e.g., during a site visit). The list of implementation activities offered here is quite detailed, and it is up to the implementation team to decide how much to invest in each activity. Not every stage will be relevant to each policy area, and the systems necessary to plan and monitor some of these stages may already be in place. The budgeting and scheduling functions should be basic management activities everywhere.

Manage Risks

The Australian *Guide to Preparing Implementation Plans* (2005) suggests that likely risks include:

- Unclear objectives and deliverables
- Unrealistic schedules
- Shortages of key resources—funds, people, equipment
- Lack of infrastructure and supports
- Lack of agency internal capacity.

Whatever the risk, the planning process needs to assess the likelihood of the risk occurring, its severity and impact, how to mitigate it, and who is responsible for preventive measures, for monitoring, and for action when it is needed.

SETTING UP TO SUCCEED

There is ample evidence that implementation is enhanced by adopting a process that involves implementers early and builds their commitment to the plan. Health care is going through a transition from a professional model that emphasizes individual responsibility, autonomy, and accountability toward an organizational one, hopefully one where organizational learning and transformation are norms. To succeed at this, a number of things need to happen, including:

1. Shared responsibility is accepted. Team leaders and members at all professional levels must come to share overall responsibility while still accepting individual responsibility for assigned tasks. The industrialization of health care often means that treatment processes are carried out by multiple actors whose actions must be coordinated.
2. Leadership takes place at multiple levels. The team involved in developing a policy must have facts about how the system works at the operational levels as well as the strategic level. Many developing countries still suffer from the system developed by the British Colonial Office for managing the Empire. Government consisted of mostly locals organized into two cadres: one, the civil service, developed policy, whereas the other, the health service, for example, implemented it. A small group of British officials controlled the flow of information from one to the other. The policy makers produced brilliant analyses that circulated in files held together with red ribbon (called *red tape* by

the English), but these analyses often proved unworkable for implementers in the field. It was an efficient way to use a small expatriate staff, but it did not necessarily produce effective delivery systems. All too many policies and plans have become "shelf art," sitting there unused because implementers do not see them as practical or relevant.

3. People understand the core business and technical processes, values, and mission of the organization. Participants must be knowledgeable and consistent in their decision making about policies and implementation. If policies and processes are not performing well, it is often useful to start a dialogue about process, values, and mission. Policies and processes do not bolt out of control. They silently drift away from the optimal as individuals and groups make incremental local adjustments in response to local events, stimuli, and negative experiences. The example above how one process moved away and failed to move back.

4. Expectations are managed. Some participants will be optimistic and expect too much, whereas others will be pessimistic or cynical and expect too little. Wilson and McLaughlin (1984) suggested that one needs to work out a psychological contract with the participants in planning that recognizes the scarcity of resources that might be involved and directly addresses the WIIFM (what's in it

The Origin of a Policy

The labor, delivery, recovery, and postpartum nursing team at a community hospital was reviewing their procedures and their cost items in order to become more competitive in their city. One policy that puzzled them was sending 100% of the placentas to the pathology laboratory after delivery. They kept asking around for the source of that rule and found that it stemmed from an incident many years earlier. At the time the daughter of the chief of obstetrics was having a difficult delivery and encountered a problem that might have been handled more effectively if the placenta from her delivery had been saved and analyzed. The angry chief thoroughly chewed out the OB nursing staff for not saving it. To avoid such a confrontation in the future, the nursing supervisor instituted the rule that all placentas would go to pathology. Both the chief of obstetrics and the nursing supervisor had long since retired, but the rule lived on. The three obstetricians currently practicing at the hospital developed a set of criteria for sending placentas to the laboratory. This new rule decreased the number of pathology reviews of placentas by 95%, resulting in substantial cost savings to the patients and the hospital.

for me?) question. **Table 12-2** provides their outline of the factors that such a psychological contract might consider. In essence, the contract specifies what each party gets from the exchange beyond monetary considerations.

5. Planning is continuous. The health care environment is continuously changing. There are many more opportunities and challenges than most organizations can take on at any one time. Through functional and cross-functional teams, managers involve providers and others in setting priorities, developing and evaluating alternatives, and meeting the many new challenges (Carroll & Edmondson, 2002).

TABLE 12-2   The Psychological Contract Under Scarce Resources

Employee Gets
- Performance standards to meet that represent realistic tradeoffs between funds, personnel, schedules, and service levels
- Personal courtesy and respect
- Supportive environment
- Meaningful and purposeful work
- Reasonable conflict and tension levels, mediated by clear standards for priority setting and evaluation of work
- Personal development opportunities
- Professional and organizational recognition for good work
- Security, as long as funds are available
- Processes for psychological contract change that reflect changing resource conditions

Organization Gets
- An honest day's work, at least
- Loyalty to the organization
- Initiative, especially in resource use
- Job effectiveness and efficiency in meeting overall organizational goals
- Flexibility and willingness to wear multiple hats under tight staffing
- Acceptance of reasonable tradeoffs among professional norms and organizational needs
- Participation in psychological contract change processes that reflect changing resource conditions

Source: Wilson & McLaughlin, 1984, p. 310.

6. Orientations are prospective rather than retrospective. Dopson and Fitzgerald (2005) and Senge et al. (1994) observed that behaviors and beliefs take time to change and require both abstract reasoning and experiential reinforcement. It is often easier to do things the way they have always been done. Looking to the past for precedent is usually a rational step in assessing a situation, but there is little assurance that what an organization has been doing is effective or will be so in the future. "Transforming leadership continually brings forward the vision of the future organization and indicates how the organization can get from where it is in the present to where it wants to be in the future" (Upshaw et al., 2006, p. 201).

7. Performance is assessed and rewarded. Effective policy change requires that the organization be prepared to commit real resources and have in place support mechanisms for recognizing creativity and innovation. Personnel evaluation processes and procedures must be in place to encourage implementers, as well as policy makers, to seek new ways to get things done and to prepare for the changing future.

THAT ALL-IMPORTANT START

Getting implementation started right is critical. If a team is involved, especially a multidisciplinary one (which would be the case for just about anything clinical), plan to offer leadership throughout the team formation cycle, which usually progresses through the following four stages:

1. Forming
2. Storming
3. Norming
4. Performing

Forming

The team needs to understand fully the factors behind the policy change and how it links to the institution's strategies. The team's initial efforts should be well-supported and include tasks that are carefully chosen to build a shared experience of success. At this stage, the team must also consider whether it includes representation of all the important implementers.

Storming

Because health care settings are complex and have many built-in tensions, the team often starts with a tendency to begin blaming, finding fault, or expressing distrust of others. The members have to be kept focused on their task until they begin to understand it and accept each other's viewpoints.

Norming

The group can set up norms of operation. For example, how decisions get made and work allocated. Do we vote? Do we have to have a consensus? What do we have to clear with higher authority? Do some professional groups have veto power?

Performing

After the barriers at each of the preceding stages are dealt with, the team can get on with its assigned tasks effectively or, having addressed them and failed to get over them, seek further guidance or facilitation.

PROVIDING FOR PERIODIC REVIEWS

Major change projects often require that multiple teams go forward in parallel. Again, one or more of these may veer off on its own path, and thus, it is important to stage periodic review sessions in which each team reports what it is doing, the progress it is making against measures such as budget and schedule, and what implementation barriers it is experiencing. This process enables senior policy overseers to assess overall progress and make adjustments to the current plan where necessary. It also allows the individual team leaders to see where they needed to interface with other teams in order to meet their objectives and how to adjust their efforts to what they learn at the review. The larger and more complex the project, the more important these periodic reviews become. For more about problems of implementation relating to project coordination and communication, it can be useful to review the literature on the fatal accidents that NASA has experienced.

IMPLEMENTING POLICIES THAT AFFECT CLINICAL DECISION MAKING

One of the more problematic areas for implementing policy involves getting professionals to change the way they carry out professional tasks. This has been a topic of concern to those who study quality of care, do continuing professional education, or sell pharmaceuticals and other supplies to the health industry. The move toward greater use of evidence-based medicine is a case in point. **Case 12-1** reports on an attempt to achieve change in the public mental health sector. Those responsible tried to do everything possible to induce change, but their results were limited. They started with strong top management support, they brought together academic experts and clinical opinion leaders to sanction adoption of the newer evidence-based practices (EBPs), and they then held training programs for those who would be the implementers; however, after their efforts had gone on a while, they reported that:

- After the key driver in the system, the top person, left, many seemed to act as if "this too would pass." The change agents noted that retraining of state agency staff was essential if implementation efforts were to be sustained.
- The middle layers of the state bureaucracy did not seem to "own" the change, perhaps because it upset existing relationships and power bases or because it was imported from another state.
- "There was a need for alignment of state-level policies, funding and systems to support implementation statewide." Tangible drivers such as changes in payer service definitions, service fees, and budget allocations were called for. Without these wake-up calls from the funders, it was easy for the implementers to argue that they were already using "best practices" and ignore the rigorous implementation guidelines associated with the evidence-based service definitions emphasized at the federal level.

This case study is very consistent with the case studies reported elsewhere. For example, Dopson and Fitzgerald (2005) provided a meta-analysis of a number of studies of implementing EBPs in the UK Health Service, in which Ferlie's (2005) concluding summary emphasized the role of leadership, organizational support, and the differences between *knowledge* (i.e., information) and *practice*.

> *In the best case examples, there appeared to be a circular relationship between research evidence and experience—they reinforced each other and were woven together. At other times, there was a tension between craft knowledge and formal evidence. It should be remembered that clinical practice contains an element of judgment and tacit knowledge more reminiscent of craft skills than traditional*

conceptions of science. It may be unwise to force a stark choice between the two modes (experience or science), but there may be a need to balance both (Ferlie, 2005, p. 188).

So knowledge in action is, for us, evidence that has been converted through social processes into locally accepted knowledge, which is then put into use and leads to evidence-based change in working practices (p. 190).

Paul Batalden at Dartmouth has suggested that professional training include a microsystem approach to continuous improvement in health care, operating alongside issues-centered and organization-centered efforts. Mohr and Batalden (2006) identified eight dimensions of an effective, improvement-oriented microsystem (a teaching clinic or hospital service):

1. Constancy of purpose
2. Investment in improvement
3. Alignment of role and training for efficiency and staff satisfaction
4. Interdependence of the care team to meet patient needs
5. Integration of information and technology into work flows
6. Ongoing measurement of outcomes
7. Support from the larger organization
8. Connection to the community to enhance care delivery and extend influence

THE POSTMORTEM

Assuming that the group doing the analysis and planning is going to be doing this kind of thing again, it is critical to review the group's own performance. This postproject analysis should be done by the planning group if the project was small- or medium-sized or by an independent evaluator if it was large or mission critical. Evaluation should study two aspects of the project—process and outcome. Process analysis should take place relatively quickly after the final report is delivered and should ask this question: "If we had to do this analysis project again, what would we do differently?" Because this can be threatening interpersonally, adding a little humor would not hurt.

The outcomes assessment part has to wait until the outcomes are evident. It can only be justified for major policy proposals that were actually implemented; otherwise, a second analysis might be needed to focus on what we might have done differently to get the proposal implemented. The failure to implement might be primarily due to outside factors. Either way one should be able to go back through the analysis and see how well the group defined the situation, assessed the technology, outlined the economics, adjusted to the political system, planned the implementation, and presented the product to the decision makers. Such a review is a key to improved organizational learning about policy analysis.

CONCLUSION

There is no silver bullet to make implementation easy; however, the elements of successful implementation are pretty well known. They involve top management consideration and support. They require understanding of the social context in which change takes place. Would-be implementers must focus on the players, their roles, their barriers to action, and the roles of leadership in bringing about change. It may be difficult to balance how much to invest in studying these influences before the policy decision is made and how much to leave until later once the political and financial compromises have been worked out. From an academic viewpoint, all of these should be worked out so that strategic policies are not derailed by the implementation details; however, decision makers are usually not comfortable with that level of detail as they deal broadly with a wide range of issues. They are very uncomfortable with surprises after the fact, but they do not want to be bogged down reading the fine print either. That is just a managerial reality. Perhaps the best answer is to turn to the experienced presenters on the team who know the behavior patterns of key decision makers and ask for their assessment of the appropriate level of detail to present at each stage.

Case 12-1

INTRODUCING EVIDENCE-BASED PRACTICE IN MENTAL HEALTH IN NORTH CAROLINA (B)

The Surgeon General's *1999 Report on Mental Health* reported that "a wide variety of community-based services are of proven value for even the most severe mental illnesses," but they were not being "translated into community settings." After this, the President's New Freedom Commission on Mental Health issued its 2003 report, *Achieving the Promise: Transforming Mental Health in America.* It noted that recovery from mental illness was now a possibility but "that for too many Americans with mental illnesses, the mental health services and supports they need remain fragmented, disconnected, and often inadequate."

One of the resulting initiatives was the national Implementing Evidence-Based Practice (EBP) Project sponsored by the Robert Wood Johnson Foundation and the Center for Mental Health Services, which is part of the Substance Abuse and Mental Health Services Administration. The intent of the project was to reduce the time it took for mental health programs to implement EBPs into mental health. The project identified six EBPs and developed implementation resource kits ("toolkits") to support their adoption. The six were as follows:

1. Assertive community treatment (ACT)
2. Supported employment
3. Medication management approaches in psychiatry
4. Illness management and recovery
5. Family psychoeducation
6. Integrated dual-disorder treatment

The Substance Abuse and Mental Health Services Administration and the National Institute for Mental Health followed up this project in 2003 with the State Implementation of

Evidence-Based Practices—the Bridging Science and Service Grant Program. North Carolina applied for Round One funding and in August 2003 the Mental Health/Developmental Disabilities and Substance Abuse Services (MH/DD/SAS) Division of the state Department of Health and Human Services received a 1-year, $100,000 grant for its North Carolina Science to Service Project (NCS2S).[2]

CHANGE CURRENTS IN NORTH CAROLINA

The state received this grant at a time when its public mental health system was experiencing considerable ferment. The state had four regional mental health hospitals which had been operating independently of its region's community-based services. In the 1980s, the state had acquired primary responsibility for funding these community mental health centers, which previously had been financed largely through centers from federal block grants.

Impetus for change was coming from several sources, but most important was the State Auditor's 2000 report *Study of the State Psychiatric Hospitals and the Area Mental Health Programs.* The report recommended that the state:

1. Define specific target populations requiring specialized services that matched each group's particular needs.
2. Develop new community-based capabilities to implement the EBPs.
3. Coordinate the funding mechanisms to assure that coordinated services were delivered to the target populations
4. Develop a state-wide training plan to support the development of new community capabilities.

[2] For a more complete description of the project, see B. Melcher and C. Rausch, North Carolina Science to Service Project, pp. 579-601, in C. P. McLaughlin and A. D. Kaluzny (eds.). (2006). *Continuous Quality Improvement in Health Care,* 3rd ed. Sudbury, MA: Jones and Bartlett, from which much of this presentation has been abstracted.

The Legislature responded by requiring an annual planning process for the mental health system. These plans, produced in 2001, 2002, and 2003, defined the target populations to be served, the service values to be promoted (person oriented, recovery oriented, community based), and the support to be provided (housing, transportation, work, and crisis response). The legislation and plans used words such as "best practices," but the 2003 plan finally cited the six EBPs as well as those considered emerging best practices.

The legislation also called for the area mental health centers to stop delivering services directly. After "divestiture," they would survive as "local management entities"(LMEs) accountable to their county commissioners and would contract out service delivery, but perform the evaluation and oversight functions that many felt had been in conflict with their service delivery roles. Some observers anticipated that these redefined LMEs, and their oversight functions would be further regionalized and undergo a transition from a quasi-governmental agency to an HMO-type structure, perhaps with capitation rather than fee-for-service Medicaid and Medicare revenues and budget-based state appropriations.

THE PROJECT

The NCS2S project was housed for convenience with the Governor's Institute on Alcohol and Substance Abuse in Research Triangle Park, NC, about 15 miles from the MH/DD/SAS Division's offices in Raleigh. The project hired the then legislative advocate and former executive director of the NC National Alliance for the Mentally Ill, as project director. The Governor's Institute also assigned staff to the project which focused on raising awareness of EBPs, conducting a needs assessment and a knowledge assessment, setting priorities, and researching adoption.

Raising Awareness

During its first year, NCS2S collaborated with just about every local stakeholder group to develop EBPs workshops and offer them at their state meetings. Representatives of national organizations and various states implementing EBPs participated and presented. The project collaborated with the Area Health Education Centers and the state association for the LMEs to present "Toolkit" workshops, which it also made available on CD-ROM. A project Web site provided definitions of these practices, fidelity scales for evaluation, answers to frequently asked questions, and links to relevant other sites.

Needs Assessments

The University of North Carolina School of Social Work conducted a needs assessment with input and guidance from a Consortium Research Committee established by the project. The assessment provided a comprehensive baseline measure of awareness about the six practices among providers, administrators, consumers, and families, and it identified perceived barriers and needs for their implementation.

Knowledge Assessments

The project staff reviewed local planning documents and found them to have little reference to the six practices or their underlying concepts. Surveys of front-line providers asked them about their "familiarity with each of the EBPs, their agency's level of provision of each EBP, their need for training in EBPs and preference for training modality, and their views on the challenges to EBP implementation, fidelity, and sustainability." They were also surveyed on the needs of the Spanish-speaking consumers in their area. The survey found considerable confusion at the provider and state bureaucracy levels about "evidence-based practices," with many claiming to be using "best practices" but not understanding the six EBPs.

Priority Setting

A committee of the consortium recommended that planning focus on two EBPs: ACT and supported employment. The final plan recommendation was delivered to the director of the Division of MH/DD/SAS on August 2, 2004. It also suggested a process to promote implementation of application research into practice.

Adoption Research

Focus groups on ACT teams suggested overall satisfaction, but perceived a need to strengthen vocational supports and to continue to study the adaptation of the ACT team concept for rural area implementation.

POSTGRANT ANALYSIS

The federal program administrators asked the NCS2S staff to offer candid observations about their experience after the grant concluded. Their response included the following:

- It takes considerable time to develop awareness and buy-in for the EBPs among constituents, especially providers.
- "Strong, consistent, visible" state leadership is essential to gain support of a broad constituency, especially the state bureaucracy. They noted that retraining of state agency staff was essential if implementation efforts were to be sustained.
- Because implementation takes place at the community level, it will be most successful where consumers and families feel ownership for EBPs and advocate for their adoption and evaluation.

CHANGING EXTERNAL CLIMATE

The policy of divestiture continued throughout this period, but there was a change of leadership in April 2004. The director of the Division of MH/DD/SAS, who was brought in from Michigan in February 2002, resigned to return to Michigan. In his Exit Communique, he noted the following (Visingardi, 2004):

The reform effort in North Carolina is indeed difficult. We may be the only state that is taking on the change process in a comprehensive manner. This is "good" because fixing only one part at a time in a system that has inter-related parts will not ultimately render a system where all the parts are aligned in such a manner that it will work well together. This is problematic due to the fact that many of the system stakeholders only are interested in and under-stand and/or value certain "parts" as opposed to the over-all system itself. The comprehensive change is "bad," as it requires virtually the entire system to develop a new foun-dation and related competencies in such as massive manner. Realizing and acting in a manner that reflects the transitional nature of the change effort mitigates the "bad." This is going to be a long-term change process that will require an adherence to the vision but an allowance for both flexibility and adjustments along the way.

DISCUSSION QUESTIONS

1. Where did the impetus for change seem to come from in this case? What was the significance of that for imple-mentation?

2. What are the strengths and weaknesses of using outsiders (division director and project director) to induce change in a mental health care delivery system?

3. What is the implication of focusing on a target popula-tion for community health centers then organized along the 1970s model? What are the implications of that change for the existing system?

4. How effective would stakeholder consortia be at induc-ing changes in treatment modalities by providers?

5. What does this case say about the role of professionals in implementing health care policy initiatives?

Part III

The Professional as a Participant

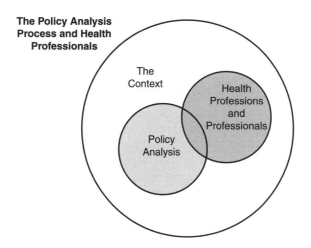

The Policy Analysis Process and Health Professionals

The Context

Health Professions and Professionals

Policy Analysis

We expect that most users of this book will be current or future health professionals. They need to understand the role of the professions and professionals in the health policy process. Although not disinterested parties, they can bring to the table their commitment, their technical expertise, and their concern for the patient. They also bring their economic interests; however, all of the other actors will be doing the same thing, and their economic interests will be known to the other parties. Likewise, health professionals must understand the positions of the others at the table and be prepared to evaluate how they are affected by various policy alternatives.

Chapter 13 looks at what alternatives and approaches are likely to work, given current U.S. political processes. Chapter 14 addresses the leadership roles open to professionals and the skills that they need to develop to perform them appropriately. Chapter 15, the concluding chapter, sums up some of the issues raised in earlier chapters and sends you on your way, hopefully as an effective future participant in the policy process. Three chapter exercises are included in this part of the book to reinforce the concepts presented throughout the book.

CHAPTER 13

What Is Likely to Work

From a policy standpoint, comprehensive coverage makes more sense, but from a political standpoint, it is unlikely to happen. We have a political system that, by its very design, is inherently conservative. It rarely takes on big, sweeping changes of any type, not just in the area of health care policy, but also in making tax policy and social policy. Having worked in the states of Louisiana and New York, I can tell you there are very few similarities in how the political systems in those states view the problem of the uninsured and how they view solutions to the problem.

> —Ken Thorpe, former Assistant Secretary for Health Policy, DHHS in the Clinton Administration and member of President Clinton's Health Care Reform Task Force (1999)

Massachusetts' experience in putting together a plan for providing health care coverage for nearly every resident that was acceptable to both political parties has been cited as a blueprint for the future. The plan included elements promoted by both sides of the political spectrum and dodged some issues that were hardest to deal with (Belluck, 2007). To a planner, that may look like a compromise, much like the ones that have put us where we are today—another case of muddling through. It certainly will attract critics who want a single-payer system as well as those that want a completely free market system. Even if the Massachusetts plan succeeds in reaching its goal of covering everyone, it may aggravate other problems. The Connector Authority has already had to make a number of agonizing compromises, one on a cap of lifetime payments and another on minimum premium levels

Although there is a building consensus for universal coverage, we might be worse off if we get it without other system changes that reduce waste, expand primary care services, and address the impact on prices of treating additional millions of low- and middle-income people.

In the field of health policy, consensus is hard to come by and even harder to sustain. There are certain conclusions, however, that seem to be inescapable:

- Health care is headed toward 20% of GDP over the next decade. There is likely to be considerable risk associated with any radical changes in that large a portion of the economy, especially for governments contending with competing issues such as international competition, immigration, terrorism, federal government deficits, and rising energy costs. It is unlikely that anyone can broker a comprehensive solution to our many intersecting health care problems.

- The race of employers away from responsibility for paying the premiums for workers, worker families, and pensioners will continue, swelling the ranks of the uninsured and generating some pressure for action on access for the uninsured. There is also evidence that insurance companies, if allowed to do selective underwriting and are not constrained by benefit mandates, will come up with less expensive products for individuals (with lesser coverage) to adapt to the changing market. The risk is that these basic packages and new exclusions will create another class of underinsured individuals, including the pregnant and mentally ill, and possibly drive up the premiums for the chronically ill and others who require more comprehensive coverage.

- The unique aspects of health care in terms of uncertainty, agency conflict, and market failure will constrain the degree to which free market solutions will take hold. They will help some, however, especially with efforts that force insurers and providers to compete on price.

- What happens with communicable diseases in other countries affects the United States much more rapidly because of global transfers of people, foodstuffs, money, and information.

- One unknown is the role of international competition in this sector. For a long time, health care was considered to be immune to globalization. Now, however, there is increasing evidence that globalization

can affect health care services in a number of ways. The flow of physicians into the United States for training and their subsequent experiences practicing here set up the potential for a competent workforce
elsewhere, as we now see returnees performing hip and heart valve
replacements in a number of countries at a third of the cost and
brokered by international middlemen. Similarly, but more darkly,
the illicit market in transplantable organs is rapidly growing, again
through middlemen. There is also the international trade in prescription drugs, which is primarily attributed to Canada but is really wider
and has great growth potential.

- The perceived instability of the Medicare "insurance" system will put
pressure on the federal government, but that reckoning will likely be
postponed because it will be beyond the re-election time horizons of
most politicians. States will be dealing with the burden of the working poor and the uninsured. That and the problems of local disasters,
especially if a pandemic occurs, will lead to pressures on the federal
government to provide more leadership. If the states are generally
successful, the federal government will not seek a comprehensive
solution. If they fail and that in turn threatens the fiscal integrity of
the states, Congress will be forced to act.

- A totally federal solution is unlikely. It is more likely that federal
legislation will enable each state to set up its own coverage system,
perhaps along the Canadian provincial model, and cobble together
funding sources such as federal block grants, Medicaid waivers, low-
level employer coverage, private insurance, and means-tested patient
payment. Then at the request of a number of players there will be
some attempt over a number of years to harmonize the individual
state systems with more and more federal government intervention
and regulation while still maintaining the appearance of 50-some
territorial and state systems.

The history of health care in the United States is that we can reach agreements that salve our consciences and deal with the worst access problems,
if we take the time to work them through. We are a wealthy nation with
lots of disposable income, but by focusing on access, we often fail to take
steps to solve major issues involving our delivery system.

The greatest uncertainties, therefore, are not on the financing side, but on
the cost control side. Our past experience with Medicare has been that

increased access has led to increased demand and increased prices (Finkelstein, 2007). Many cost-oriented measures that seem to work over time have been described previously. They could involve the following:

1. Removing provider incentives and opportunities for overutilization
2. Reducing contribution margins and incomes of providers and suppliers to levels comparable with other professional services through administered pricing or competition
3. Reducing the costs of malpractice coverage and the need for defensive medicine
4. Allowing more international competition to drive down prices
5. Constraining treatment choices to those that are most effective and efficient
6. Encouraging labor substitution for those process steps that can be made routine
7. Empowering primary care providers to control utilization and self-referral
8. Increasing the supply of providers to levels available in other countries
9. Allowing some longer waiting periods for elective procedures to slow consumption
10. Increasing use of information technology to avoid waste and medical error, but also trying to avoid the implementation of these systems in ways that are anticompetitive at both the provider and equipment supplier levels
11. Employing community rating and no-fault health care insurance, tempered by tiered premium systems for those continuing high-risk behaviors
12. Restoring more volunteerism to the health care sector.

If international pressures ease and states find that they must demand more stringent measures from Washington or if there is an economic meltdown, then we are likely to see further implementation of measures with more impact. They could include the following:

- Mandated health insurance for all
- Full transparency in health care pricing, including bundled prices for all stages of a specific medical condition

- Legislation to amend the Employee Retirement Income Security Act (ERISA) to remove that exemption of self-insured plans from state jurisdiction
- Regionalization of care for complex or rare medical conditions, requiring greater patient travel but producing much less waste and better outcomes
- Stronger control of the referral process by primary care providers
- Other aspects of value-based competition (Porter & Teisberg, 2006) in the marketplace, including the following:
  - Integrated IT systems reporting bundled prices and quality performance
  - Attention to the total process of care, making it better coordinated and more effective
  - Risk pools for those at high risk, perhaps leading to community rating via the back door
  - Shifting the direct costs of medical error back onto the provider institutions rather than the patient or payer
  - Shifting research budget priorities from developing and evaluating new treatments to evaluating methods already in use
  - Limitations on allowable price discrimination, perhaps along the lines of the Robinson-Patman antitrust law, but applied to individuals
  - Phasing out of corporate practice of medicine laws and other restrictive regulations to open up competition on price and results. This needs to be accompanied by licensure procedures that are more closely linked to performance.

Are we saying that the future of our health care depends more on what happens to our supply of foreign oil or to the willingness of others to underwrite our debt—factors that if they change significantly could precipitate an economic breakdown—than on our own democratic processes? That is possible. Noted health economist Victor Fuchs (2002) has suggested that major health system change such as national health insurance will come only after the "kind of change that often accompanies a war, a depression or large scale civil unrest" (p. 1824).

WORKING OUT YOUR OWN SCENARIOS

We can push the policy envelope by considering some extreme scenarios against the status quo and seeing what kind of a health care system might result; however, as noted in Chapter 7 on technological forecasting, getting single-event estimates is only one step in the process. An event may be acceptable on its own, but its interaction with other events may result in an aggregate outcome that is totally unacceptable. For example, encouraging kidney transplants for end-stage renal disease patients is one thing, but if the supply is totally inadequate and that promotes a sizable international traffic in involuntarily harvested human kidneys, would that be unacceptable? Later here we have set up an illustrative example with multiple scenarios to compare.

Let's look at the following five scenarios, three of which are extreme:

A. Extrapolating current trends
B. Extreme reliance on free market
C. Extreme industrialization
D. National economic crisis resulting in major tax code reform
E. The Emanuel-Fuchs proposal

By way of illustration, we have provided event predictions for 15 boxes in **Table 13-1** for the first four of these scenarios. A rational person can certainly come up with others, and thus, we have included Table 13-2, which encourages you to build your own, redefining the scenarios and then assessing the impact of a set of events that you are free to augment.

Scenario A: The Status Quo Extrapolated

As you look down column *A* of Table 13-1, you see that not much new is happening to reduce costs. We might expect to see some responses as funding becomes more and more of a problem, namely, reductions in malpractice insurance costs and international competition to reduce prices of some procedures. There are also possibilities that as consumers and insurers find it harder and harder to pay their bills, provider incomes will fall further, along with institutional contribution margins. Information technology (IT) will move into place, but it may still be subject to the complaint of Brailer that despite increased deployment of health IT, the motivation to share information in still lacking (Cunningham, 2005). Thus, one might see some internal waste and medical error reduced, but a very high investment cost

TABLE 13-1   Building Some Scenarios for Cost Reduction

Change Scenario	A	B	C	D	E
1. Remove provider incentives to overutilize	N	N	N	Y	
2. Major changes in staffing requirements	N	Y	Y	Y	
3. Major reductions in provider and staff incomes and contribution margins	?	Y	N	Y	
4. Reduced costs of malpractice coverage	Y	?	Y	Y	
5. International competition reducing prices	Y	Y	?	?	
6. Constraining treatment choices to those most effective and efficient	N	N	Y	Y	
7. Encouraging labor substitution where process can be industrialized	N	Y	Y	Y	
8. Empowering primary car providers to control utilization and self-referrals	N	N	Y	Y	
9. Increasing supply of providers to levels in other countries	N	Y	N	?	
10. Increased waiting periods and other devices to increase competition	N	N	Y	Y	
11. Increasing use of IT to reduce waste and medical error without constraining competition	?	Y	N	?	
12. Global budgeting of hospitals and other institutions to ration capital, perhaps on a regional basis	N	N	Y	Y	
13. Community rating and no-fault health insurance, perhaps with tiered premiums	N	N	N	Y	
14. Stripping away less essential services or covering outside health insurance system	?	?	Y	Y	
15. Return of more voluntarism in the health sector	N	Y	N	N	

Y = likely, N = not likely, and ? = not predicted

Scenario A is the extrapolation of the current trends in the current system.

Scenario B is the case of an extremely strong move toward a free market health care system.

Scenario C is the case of an extremely strong move in the direction of industrialization and corporate governance of health care.

Scenario D is the case of a major economic crisis that leads the country to a major overhaul of government programs, including health care, and major changes in the tax code such as shift from the income tax to a value-added or some other form of consumption tax.

Scenario E provides all citizens a voucher for basic health coverage replacing current insurance and Medicaid and ultimately Medicare. It would be financed with a value-added tax and add administrative systems to oversee coverage, technology assessment and quality measurement and to replace the current tort system for malpractice with administrative law.

and then find relatively little immediate impact on operating cost. Some major changes might occur on the funding side, so you might want to repeat the exercise with an added set of rows representing programmatic changes on the funding side.

Scenario B: Extreme Reliance on the Free Market

Here we would be likely to see little or no action to reduce costs, except to increase the competitive pressures from foreign competition and to increase the supply of providers. The primary argument for consumer-centered health care—that consumers will make choices to lower their own costs of care—is not addressed in this listing. Again, you might want to repeat the exercise with some events related to consumer-driven health care as an additional set of rows; however, the lower the resulting profit margins and professional incomes, the more providers are likely to improve efficiency to compete on cost, resulting in staffing changes, better use of information technology for scheduling and coordination, and more use of volunteers.

Scenario C: Extreme Industrialization

Under the corporate, industrializing scenario, the resulting oligopolistic firms will likely try to resist and/or seek protection from a number of cost-reduction pressures, such as foreign competition and increasing the supply of providers. At the same time, they will likely make a number of internal policy choices that limit provider options, restrict capital investment, constrain institutional budgets, and break jobs down into repetitive tasks doable by lower level, lower paid personnel. They will also be likely to resist and lobby against measures to limit overutilization, as long as those limits affect their revenues.

Scenario D: National Economic Crisis Resulting in Major Tax Code Reform

In this scenario, the nation is in severe economic difficulties and radical change is in the air. The number of uninsured has skyrocketed, and something has to be done. That is when federally administered universal coverage might have a chance of coming in, especially if the tax system were to be restructured at the same time to emphasize consumption-based taxation and eliminate the health care income tax deductions. At the same time, there is likely to be a much higher level of regulation affecting choices of treatments, capital availability, and staffing coupled with community rating. Resources will be very tight; thus, waiting lines will lengthen, and there will be pressures to put hospitals on fixed budgets, reduce services that are not absolutely necessary, and concentrate specialized treatment capacities to increase throughput and effectiveness.

Scenario E: Emanuel and Fuchs Proposal

In a one-page *Fortune* article, Emanuel and Fuchs (2006) suggested, "How to cure U.S. health care." They offered a comprehensive five-part program, the centerpiece of which would be a health care voucher for every citizen currently under 65 years old. It would cover currently accepted levels of care with existing or new health plans. Each individual would then have a choice of 5 to 10 plans that would have to accept all comers.

The vouchers would be paid for by an earmarked 10% value-added tax that would be offset by replacing current employment-based insurance premiums, Medicaid expenditures, and individual and corporate tax deductions for health care premiums. Medicare recipients would be grandfathered (so to speak) under the current system, but those in the new program would stay with it past 65 years old, and Medicare would gradually be phased out.

To administer it, there would be a new system of federal and regional boards, much like the Federal Reserve System, to provide accountability, specify and modify the benefit package, and oversee technology assessment and quality evaluations. Malpractice cases would be assigned to a separate administrative system that would adjudicate and pay claims and oversee linkages to quality measurement and the licensure process. We have left column *E* of Table 13-1 blank for you and your colleagues to assess and fill in.

Interpreting Table 13-1

As you can see, virtually every scenario has elements that U.S. patients would strongly object to and is likely to generate strong opposition from one or more interest groups. That is why the most radical departures from current trends of more intramarket competition and more industrialization are likely to occur only if there is a general meltdown of the economic system, evoking new, strong domestic leadership with the will to take the government in a very different direction; however, it is apparent that each of the first three scenarios is weak in terms of its likely effects on health care costs, and ultimately, draconian measures may be taken. In other words, nothing is likely to work until the society either runs out of money or reaches some consensus as to when enough health care is enough. Economists differ on whether that will be 10, 20, or 25 years from now (Hall & Jones, 2007).

CHAPTER EXERCISE: WORKING WITH YOUR OWN SCENARIOS

We purposely offered scenarios that omitted some key policy possibilities (like consumer-oriented health care) in hopes that you and your associates would undertake your own evaluative process and (1) flesh out your own list of changes to be tried, (2) match them against your own list of scenarios, (3) debate the effects of each change on the outcome of each scenario, and (4) come up with your own concepts of what would or would not work in the United States under various conditions. **Table 13-2** is provided for that purpose. We do not have pat answers. Most have been tried somewhere in the world with mixed results. What would you want the United States to try next, perhaps on a small scale, to see how it works here?

SO, WHAT IS LIKELY TO WORK?

One takeaway from this exercise is that quite radical change is unlikely to happen until the U.S. economy is threatened by other events, and health care is seen as a part of the total package of changes that includes revisions in our tax code and is part of a compromise designed to deal with bigger overall problems. Short of that, we are likely to see incremental changes with a forecast increase in the proportion of the gross domestic product devoted to health care. Regardless of the party in power, health care is likely to take a back seat to national security, immigration reform, reduced dependence on foreign oil and the related replacement of much of our automotive stock, and inflationary pressures because of lack of savings and the rising cost of interest necessary to attract foreign capital. The one likely exception may be efforts to extend some form of coverage to all, especially to more children. Along the way, we will probably see some offsetting federal efforts to strip out of Medicare and Medicaid some services that are not essential to health and safety in the short run, some positive effects from prevention programs, and increased experimentation with pay-for-performance. In the short run, maintaining even the current level of covered lives will come from the efforts of state and local governments. These efforts will probably center on cost-effective, basic-level health insurance pools that small businesses and by some of the working poor can afford. The pressure on both low-income working families and older people to pay a higher percentage of their income for health care will continue, and the benefits available to the disabled and the unemployed are likely to atrophy further.

TABLE 13-2 Your Exercise on Building Cost Reduction Scenarios

Change Scenario	A	B	C	D	E
1. Remove provider incentives to overutilize	N				
3. Major reductions in provider and staff incomes	?				
	?				
5. Reduced costs of malpractice coverage	Y				
7. Constraining treatment choices to those most effective and efficient	?				
16. Encouraging labor substitution where process can be industrialized					
17. Empowering primary care providers to control utilization and self-referrals					
18. Rationing capital available to institutions					
21. Increased waiting periods and other devices to increase competition					
22. Increasing use of IT to reduce waste and medical error without constraining competition					
23. Global budgeting of hospitals and other institutions, perhaps on a regional basis					
24. Community rating and no-fault health insurance, perhaps with tiered premiums					

Y = likely, N = not likely, and ? = not predicted

Scenario A is the extrapolation of the current trends in the current system.

Scenario B _____.

Scenario C _____.

Scenario D _____.

Scenario E _____.

Why Not an Unraveling?

In January 2006, in advance of President Bush's State of the Nation speech, *The Economist* published a scathing review of the U.S. health care system, including a forecast of a "great unraveling."

> *With employers limiting their commitments and government unable to fund its commitments, America's health system will unravel—perhaps not this year or next, but soon. Few health experts deny this. Nor do they disagree much on the sources of the problem. Health markets are plagued with poor information, inadequate competition and skewed incentives.*

We suspect that such an outcome is still a number of years away for the following reasons:

- Measures undertaken in the interim will have some effect.
- Overall growth and efficiency improvement in other sectors would enable consumers to choose to allocate a larger proportion of the gross domestic product to their health care.
- Inflation in other sectors, such as energy, could divert interest and support.
- Employment in the health sector is healthy.
- Temporizing is the name of the game.

Measures Undertaken Will Have Some Effect

Although measures such as consumer-driven health care and the growth of integrated health systems are unlikely to solve the problems of the health sector, they will, like other measures before them, have some effect in slowing the rate of growth. Efforts to improve quality of care and introduce evidence-based medicine will have some impact and so will efforts to get comparative information to consumers and payers. Reductions in provider incomes, although personally painful, are unlikely to reduce the care available and may increase productivity. Introduction of IT may do the same. Given enough time, these many small improvements will have some cumulative effect, especially if institutions focus on a more limited range of patients and diseases and gain more efficiency for themselves.

Inflation in Other Sectors Could Offset the Impact of Health Care Growth

Despite the opposition of the Federal Reserve, politicians may find it advantageous to allow a higher level of inflation in the economy, bringing growth to the rest of the economy and to tax revenues. If there are some constraints on health care expenditures at the same time, the inflation rate in the overall economy might approach or surpass that of the health care sector and reduce the burden of added costs. International lenders may require more repayment of loans and force more favorable exchange rates, raising the costs of foreign goods, so that health care does not seem quite so expensive in comparison.

Employment in the Health Sector Is Healthy

As the proportion of national income devoted to health care increases, we will see more and more employment in that sector. Like most other service sectors, health care employs a large number of individuals of moderate and low income. Continuing industrialization will mean that some higher income workers will be displaced by lower income workers as some tasks become rationalized and can be handled routinely.

One risk to the country of having health care get so big is that a large proportion of the population will have their aspirations tied to the growth of that sector. Major cutbacks in expenditures, whether caused by improved quality and productivity or taken arbitrarily, will trigger a pushback by the affected employees. The growth of the health care sector is not a negative event from an employment point of view, especially as manufacturing and information-related service jobs continue to move out of the country.

Some economists are beginning to argue that health care expansion is the key to maintaining employment and that a substantial proportion of the population will be willing to spend a greater proportion of their income on health care because they attach a high subjective utility to their own longevity and care (Cutler et al., 2006; Hall & Jones, 2007). The problem with such growth is that it will continue to force the transfer of wealth away from the young, the healthy, and the poor and toward the older population, the sick, and the professionals. At some point, those footing the bill will begin to object strongly to these transfers, and we will see much more stringent measures to control expenditures and reduce those transfer rates (Kolata, 2006b). This is especially likely to create a political backlash if the income gap between low-wage workers and higher income knowledge workers and managers continues to expand.

Temporizing Is the Name of the Game
Enough said.

CONCLUSION

The United States is unlikely to undertake major health care reforms at the federal level in the near future. The states will continue to lead the reform effort, but focus primarily on improved access. A number of tweaking changes to reduce costs will move forward, but major cost reductions will not take place until the states get into financial trouble. Only if there is a general economic recession and a problem financing state budgets and the national debt are there likely to be radical changes. Employers may support the notions of value-based care, especially transparency in pricing, and an end to price discrimination. The position of specialists is likely to weaken as primary-care providers are asked to reduce waste and improve efficiency, and capital-intensive, rare, and complex procedures are concentrated at selected sites, often outside traditional market areas.

This chapter emphasized the importance of putting event forecasts into scenarios to highlight how events and measures will interact. Five illustrative scenarios were considered dealing with the status quo ante, more industrialization, more governmental involvement, and more of a free market; however, even these were not examined exhaustively, and further examination would be expected.

Available measures and expected adjustments are likely to delay the anticipated "unraveling" of the health care system. As it grows, people may become increasingly concerned about upsetting the economy with radical measures. The issue that will have to be faced will not be the size of the sector, but the distributional effects of its growth, the equity concerns of transfers of income from the young on behalf of the old and from the poor and middle class toward the wealthy. These will generate pressures to reduce waste and overall cost in the health sector as payers resist further premiums or taxation.

CHAPTER 14

Health Professional Leadership

Normal is getting narrower and narrower.

—Personal observation by an
experienced nurse practitioner

Health professionals are important to health policy processes. They bring their experiences, their knowledge of both science and art, their ability to distinguish between the two, and their commitment to the patient. Typically, they also bring a commitment to lifelong learning. The power of the professions, especially physicians, has been waning of late, but that has a lot to do with the height of their dominance in the past. In an open, market-driven, information-rich society, the kind of monopoly power described by Starr (1982) is not sustainable. Health professionals now need to undertake new leadership roles or else their status will be further undermined by those actively seeking a greater share of the pie. Given the forecasts that the health care sector will comprise 20% of the U.S. economy in 2015, health care policy leadership is sure to draw a crowd of interested parties.

DISINTERESTEDNESS

Much of the diminished respect for health professionals stems from the public's perception of a loss of disinterestedness. The current fashion in economics seems to deny the concept of disinterestedness—the concept of lack of bias and freedom from special interest, the ability to set aside one's own interests and to seek the best possible outcome for others. One symptom is the oft-repeated phrase, "All they care about is money." Money is harder to come by in most parts of the health care system because of utilization controls and deep discounts to health care plans, and thus, increased concern is understandable; however, that is not reassuring to the public. Much of the literature on the rising costs of care blames the current fee-for-service system for making it in the providers' interest to promote overutilization. Schlesinger (2002) argued that this loss of faith seemed to intensify with the advent of Medicare and Medicaid and that that has led to a loss of political power as well. One parameter of successful professional leadership will be the ability to engender faith that the professional and the profession have the interests of other constituencies in mind.

INFORMATIONAL CREDIBILITY

Earlier chapters noted how disintermediation in general and direct-to-consumer advertising in particular were affecting the informational monopoly of the health professions. This is not a one-way street. The claims and counterclaims of the various interested parties can be hard to sort out. One leadership role for the health professional is to guide the general public through that welter of information. This is not just a physician's task. It involves all health professionals. An article in *Business Week* asks, "How Good Is Your Online Nurse?" It compares the online patient portals of the three largest health insurers: Wellpoint, United Health Group, and Aetna (Weintraub, 2006). The trends reported included greater integration with patient records, more add-on purchased counseling, and more personalized responses. It concluded, "A bit like Big Brother? Sure. But as health care gets more complex, it's comforting to have a virtual coach" (p. 89). Despite the word nurse in the title, the article compares the companies' automated systems tailoring the information. One insurer did offer written and telephone nutritional consultations for a fee, but the professional component was largely invisible in the process. Maintaining the power of the professions in the future will take substantial effort to maintain acceptance as a unique and relevant information domain. There is relatively little art in computerized communications, and the public might well want more in the way of art, if it is offered. A counterexample is the rise of boutique medical services, which offer more access and attention for an annual fee. Conceding the informational domain to others is risky. Procedural control alone is a slender reed on which to stake the future of a profession.

TO INFLUENCE GLOBALLY, START LOCALLY

The health professional's power to participate effectively in the political process is earned through leadership in one's profession, one's institution, and in one's community. True, some leaders and spokespersons appear to have burst onto the national scene directly—Dr. David Brailer in government and health information technology, for example, and Dr. Atul Gawande with his *New Yorker* articles and his book, *Complications* (2002)—but most rise slowly through the ranks of their profession as team players. The routes to leadership positions are varied. Health professionals are in leadership roles in medical centers, community hospitals, government agencies, and insurance companies. Each presumably came by his or her position by training, intelligence, hard work, and usually trustworthiness. They were able to convince others to work beside them and for them because they could be trusted to take the interests of others into account.

Leadership career paths often overlooked in the health policy arena are those in corporations and as entrepreneurs. A number of very influential health professionals have stopped delivering care directly and have moved into the management of health institutions, insurance companies, occupational health, medical device and supply companies, pharmaceutical companies, and government agencies. They represent those institutions but seem able to do so without negating the trust of health care decision makers. Their leadership roles may have been thrust on them, or they may have sought them. In either case, they took a prepared mind and a sense of what they want to accomplish in their arena of health care policy.

The press seems to emphasize the importance of careers in publicly held companies, as considerable wealth can be created by developing a company and taking it public. After the company goes public, however, it is beholden primarily, if not solely, to one set of stakeholders, the stockholders; therefore, there is still a major role in health care for the not-for-profit organization that does not have stockholders and can balance a number of competing interests. A deeper knowledge of not-for-profit organizations and their behaviors is necessary for determining their role in setting and implementing health policy. This is especially true of entrepreneurial not-for-profit organizations that can participate in the marketplace as fully as a stock corporation, provided that they do not need to raise large amounts of capital quickly. Leaders must understand the similarities and differences in how these types of organizations function. The term *governance* is often applied to the roles of management, staff, and boards in both for-profit and not-for-profit organizations. The professional leader must be able to function effectively and help govern effectively in one or the other or both.

RISK TAKING

Moving out of a traditional professional role requires being able to deal with new classes of risks and to accept success, failure, or both. There are many successful health professional entrepreneurs and leaders and some unsuccessful ones. Recent events have shown us situations where successful professional leadership has been followed by failure. An example is the rise of large physician practice management organizations that grew very rapidly in the 1990s but failed as their leaders strayed from their areas of expertise and listened, not to their customers, but to those who were concerned only with increasing stock prices.

HEALTH POLICY ANALYSIS: A RELEVANT SCHOOL FOR LEADERSHIP

Participating in policy discussions and analyses can also help prepare one for leadership. By reviewing and critiquing the alterative scenarios provided by scholars—such as the consumer-oriented free-market approach of Herzlinger (1997) versus the community-based planning approach of Shortell et al. (1996) versus new approaches being undertaken by the various states—one can learn a great deal. These debates offer a number of possible intellectual leadership roles for trained policy analysts with professional backgrounds and skills.

Evaluating the alternatives calls for an understanding of the types of risks that health care organizations and health care managers may choose to handle or not handle in the design of their system. These risks have been described as follows (McLaughlin, 1997; McLaughlin & Kaluzny, 1997):

- Underwriting
- Marketing
- Clinical operations
- Financial
- Regulatory
- Integrative.

The would-be professional leader has to think through the following questions:

- Which of these risks am I now comfortable handling?
- Which other ones do I need and want to learn to handle?
- How can I use my work or educational experiences to learn to handle those that I want or need to handle?

This exercise can help the potential professional leader outline what he or she needs to learn about managerial skills and activities. One must learn to analyze the various organization forms used for health care delivery in terms of how they allocate these risks and facilitate their handling.

GOVERNANCE

Not only must health care professional leaders manage, but they must also provide what Karl Weick (1995) called *sense making* for those being led. They must be able to understand and articulate the role of the governance process in their operation. Health care professionals guard and maintain the technological core of health care organizations. They demand a role in their governance processes and governance mechanisms, which are the keys to effective technical and organizational change. Their leaders must understand how these processes operate and how their professions and other actors can best work together in the policy-making process. Through understanding the risks to be encountered, analyzing the nature of local markets and delivery organizations, and meeting the governance needs of organizations delivering care, health profession leaders can become equipped to analyze and improve local health care systems.

PLANNING ALTERNATIVES

Professional leaders must be able to analyze issues of health care policy for specific communities and specific segments of health care. These have to be analyzed against specific public health criteria of quality, access, and cost. Here health policy intersects with the issues of quality and quality improvement; however, one can also master less familiar risks, such as underwriting (including pricing). Leaders must consider quality measurement and improvement and disease-management approaches. Imbedded in such studies are opportunities to develop insights about the ability or inability of organizations to handle high levels of inherent variability in definitions, patients, events, costs, etc. This needs to be a continuing theme in analysis, one relating back to the issues of art versus science and Deming's (1986) notions about special cause variation and common cause variation. Health care professions have historically treated all situations, whether art or science, as if they were science. Consequently, they have assumed that any negative consequences were the result of special cause variation, holding the individual practitioner responsible for adverse events. What future managers have to learn from the Deming approach is that health care is a field that will have high variability, even without special cause variation, and that administrative systems have to be tailored to that reality. Success in health care is as much dependent on a team's functioning in an effective system as it is on any individual professional. As Deming noted, "The system is the problem." To which we would add, "Especially if it fails to handle inherent variability fairly and effectively." Professional leaders must come to understand that assessing and adapting to this inherent variability is a key element of the manager's role in health care delivery whether it is organized for craft or mass customization.

COMMUNITIES

If professionals are to manage the health of populations rather than just individuals, they must develop a sense of how that can be done in a community setting. To do that, they must experience and participate in change processes undertaken by groups involving payers, providers, public health agencies, and patient organizations in their community. They need to understand the limits of community-based cooperation and planning in a market-driven health care system. Leaders must also be able to develop sufficient respect among their colleagues to be trusted with data needed for community health improvement when it might otherwise be seen as proprietary information for competitive use.

ENHANCING THE PROFESSIONAL'S ROLE

Professional performance in health policy roles can be enhanced in a number of ways, including the following:

- Preparation
- Skills development
- Training others
- Networking
- Practicing leadership.

Preparing to Learn and to Lead

Professionals need opportunities to adapt to policy analysis roles above and beyond those normally associated with clinical care. Potential leaders have to walk in the shoes of those who are leading, to consider the multiple sides of the issues, to use hard facts and fit them into conceptual and mathematical models that allow one to reduce and refine the array of available alternatives, and to recommend those that are likely to succeed in a given environment. Health policy analysis invites the potential leader to step back from narrow professional roles, think in terms of what is best for the patient and for society, and see the changes in health care more in the sweep of time. Intellectual integrity is also needed as a bulwark against being swept along with the fads.

One very important role for the health care professional is as a team member. Policy analysis teams require a wide range of skills including management, economics, operations, and medicine. As the owners of the technological core of medicine, health care professionals can always claim a place at the table; however, they must also be prepared to contribute to the overall progress of process analysis and improvement efforts. Their participation can be enhanced by a number of skills, typically including how to lead teams, how to analyze processes, how to implement change, and how to evaluate outcomes.

Developing Skills

The policy analyst must also understand the financial implications of what is being discussed; think in terms of markets and competition; adjust to social, economic, and political change as they play out in U.S. society; analyze and optimize processes; and motivate individuals and teams. All of these move in the direction of exhibiting competence, demonstrating mastery and gaining respect of one's peers and colleagues so that one can be eligible to be a contributor on a top management or decision-making team.

Training Others

One function of professional leadership is training the next generation of professionals. For example, if health policy is going to focus on motivating the system to reduce waste as suggested by Porter and Teisberg (2006), then the present and the next generation is going to have to think in terms of value-based patient care and focus on managing the entire medical condition from start to finish. Paul Batalden and others from Dartmouth have already started to incorporate this into their training of physicians there and elsewhere. They refer to it as employing microsystem-centered strategies as compared with organization-centered or issue-centered strategies for process improvement (Mohr & Batalden, 2006). They suggest that there are eight dimensions of effective microsystems (Mohr et al., 2006, p. 408):

1. Constancy of purpose
2. Investment in improvement
3. Alignment of role and training for efficiency and staff satisfaction
4. Interdependence of the care team to meet patient needs
5. Integration of information and technology into workflows
6. Ongoing measurement of outcomes
7. Supportiveness of the larger organization
8. Connection to the community to enhance care delivery and extend influence.

These eight dimensions align very well with the concepts of the value-based competition model (Porter & Teisberg, 2006). Adopting their approach in both clinical process improvement and in clinical training is one way to walk the talk, to learn the full implications of such an approach, and to develop the skills and insights applicable at higher levels of policy analysis. If one does not normally use something, one of the best ways to come to understand it fully is to try to teach it to others.

Networking

An intriguing part of health policy analysis is that it takes place in a virtual network of participants, professions, and organizations. One learns in the process of survival how to function in this new world. One sees how influence is exerted nationally and locally and in one's work group by knowing when to speak up and when to hold back, when to be the advocate and when to be the analyst, and how to support and move forward the multidisciplinary team—the key element of health care leadership for many years to come. By doing so, one develops skill at working with other disciplines and the contacts that become important assets as one attempts to exert leadership at higher and higher levels in the policy analysis process.

Practicing Leadership

Potential professional leaders have many opportunities to experiment with leadership roles in their interactions with program peers inside and outside their usual work setting. They can try out new concepts and compare experiences with their colleagues. Buttressed by the knowledge and skills gained, they can gradually assume leadership based on competency and commitment to personal and institutional change. One need not wait for a senior management opening to put that new knowledge to use.

CHAPTER EXERCISE: GENDER DISCRIMINATION ISSUES IN HEALTH CARE

One of the issues that this book has not emphasized so far is gender discrimination in health care. Questions include:

1. Are the diseases affecting only women as carefully researched and treated as those affecting only men?
2. Women have smaller current incomes than men, especially single older women. How does this affect their access to care? For example, how does the movement from employment-based health insurance to individual policies comparatively affect women?
3. We have witnessed sex discrimination against women professionals who our in are family. Have you witnessed or experienced sex discrimination professionally? What happened?

Prepare a working definition of and a subsequent policy recommendation concerning one or more gender issues in health care and come prepared to discuss it.

CONCLUSION

Professionals can play a very important role in policy analysis; however, they need to acquire not only the knowledge outlined in this text, but also those skills necessary to achieve positions of leadership in health policy making. They, especially physicians, must learn to take a disinterested view in many of their interactions with others, offsetting the growing public perception that they are much too concerned with the monetary aspects of care. If they fail to do so, their professional and political influence will continue to wane as their informational and procedural monopolies weaken.

Professionals must start by influencing health policy locally. They have to gain experience and leadership skills at that level before moving up to higher levels. As they move up, they will learn about the governance processes of both for-profit and not-for-profit organizations and the suitability of each for specific purposes. They will gain knowledge about managing nonclinical types of risks in the health care setting and about how to become a member of a team that can deal with the entire medical condition rather than their profession's aspect of it. Learning by doing is available in all settings, especially in training newer health professionals, improving local care processes, and health policy analysis at the community level. There is plenty of room for professional leaders in the health policy process, if they are willing to invest time and effort into learning to manage and lead it.

CHAPTER 15

Conclusion — All Those Levers and No Fulcrum

The pragmatic method is primarily a method of settling metaphysical disputes that otherwise might be interminable. Is the world one or many?—fated or free?—material or spiritual?—here are notions either of which may or may not hold the good of the world; and disputes over such notions are unending. The pragmatic method in such cases is to try to interpret each notion by tracing its respective practical consequences. What difference would it practically make to any one if this notion rather than that notion were true? If no practical difference whatever can be traced, then the alternatives mean practically the same thing, and all dispute is idle. Whenever a dispute is serious, we (need to) be able to show some practical difference that must follow from one side or the other's being right.

    — What is Pragmatism (1904), from series of eight lectures dedicated to the memory of John Stuart Mill, *A New Name for Some Old Ways of Thinking,* in December 1904, from William James, Writings 1902–1920, The Library of America; Lecture II

WHERE TO STAND

As the first part of this book illustrates, we are offered many, many levers that we might use to try to move health care delivery in one direction or the other. All levers, however, require a strong fulcrum, a solid base against which the lever's force can be exerted. In the United States, there is a clear absence of a reliable fulcrum. The federal government is the least reliable of all. Bureaucrats know that the efforts of lobbyists, senior White House staffers, or chairs of congressional committees can undermine in a few days what has taken months of study and consensus-building to achieve. At worst, one's program, even one's agency, can disappear from the budget overnight. State offices are subject to the same risks, although the governors sometimes stand more firmly because the state must meet its financial obligations, rather than print money or borrow more heavily.

Other potential fulcrums are likewise unreliable. Insurers pass on added costs. Providers continue to maximize revenue. Employers opt out of defined benefit programs. More and more patients go bare (i.e., without insurance). More and more of the costs of providing coverage and care accrue to state and federal governments through Medicare, Medicaid, and other programs. Thus, the downward spiral continues.

Fitting Into Our Culture of Individualism

There are practical, pedagogical reasons for the on-one-hand and on-the-other-hand approach Harry Truman objected to when he called for a "one-handed" economist. Each of us brings a value system to any policy analysis, and those values inevitably get mixed up with the objective information that a scholarly approach offers decision makers. We are therefore understandably reluctant to declare one approach, one solution, one system to be absolutely and unequivocally superior.

It is clear, however, that there are things that fit well into the culture of the United States, and others that do not. One of our current cultural problems is that loud sets of voices are calling for one extreme or another with almost religious zeal. Reagan (1999) pointed to the horns of one health care dilemma. On one hand, some would prefer that the federal government be the single purveyor of health care, but in a country that has long valued individualism and a free-market economic system, it seems that there has to be some acceptance somewhere of some market forces in the process. On the other hand, it is clear that health care has been and will continue to be a highly imperfect marketplace. No matter how much information U.S. consumers receive, it is unlikely to be sufficient for them to make good decisions about all aspects of personal health care. Furthermore, it is clear that many segments of U.S. society cannot generate sufficient income to participate in that marketplace, whereas others may lack the cognitive skills or other attributes necessary to participate fully and effectively in an unfettered health care market. Advocates of a single-payer system, who have been fond of saying that the United States is the only developed country without a national health system, are unlikely to see the United States fall in line with other nations anytime soon. Yet the current dependence on employers as the basic source of funding for care for workers and their families, while working and especially during retirement, is collapsing in the face of increasing international competition.

The Limits of the Free-Market Approach

Those who argue that insurance, because it insulates health care consumers from any economic consequences, has been responsible for waste and overutilization have a strong point. Their efforts to shift more costs to the consumer will pay off some in terms of reduced utilization. There are three issues with that approach, however, in addition to the risk that for lower income individuals it will likely lead to underutilization with negative long-term consequences. The first is that much of its impact may already have been achieved with the increases in deductibles and co-pays already in force, and the marginal effect may be much smaller than anticipated. Second, information on quality and price is so opaque that the market cannot function very effectively until major changes take place to get realistic and relevant information into the hands of the consuming public. Those changes do not yet seem to be underway with respect to (1) hospital prices and (2) quality outcomes for specific physicians.

The third constraint on the free-market approach is that some purchasers are quite capable of researching a medical condition and some are not. Even for the population that is capable (and those supporting a single-payer system have often underestimated the ability of today's public to research health care and understand what they find), this is not a cross-sectional problem, but a serial one. With one episode of care, the consumer may seek to make an informed market decision, because he or she:

- Has the technical information and the background to interpret it
- Has the market information on price and quality of providers of care for this medical condition
- Has the mental acuity to interpret it and make an appropriate decision
- Feels confident enough in their knowledge to act on it
- Has access to a primary care provider to test out their conclusions.

Yet six months later, he or she may have a set of symptoms that leaves them completely baffled and they have to rely completely on the recommendations of their primary care provider or a local specialist, especially if they are in pain and sedated at that moment. Yes, they may be capable of rational consumer decision-making behavior in the first instance, but not in the latter. In the second situation, they are going to have to rely on their agents, their physician, and, to a lesser extent, their insurer for such a decision.

If one has lived with gout for years, for example, they may be about as knowledgeable about the condition as most providers, but what if they then have intestinal polyps and their personal physician sends them to a specialist who says, "I have this new technology that is less invasive than what is usually done and insurance will pay for it and you are a perfect candidate for it"? Are they going to demur and go out and do a survey of methods and the market? Probably not. More likely, they will say yes and then look it up when they get home. If they cannot find out much about what it will cost and how effective it is and they are told that it is safe, then they are likely to keep the appointment and let their insurer cover it— especially if they have other things to worry about, like a consulting report that is due. The impact on health care costs of the market approach will be felt, but it will also be limited.

THE PHYSICIAN'S DILEMMA

What will these proposed changes do to the status of American physicians? Many of them would clearly contribute to the industrialization of the health care sector and weaken physician bargaining power. For example, if most medical centers were required to quote a single price up front for treating a medical condition and that single price covered the professional, technical, and inpatient components of that treatment, the physicians would have to bargain for their share, and they would likely be in a relatively weak position. In fact, it seems likely that specialists ultimately would be placed on salary in community settings, just as they currently are in many academic medical centers. Some physicians might counter this development by setting up their own specialty hospitals, but one might anticipate further Stark amendment-type constraints if that response became very widespread.

More information on process, price, and quality, more bundling of pricing, more evidence-based protocols, requirements for reduced waste and more intense case management would all in part constrain physician autonomy. At some point, health system policy makers will have to reconsider the patient–physician relationship and its attendant agency issues and try to reach an appropriate balance between industrialization and professionalism. One answer is for physicians to provide more assertive leadership when it comes to defining and maintaining the physician's role, especially the role of the primary provider, without trying to get back to the old monopolistic mind set that once tainted state and local American Medical Association efforts.

THE ERISA PROBLEM

Trying to make rational sense out of the health care system is difficult enough, but effectively having two complete sets of regulatory requirements, one under state insurance laws and one under ERISA, does not make sense, especially because the current responsibility for health and welfare in the United States rests principally with the states. At the time that the ERISA law was passed, it was necessary as an enabler of nationwide collective bargaining by large employers and large industrial unions, but in an era when we have so many "model uniform codes" for so many types of commercial and personal business transactions, it would not seem to be an insurmountable obstacle to come up with and adopt a model uniform code for employer-based health insurance. The likely fly in the ointment is the health insurance industry itself, as the dual system blunts the ability of the states to attempt any universal or mandated coverage requirements; however, the benefits of a uniform system are so great that legislatures, unions, and major corporations might be persuaded to fall in behind it and move it ahead.

CHAPTER EXERCISE: TRADEOFFS

It is popular to talk about a country, if not a world, divided over values, but that is not the entire story. This book illustrates that there are many tradeoffs—tradeoffs everywhere one turns. **Table 15-1** lists a number of these showing the two sides, the impacts of the current status quo, and some possibilities for responding to them. The fact that these tradeoffs have been issues for as long as they have shows that they are currently at an equilibrium position (or an impasse). Some would argue that having a less than rational system with unresolved conflicts and continuing inefficiencies is not all bad because it provides high-income employment. It does that, but one might also question how productive much of that employment is.

In Table 15-1 a number of potential tradeoffs were purposely omitted. Add others as you identify them. Add new lines for those additional tradeoffs that you perceive to be important in the near future and come to class prepared to discuss your candidates for inclusion.

CONCLUSION

We expect that managing tradeoffs, rather than implementing radical changes, will be grist for health policy analysts' mill for some years to come. Each time a new program or regulation is proposed to deal with one aspect of health care access, cost, and quality, the policy analyst must present to the interested parties the tradeoffs that have to be made, their magnitude, and their consequences, intended and otherwise. The policy analyst will have to look at the desired impact, the unintended consequences, the distributional effects, the ethical issues, the technologic impact, the financial feasibility, the political feasibility, and the best way to implement the proposal, and from that come up with a justified recommendation to the parties involved, the politicians, and the public. Such analyses do not necessarily lead to earth-shaking decisions, but they are necessary if we are to make things better rather than worse. There will be much work to do. How successful it will be, in all likelihood, will be a matter of leadership as much as anything else; however, those who would lead, especially from a professional position, must participate both in effective analysis and in rational leadership.

TABLE 15-1   Illustrative List of Tradeoffs, Impacts, and Some of the
Proposed Solutions

Tradeoff	Versus	Current Impact	Proposed Solutions
First-dollar coverage	Catastrophic insurance	Many see payouts, motivating participation, but not enough money for both	Major medical option Means testing (spend-downs and Medicaid) Risk pools for high-risk patients
Universal coverage	Willingness to pay	Uninsured, underinsured High administrative costs Government, which is already covering up to 45%, continuing to gather more under tent	More categorical programs Basic coverage package, plus add-ons Expand programs such as the State Children's Health Insurance Program (SCHIP) to cover more individuals
Selective underwriting	Community rating	Adverse selection Lifetime limits Prevention disincentives	Minimum coverage for all with add-ons allowed
New drug safety and efficacy	Rapid deployment of effective technology	Current focus on drugs for continued use A lack of new drugs to fight acute illnesses	Sponsored development Stronger postmarketing surveillance
Direct-to-consumer advertising	Health education campaigns	Higher drug costs Overutilization Misallocated research funds Disease mongering	Constraints on proportion of costs in advertising Redefining health Health education (counter detailing)

(continues)

TABLE 15-1   Illustrative List of Tradeoffs, Impacts, and Some of the Proposed Solutions *(continued)*

Tradeoff	Versus	Current Impact	Proposed Solutions
Liability for vaccines' effects	Vaccine development and production capacity	Inability to respond to surges in demand Failure to develop new vaccines and production methods	Limited liability Support for not-for-profit producers Subsidies for standby capacity
Linked electronic medical records	Consumer privacy	Medical errors Duplicate tests Slow responses to acute problems	Designing in privacy safeguards Firewalls
Needs to train new health professionals	Desire to increase faculty incomes and cross-subsidize research	Overstressed learners Poorer quality of care	Better funding of supervision Reduced charges for learner-produced services
Customized care for complex patients	Strong move toward use of evidence-based practices Friction between suits and coats	High variability of practice patterns	Stronger physician and government leadership Exception reporting Better evaluation, communication, and dissemination
Use of high end technology in low end settings	Rapid testing and deployment Visibility of large medical centers	High treatment and capital costs Resistance to disruptive technology	Development of more flexibility in system capacities and operating costs
Investment driven by utilization growth	Certificate of need	Efforts to increase demand Duplication of services Reduced competition	Wider disease-specific catchment areas Capital rationing Global budgeting

References

AAMC (Association of American Medical Colleges). (2005). Calls for modest increase in medical school enrollment. Press release retrieved at www.aamc.org/newsroom/pressrel/2005/05022.

Abelson, R. (2006a, March 8). Pay method said to sway drug choices of oncologists. *New York Times.* Retrieved March 9, 2006 from www.nytimes.com/2006/03/08/health/08docs.

Abelson, R. (2006b, June 28). Charities tied to doctors get drug industry gifts. *New York Times.* Retrieved June 28, 2006 from www.nytimes.com/2006/06/28/business/28foundation.

Abelson, R. (2006c, June 22). Doctors' average pay fell 7% in 8 years, report says. *New York Times.* Retrieved June 22, 2006 from www.nytimes.com/2006/06/22/business/22doctors.

Abelson R. (2006d, August 18). Heart procedure is off the charts in an Ohio city. *New York Times.* Retrieved August 18, 2006 from www.nytimes.com/2006/08/18/business/18stent.

Ackerman, F., & Heinzerling, L. (2004). *Priceless: On knowing the price of everything and the value of nothing.* New York: The New Press.

American Academy of Family Physicians. (2004, July 22). Premier medical organizations announce formation of Physicians Electronic Health Record Coalition. Press release retrieved June 10, 2005 at www.aafp.org/online/en/home/press/aafpnewsrelease/july04/ehrcoalition.

American Academy of Pediatrics. (2007). *What is a medical home?* Retrieved February 1, 2007 from http://www.medicalhomeinfo.org/health/general.

American Case Management Association. (2006). *Definition* Retrieved April 21, 2006 from http://www.acmaweb/section.

Altman, S. H., Shactman, D., & Eilat, E. (2006). Could U.S. hospitals go the way of U.S. airlines? *Health Affairs, 25,* 11–21.

AMA v. U.S. (1943). American Medical Association v. United States. 1942. and Medical Society of the District of Columbia v. United States 317 U.S. 519.

Anderson, G. F., Frogner, B. K., Johns, R. A., Reinhardt, U. E., (2006). Health Care Spending and Use of Information Technology in OECD Countries. *Health Affairs, 25*(3): 819–831.

Anderson, G.F., Reinhardt, U.E., Hussey, P. S., & Petrosyan, V. (2003). It's the prices stupid: Why the United States is so different from other countries. *Health Affairs, 22,* 89–105.

Aos, S., Mayfield, J., Miller, M., & Yen, W. (2006). *Evidence-based treatment of alcohol, drug, and mental health disorders: Potential benefits, costs, and fiscal impacts for Washington state.* Olympia, WA: Washington State Institute for Public Policy.

Armstrong, D. (2006, December 13). Drug firm's cash sways debate over test for pregnant women. *The Wall Street Journal,* pp. A1, A12.

Arrow, K. J. (1963). Uncertainty and the welfare economics of medical care. *American Economic Review, 53,* 941–973.

Baker, F., Sheldon, A. C., & McLaughlin, C. P. (1970). *Systems analysis and medical care.* Cambridge, MA: MIT Press.

Basch, P. (2006, September 10). Pay-for-performance: Too much of a good thing— or too worried about the wrong things? *Health Affairs eLetters.* Retrieved January 6, 2007 from http//content.healthaffairs.org/cgi/eletters/25/5/w412.

Bates, D. W. (2005). Physicians and ambulatory electronic health records. *Health Affairs, 24,* 1180–1189.

Becker, H. (Ed.). (1955). *Prepayment and the community.* New York: McGraw-Hill.

Bellomo, R., Goldsmith, D., Uchino, S., Buckmaster, J., Hart, G.K., Opdam, H., et al. (2003). A prospective before-and-after trial of a medical emergency team. *Medical Journal of Australia, 179(6),* 283–287.

Belluck, P. (2007, January 10). Massachusetts could serve as a guide in California's health insurance bid. *New York Times.* Retrieved January 11, 2007 from www.nytimes.com/2007/01/10/us/10mass.

Berenson, R. A., Bodenheimer, T., & Pham, H.H. (2006). Specialty-service lines: Salvos in the new medical arms race. *Health Affairs, 25,* W337–W343.

Berwick, D. M., Calkins, D. R., McCannon, C. J., & Hackbarth, A. D. (2006). The 100,000 lives campaign: Setting a goal and deadline for improving health care quality. *Journal of the American Medical Association, 295,* 324–327.

Birnbaum, J. L. (2004, October 3). Cost of Congressional campaigns skyrockets. *Washington Post,* p. A08.

Blakely, B.G. (2006). Testimony before the U.S. Senate Special Committee on Aging, Washington, DC, The Globalization of Health Care: Can Medical Tourism Reduce Health Care Costs? June 27, 2006, by Bonnie Grissom Blackley, Benefits Director, Blue Ridge Paper Products Inc. Retrieved April 23, 2007 at http://aging.senate.gov/public/index/cfm?Fuseaction=Hearings. Detail&HearingID=182.

Blendon, R. J., Young, J. T., DesRoches, C. M., Osborn, R., Scoles, K. L., & Zapert, K. (2002). Inequities in health care: a five country survey. *Health Affairs, 21*(3), 182–191.

Bodenheimer, T. S. & Grumbach, K. (2005). *Understanding health policy: A clinical approach* (4th ed.). New York: McGraw-Hill, Lange Medical Books.

Borger, C., Smith, S., Truffer, C., Keehan, S., Sisko, A. et al. (2006). Health spending projections through 2015: Changes on the horizon. *Health Affairs, 25 (2),* W61–W73.

Bower, A. G. (2005). Perspective: Federal investment in health information technology: How to motivate it? *Health Affairs, 24,* 1263–1265.

Bradshaw, P. L., & Bradshaw, G. (2004). *Health policy for health care professionals.* London: Sage.

Brown, L. D. (2006, April 11). Impermanent politics: The Hillsborough County health care plan and community innovation for the uninsured. *Health Affairs Web Exclusive, 25,* W162–W172.

Buist, M. D., Moore, G. E., Bernard, S. A., Waxman, N. P., Anderson, J. N., & Nguyen, T.V. (2002). Effects of a medical emergency team on reduction of incidence of and mortality from unexpected cardiac arrests in hospital: preliminary study. *British Medical Journal, 324,* 387–390.

Bunker, J. P., Barnes, B. A., & Mosteller, F. (1979). *The costs, risks and benefits of surgery.* Princeton, NJ: Princeton University Press.

Cabinet Implementation Unit. (2005). *Guide to preparing implementation plans.* Canberra, Australia: Department of the Prime Minister and Cabinet.

Calkthan, D. (1991). Commentary: Ethics and priority setting in Oregon. *Health Affairs ,*10(2): 78–87.

Callaghan, P. (2006, February 16). One Democrat stands in the way of Washington state tobacco bill. *Tacoma News Tribune.* Retrieved October 14, 2006 from www.shns.com/shns/g_index2.cfm?action=detail&pk=CALLAGHAN-02-16-06.

Cannon, M. F., & Tanner, M. D. (2005). *Healthy competition: What's holding back health care and how to free it.* Washington, DC: The Cato Institute.

Carroll, J. S., & Edmondson, A. C. (2002). Leading organizational learning in health care. *Quality and Safety in Health Care, 11,* 51–56.

Causin, T., Moore, M., et al. (2005). Assessment of US Senate campaign expenditures in 2000, 2002 and 2004, with predictions for 2006. Center for Communication and Civic Engagement Working Paper #2005–2. Retrieved January 30, 2007 from http://uwnews.washington.edu/ni/relatedcontent/2005/December/rc_parentID13896_thisID13934.pdf

Centers for Disease Control and Prevention. (1991). Effectiveness in disease and injury prevention use of folic acid for prevention of spina bifida and other neural tube defects: 1983–1991. *MMWR Weekly, 40,* 513–516.

Centers for Disease Control and Prevention. (2000). Folate status in women of childbearing age: United States 1999. *MMWR Weekly, 49,* 962–965.

Centers for Disease Control and Prevention. (2004). Spina bifida and anencephaly before and after folic acid mandate: United States, 1995–1996 and 1999–2000. *MMWR Weekly, 53,* 362–365.

Centers for Disease Control and Prevention. (2006). National, state, and urban area vaccination coverage among children aged 19–35 months: United States 2005. *MMWR Weekly Rep, 55,* 988–993.

Champlin, L. (2006, June 6). CMS to allow specialty hospitals to proceed. *AAFP News Now.* Retrieved from www.aafp.org/online/en/home/publications/news/news-now/government-medicine/2.

Choudhry, S., Choudhry, N. K., & Brennan, T. A. (2005, August 9). Specialty vs. community hospitals: What role for the law? *Health Affairs 24,* W5–361–372.

Christensen, C., Bohmer, R. M. J., & Kenagy, J. (2000). Will disruptive innovations cure health care? *Harvard Business Review, 78(5),* 102–111.

Cleverley, W. O., & Cameron, A. E. (2003). *Essentials of health care finance* (5th ed.). Gaitherstown, MD: Aspen Publishers.

Clinton, H. R. (2003). *Living history.* New York: Scribner.

Clinton, H. R. (2004, April 18). Now can we talk about health care? *New York Times Magazine,* pp. 26–31, 56.

Cogan, J. F., Hubbard, R. G., & Kessler, D. P. (2005). *Healthy, wealthy and wise: Five steps to a better health care system.* Washington, DC: AEI Press.

Cooper, M., & Chan, S. (2006, November 28). Panel said to call for closing 9 New York hospitals. *New York Times.* Retrieved November 28, 2006 from www.nytimes.com/2006/11/28/nyregion/28hospitals.

Coye, M. J., & Kell, J. (2006). How hospitals confront new technology. *Health Affairs, 25,* 163–173.

Cunningham, R. (2005). Action through collaboration: A conversation with David Brailer. *Health Affairs, 24,* 1150–1157.

Cutler, D. M., Rosen, A. B., & Vijan, S. (2006). The value of medical spending in the United States 1960–2000. *New England Journal of Medicine, 355,* 920–927.

Daniels, N. (2006). Toward ethical review of health system transformations. *American Journal of Public Health, 98,* 447–451.

Davis, F. D. (1989). Perceived usefulness, perceived ease of use, and user acceptance of information technology. *MIS Quarterly, 13,* 319–340.

Davis, K. (2004). Consumer-directed health care: Will it improve health system performance? *Health Services Research, 39*(4, Pt. II):1219–1233.

Davis, K., Schoen, C., Schoenbaum, M. S., Audet, A-M. J., Doty, M. M. & Tenney, K. (2006). *Mirror, mirror on the wall: An update on the quality of American health care through the patient lens.* New York: The Commonwealth Fund.

Deming, W. A. (1986). *Out of crisis.* Cambridge, MA: MIT Center for Advanced Engineering Study.

Donabedian, A. (1980). The definition of quality and approaches to its assessment. *Explorations in quality assessments and monitoring* (Vol. 1, pp. 95–99). Ann Arbor, MI: Health Administration Press.

Dopson, S., Lacock, L., Gabbay, J., Ferlie, E., & Fitzgerald, L. (2005). Evidence-based health care and the implementation gap. In Dopson, S., & Fitzgerald, L. (Eds.) *Knowledge to action? Evidence-based health care in context.* Oxford, UK: Oxford University Press, pp. 182–197, pp. 28–47.

Doran, T., Fullwood, C. A., Gravelle, H., Reeves, D., Kontopantelis, K., et al. (2006). Pay-for-performance program in the United Kingdom. *New England Journal of Medicine, 355,* 375–384.

Dror, Y. (1969). *The prediction of political feasibility.* Santa Monica, CA: The RAND Corporation.

Dror, Y. (1988). Uncertainty: Coping with it and with political feasibility. In H. J. Miser & E. S. Quade (Eds.). *Handbook of systems analysis: Craft issues and procedural choices.* New York: Elsevier Science Publishing, pp. 247–281.

Drucker, P. F. (1974). *Management: Tasks, responsibilities, practices.* New York: Harper & Row.

Economist, The. (2006, January 26). Editorial: Desperate measures. Retrieved June 10, 2006 from www.economist.com/world/PrinterFriendly.cfm?story_id=4326968.

Einthoven, A. C., & Tollen, L. A. (2005). Competition in health care: It takes systems to pursue quality and efficiency. *Health Affairs, 24*(Suppl. 3), W5-420–W5-433.

Emanuel, E., & Fuchs, V. (2006, November 13). How to cure U.S. health care. *Fortune,* p. 78.

Epstein, A. M. (2006). Paying for performance in the United States and abroad. *New England Journal of Medicine, 355,* 406–408.

Epstein, A. M. (2007). Pay for performance at the tipping point. *New England Journal of Medicine, 356,* 515–517.

Food and Drug Administration. (1993). Food standards: Amendment of the standards of identity for enriched grain products to require addition of folic acid. *Federal Register, 58,* 53305–53312.

Feldstein, M. (2005a). Rethinking social insurance. Retrieved November 18, 2006 from http://www.nber.org/feldstein/aeajan8.pdf.

Ferdows, K. (2006). Transfer of changing production know-how. *Production and Operations Management, 15,* 1–9.

Ferlie, E. (2005). Conclusion: From evidence to actionable knowledge. In Dopson, S., & Fitzgerald, L. (Eds.) *Knowledge to action? Evidence-based health care in context.* Oxford, UK: Oxford University Press, pp. 182–197.

Finkbonner, J., Pageler, M., & Ybarra, V. (2001). *Final report: State board of health priority: Health disparities.* Olympia, WA: Washington State Board of Health.

Finkelstein, A. (2007). The aggregate effects of health insurance: Evidence from the introduction of Medicare, *Quarterly Journal of Economics, 122 (1),* 1–37.

Fisher, E. S., Wennberg, D. E., Stuckel, T. A. & Gottlieb, D. J. (2004, October 7). Variations in the longitudinal efficiency of academic medical centers. *Health Affairs Web Exclusives,* Var 19–32. Retrieved 04/20/07 at www.healthaffairs.org/RWJ/variations_Fisher.pdf.

Food Standards Agency Board. (2006). Agency board discusses folate and health. Retrieved May 5, 2006 from http://food.gov.uk/news/newsarchive/2006/apr/folatehealth?view.

Fox, D. M., & Leichter, H. M. (1991). Rationing care in Oregon: The new accountability. *Health Affairs,* 10 (2), 7–27.

Freidson, E. (2001). *Professional power: The third logic.* Cambridge, UK: Polity Press.

Freudenheim, M. (2006a, January 26). Prognosis is mixed for health savings. *The New York Times.* Retrieved January 26, 2006 from www.nytimes.com/2006/01/26/business/26accounts.

Freudenheim, M. (2006b, May 25). The check is not in the mail. *The New York Times.* Retrieved May 25, 2006 from www.nytimes.com/2006/05/25/business/25insure.

Friedman, T. L. (2005). *The world is flat: A brief history of the twenty-first century.* New York: Farrar, Straus, and Giroux.

Frist, B. (2002). Public health and national security: The critical role of increased federal support. *Health Affairs, 21(6),* 117–130.

Frogner, B. K., & Anderson, G. F. (2006). *Multinational comparisons of health systems data 2005.* New York: The Commonwealth Fund.

Fuchs, V. R. (2002). What's ahead for health insurance in the U.S. *New England Journal of Medicine, 346,* 1822–1824.

Fuhrmans, V. (2007a, January 19). California gets health response. *The Wall Street Journal, 249,* p. A10.

Fuhrmans, V. (2007b, January 10). A novel plan helps hospital wean itself off pricey test. *The Wall Street Journal, 249,* pp. A1, A11.

Galvin, R. S., & Delbanco, S. (2006). Between a rock and a hard place: Understanding the employer mind set. *Health Affairs, 25,* 1548–1555.

Gardner, E. S., Jr., & McLaughlin, C. P. (1980). Forecasting: A cost control tool for health care managers. *Health Care Management Review, 5,* 31–38.

Gaull, G. E., Testa, C. A., Thomas, P. R., & Weinrich, D. A. (1996). Fortification of the food supply with folic acid to prevent neural tube defects is not yet warranted (fortifying policy with science—the case of folate). *The Journal of Nutrition, 126,* 773S–780S.

Gawande, A. (2002). *Complications: A surgeon's notes on an imperfect science.* New York: Henry Holt and Company.

Gaynor, M. (2006). What do we know about competition and quality in health care markets? NBER Working Paper 12301. Retrieved November 12, 2006 from www.nber.org/papers/w12301.

Gilfillan, S. C. (1952). The prediction of technical change. *Review of Economics and Statistics, 34 (4),* 368–385.

Gilliam, F. D. (2005, December 6). Framing health care reform for public understanding and support. Presentation delivered at Health Legislative Conference, Seattle, WA. Retrieved January 30, 2007 from http://depts.washington.edu/rchpol/docs/legcon05/Gilliam.ppt#1.

Gingrich, N. (2003). *Saving lives and saving money.* Washington, DC: Alexis de Tocqueville Institution.

Gingrich, N., & Kennedy, P. (2004, May 3). Operating in a vacuum. *New York Times,* p. A23.

Goddard, B. (1998, March 25). Public policy advocacy campaigns. Speech delivered at Duke University, Durham, NC. Retrieved January 30, 2007 from www.pubpol.duke.edu/centers/dewitt/papers/archive/15/15_2.doc.

Gogoi, P. (2006, February 27). Steering patients through the system. *Business Week,* p. 80.

Goldman, D. P., Shekelle, P. G., Bhattacharya, J. Hurd, M., Joyce, G F., Lakdawalla, D.M. et al. (2004). *Health status and medical treatment of the future elderly: Final report.* Santa Monica, CA: The RAND Corporation, TR-169-CMS.

Goldman, D. P., Shang, B., Bhattacharya, J., Garber, A.M., Hurd, M. Joyce, G.F., et al. (2005). Consequences of health trends and medical innovation for the elderly of the future. *Health Affairs, 24*(Suppl. 2), W5-R5–W5-R17.

Goldsteen, R. L., Goldsteen, K., Swan, J. H., & Clemena, W. (2001). Harry and Louise and health care reform: Romancing public opinion. *Journal of Health Politics, Policy and Law, 26,* 1325–1352.

Greenwald, L., Cromwell, J., Adamache, W., Bernard, S., Drozd, E., et al . (2006). Specialty versus community hospitals: Referrals, quality and community benefits. *Health Affairs, 25,* 106–118.

Grol, E. (2006). *Quality development in health care in the Netherlands.* The Commonwealth Fund. Retrieved June 5, 2006 from www.cmwf.org/publications/publications_show.htm.

Grosse, S. D., Waitzman, N. J., Romano, P. S., & Molinare, J. (2005). Reevaluating the benefits of folic acid fortification in the United States: economic analysis, regulation and public health. *American Journal of Public Health, 95,* 1917–1922.

Grossman, J. M., & Reed, M. C. (2006). *Clinical information technology gaps persist among physicians: Issue brief no. 106.* Washington, DC: Center for Studying Health System Change.

Guterman, S. (2006). Specialty hospitals: A problem or a symptom? *Health Affairs, 25,* 95–105.

Hackbarth, G., & Milgate, K. (2005). Perspective: Using quality incentives to drive physician adoption of health information technology. *Health Affairs, 24,* 1147–1149.

Hacker, J. S. (1997). *The road to nowhere: The genesis of President Clinton's program for health security.* Princeton, NJ: Princeton University Press.

Hadler, N. M. (2004). *The last well person: How to stay well despite the health-care system.* Montreal: McGill-Queens University Press.

Haislmaier, E. F. (2006). The significance of Massachusetts Health Reform. Web Memo #1035. Washington, DC: The Heritage Foundation. Retrieved January 3, 2007 from www.heritage.org/Research/HealhtCare/wm1035.cfm.

Hall, R. E., & Jones, C. I. (2007). The value of life and the rise in health spending. *Quarterly Journal of Economics, 122,* 39–72.

Halverson, P. K., Kaluzny, A. D., McLaughlin, C. P., & Mays, G. P. (eds.). (1998). *Managed care and public health.* Gaithersburg, MD: Aspen.

Halvorson, G. C. (2005). Perspective: Wiring health care. *Health Affairs, 24,* 1266–1268.

Hansmann, H. (1996). *The ownership of enterprise.* Cambridge, MA: The Belknap Press of Harvard University Press.

Havighurst, C. C. (2005). Monopoly is not the answer. *Health Affairs* Web Exclusives, W5-373.

Heath, I. (2005). Promotion of disease and corrosion of medicine. *Canadian Family Physician.* Retrieved June 10, 2006 from www.cfpc.ca/cfp/2005/Oct/v0151-oct-editorials-2.

Henderson, J. W. (2002). *Health economics and policy* (2nd ed.). Cincinnati, OH: Southwestern/Thomson Learning.

Hertkampf, E. (2004). *Folic acid fortification: Current knowledge and future priorities (discussion paper).* Santiago, Chile: Institute of Nutrition and Food Technology, University of Santiago.

Herzlinger, R. E. (1997). *Market driven health care.* Reading, MA: Addison-Wesley.

Hibbard, E. D., & Smithells, R. W. (1965). Folic acid metabolism and human embryopathy. *Lancet, 1,* 1254–1256.

Hillestad, R., Bigelow, J., Bower, A., Girosi, F., Meili, R. et al. (2005). Can electronic medical record systems transform health care? Potential health benefits, savings and costs. *Health Affairs, 24,* 1103–1117.

Himmelstein, D. U., & Woolhandler, S. (2005). Perspective: Hope and hype: Predicting the impact of electronic medical records. *Health Affairs, 24,* 1121–1123.

Holahan, J., & Cook, A. (2005). Changes in economic conditions and health insurance, 2000–2004. *Health Affairs,* Web Exclusives W5.498–W5.508.

Holstein, W. J. (2006, December 31). For better care, work across lines. *New York Times.* Retrieved January 15, 2007 from www.nytimes.com/2006/12/31/jobs/31advi.html.

Homer, J. B., & Hirsch, G. B. (2006). System dynamics modeling for public health background and opportunities. *American Journal of Public Health, 96,* 452–458.

Houghton, A. (1995, September 28). In memoriam: The Office of Technology Assessment, 1972–1995. *House of Representatives—Congressional Record, Extension of Remarks* (pp. E1868–1870). Retrieved from www.wws.princeton.edu/ota/ns20/hough_n.html.

Hubbard, A. R. (2006, April 3). The Health of a Nation. *New York Times,* p. A17.

Hubbard, R. G. (2006, January 30). Health care, heal thyself. *National Review Online.* Retrieved April 17, 2006 from http://www.nationalreview.com/coment/hubbard200601300837.asp.

Hurley, R. E., Pham, H. H., & Claxton, G. (2005). A widening rift in access and quality: Growing evidence of economic disparities. *Health Affairs, 24*(Suppl. 3): W5-566–W5-576.

Institute for Healthcare Improvement. (2006, June 14). IHI announces that hospitals participating in 100,000 Lives Campaign have saved an estimated 122,300 lives. Retrieved July 23, 2006 from http://www.ihi.org/NR/rdonlyres/1CS51BADE-OF7B-4932-A8C3-OFEFB-654D747/0/100kLivesCampaignJune14MilestonePressRelease.pdf.

Institute for Health Care Improvement. (n.d.). 100,000 Lives Campaign: Lives saved FAQ. Retrieved July 23, 2006 from http://www.ihi.org/NR/rdonlyres/0FC36040-53FB-4B06-A95E-7E2D5055A154/0/LivesSavedCalculationFAQ.doc.

Institute of Medicine. (2000a). *Bridging disciplines in the brain, behavioral and clinical sciences.* Washington, DC: The National Academy Press.

Institute of Medicine. (2000b). *To err is human: Building a safer health system.* Washington, DC: The National Academy Press.

Institute of Medicine. (2001). *Crossing the quality chasm: A new health system for the 21st century.* Washington, DC: The National Academy Press.

Jacobson, M., O'Malley, A. J., Earle, C. C., Pakes, J., Gaccione, P. & Newhouse, J. (2006). Does reimbursement influence chemotherapy treatment for cancer patients? *Health Affairs, 25,* 437–443.

Jones, A. P., Homer, J. B., Murphy, D. L., Essien, J. D., Milstein, B., & Seville, D. A. (2006). Understanding diabetes population dynamics through simulation modeling and experimentation. *American Journal of Public Health, 96,* 488–493.

Jonsson, P. (2006, Sept.29). Union blocks foreign healthcare plan. *Christian Science Monitor,* p. 2. Retrieved October 11, 2006 at www.csmonitor.com/2006/0929/p02201-usec.

Junod, S. W. (2006). *Folic acid fortification: Fact and folly.* U.S. Food and Drug Administration. Retrieved January 7, 2006 from http://www.fda.gov/oc/history/makinghistory/folicacid.html.

Kaiser Commission on Medicaid and the Uninsured. (2005, November). *The uninsured and their access to health care.* Washington, DC: Kaiser Family Foundation.

Kaiser Commission on Medicaid and the Uninsured. (2006, October). *The uninsured and their access to health care.* Washington, DC: Kaiser Family Foundation.

Kaplan, R. M. (1995). Utility assessment for estimating quality-adjusted life years. In Sloan, F.A. (Ed.). *Valuing health care: Cost, benefits and effectiveness of pharmaceuticals and other medical technologies.* Cambridge, UK: Cambridge University Press, pp. 31–60.

Kerridge, R. K., & Saul, W. P. (2003). The medical emergency team, evidence-based medicine and ethics. *Medical Journal of Australia, 179,* 313–315.

Kibbe, D. C., & McLaughlin, C. P. (2004). Getting from A to C: Lifecycle lessons for e-health deployment. *International Journal of Electronic Healthcare, 1,* 127–138.

Kiewra. K. (2004, Fall). What price health? *Harvard Public Health Review.* Retrieved April 30, 2007 at www. hsph.harvard.edu/review/review_fall_04/risk_whatprice.html.

Kindig, D. A. (2006). A pay-for-population health performance system. *Journal of the American Medical Association, 296,* 2611–2613.

Kingdon, J. W. (1984). *Agendas, alternatives, and public policies.* New York: HarperCollins Publishers.

Kleinke, J. D. (2005). Dot-gov: Market failure and the creation of a national health information system. *Health Affairs, 24,* 1246–1262.

Kolata, G. (2006a, May 21). If you've got a pulse, you're sick. *New York Times.* Retrieved May 22, 2006 from www.nytimes.com/2006/05/21/weekinreview/21kolata.

Kolata, G. (2006b, August 22). Making health care the engine that drives the economy. *New York Times.* Retrieved August 22, 2006 from www.nytimes.com/2006/08/22/health/policy/22pros.

Kosar, K. R. (2006). *Regular vetoes and pocket vetoes: An overview.* Washington, DC: Congressional Research Service.

Kuhnhenn, J. (2006, September 16). White House race may cost hopefuls $500m (presidential election campaign fund in need of reform?). Associated Press. Retrieved on October 8, 2006 from http://www.freerepublic.com/focus/f-news/1702769/posts.html.

Lamson, E., & Colman, V. (2005). *Nutrition and physical activity: A policy resource guide.* Washington State Department of Health. Retrieved January 31, 2007 from www.doh.wa.gov/cfh/steps/publications/nutrition_activity_policy_guide_final.pdf.

Leape, L. L., & Berwick, D. M. (2005). Five years after to err is human: What have we learned? *Journal of the American Medical Association, 293,* 2384–2390.

Leary, W. E. (1995, September 24). Congress's science agency prepares to close its doors *New York Times,* p. 26. Retrieved March 5, 2006 from www.wws.princeton.edu/ota/ns20/nyt95_n.html.

Leavitt, M. O. (2006a). Letter from Secretary Mike Leavitt to CEOs. Retrieved January 30, 2007 from www.hhs.gov/transparency/employers/ceo.

Leavitt, M. O. (2006b). *Better care, lower cost: Prescription for value-driven health care.* Washington, DC: Department of Health and Human Services. Retrieved January 30, 2007 from www.hhs.gov/transparency.

Levitt, S. D., & Dubner, S. J. (2005). *Freakonomics.* New York: HarperCollins Publishers.

Lewin K. (1951). *Field theory in social science.* New York: Harper and Row.

Lindenauer, P. K., Remus, D., Roman, S., Rothberg, M.B., Benjamin, E.M., et al. (2007). Public reporting and pay for performance in hospital quality improvement. *New England Journal of Medicine, 356,* 486–496.

Lohr, S. (2005, February 17). Health industry under pressure to computerize. *New York Times.* Retrieved at www.nytimes.com/2005/02/19/business/19health.html.

Lyall, S. (2006, April 13). Court backs Briton's right to a costly drug. *New York Times.* Retrieved from www.nytimes.com/2006/04/13/world/europe/13britain.html.

MRC Vitamin Study Research Group. (1991). Prevention of neural tube defects: Results of the Medical Research Council Vitamin Study. *Lancet, 338,* 131–137.

MacRae, D. (1976). *The social functions of social science.* New Haven, CT: Yale University Press.

Mandel, M. (2006, September 27). What's really propping up the economy. *Business Week,* pp. 55–62.

Mattoo, A., & Rathindran, R. (2006). How health insurance inhibits trade in health care. *Health Affairs, 25,* 358–368.

Max, W. (2004). Economic analysis. In health care. In Harrington, C. and Estes, C. L. (Eds.). *Health policy: Crisis and reforms in the U.S. health care delivery system* (4th Ed.). Sudbury, MA: Jones and Bartlett, pp. 260–270.

Mayer, T. R., & Mayer, G. G. (1985). HMOs: Origins and development. *New England Journal of Medicine, 312,* 590–594.

Mays, G. P., McHugh, M. C., Shim, K., Perry, N., Lenaway, D., et al. (2006). Institutional and economic determinants of public health system performance. *American Journal of Public Health, 96,* 523–531.

McClellan, M. B. (2005, May 26). Tax exemption for hospitals and payment for uncompensated care, testimony to House Committee on Ways and Means. Retrieved January 20, 2007 from www.cms.hhs.gov/apps/media/press/release.asp.

McGinnis, J. M., & Foege, W. H. (1993). Actual causes of death in the United States. *Journal of the American Medical Association, 270,* 2207–2212.

McLaughlin, C. P. (1984). *The management of nonprofit organizations.* New York: John Wiley & Sons.

McLaughlin, C. P. (1997). Management in practice: A case of risks and rewards. In K. A. Miller & E. K. Miller (Eds.), *Making Sense of Managed Care. Vol. III: Operational Issues and Practical Answers.* Tampa, FL: American College of Physician Executives, pp. 99–113.

McLaughlin, C. P. (1998). Evaluating the quality control system for managed care in the United States. *Quality Management in Health Care, 7,* 38–46.

McLaughlin, C. P., & Kaluzny, A. D. (1994). *Continuous quality improvement in health care: Theory, implementation and application.* Gaithersburg, MD: Aspen Publishers.

McLaughlin, C. P., & Kaluzny, A. D. (1997). Total quality management issues in managed care. *Journal of Health Care Finance, 24,* 10–16.

McLaughlin, C. P., & Kaluzny, A. D. (1998). Managed care: The challenge ahead. *OR/MS Today, 25 (1),* 24–27.

McLaughlin, C. P., & Kaluzny, A. D. (2006). *Continuous quality improvement in health care: Theory, implementation and application* (3rd ed.). Sudbury, MA: Jones and Bartlett.

McLaughlin, C. P., & Sheldon, A. (1974). *The future and medical care.* Cambridge, MA: Ballinger.

McLaughlin, C. P., Kaluzny, A. D., Kibbe, D. C., & Tredway, R. (2005). Changing roles for primary-care physicians: Addressing challenges and opportunities. *Healthcare Quarterly, 8(2),* 70–78.

McNamara, R. M. (2006). *Emergency medicine and the physician practice management industry: History, overview and current problems.* American Academy of Emergency Medicine. Retrieved June 6, 2006 from www.aaem.org/corporatepractice/history.shtml.

Medical Board of California. (2006). *Corporate practice of medicine.* Retrieved June 5, 2006 from www.medbd.ca.gov/Corporate_Practice.htm.

Melcher, B., & Rausch, C. (2006). North Carolina science to service project. In McLaughlin, C. P., & Kaluzny, A. D. (Eds). *Continuous quality improvement in health care: Theory, implementation and application* (3rd ed.). Sudbury, MA: Jones and Bartlett, pp. 579–601

Mendelson, D. N., Abramoff, R. G., & Rubin, R.J. (1995, September). State involvement in medical technology assessment. *Health Affairs,* 14 (2), 83–98.

Messonnier, M. L., & Zhou, F. (n.d., 2006 or later). Review of economic studies of varicella zoster vaccine. Retrieved April 30, 2007 at www.cdc.gov/nip/ACIP/slides/Oct6/01_Herpes_Zoster/zoster_3-messonnier.pdf.

Middleton, B. (2005). Perspective: Achieving U.S. health information technology adoption: The need for a third hand. *Health Affairs, 24,* 1269–1272.

Miller, R. H., West, C., Martin-Brown, T., Sim, I. and Ganchoff, C. (2005). The value of electronic health records in solo or small group practices. *Health Affairs, 24,* 1127–1137.

Milstein A., (2006). American surgical emigration is a treatable symptom. Testimony before the U.S. Senate Special Committee on Aging, Washington, DC, The Globalization of Health Care: Can Medical Tourism Reduce Health Care Costs? June 27, 2006, Retrieved April 23, 2007 at http://aging.senate.gov/public/index/cfm?Fuseaction=Hearings.Detail&HearingID=182.

Mohr, J. J., & Batalden, P. (2006). Integrating approaches to health professional development with improving patient care. In McLaughlin, C. P., & Kaluzny, A. D. (2006). *Continuous quality improvement in health care: Theory, implementation and application* (3rd ed.). Sudbury, MA: Jones and Bartlett, pp. 281–317.

Mohr, J. J., Batalden, P., & Barach, P. (2006). Inquiring into the quality and safety of care in the academic clinical care microsystem. In McLaughlin, C. P., & Kaluzny, A. D. (2006). *Continuous quality improvement in health care: Theory, implementation and application* (3rd ed.). Sudbury, MA: Jones and Bartlett, pp. 407–423.

Morgan, M. G. (1995, August 2). Death by congressional ignorance: How the Congressional Office of Technology Assessment—small and excellent—was killed in the frenzy of government downsizing. *Pittsburgh Post Gazette.* Retrieved March 5, 2006 from www.wws.princeton.edu/ota/ns20/ota95_n.html.

Morrison, A., & Webb, K. (2004). Bicycle helmet standards and hockey helmet standards: Two approaches to safety protection. Chapter 11 in Webb, K. (Ed.). (2004). *Voluntary codes: private governance, the public interest and innovation.* Ottawa, Canada: Carleton University Research Unit for Innovation, Science and Environment.

Mullaney, T. J. (2006, June 26). The doctor is (plugged) in. *Business Week,* pp. 56, 58.

Naim, M. (2005). *Illicit: How smugglers, traffickers, and copycats are hijacking the global economy.* New York: Doubleday.

National Association of State Budget Officers & National Governor's Association. (2006). *The fiscal survey of states.* Retrieved January 30, 2007 from www.nasbo.org/Publications/PDFs/FiscalSurveyJune06.pdf.

National Committee for Quality Assurance. (2006). *The State of Health Care Quality: 2005.* Washington, DC: NCQA. Retrieved April 20, 2006 from www.ncqa.org.

NICE. (2006). NICE issues statement following ruling of appeal court in Herceptin case. National Institute for Health and Clinical Excellence. Retrieved May 14, 2006 from www.nice.org/page.aspc?0=306959.

Nichols, L. (2006). Personal communication.

Newhouse, J. (2001). Medical care price indices: Problems and opportunities. NBER Working Paper 8168. Retrieved July 6, 2006 from www.nber.org/papers/8168.

Oberlander, J. (2003, August 27). The politics of health reform: Why do bad things happen to good plans? *Health Affairs* Web Exclusive, W3-391–W3-404.

Office of Management and Budget. (1972). *Circular No. A-94 guidelines and discount rates for benefit-cost analysis of federal programs.*

Office of Minority Health. (2001). *National standards for culturally and linguistically appropriate services in health care: final report.* Washington, DC: U.S. Department of Health and Human Services. Retrieved December 28, 2006 from www.omhrc.gov/assets/pdf/checked/finalreport.pdf.

Office of Technology Assessment. (1980). *The implications of cost-effectiveness analysis of medical technology, Background Paper #1: Methodological Issue and Literature Review.* Washington, DC: OTA, Congress of the United States.

Oliver, T. R. (2006). The politics of public health policy. *Annual Review of Public Health, 27,* 195–233.

Oliver, T. R., & Singer, R. F. (2006). Health services research as a source of legislative analysis and input: the role of the California Health Benefits Review Board. *Health Services Research, 41*(Pt. II), 1124–1158.

Palca, J. (1992). Agencies split on nutrition advice. *Science, 257,* 1857.

Park, C. H. (2000). Prevalence of employer self-insured health benefits: National and state benefits. *Medical Care Research and Review, 57,* 340–360.

Parks, J. (2006, Sept.13). First employers send your jobs overseas. Guess what? You're next. *AFL-CIO Now Blog.* Retrieved October 11, 2006 at http://blog.aflcio.org/2006/09/13/first-employers-sent-your-job-overseas-guess-what-you-are-next.

Pauly, M. V. (1995). Measuring health care benefits in money terms. In Sloan, F.A. (Ed.). *Valuing health care: Cost, benefits and effectiveness of pharmaceuticals and other medical technologies.* Cambridge, UK: Cambridge University Press. pp. 99–124.

Pear, R. (2006, April 11). Employers push White House to disclose Medicare data. *New York Times.* Retrieved April 11, 2006 at www.nytimes.com/2006/04/11/washington/11medicare.html.

Peterson, M. A. (1995). How health policy information is used in Congress. Mann, T. E., & Orenstein, N. J. (Eds.). *Intensive care: How congress shapes health policy.* Washington, DC: AEI/Brookings.pp. 79–125.

Peterson, M. A. (2006, December 12). The blue sky initiative: A description and a challenge. Presentation at the Washington Health Legislative Conference. Retrieved April 22, 2007 at http://depts.washington.edu/rchpol/docs/legcon06/Peterson.pdf.

Portela, M. C. (1995). *A Markov model for the estimation of costs in the treatment of AIDS patients.* Unpublished PhD dissertation, Department of Health Policy and Administration, School of Public Health, University of North Carolina at Chapel Hill.

Porter, M. E., & Teisberg, E. O. (2006). *Redefining health care: Creating value-based competition on results.* Boston: Harvard Business School Press.

Priester, R. (1992). A values framework for health system reform. *Health Affairs, 11,* 84–107.

Purchase, B. (2004). The Political Economy of Voluntary Codes. In Webb, K. (Ed.). (2004). *Voluntary codes: private governance, the public interest and innovation.* Ottawa, Canada: Carleton University Research Unit for Innovation, Science and Environment, pp. 77—95.

Rao, R. (2006). Testimony before the U.S. Senate Special Committee on Aging, Washington, DC, The Globalization of Health Care: Can Medical Tourism Reduce Health Care Costs? June 27, 2006, by Rajesh Rao, CEO, IndUShealth. Retrieved April 23, 2007 at http://aging.senate.gov/public/index/cfm?Fuseaction=Hearings.Detail&HearingID=182.

Reagan, M. D. (1999). *The accidental system: Health care policy in America.* Boulder, CO: Westview Press.

Reed, M. C, & Grossman, J. M. (2006). *Growing availability of clinical information technology in physician practices: Data bulletin no. 31.* Washington, DC: Center for Studying Health System Change.

Reinhardt, U. E. (2006). The pricing of U.S. hospital services: Chaos behind a veil of secrecy. *Health Affairs, 25,* 57–69.

Richmond, J. B., & Fein, R. (2005). *The health care mess: How we got into it and what it will take to get out.* Cambridge, MA: Harvard University Press.

Robert Wood Johnson Foundation. (2000). *Advances, 1,* 1.

Robinson, J. C., & Dratler, S. (2006). Corporate structure and capital strategy at Catholic Health West. *Health Affairs, 25,* 134–147.

Rogers, E. M. (1983). *Diffusion of innovations.* Glencoe, NY: The Free Press.

Romano, P. S., Waitzman, N. J., Scheffler, R.M., & Pi, R. D. (1995). Folic acid fortification of grain: An economic analysis. *The American Journal of Public Health, 85,* 667–676.

Rosenthal, J., & Booth, M. (2005, October). *Maximizing the use of state adverse event data to improve patient safety.* Portland, ME: National Academy for State Health Policy. Retrieved December 3, 2006 from http://www.nashp.org/Files/Patient_Safety_GNL61_for_web.pdf.

Rosenthal, M., & Milstein, A. (2004). Awakening consumer stewardship of health benefits: prevalence and differentiation of new health plan models. *Health Services Research, 39*(4, Pt. II), 1055–1170.

Rosenthal, M. B., Zaslavsky, A., & Newhouse, J. (2005). The geographic distribution of physicians revisited. *Health Services Research, 40*(6 Pt. 1), 1931–1952.

Rychlik, R. (2002). *Strategies in pharmacoeconomics and outcomes research.* Binghamton, NY: Pharmaceutical Products Press/Haworth Press.

Sahney, V. K. (1993). Evolution of hospital industrial engineering: From scientific management to total quality management. *Journal of the Society for Health Systems, 4,* 3–17.

Saul, S. (2006, May 4). Doctors object to gathering of drug data. *New York Times.* Retrieved May 8, 2006 at http://www.nytimes.com/2006/05/05/business/04prescribe.html .

Savas, E. S. (1978). On equity in providing public services. *Management Science,* 800–808.

Schechter, M. (2001). Retrieved May 10, 2006 from www.fda.gov/OHRMS/DOCKETS/AC/01/slides3678sl_03-schechter.ppt.

Schick, A. (1995). How a bill did not become a law. In Mann, T. E., & Orenstein, N. J. (Eds.). (1995). *Intensive care: How congress shapes health policy.* Washington, DC: AEI/Brookings, pp. 227–272.

Schlesinger, M. (2002). A loss of faith: The source of reduced political legitimacy for the American medical profession. *The Milbank Quarterly, 80,* 185–235.

Schoen, C., Osborn, R., Huynk, P. T., Doty, M, David, K. et al. (2004, October 28). Primary care and health system performance: Adults' experiences in five countries. *Health Affairs Web Exclusive,* W4-487–W4-503.

SCI. (2006). *The state of the states.* Seattle, WA: AcademyHealth.

Senge, P. M., Kleiner, A., Roberts, C. Ross, R., & Smith, B. (1994). *The fifth discipline fieldbook: Strategies and tools for building a learning organization.* New York: Doubleday/Currency.

SerVaas, S., & Perry, P. (1999). A flaming failure. *Saturday Evening Post, 27(5)62*–ff.

SHADAC. (2006). *The state of kids coverage, August 2006.* Minneapolis, MN: State Health Access Data Assistance Center.

Shekelle, P. G., Ortiz, E., Newberry, S.J., Rich, M.W., Rhodes, S.L. et al. (2005). Identifying potential health care innovations for the future elderly. *Health Affairs, 24*(Suppl. 2), W5-R67–W5-R76.

Shortell, S. M., et al. (1996). *Remaking health care in America: Building organized delivery systems.* San Francisco: Jossey-Bass.

Skocpol, T. (1996). *Boomerang: Health care reform and the turn against government.* New York: W.W. Norton & Company.

Sloan, F. A. (Ed.). (1995). *Valuing health care: Cost, benefits and effectiveness of pharmaceuticals and other medical technologies.* Cambridge, UK: Cambridge University Press.

Sloan, F. A. (2003). Arrow's concept of the health care consumer: A forty-year retrospective. In Hammer, P. J., Haas-Wilson, D., Peterson, M. A., & Sage, W. M. (2003). *Uncertain times: Kenneth Arrow and the changing economics of health care.* Durham, NC: Duke University Press, pp. 49–59.

Solomon, J. (2007). *Health insurance "connectors" should be designed to supplement public coverage, not replace it.* Washington, DC: Center on Budget and Policy Priorities. Retrieved from http://www.cbpp.org/1–29–07/health.

Solomon, D., & Wessel, D. (2007, January 19). Health-insurance gap surges as political issue. *The Wall Street Journal, 249,* pp. A1, A12.

Sowell, T. (2002). *A conflict of visions: Ideological origins of political struggles.* New York: Basic Books.

Stanton, M. W. (2004). Hospital nurse staffing and quality of care. *Research in Action, Issue 14,* 1–9. Retrieved from www.ahrq.gov.

Starr, P. (1982). *The social transformation of American medicine.* New York: Basic Books.

State Health Facts. (2005). Percentage point change among nonelderly by coverage type, 2000–2004. Retrieved December 22, 2005 at www.statehealthfacts.kff.org/cgi-bin/healthfacts.cgi?

State Health Facts. (2006). Rate of child deaths per 100,000 population, 2003. Retrieved December 15, 2006 at www.statehealthfacts.kff.org/cgi-bin/healthfacts.cgi?

State Health Facts. (2007). Heart disease death rate per 100,000 population, 2003. Retrieved April 25, 2007 at www.statehealthfacts.kff.org/cgi-bin/healthfacts.cgi?

Stensland, J., & Winter, A. (2006). Do physician-owned cardiac hospitals increase utilization? *Health Affairs, 25,* 119–129.

Sterling, B. (1996). *Holy fire.* New York: Spectra.

Sterman, J. D. (2006). Learning from experience in a complex world. *American Journal of Public Health, 96,* 505–514.

Strauss, W., & Howe, N. (1991). *Generations: The history of America's future, 1584 to 2069.* New York: William Morrow.

Taylor, R., Bower, A., Girosi, F., Bigelow, J., Fonkych, K., & Hillestad, R. (2005). Promoting health information technology: Is there a case for more-aggressive government action? *Health Affairs, 24,* 1234–1245.

Texas Medical Board. (2006). *Corporate practice of medicine.* Retrieved June 5, 2006 from www.tmb.state.tx.us/professionals/licensed/cpg.php.

Texas Health and Human Services Commission. (2007). HHSC stakeholder public forum: Medicaid Reform—Preparing for the 80th Legislative Session, January 8, 2007. Retrieved January 30, 2007 from www.hhsc.state.tx.us/medicaid/reform.

Thorpe, K. (1999, Fall). Interview by Rhonda Mullin, *Public Health (Emory).* Retrieved February 27, 2006 from www.whsc.emory.edu/_pubs/ph/fa1199/policy.html.

Tomkins, C. P., Altman, S. H., & Eilat, E. (2006). The precarious pricing system for hospital services. *Health Affairs, 25,* 45–56.

Tonelli, M., Winkelmayer, W. C., Jindal, K. K., Owen, W. F., Jr., & Manns, B. J. (2003). The cost-effectiveness of maintaining higher hemoglobin targets with erythropoietin in hemodialysis patients. *Kidney International, 64,* 295–304.

Torenvlied, R., & Thomson, R. (2003). Is implementation distinct from political bargaining? A micro-level test. *Rationality and Society, 15,* 64–84.

Tornatzky, L. G., & Klein, R. J. (1982). Innovation characteristics and innovation adoption-implementation: A meta-analysis of findings. *IEEE Transactions on Engineering Management, EM-29,* 28–45.

Torrey, E. F. (1997). *Out of the shadows: Confronting America's mental illness crisis.* New York: John Wiley and Sons.

United Network for Organ Sharing. (2006). *How the transplant system works: Matching donors and recipients.* Retrieved March 3, 2006 from www.unos.org.

University of Birmingham. (2003). *A training manual for health impact assessment.* Birmingham, UK: Health Impact Assessment Unit.

Upshaw, V. M., Kaluzny, A. D., & McLaughlin, C. P. (2006). CQI, transformation and the "learning organization." In C. P. McLaughlin & A. D. Kaluzny (Eds.), *Continuous quality improvement in health care: Theory, implementation and application* (3rd ed,). Sudbury, MA: Jones and Bartlett, pp. 191–210.

Victor, B., & Boynton, A. C. (1998). *Invented here.* Boston: Harvard Business School Press.

Virginia Mason Medical Center. (2006). *Improvement report: Prevent avoidable codes with a medical emergency team.* Institute for Health Care Improvement. Retrieved from July 22, 2006 from www.ihi.org/IHI/Topics/CriticalCare/IntensiveCare/Improvements/ImprovementStories/InitiatingMETSuccessesAndChallenges.htm.

Visingardi, R. J. (2004, March 18). *Exit communiqué.* Raleigh, NC: North Carolina Department of Health and Human Services, Division of Mental Health, Developmental Disabilities Services.

Vladeck, B. C. (2006). Paying for hospitals' community service. *Health Affairs, 25,* 34–43.

Walker, J. M. (2005). Perspective: Electronic medical records and health care transformation. *Health Affairs, 24,* 118–1120.

Walker, J., Pam, E., Johnston, D., Adler-Milstein, J., Bates, D. W., & Middleton, B. (2005). The value of health care information exchange and interoperability. *Health Affairs Web Exclusives.* Retrieved January 19, 2005 from www.content.healthaffairs.org/cgi/content.

Walley, T., Haycox, A., & Boland, A. (2004). *Pharmacoeconomics.* Oxford: Churchill Livingstone/Elsevier.

Ward, W. J., Jr., Spragens, L., & Smithson, K. (2006). Building the business case for quality. *Healthcare Financial Management, 60,* 92–98.

Washington State Board of Health. (2003). *Nationwide survey of state boards of health.* Retrieved April 23, 2007 from www.sboh.wa.gov/Pubs/documents/StateBoardsReport_Final.pdf.

Weick, K. E. (1976). Educational organizations as loosely coupled systems. *Administrative Science Quarterly, 21,* 1–19.

Weick, K. E. (1995). *Sensemaking in organizations.* Thousand Oaks, CA: Sage.

Weinstein, S. M., & Stason, W. B. (1977). Foundations of cost-effectiveness analysis for health and medical practices. *The New England J. of Medicine, 296,* 716–721.

Weintraub, A. (2006, February 20). How good is your online nurse? *Business Week,* pp. 68–69.

Weissert, C. S., & Weissert, W.G. (2002). *Governing health: The politics of health policy.* Baltimore, MD: The Johns Hopkins University Press.

Welch, H. G., Schwartz, L., & Woloshin, S. (2007, January 2). What's making us sick is an epidemic of diagnoses. *New York Times.* Retrieved January 2, 2007 from www.nytimes.com/2007/01/02/health/02essa.html.

Wennberg, J. E., Fisher, E. S., & Skinner, J.S. (2002, February 13). Geography and the debate over medicare reform. *Health Affairs Web Exclusive,* W96–W114.

Wessel, D., Wysocki, B., Jr., & Martinez, B. (2006, December 19). As health middlemen thrive, employers try to tame them. *The Wall Street Journal, 248,* pp. A1, A4.

West, D. M., & Francis, R. (1995). Selling the contract with America: Interest groups and public policymaking. Paper delivered at the Annual Meeting of the American Political Science Association, Chicago, August 3 through September 3.

Westley, M. E. (2007). Personal communication.

Wilson, M. P., & McLaughlin, C. P. (1984). *Leadership and management in academic medicine.* San Francisco: Jossey-Bass.

Woolhandler, S., Campbell, T., & Himmelstein, D.U. (2003). Costs of health care administration in the United States and Canada. *The New England Journal of Medicine, 249,* 768–775.

World Health Organization. (1999). *Health impact assessments: Main concepts and suggested approach (the Gothenberg Consensus Paper).* Brussels: European Centre for Health Policy, WHO Regional Office for Europe.

Index